COMPENSATORY JUSTICE

NOMOS

XXXIII

NOMOS

Harvard University Press

The Liberal Arts Press

Atherton Press

Aldine-Atherton Press

Lieber-Atherton Press

New York University Press

NOMOS XXXIII

Yearbook of the American Society for Political and Legal Philosophy

COMPENSATORY JUSTICE

Edited by

John W. Chapman, *University of Pittsburgh*

New York and London: New York University Press · 1991

Compensatory Justice: NOMOS XXXIII
edited by John W. Chapman
Copyright © 1991 by New York University
Manufactured in the United States of America

Library of Congress Cataloging-in-Publication Data
Compensatory justice / edited by John W. Chapman.
     p. cm. — (NOMOS ; 33)
    "Began with presentations and commentaries at the meeting of The
American Society for Political and Legal Philosophy held in conjunction with
the annual meeting of the Association of American Law Schools in New
Orleans, 5–8 January 1989"—Pref.
    Includes bibliographical references and index.
    ISBN 0-8147-1453-6 (cloth)
    1. Compensation (Law)—Philosophy—Congresses. I. Chapman, John
William, 1923– . II. Series.
K970.C66 1991
340'.1—dc20   91-14121
                                           CIP

New York University Press books are printed on acid-free paper,
and their binding materials are chosen for strength and durability.

CONTENTS

PART III: COMPENSATORY AND DISTRIBUTIVE JUSTICE

PART IV: THE TAKINGS ISSUE

PART V: LEGAL CULTURES

CONTRIBUTORS

ELIZABETH ANDERSON
Philosophy, University of Michigan

RANDY E. BARNETT
Law, Illinois Institute of Technology

JAMES S. FISHKIN
Political Science, University of Texas, Austin

GERALD F. GAUS
Philosophy and Political Science, University of Minnesota, Duluth

ROBERT E. GOODIN
Philosophy, Australian National University

DAVID JOHNSTON
Political Science, Columbia University

SAUL LEVMORE
Law, University of Virginia

LOREN E. LOMASKY
Philosophy, Bowling Green State University

STEPHEN R. MUNZER
Law, University of California, Los Angeles

ELLEN FRANKEL PAUL
Political Science, Bowling Green State University

ix

MARGARET JANE RADIN
Law, Stanford University

CAROL M. ROSE
Law, Yale University

CASS R. SUNSTEIN
Law and Political Science, University of Chicago

PREFACE

This thirty-third volume of NOMOS began with presentations and commentaries at the meeting of The American Society for Political and Legal Philosophy held in conjunction with the annual meeting of the Association of American Law Schools in New Orleans, 5–8 January 1989. As required by our constitution, the topic considered at the meeting, "Compensatory Justice," was selected by the vote of the Society's members. We are grateful to Jules L. Coleman of the Yale Law School for having organized the program for our meeting.

At the thirty-fifth annual meeting of the Society, held in Atlanta in September 1990, John Chapman retired from the editorship of NOMOS. The Council and the President of the Society appointed Ian Shapiro of Yale University as the new Editor. His first volume of NOMOS will be number XXXVI, to be published in the spring of 1994. We thank him for taking on this important and demanding job.

J.W.C.

INTRODUCTION

JOHN W. CHAPMAN

NOMOS XXXIII opens with an exploration of the significance of rights for compensatory justice. Loren E. Lomasky offers an array of fiendishly illuminating variations on Joel Feinberg's famous backpacker who breaks into and ransacks a cabin to save his life. How should we understand this action and the rights that are involved in it? Lomasky urges us to look upon ourselves as "project pursuers," who have lives to lead that can only be our own. And each of us has a "maximally weighty duty" not to harm others by infringing on their rights, rights they have as fellow project pursuers. But rights may be infringed to avoid "catastrophic moral horror" and death, as in the case of the backpacker. In his case, justified invasion of the rights of the cabin's owner created a moral disequilibrium that only compensation can restore. Rights may be justly invaded. But justification does not suspend dutiful compensation, as some moral philosophers would have us believe.

Gerald F. Gaus says no to the question that forms the title of his chapter "Does Compensation Restore Equality?" In the course of his analysis Gaus rejects an Aristotelian conception of compensatory justice and a purely instrumental account of rights, which he says that Lomasky endorses. Gaus affirms a "Liberal Principle" of noninterference, in the light of which some in-

1

fringements of rights may be justified and compensated for. But we must distinguish between infringements that are "harms" and those that are "wrongs." Wrongs exhibit disrespect for moral agents and as such cannot be compensated for, as is the case with harms. Wronging a person renders a return to moral equality impossible. Gaus's closing sentence reads, "Although aggressors can repay victims for the harm done, transfer of resources cannot right a wrong."

The chapters of Part 2 attempt to cope with the historical dimensions of compensatory justice. James S. Fishkin says, "Justice between generations confronts us with the issue of how to think about the interests of possible people." He holds that interests may be conceived of as either "identity-specific" or "identity-independent." Both ways of thinking have their difficulties. "Identity-specific" claims to compensation run into the difficulty that the people harmed or compensated may not be the same. On the other hand, the "identity-independent" understanding of the human condition suffers from the typical utilitarian insensitivity to the ultimate separateness of persons. What to do? Fishkin closes by suggesting that we need to think through the defensibility of some forms of group compensation, a proposal that he had previously ruled out of order.

Ellen Frankel Paul begins her analysis by stating the case against "set-asides." They are essentially "perverse." This is because they benefit the least disadvantaged, not the most disadvantaged, in the group to whom compensation is offered. Moreover, set-asides create a new generation of victims. Her reflections on the issues generated by the problem of set-asides lead Paul to formulate a generalization on the historical dimension of compensatory justice: "A theory of compensatory justice of the Aristotelian, individualistic sort, seems to break down under the burden of enormous, multifarious, sometimes even mutually negating injuries suffered in the past." Frankel moves on from this conclusion to consider advocates of group compensation. She finds that none has developed a "theory" of compensatory justice for groups, that is, set forth the criteria whose application would enable us to decide which groups, if any, deserve recompense. She next takes up the matter of "reparations." She thinks the compensatory scheme devised for the Japanese interned by the United States government during the Second World War is "both theoretically sound and practically manageable." The reparations made by the Federal Republic of Germany to the Jews also meet with her approval. However, with reference to the atrocities committed in the USSR she affirms that "a theory of compensatory justice seems utterly to collapse under the weight of this history." Her final word is that "compensatory justice certainly has its limitations."

Part 3 has to do with the relations between compensatory and distributive justice. It may seem at first sight that they are at odds, that "compensation strives to preserve what redistribution strives to change." Not so, argues Robert E. Goodin. Properly understood, compensation is quite compatible with redistribution of a certain kind. Goodin goes on to say that compensatory action cannot be justified on the ground that it is designed to restore a just distribution. But it can be justified as serving to enable people to plan their lives in a reliable manner. "On my theory of compensation, what is sacrosanct is not the preexisting distribution but rather preexisting expectations and the plans and projects that people have built around them." This is the moral principle, according to Goodin, that compensatory justice is based on. The very same principle may apply to distributive justice in at least some of its redistributive applications. "The reason we should redistribute resources to meet people's basic needs is that without those resources the psychological prerequisites of planning one's life are lacking." Compensatory and distributive justice have similar foundations and aims.

Moral philosopher Elizabeth Anderson thinks Goodin's analysis is overly simplified. She reads him as commited to "parsimony as a fundamental aim of moral theory." In her view it is not the case that "reliance" is the one true justification for compensation. According to Anderson, "Compensatory schemes are justified not just because they enable people to carry out plans they have already made, but because they provide people with some of their basic needs and because they promote autonomy." Moreover, the status quo that compensatory measures seek to restore may well contain redistributions already made or provisions for them. Furthermore, Anderson says that "the rules of justice are more than devices for generating independently de-

sirable outcomes. They also express moral principles." For Anderson, our moral thinking and our legal system correctly display a division of labor between compensatory and distributive
justice. We live in the midst of moral diversity and complexity.
"A parsimonious moral theory is suitable only to a lean and
barren moral life."

Our legal commentator, Saul Levmore, would seem to be
pretty much in agreement with the essentials of Anderson's
position. In the very first paragraph of his commentary on
Goodin, he points out that "liability rules deter certain activities,
and the law must use *other* tools to redistribute or its deterrence
aim will not be accomplished." Our liability rules have important "incentive" aspects and effects. To neglect these will not do.
Attention to incentives readily explains why governments compensate in some cases and not in others. "A government that
does not pay for the food it takes will soon find itself without
food because private citizens will cease planting and harvesting."
It is not only the Anglo-American laws on compensation that
make a good deal of sense in a "perspective that is dominated
by or at least includes deterrence considerations." This is why
fishermen were compensated for losses caused by an oil spill. A
wide range of legal systems sees matters in the same light.

The contributors to Part 4 confront the takings issue head
on. And to resolve that issue we need a theory of property.
According to Stephen R. Munzer, "a pluralist theory of property rights yields the soundest approach to takings and compensation." Munzer proceeds to articulate his theory in terms of
three principles: utility and efficiency; justice and equality; and
desert based on labor. Along the way he points out that "most
takings that occur in the United States lack any clear redistributive purpose." Munzer's presentation of his theory runs as follows. The amalgamated principle of utility and efficiency is
based on the proposition that they have in common "individual
preference-satisfaction." The second principle, justice and
equality, is interpreted to mean that unequal property holdings
are acceptable so long as everyone has a minimum and "the
inequalities do not undermine a fully human life in society."
Munzer's third principle, desert based on labor, is founded on a
conception of persons as responsible agents who should get

what they deserve. Munzer affirms that these principles are "independent and irreducible." Much of the rest of Munzer's chapter deals in an elaborate and subtle manner with the application of his theory of property to the problem of takings, that is, with how we should deal with government actions that adversely affect private holdings. He thinks that the government should sometimes compensate for takings and offers a formula, based on his theory of property, that should enable us to identify those situations in which compensation is called for and those in which it is not.

In her commentary on Munzer's analysis, Carol M. Rose asserts that his three principles of property collapse into the first, namely, preference satisfaction. That our property system is to some degree "pluralistic" arises from the presence of an older conception of property. This is property as "propriety," as appropriately connected with status and authority. In the course of her analysis Rose points out that a property system maximizes preference satisfaction by making resources more valuable. In her view Munzer's principle of justice works to promote satisfactions by encouraging enterprise and investment. As for the principle of desert, it operates to elicit effort and that makes for the increase of satisfaction. The components of private property as we have come to know it all hang together for the purpose of advancing human welfare. The older conception of property, property as "propriety," had a quite different purpose, namely, the appropriate support for authoritative stations in society. In the "civic republican," far less hierarchical philosophy of life, property performed a similar function; it provided personal independence, considered necessary for political autonomy. These older ways of conceiving of property survive in the modern welfare state's concern for human dignity and decency. But we also think that uncompensated "takings" would violate the very purpose of private property, utility maximization. Rose holds that "these different postures toward property are not compatible." Their coexistence makes for our "extremely confused" law of "takings."

In "Diagnosing the Takings Problem," Margaret Jane Radin announces that our legal "malaise" about takings arises because we cannot tell with "satisfactory certainty" which government actions constitute takings and which do not. In part our malaise springs from the search for a "coherent master-rule," a rule that cannot be found. According to Radin, "Situated moral judgment is required." And a review of relevant cases leads Radin to the conclusion that "so far no one has been able to reduce these conventional, intuitive, contextually contingent baseline judgments to a set of formal rules." With reference to the historical dimension of compensation, Radin says, "In the institution of property, corrective justice has its day but fades, continually overshadowed by present realities. This is a vital pragmatic compromise." Indeed, intuition, context, and compromise pervade the decisions having to do with takings. Political context and political theory also enter into the judicial equation. She refers to "contextualized pragmatic decisions." Our ideal of the "rule of law" drives us to transcend this kind of adjudication, but to no avail. Insofar as theories of property, politics, and personhood remain contested, the takings issue cannot be definitively resolved. Uncomfortable though it may be, the best we can have we already have, the "pragmatic practice of situated judgment." By way of conclusion to her analysis, Radin proclaims that in the takings issue, "here as elsewhere in the law, we should recognize the pragmatic nature of the enterprise."

Part 5 addresses the problem of differing "legal cultures," a legalistic way of referring to differing political theories or philosophies of life. Cass R. Sunstein informs us at the outset of his contribution that in our legal culture, "Principles of compensatory justice are the defining feature of the common law of tort, contract, and property." But in today's world, a world infested with "regulatory harms," application of these principles generates perverse results. As alternatives to our inherited principles of compensatory justice Sunstein puts forward the principles of "risk management" and "nonsubordination." According to Sunstein, subordination exists where and when "a difference irrelevant from the moral point of view has been turned, without sufficient reason, into a social disadvantage in important spheres of life." Sunstein proceeds by way of a critique of the law having to do with small claim class actions, probabilistic torts, and regulatory harms. By way of an example of how compensatory thinking makes for trouble he points to the recalling of automobiles, "an irrational way to reduce automobile accidents and injuries." With reference to the practice of racial discrimination, Sunstein says that "the requirement of discriminatory purpose is a clear outgrowth of compensatory principles." Indeed, "the problem of inequality is not at all understandable in traditional compensatory terms." Concepts of compensatory justice do not accord well with "affirmative action" programs, because "the problem of racial discrimination is systemic rather than episodic in character." Here, in particular, Sunstein's thinking seems to be inspired by the work of John Rawls. In the remainder of the chapter Sunstein explains how the principles of "risk management" and "nonsubordination" might be institutionalized.

Hayek's philosophy of life, not Rawls's, appears to be the inspiration for Randy E. Barnett's critique of Sunstein. He says, to begin with, that "what is missing from Sunstein's account is the rights-based nature of the common law of tort, contract, and property." A liberal conception of justice informs the Anglo-American legal system. And, "Compensation for objective wrongs rather than for subjective 'injuries' is fundamental to the liberal conception of justice." Sunstein's conception of compensatory justice is flawed insofar as it makes injury and not violation of rights the criterion to be applied in identification of the ground for compensation. The rights that Barnett has in mind are not "Holmesian legal rights," defined entirely in terms of remedies. In the liberal conception of justice, as Barnett understands it, legal rights can be appraised "against a normative framework of individual background rights." Barnett holds that "to implement legal theories such as risk management and nonsubordination means abandoning important aspects of the liberal conception of justice and the rule of law." Barnett moves on to an exposition of the limits of judicial competence from which he extracts the proposition that "to concede that a particular legal theory cannot be couched in terms of a claim of right is to concede that such a claim does not belong in a court of law." Sunstein's "limits of compensatory justice," in this perspective, "may simply reflect the limits of judicial competence." Now Barnett's Hayekian understanding of the human condition comes fully into view. In the face of the "polycentric issues" that modern societies confront, not only are courts incompetent, but so are legislatures and administrative agencies as well. Only the free market based on "several property" can cope with the "pervasive problems of knowledge, interest, and power." To plan and to manage society and its development along the lines proposed by Sunstein is to commit what Hayek called "the fatal conceit." In Barnett's eyes, to supplant the liberal conception of justice and the rule of law with principles of risk management and nonsubordination is simply too risky a proposition. Best to hold fast to the liberal legal culture of individuated rights. Rights are the motor that runs Hayek's philosophy of life, which I think best described as "evolutionary utilitarianism."

If Rawls inspires Sunstein and Hayek inspires Barnett, then Amartya Sen is the thinker to whom David Johnston is best compared. Johnston's analysis and appraisal of Cass Sunstein's thinking is so closely reasoned that it defies compact summary. He begins by contending that Sunstein "conflates" questions about legal cultures with questions about the purposes of law. The latter are political, not legal questions. The disarray in the realm of compensatory justice arises from disagreement over the proper purposes of government, that is to say, it is a disagreement in political theory. We are living in a world inhabited by two visions of state and society. These are classical liberalism and managerialism. Classical liberalism is based on "the idea of a person as an agent of choice who is responsible for his or her own voluntary actions and their effects, but not for effects or events over which he or she has no control." Johnston would have us cling so far as possible to this ideal of personality. In the managerial philosophy of life, groups, regulations, and administrative agencies make their appearance. In fact, we live in a world that is more managerial than classical liberal, sociologically speaking. According to Johnston, "the idea of individual responsibility, though not abandoned, declined in importance for those who endorsed the managerial view." Johnston says that compensatory justice as we know it is much in line with liberal aspirations, and further that "Sunstein offers no alternative to the compensatory model . . ." With reference to Sunstein's principle of "risk management," Johnston concludes that "the point is not to go beyond compensatory justice, but to modify it." As to Sunstein's principle of "nonsubordination,"

Johnston asks, to what sort of equality does it point? Perhaps to some kind of "equality of result." In any event Johnston advances a conception of equality that derives from classical liberalism in that it has freedom built right into it. People are equal if they can deal with one another and their affairs on a genuinely voluntary basis. This means they must possess all kinds of skills—Sen would say "abilities." Our main objective should be "to cultivate the capabilities that enable individuals to become responsible agents of choice." In the end we are not faced with an outright choice between the liberal and managerial philosophies of life. Given a liberal interpretation of the idea of equality, all we confront are problems of judicious promotion and application. In David Johnston's world issues of compensatory justice would remain, but surely decline in importance.

PART I

RIGHTS AND
COMPENSATORY JUSTICE

1

COMPENSATION AND
THE BOUNDS OF RIGHTS

LOREN E. LOMASKY

I

Joel Feinberg tells the following story:

> Suppose that you are on a backpacking trip in the high mountain
> country when an unanticipated blizzard strikes the area with such
> ferocity that your life is imperiled. Fortunately, you stumble onto
> an unoccupied cabin, locked and boarded up for the winter,
> clearly somebody else's private property. You smash in a window,
> enter, and huddle in a corner for three days until the storm
> abates. During this period you help yourself to your unknown
> benefactor's food supply and burn his wooden furniture in the
> fireplace to keep warm. Surely you are justified in doing all these
> things, and yet you have infringed the clear rights of another
> person.[1]

Feinberg's gloss on the tale is thoroughly persuasive. Only an
exceptionally rigorous Kantian or libertarian would deny that
the backpacker's conduct is, under the circumstances, eminently
warranted.[2] Yet this poses a difficult problem for proponents of
strong rights. If it is rationally justifiable to violate someone's
rights when the stakes are high enough, then how are we to

13

construe the role of rights in the overall moral economy? If they do not absolutely bar rights-traducing conduct, then one might think that they serve primarily as markers for generally impermissible conduct. As such, they appear to be not much different from the act utilitarian's "rules of thumb," mostly reliable guides for conduct but certainly not unbridgeable nor, significantly, moral commodities that carry their own independent force.[3]

Feinberg borrows from Judith Thomson the distinction between *violating* a right and *infringing* a right: "Suppose that someone has a right that such and such shall not be the case. I shall say that we infringe a right of his if and only if we bring about that it is the case. I shall say that we violate a right of his if and only if *both* we bring about that it is the case *and* we act wrongly in so doing."[4] The distinction seems to be convenient in the present case. Feinberg and Thomson can classify the backpacker's actions as constituting an infringement but not a violation, thereby shielding his conduct from any imputation of moral wrong.

The result is not, however, achieved without considerable cost. For what follows is this: from the fact that *A* has a right that such and such shall not be the case, and that *B* brought it about that such and such is the case, no conclusion to the effect that *B* has done anything improper is warranted, not even a provisional conclusion. Some breaches of rights are merely infringements and others are violations; in the absence of specific *additional* evidence to the effect that *B* acted wrongly we have no reason to find anything amiss in the (for all we know) mere infringement. But if that additional evidence constitutes an *independent* reason for holding that *B* acted wrongly, then the fact that *B* brought it about that a right of *A* failed to be satisfied would seem to be strictly irrelevant to our moral appraisal of *B*'s action.

An analogy helps clarify the point. Some acts of crossing the street are innocuous while others constitute jaywalking. Jaywalkers are culpable but nonjaywalking street-crossers are not. Simply from the fact that *B* crossed the street, nothing whatsoever can be concluded about *B*'s culpability or lack of same. To draw that further judgment we must first determine whether *B* has jaywalked. It follows that *having crossed the street* does not figure significantly in directing our evaluations while *having jaywalked* does. Correspondingly, if Thompson's distinction is accepted it would seem that *having infringed a right* will not figure significantly in our moral appraisals; all the work will be done by the "act wrongly in doing so" clause. Surely, though, this is not how most of us think that rights function. Rather, we suppose that one has provided an extremely powerful, if not absolutely decisive, reason for holding *B*'s conduct to be morally defective if one shows that B's action was contrary to *A*'s right. So again we confront the question: if rights may permissibly be infringed, where does that leave the stringency of rights?

Rather than concede the leakiness of rights and thus take the first step onto the slippery slope, one might instead deny that the backpacker has infringed, let alone violated, anyone's rights. The cabin owner, it is said, possesses a *prima facie* right that her property not be put to the use of another without her consent, but the full specification of her property right includes various emergency clauses covering situations such as that encountered here. The suggestion is implausible. Feinberg notes, "It is, of course, possible to *say* these things, but only at the cost of rejecting the way most of us actually understand the rights in question. We would not think it inappropriate to express our gratitude to the homeowner, after the fact, and our regrets for the damage we have inflicted on his property. More importantly, almost everyone would agree that you owe *compensation* to the homeowner."[5]

Feinberg's point is that rights that are no more than *prima facie* do not leave a claim for compensation in the wake of their being overridden. For example, an heir's *prima facie* right to the substance of an estate can be blocked by the existence of creditors' claims. If so, the creditors owe nothing to the heir, not even gratitude. The case of the imperiled backpacker does not seem to be of this kind. Although his use of the cabin was entirely justifiable, it nonetheless leaves a moral imbalance for which compensation is the indicated remedy. However, that too generates difficulties. The backpacker did nothing wrong in making use of the cabin; on what grounds then can it be maintained that he has created a moral debt that must be compensated? Suppose instead that a meteor had fallen on the cabin.

That would be bad luck for its owner, perhaps calling for our sympathy or even charitable relief, but no one of us individually nor all of us collectively would be under an obligation to tender compensation. People, unlike meteors, can not only harm people but also wrong them. When they do, they incur an obligation to make good the wrong by rendering the injured party whole.[6] However, in the present instance the backpacker seems to be no more liable to criticism than the errant meteor. What then can be the moral foundation of a compensation requirement? Or, to put it another way, if wrongful action is not necessary to trigger the compensation requirement, how otherwise can a duty to compensate arise?[7]

I believe that Feinberg is correct in all of the following: (1) the backpacker does not act wrongly by breaking into the cabin and using its resources to sustain himself; (2) the backpacker does, however, thereby infringe the clear rights of another person; and (3) the backpacker owes compensation to the cabin owner. The task of this chapter is to develop an understanding of rights in which all three of these contentions are supportable. That task becomes trivial if rights are taken to be no more than the consequentialist's usually trustworthy markers of where utility might profitably be accrued, or if the fact of a right's infringement were not in and of itself a powerful, though not absolutely decisive, reason for holding that the infringer has acted wrongly. So let me be more precise: I shall attempt to show that a theory of maximally stringent, nonconsequentialist rights accommodates itself to Feinberg's backpacker.

I begin in section II by telling several stories in which the protagonist is an imperiled backpacker. Their several upshots help locate the salient moral issues to be addressed by a theory of strong rights. Section III offers a sketch of that theory, and IV shows how wrongful rights infringements generate a moral imbalance for which compensation (and, in some cases, punishment) is the appropriate response. In section V I argue that limitations on the scope of rights issue from the underlying account of practical reason from which those rights are derived: a theory that takes rights to be *maximally weighty* moral claims cannot reasonably take the scope of rights to be similarly maximal. That is because rights have purchase on our conduct only insofar as those who transact with rights holders do not thereby forfeit their stake in the regime of rights itself. That introduces the analysis in section VI of compensation for justifiable incursions on rights. Exigent circumstances can place a person beyond the outermost boundary at which that person has reason to accede to the individuals' otherwise legitimate rights claims. However, once exigency has passed, the parties may find themselves again in circumstances such that each has reason to acknowledge the others' rightful holdings. Such acknowledgment may require rectification of previous inroads on those holdings. That is why Feinberg's backpacker has a duty to compensate the cabin owner. However, not all inroads on the assets of others create claims for subsequent compensation, and in section VII I argue that this is how we should understand minimum welfare entitlements. Section VIII appends a brief conclusion.

II

1. The Surrogate Transaction Ploy

Had the backpacker been able to ring up the cabin owner on a cellular telephone carried along for just such emergencies, he could have offered to pay her a reasonable sum for room and board while he waited out the storm. Only a moral monster would decline to allow the use of the cabin under these circumstances. Since very few people are moral monsters, it is likely that they would have struck a respectably capitalistic bargain whereby the backpacker survived and the property owner is adequately remunerated. Unfortunately, on this particular backpacking trip no cellular telephone was at hand. Still, based on probabilities, the backpacker can reasonably impute the cabin owner's assent to the transaction they *would have* made. Therefore, he does no wrong when he breaks into the cabin, burns selected pieces of furniture for warmth, etc. Compensation due after the fact is to be understood as the hypothetical contract's quid pro quo.

Property holdings are, after all, not sacrosanct. Millions of times each day they migrate from one person to another as property is bought and sold. The surrogate transaction version appeals because it models the backpacker's actions on familiar commercial transactions. Nonetheless, it is defective.

First, if the surrogate transaction model were appropriate, it would not be the case that the backpacker infringes the cabin owner's rights. A person may freely burn furniture for which he has paid or, as in this case, for which he has transacted to pay in the future. Compensation, though, is not the same as paying a purchase price, and it is the former that is exacted from the backpacker.

But second, the transaction model does not begin to get off the ground. Even a *certainty* that you would consent to a particular transaction were the terms put to you does not entitle me to force that transaction on you. For example, I might know that, for a payment of ten thousand dollars, you would gladly assent to my painting a mustache on the picture of Immanuel Kant hanging on your wall. Nonetheless, I am not at liberty to deposit that amount in your bank account and then, without first asking you, commence my graffiti attack. Actual agreement is to the point but hypothetical agreement is not.[8]

Third, neither hypothetical *nor* actual consent on the part of the cabin owner seems requisite to justify the backpacker's incursion. Suppose that on the door of the cabin is a sign reading "WARNING!!! This cabin may not be entered by anyone, ever! I don't care if you're here because of avalanche, blizzard, flood, nuclear holocaust, or whatever; just go. THIS MEANS YOU!" Now the evidence is very strong that the owner would not agree to provide shelter; must the backpacker therefore consign himself to the blizzard? Certainly not. He is justified in entering the cabin by virtue of his extreme *need*, not because of what its owner did or would agree. Indeed, as Thomson notes, the backpacker's need for shelter morally forces the hand of the owner: "Suppose that I have a device in place, by the activation of which I can prevent you from burning my chair—for example, pressing the switch will cause all the furniture to be coated with fire-proof foam. Would it be morally permissible for me to activate that device? Surely not; surely it would be wrong to prevent you from burning the chair."[9]

It may therefore seem that (appropriately grave) need, and

need alone, suffices to justify incursions. But that judgment is contravened by the following story.

2. *The Imperiled Thrill-Seeking Backpacker*[10]

As it happens, our backpacker is no stranger to perilous escapes. He does not much care for hiking. Rather, it is the thrill of living on the edge that sets his juices bubbling. If the weather is clement, he sinks into his La-Z-Boy recliner and watches "Miami Vice" reruns. But when he hears reports of impending storms, he dons his gear and sets out for the high country. This happens to be the forty-third time he has braved a blizzard. On each previous occasion he has chanced upon an unoccupied cabin in which to find refuge. His luck once again holds good. He breaks into the cabin, helps himself to its food stocks, burns furniture for warmth, and so on. As with the prior forty-two episodes, he pays liberal compensation after the event.

In this emendation of Feinberg's example, the backpacker's conduct is not innocent. Although it remains true that he would have died had he not entered the vacant cabin, he nonetheless acts impermissibly. His trespass wrongs the cabin owner. Nor does his willingness to pay compensation erase that wrong.

It might be objected that the thrill-seeking backpacker has indeed acted wrongly, but the wrong he commits is not the act of trespass. Once caught up in the blizzard he has no reasonable alternative but to enter the cabin. Rather, it can be claimed, the flaw in his conduct occurs prior to his endangerment. By heading out into the storm with the intention of turning another's property to his use, he undertakes, under circumstances in which no excusing conditions operate, to infringe rights.

I believe that this misconstrues the nature of the transgression. The claim is that the backpacker is guilty of intending to perform an impermissible action, yet how can that be? If the *actual* entry into the cabin is morally unobjectionable, then acting with the intention (or hope) of securing entry cannot be to intend what is wrong. And even if the backpacker sets out, so to speak, on the wrong foot, that initial moral error is something different from the one eventually committed: viz., violation of the cabin owner's rights. To put oneself in a situation where one will be powerfully tempted to help oneself to another's goods may be perverse, but that is not tantamount to actually violating someone's rights. Rather, it is the failure to resist the temptation that upsets the moral balance. So, had the backpacker realized at the last minute that he could not permissibly break into the cabin and then resolutely refrained from doing so, he could be convicted of having acted imprudently or even tragically, but not of having offended against the rights of others.

Therefore, though the judgment may seem harsh, the ultimate wrong action committed by the backpacker is his breaking into the cabin. Moreover, that is the only aspect of his conduct that violates the rights of anyone else. One might say that it would have been worse overall, worse from the perspective of the universe, had he allowed himself to perish in the storm, but that is strictly irrelevant to his transgression vis-à-vis the cabin owner. The latter's complaint concerns the destruction of her property. In this version of the story the backpacker cannot maintain that it was justifiable under the circumstances, and that he need only tender compensation fully to restore the moral equilibrium.

The moral of the story is that not all suitably grave needs serve to exonerate rights infringements. Rather, if the need is one that predictably and reasonably could have been averted or met by the agent himself, then he is not at liberty to convert the rightful holdings of others to his own use. The thrill-seeking backpacker reasonably could have done so; thus he is at fault.[11]

3. The Entrepreneurial Rescue Service

Backpacking has become exceedingly popular, and a great number of people head for the hills. They are not always wise in choosing how or when to do so, and many find themselves at risk. This circumstance is not lost on aspiring capitalists who detect an opportunity for profit. One incorporates Rachel's Rescue Service. Her bright idea is to construct a series of aptly situated havens where hikers can find food, shelter, and in-room movies with which to wile away the hours. A fee list detailing the charges for these various services is prominently displayed on the door, which is activated by insertion of any major credit card. These services are expensive, considerably in excess of the replacement cost of goods consumed, but of course the company has to recover its capital investment and all other business expenses to remain a going concern. In fact, Rachel's after-tax profits are in line with those of other small businesses in the area.

Once again our backpacker is overtaken by a blizzard which, unlike that of the previous story, was completely unexpected. Fortunately, he comes upon an unoccupied cabin. Perhaps not so fortunately, that cabin is located next to a Rachel's Rescue Service hostel. The backpacker can save himself either by breaking into the unoccupied cabin or by patronizing Rachel's establishment. If he elects the former, he will, of course, be required to compensate the cabin's owner for the damage he causes. However, the tariff will be only a tenth or so of what Rachel charges for equivalent provision. The backpacker can afford the fee but naturally prefers to spend less rather than more. After taking a few seconds to weigh the alternatives, he breaks into the cabin.

The backpacker has acted improperly. He was obliged, if he wished to save himself, to pay the going rate. Some, though, will take issue with this conclusion. They might argue in this way: "We all agree that if there had been no branch of the rescue service in the vicinity, the backpacker would have been blameless in breaking into the cabin. Once he subsequently provides full compensation to its owner, no one would have any legitimate complaint. But if that is so, the presence of an alternative refuge is immaterial. The cabin owner is no worse off in virtue of the entry and subsequent compensation for damages than she would have been in the absence of the commercial establishment. Thus, she is not wronged by the backpacker. Neither is Rachel's Rescue Service wronged; it had no right against the backpacker that he purchase its services. Therefore, the backpacker wrongs no one by using the cabin."

The argument is invalid because it invokes the wrong comparison. The backpacker needs refuge, and so he may justifiably do *something* to secure that refuge. That he may do *anything* that will bring about that end does not follow. Damage to a cabin is damage to a cabin, but whether it constitutes a morally derelict action depends on whether it was justifiable under the circumstances that actually obtained. In the present circumstances, unlike those of Feinberg's original version, the backpacker is able to save himself without traducing anyone's rights. Therefore, he may not break into the cabin.

This story too has a moral. One may permissibly infringe the rights of another to secure what is urgently needed, but not when it is feasible both to satisfy that need and to respect rights. That is true even when respecting rights comes at substantial cost—though, as the next story implies, not true irrespective of the cost level. Note that breaking into an unoccupied cabin might be the course of action that maximizes the total happiness enjoyed by all affected parties; it remains impermissible. Its wrongness is not the outcome of a delicate utilitarian calculus. Rather, it issues directly from the stringency of rights.[12]

4. The Avariciously Entrepreneurial Rescue Service

Same story as previously, except that Rachel has upped the ante. She now extracts for entry into one of her havens 80 percent of the customer's net assets plus a similar percentage of all his future earnings. She is known to be able to implement compliance with such contractual undertakings through her remarkably persuasive ("Here's an offer you can't refuse") enforcement director. The backpacker weighs his alternatives and breaks into the unoccupied cabin.

The conclusion to be drawn is sensitive to the precise extent of the burden, but we probably should judge that the backpacker does no wrong. True, he could have saved himself without infringing any rights, but the upshot would be that the remainder of his life would be miserable. While one may, under certain conditions, be morally obliged to accept a miserable life for oneself,[13] those conditions do not seem to obtain here. The guiding idea, roughly, is that individuals' duties not to transgress the rights of others either entirely disappear or else are considerably weakened when respect for rights would put the individual below the baseline of being able to lead a decent life. Moreover, those who would claim rights against others are rationally obliged to recognize that those others' reasons for compliance are a function of where they are situated with respect to that baseline. The bargain that Rachel proposes is outrageously harsh, and the cabin owner cannot justifiably complain against the backpacker that he declined to embrace it.

5. The Overcompensating Backpacker

Same as the third story except that the backpacker is a more ingenious contriver of alternatives. Rather than pay Rachel's fee, he breaks into the cabin and subsequently tenders its owner triple damages. The owner is thereby raised to a higher indifference curve than if the cabin had been untouched, and the backpacker is also better off than had he patronized Rachel's Rescue Service. Only Rachel does less well, but she had no right against the backpacker for his business.

The backpacker has wronged the cabin owner. That is true even if the owner turns out to be pleased, on balance, with the way things worked out. Just as imputed hypothetical consent does not legitimize forced transactions (see the first story), neither are they legitimized by an overall utility gain accruing to the person whose rights have been infringed. One is not at liberty to make people better off by breaching their rights.[14] Of course the cabin owner may choose to forgive the infringement of her rights, but the essential point is that forgiveness of the offense would not be possible unless an offense had occurred. The moral—our final one—is that the stringency of rights is such that they can block not only courses of action that survive the consequentialist's delicate balancing but even alternatives that would render every party better off, where being better off is understood in terms of the familiar welfarist indifference

curve apparatus. That underscores the difficulty of understanding how rights can justifiably be infringed.

III

It goes without saying that theorists do not concur on any single
univocal statement of what rights are, who has them, and why.
I shall not try to develop that characterization here.[15] Rather, I
pick up some cues familiar from the literature. Robert Nozick
characterizes rights as "side constraints,"[16] Ronald Dworkin as
"political trumps."[17] The two locutions point in essentially the
same direction but are distinct. A side constraint dictates that
certain courses of action are out of bounds, simply not to be
employed within the domain over which the constraint operates. A trump, though, as any bridge player knows, can be
overtrumped—frequently if one is having a bad day. Nonetheless, both Nozick and Dworkin agree that rights establish morally potent boundaries that others are not at liberty to cross to
achieve otherwise desirable outcomes.

Though some theorists take exception to this characterization,[18] I follow Nozick/Dworkin in understanding rights to be
maximally weighty moral claims, claims powerful enough to block
utility-maximizing moves. It therefore becomes problematic why
one should acknowledge the existence of such claims. What
reason could we have to accede to securing less overall value
when more is attainable?

Only an abbreviated answer can be supplied here.[19] It com-
mences from the understanding of individuals as *project pursuers,* as agents committed to acting on behalf of enduring ends
that are distinctively their own. These ends are a source of
individuated, *personal* value in that they afford agents reason to
value certain states of affairs and disvalue others, which, in the
absence of those commitments, they would not have equivalent
reason to value/disvalue. Person *A*, therefore, may have overwhelmingly good reasons to value the advancement of some
end that to *B*, for equally good reasons, is an object of indifference or loathing. Projects have directive force with respect to
agents' subsidiary valuations and furnish recognizable coherence and continuity—what we may call *meaning*—to an individ-

ual's life. It follows that, contrary to the claims of consequential-
ists, project pursuers do not have reason to subscribe to some
monolithic impersonal standard of value that would arbitrate all
interpersonal conflicts without reference to the particularities of
individuals' personal projects. Rather, a project pursuer has
reason, individuated practical reason, to take his own distinctive
commitments as affording a rational motivation for their ad-
vancement-by-him.

The world, of course, contains many project pursuers, each
with his own directive ends, and each of whom has reason to lend
special weight to those ends. If I am not utterly myopic, I
recognize that the value I attach to my ability to act in pursuit
of my own projects will not afford you equally compelling reason to value my ability to pursue my projects. Rather, I shall
acknowledge that you have reason to lend differential weight to
those ends that are especially salient to you. Within this understanding of individuated practical reason there exists the potential for incessant conflict, for the Hobbesian war of all against
all. But also latent within it is a basis for accommodation. Although neither you nor I has reason to be impartial between
advancement of his own ends and advancement of the other
person's ends, we each have reason to acknowledge the rationality from the perspective of each person of lending special weight
to the values constituted by that individual's personal projects.

As a project pursuer, I require secure possession of moral
space within which I am at liberty to act on the basis of those
ends that specially matter to me. You require similar moral
space within which to pursue your own projects. Because our
situations are symmetrical, we each have reason—personal reason—to value the other's noninterference. Therefore, over a
wide (though not unlimited; see below) range of situations in
which we might find ourselves, we each have reason to value a
moral order characterized by mutual restraint. Within that order I will not be obliged to set aside my own cherished ends to
advance yours, but I will be required to refrain from trampling
on your activities. Basic rights duly emerge as affording what I
have elsewhere characterized as "those moral constraints that
impose minimal demands on the forbearance of others such
that individuals can pursue projects amidst a world of similar

beings, each with his own life to lead, and each owing the same measure of respect to others that they owe to him."[20]

Rights so understood establish a moral baseline. We can, and doubtless should, do more than merely respect the rights of others, but we may not do *less*. The feasibility of acting effectively on behalf of projects that are distinctively one's own is predicated on the maintenance of a system of generalized non-interference. No one is thereby guaranteed success in achieving his ends, but it would be unreasonable to require of other project pursuers that they provide guarantees. They have their own affairs to attend to. All that can reasonably be demanded from everyone is commitment to a policy of reciprocal restraint. Because the alternative is the Hobbesian jungle, the demand has considerable urgency. Rights thus take the form of side constraints that establish the boundaries within which one is at liberty to pursue those ends that personally matter most. They are maximally weighty moral claims not because respect for rights is the be-all and end-all of living well, but because they ground the possibility of leading good lives in civil society.

IV

Rights *must* be respected, but sometimes they are not. So it is important to develop not only the primary theory of what duties people owe to others but also the secondary theory of what duties they owe to others in virtue of failing to comply with their primary duties. If *B* smashes the windows of *A*'s donut shop, thereby violating *A*'s rights, *B*'s offense is not some generalized blow against impersonal value. Rather, the complainant in the first instance is *A*. It is *A*, not the universe, who is wronged. The moral imbalance that comes to obtain between victim *A* and victimizer *B* is not simply a function of the fact that *A* has become worse off and *B*, perhaps, better off. Had instead a meteor fallen on *A*'s donut shop, that would have been bad luck for *A* and a windfall gain for *B*, *A*'s competitor in the donut business, but it would not establish any particular tie of obligation between them, any debt owed by *B* to *A*. Nor can we explain the relation by adding that *A*'s loss is caused by *B*'s deliberate action. If *B* had contrived a better donut recipe and thereby driven *A* into bankruptcy, that would be an *evil for A* but not an *evil done to A* by *B*. It is only insofar as *B* transgresses the side constraints constituted by *A*'s rights that *B* becomes *A*'s moral debtor.

This debt has several dimensions. First, and seemingly least controversial, *B* is obliged to render *A* whole, to transfer resources to *A* adequate to make *A* at least as well off as before the transgression occurred. Jules Coleman has, however, questioned this understanding:

> If there is a wrongful loss, it ought to be annulled; the same goes for wrongful or unwarranted gains. Nevertheless, the principle of corrective justice which enables us to identify compensable losses and unjust enrichments does not commit us to adopting any particular mode of rectification. The principle that determines which gains and losses are to be eliminated does not by itself specify a means for doing so. Presumably there is more than one way of rectifying undeserved gains and losses.[21]

So, for example, it is entirely immaterial as a strict matter of corrective justice whether compensation for wrongful losses is paid by the victimizer or is instead provided by a social insurance fund.[22]

In effect, Coleman denies that any special moral relation between the victim and victimizer has come to obtain in virtue of the encroachment. But that leaves as puzzling only his attention specifically to *wrongful* losses. Why should we not instead focus our attention on all and only those losses that result in a pattern of holdings that our favored distributional model classifies as subpar? *A*'s loss is just as real, just as salient to *A*, if it resulted from a wayward meteor as if it were the product of *B*'s vandalism. In each case *A* has equivalent reason to value rectification. If the point of taking action is to relieve *A*'s distress, it makes just as much sense to afford *A* recovery from meteors as from the rights-infringing actions of other people. Insurance, whether collectively provided or purchased on the market by individuals, is an appropriate response to the risk of losses.

That, however, is to leave an important element out of the equation. It is to treat an issue in *compensatory justice* as if it were instead a matter of *distributive justice*. Some believe that there are collectively shared duties to promote economic equality or to enhance the position of the least well off; others reject such notions. However, that should be recognized as being a different issue from whether A ought to recover specifically for a wrongful loss. Criteria of distributional justice are impersonal; they apply, if they apply at all, to everyone in the same way. Compensatory justice, though, is essentially perspectival. The only reason why the wrongfulness of A's loss can be relevant is because it validates the existence of a complaint A has specifically against the perpetrator of that loss, B. It is not the existence of the loss as such that generates the complaint; wrongful losses are no worse simply *as losses* than are those that arise innocently. Rather, the moral equilibrium is upset by the deficiency in B's conduct, and that is why the onus of providing rectification or compensation[23] properly falls on B. The controlling idea is not that (B and) everyone has an open-ended duty to repair unfortunate circumstances, but that each person has a maximally weighty duty to avoid damaging others through rights-infringing conduct.

The point can be put yet more sharply. Suppose that B attempts to sabotage A's product by pouring massive quantities of oat bran into A's donut batter; as it turns out, A's business now booms as cholesterol-conscious snackers now flock to A's shop. A has not been harmed[24] but rather benefited. Should we say that A has no legitimate complaint against B? I think not. B has not caused A any wrongful loss, but he has nonetheless *wronged* A. B has not afforded to A the deference due to a rights holder, and thus generates a moral imbalance between them. A may have no reason to complain of the *outcome* that has fortuitously emerged, but he has reason to be indignant about the means through which that outcome eventuated. To assess punitive damages against B or otherwise to respond to the legitimacy of A's complaint against B would not be improper. Notice that the issue remains within the domain of compensatory/corrective justice in that a breach by one party vis-à-vis another is held to be a proper basis for compelling a transfer of resources between them.

The point should not be obscured by the fact that rights violators are not only compelled to make restitution to their victims but are also sometimes *punished* for crimes "against the state." An offense done to a particular individual is, secondarily, a breach of the general moral order. Because we all have reason to value maintenance of that order, those who are not directly victimized may nonetheless have reason to take an interest in rights violations. Not every offense has generalized import, but some do. Those we may properly punish.[25] But it should be recognized that this secondary response is derivative from the primary victimization, whether retrospective or prospective,[26] of particular individuals. Only because offenses generate in the first instance a moral imbalance between victim and victimizer do they have an import that extends beyond those parties.

V

I have argued that rights entail maximally weighty moral demands. It does not follow, however, that their *scope* is maximal. Nothing in the preceding argument implies that individuals' reasons to forbear in their dealings with others obtain under all conceivable circumstances. Indeed, it points in the opposite direction. Recall that rights emerge as a function of individuals' interest in being able to live as project pursuers. If, however, scrupulous regard for another's moral space would directly jeopardize one's own standing as a project pursuer, then all bets are off. The generalized version of this unfortunate circumstance is, of course, Hobbes's state of nature where life is "solitary, poor, nasty, brutish, and short" because no one acknowledges any restriction on his liberty to "use his own power, as he will himself, for the preservation of his own nature; that is to say, of his own life; and consequently, of doing any thing which in his own judgment and reason, he shall conceive to be the aptest means thereunto."[27]

Feinberg's imperiled backpacker finds himself in a rather different sort of state of nature, but the threat it poses to "his own nature" is no less authentic. He will be unable to live as a project pursuer, indeed be unable to live,[28] unless he appropriates another's rightful holdings. Therefore he has overriding reason to break into the vacant cabin although he thereby infringes its owner's property rights. That conclusion should not be viewed as in any way undermining the preceding argument for the general applicability of rights. Quite the reverse; just those considerations that underlie the rationality of respecting rights in less precarious circumstances here imply the reason-ableness of infringing them. What has changed are the back-ground conditions, not the underlying rationale.

The result is congruent with the familiar Humean contention that principles of justice apply only in circumstances of relative scarcity. If all goods are abundant to the point of satiation, justice becomes otiose; if they are so scarce that chances for survival dim, principles of justice lose their rational purchase on the conduct of individuals. I suggest that for Hume's "justice" we substitute "rights." The backpacker has passed beyond rela-tive scarcity to dire need; that justifies his setting aside the regulative demands constituted by the rights of others.

It can be objected that no such sweeping conclusion follows from the slender evidentiary base afforded by the imperiled backpacker. There are two important respects in which that case can be held to be exceptional. First, the rights infringement in question extends only to property holdings, and those of a rather negligible sort. (How dearly is the average wooden chair in the average cabin likely to be prized?) Even if it is acceptable under conditions of exigency to encroach on property, that incursions on liberty or life are licit does not follow. Second, the case is described as one in which compensation after the fact is feasible. Even if compensation does not erase a prior moral transgression, it certainly eases its sting. However, losses, espe-cially momentous ones, that for one reason or another cannot be compensated, are a different matter. We might therefore hold that it is permissible to infringe rights to alleviate a grave need if compensation will subsequently be made, while rights infringements that do not admit of after-the-fact compensation are barred.

Both contentions are, to an extent, credible. There is a dis-cernible moral difference between burning a chair and burning a person, and any theory that insists on subsuming the two under the same strictures is a nonstarter. Loss of property typi-cally impinges less critically on an individual's ability to live as a project pursuer than does loss of liberty or life. Similarly, it is of undeniable moral significance whether intrusions on rights are compensated; that is why, after all, we have reason to be concerned with principles of compensatory justice. Damages that are subsequently compensated pose a lesser threat to one's prospects for successful project pursuit than do those for which no compensation is tendered. We would expect different principles to apply to these readily distinguishable cases. Without attempting to erect an elaborate casuistry of justifiable rights infringements, one can reasonably maintain that the benchmark for permissible rights infringements will be set higher for harms to person than harms to property, for uncompensatable transgressions than those for which compensation is feasible. Nonetheless, I contend that even infringements of the right to life—which, necessarily, are uncompensatable to the victim—can be rationally justifiable under conditions of extreme urgency.

Consider this case which is far from the original example:

> The terrorist has planted a bomb somewhere in the city. He threatens to detonate it unless his demands are met. As it happens, those demands are unmeetable. As it also happens, an expert marksman is on the scene. Unfortunately, the terrorist is shielded by a purely innocent hostage—in this sort of example the hostage is *always* purely innocent—a child perhaps. If the bomb is detonated it will destroy a busy shop/a city block/half the city. The terrorist's threat is entirely credible. Should the marksman shoot through the child to kill the terrorist?

I maintain that he should. In this sort of scenario the recriprocal accommodation that characterizes a regime of rights has broken down, admittedly through no fault of the hostage. We are plunged into what Nozick calls a situation of "catastrophic moral horror."[29] Nozick's expressed disinclination to consider such cases has led some people to suppose that they represent a hole in the theory of rights as side constraints. No such conclusion is warranted. Catastrophic moral horror should be understood not as an exception within the theory of rights but rather as situated beyond its borders. The same considerations that generate the stringency of rights also demarcate, though admittedly not with exactitude, the bounds of their applicability. It would be irrational to accept the principle, "Respect rights though the heavens may fall," if the point of endorsing rights is to ensure for persons that the heavens will not fall on them. But not only catastrophic moral horror presses one to the outer bounds of rights; the quite ordinary instance of Feinberg's imperiled backpacker does so as well.[30]

That is not to say that individuals never have good reason to accede to great losses, even loss of life, so as not to impose substantial disabilities on others. That may be Hobbes's contention, but he attaches his account of moral obligation to a suspect, purely egoistic theory of rational motivation. To the contrary, self-sacrifice may be noble, may even be morally mandatory. Suppose that the only means by which I can stay alive is to undertake an inordinately costly medical regimen that will leave my family destitute and with minimal prospects of future happiness. Perhaps the money is mine, so that I have a straightforward right to spend it on myself. Nonetheless, for me to do so would be wrong; I have exceedingly good reason not to undertake the medical regimen even though I shall therefore die. Similarly, Gary Cooper may have good reason to confront the desperados at high noon rather than run, despite the fact that it is likely that he will be killed unless he leaves town. In the former case self-sacrifice is, I believe, morally mandatory; in the latter it's a tough call between saying that Gary Cooper is fulfilling a moral duty and classifying his actions as supererogatory.

What is significant about these examples is that they are constructed on foundations of preexistent personal relations and special duties that generate moral reasons above and beyond those constituted by bare recognition of the rights of others. Parents and sheriffs have reason to regard themselves as bound by considerations that would not apply to them in the absence of such special relations. The general theory of rights, however, presupposes no such special relations. Indeed, a helpful way to understand the extent of the requirements generated by rights is to ask: What degree of reciprocated deference do I have reason to extend to persons with whom I have no special sympathy, to persons whose projects I view with disinterest or even disdain? The answer, I have argued, is: minimal forbearance. By way of contrast, my reasons to act on behalf of persons whose fate matters much to me, or to fulfill the requirements of an office to which I have committed my energies, are significantly more extensive. Although I am obliged to sacrifice my life to save my family from destitution, I need not do so to spare the person who invented Muzak.

VI

Rights may permissibly, or even mandatorily, be infringed to avert both catastrophic moral horror and the less dramatic plight of imperiled backpackers. That is not, of course, to sanction the once-and-for-all destruction of the regime of rights but rather its temporary suspension. When crisis looms, rights are consigned to the background, but from that vantage they nonetheless tug on us, though as aspiration rather than achievement. We shoot through the child at the terrorist in order to restore a moral order in which children will not be wrongfully killed. Backpackers may permissibly help themselves to the property of cabin owners if they do so with an intention of subsequently reestablishing a balance in which each party will have reason to accede to the rights of the other.

Requiring compensation or punishment in response to wrongful rights infringements is easily understood as a balance-restoring move. The aggressor has secured illicit advantage through inflicting damage on his victim. Compensation restores, if not completely and perfectly then at least somewhat, the victim's losses by transferring resources from the individual against whom the complaint is aptly lodged to the injured party. It thereby moves both parties back in the direction of the status quo ante. Punishment expresses the social determination that individuals may not profit from infringing the protected moral space of others; it does so by imposing on the aggressor burdens instead of the sought-after benefits. Although punishment does not afford the victim any tangible gain, it expresses recognition of his standing as a being entitled to respect, recognition of the fact that he is not a moral nonentity. That too is something that individuals have reason to value.

To understand how justifiable rights infringements also generate a demand for compensation is less easy. The problem is this: one who justifiably infringes does nothing wrong. But if no wrongful action was committed, then it would seem that no moral disequilibrium needs mending. A world in which all parties do what they have eminently good reason to do, in which none of them does what is morally impermissible, is a world that is as good as it gets! Imposed transfers in this world can only have the effect of movement away from, not toward, moral equilibrium.

This appears to be the view of Philip Montague, who contends:

> I would like to suggest that if A does in fact act permissibly in burning B's furniture, then he does not owe B compensation for the loss. My reasons for saying this refer back to the beginning of this discussion, when it was pointed out that someone who simply *vandalizes* another's property does owe compensation for whatever he destroys or damages. It strikes me as extremely implausible to regard both the vandal and A in our example as owing compensation.[31]

It would be bizarre, Montague suggests, to treat the backpacker, the man who has done nothing wrong, in the same way the vandal is treated. A theory that imposes equivalent burdens on malefactors and the innocent is fundamentally flawed.

One response to Montague is that the vandal, unlike the backpacker, is liable to punishment. The point is well taken and important, but it fails to address the central issue. Punishment is an additional burden beyond mandated compensation. The problem, though, is to understand why *any burden* should be placed on the guiltless backpacker, not why he should be immune from the punitive response visited on the vandal.

Here is a different response: once the backpacker breaks into the cabin, it is a fait accompli that *some* innocent party will be burdened. Either the backpacker bears the loss or the owner does. Therefore, it cannot be a moral requirement that no innocent party lose out as a consequence of his own blameless conduct. All that remains open for decision is how the loss is to be apportioned. To escape the fate of Buridan's ass, some apportionment rule is needed: we can allow all losses to lie where they fall, shift all losses away from where they fall, or on each occasion flip a coin.[32] If these decision procedures are seen to suffer from arbitrariness, it can be recommended that, as most in keeping with principles of formal justice, allotted burdens be proportionate to each party's degree of wrongdoing. Since, in the present case, no one has acted wrongly, the backpacker and owner are moral equals, and therefore each should bear half of the loss.[33]

That is to take a wrong turn. Implicit in the preceding paragraph is the assumption that moral arbitration is properly carried out from the perspective of a detached, disinterested observer whose concern is to rearrange holdings to fit with an impersonal standard of moral worthiness.[34] But neither of the parties to the affair has reason to adopt that perspective. Both the backpacker and the owner are *interested* parties and, as such, they lack reason to accede to determinations that issue from a thoroughly impersonal standard. Rather, each can reasonably take his own interest in living as an unimpeded project pursuer to be a crucial determinant of what is justifiable to him.

Feinberg's backpacker needs the shelter that the cabin affords and so has overwhelmingly good reason from his perspective to break in. It is not, of course, a matter of corresponding urgency to the owner that the packpacker break in. She may take no interest whatsoever in stranded hikers or merely display the level of moderate concern that one typically has for some anonymous person's distress. Because the backpacker's intrusion sets back her interests, we can represent the owner's instinctive first response as a demand that the backpacker not intrude. However, the owner does not suffer from solipsism, so she realizes that the backpacker lacks reason to accede to that demand. She acknowledges that a requirement of nonentry is unjustifiable from the perspective of the backpacker. Because it cannot be justified to the backpacker, the owner cannot claim that the backpacker acted wrongly in using the cabin.

That, though, is not the end of the story. Once shelter has been secured, there the question remains of who should bear the resultant losses. The backpacker's first move might be to reflect, "I have not acted wrongly and therefore should have no burden imposed on account of my entirely innocent action." However, the backpacker also is not a solipsist. He understands that the owner has a life of her own to lead and therefore has reason from her own perspective to disvalue the damage done to her holdings. So he concedes the warrantability of the following response offered by the owner: "I acknowledge that you had overwhelmingly good reason to make use of my cabin. But those are *your* reasons, not mine. Your interest in living as a project pursuer has been advanced but mine has been retarded. I too am entirely innocent in the affair; why then should I, rather than you, be obliged to bear the resultant disadvantage?"

It might appear that an impasse has been reached; each actor properly takes himself to be blameless, and each is, all else equal, disinclined to bear costs consequent on blameless conduct. However, not all else is equal. Those costs have not simply fallen from the skies, as they literally do when a meteor falls on a cabin. Rather, they have been occasioned by the backpacker's actions in service of his own continuing capacity to live as a project pursuer. While everyone might have *some* reason, even if vanishingly small, to take an interest in the backpacker's well-being, he is the one for whom that is a *commanding* interest.[35] It is *his* projects, *his* life, that the blizzard jeopardizes. Therefore, *he* has powerful reasons to bear costs to preserve himself, reasons that cannot be universalized, in all their power, to everyone.

Individuals need various goods to live successfully as project pursuers. Some can only be provided by themselves for themselves, for example self-respect. Others can only be provided by others, for example friendship and, crucially noninterference. Yet others can be provided either by the agent himself or by others: an adequate level of material well-being typically falls into this category. The principle via which the impasse between the backpacker and owner is broken is that, where a good is such that either the agent himself or others are able to make provision, the onus properly falls on the agent. That principle derives from the individuated nature of practical reason within which each project pursuer has reason to lend special weight to the ends that are distinctively his own.[36]

It is now not difficult to pinpoint the defect in Montague's argument. He assumes that the relevant moral consideration is simply who, if anyone, has acted wrongly. However, from the perspective of the involved parties what is of primary significance is not some god's-eye-view estimation of moral rectitude but rather their ability to act on behalf of those ends that specially matter to them. The backpacker serves his own ends by breaking into the cabin; costs are thereby generated. On whom should they fall? The indicated answer is that they are properly to be borne by the backpacker. It is he who has reason to take the creation of those costs for the sake of saving his skin to be a splendid bargain. Thus he has reason, reason that derives from his own perspective, to acknowledge that the onus properly falls on him, not the owner.

VII

I append a corollary intended to reinforce the results of the preceding analysis by showing their affinity to a related limitation in the scope of rights.

Most people believe that individuals in exigency can justifiably claim from others as a matter of right the provision of needed welfare goods. For some theorists the proposition is unproblematic. They can directly appeal to elaborate criteria of distributive justice or some antecedent equality presumption to justify transfers from the more to the less well off. However, for classical liberals who insist on the paramount status of noninterference and who find theories of distributive justice to be unpersuasive, mandatory transfers are problematic. Why, in the absence of any determination of fault or particular obligation, should one group of individuals be required to transfer their holdings to another? Each person has a primary interest in advancing the ends constituted by his own projects; how then can forced redistribution be justified to the less-than-willing provider? For the more well-off to make charitable provision for the less fortunate may be salutary, but that is a long step from the conclusion that provision is warranted as a matter of basic rights.

Again, the problem is best approached from the perspective of the individuated practical reason of the different involved parties rather than in terms of some impersonal allocative standard. Each individual has reason to value the noninterference

of others. Under a wide—but, as we have seen, not unbounded
—range of circumstances, that translates into a reciprocal interest in pledging noninterference subject to the receipt of same.
Specifically, and in parallel with the preceding discussion, the
boundaries are established by the ability of the respective parties
each to live as a project pursuer. I may have compelling reason
to value your not encroaching on my person or property, but
what reason do you have to accede? If the predictable consequence of your acquiescence would be to fall below the baseline
of being able to act effectively in the service of your own ends,
the indicated answer is: precious little. Moreover, because I
acknowledge your primary interest in advancing your own projects, I must concede, if I am rational, that you lack sufficient
reason to sacrifice your own prospects for the sake of those
resplendent ends that happen to be mine. Consequently, I have
practical reason to acknowledge the cogency of your unwilling-
ness to tender me the noninterference I crave unless you somehow are ensured provision of a level of welfare goods adequate
to safeguard minimally decent life prospects.

That is not to write a blank check. It conveys no entitlement
to any level of well-being higher than that of the baseline. Hence
it should not be understood as motivated by an egalitarian im-
pulse or any other impersonal standard of just distribution. Nor
does it disregard the principle that, for goods that can be supplied either by oneself or by someone else, the primary onus
falls on the agent to secure that which he needs.[37] The claim for
provision by others is contingent, kicking in only when an individual is genuinely unable to secure for himself a minimal level
of well-being. But though contingent and strictly limited to the
relief of exigency, it nonetheless constitutes a claim that can
justifiably be asserted as a matter of right.[38]

The connection to the preceding analysis of compensation
can be yet more tightly drawn. I demand of you noninterference with my efforts. If your straits are dire, noninterference
may come at a cost too great for you reasonably to assume. The
situation is transformed into one in which you have good reason
to forbear in your relations with me if I transfer resources to
you adequate to *compensate* you for your forbearance. Admittedly, this is to play on words. "Compensation" so understood is

not, as previously, a penalty payment consequent on some prior infringement. It is more like compensation in the sense of *remuneration*. The employer compensates the worker for hours put in on the job, but there is no suggestion that the employer has in any way been responsible for some antecedent breach in the moral order.[39] However, it is not pure equivocation. Compensation in the wake of an infringement of rights is a move toward *restoration* of a moral order; compensating individuals via welfare payments for their forbearance is a necessary precondition for the *creation* of a moral order such that each has reason to acknowledge the moral space of the other.

The two preceding paragraphs stylized the interchange as a two-party transaction. That made for simplicity, but simplicity comes at a cost. In a multiperson world, I will not rationally be obliged to acknowledge your claim on my resources. Rather, I can eloquently object, "Why me?" That is, why should your demand not be pressed on some one of the myriad of other people who are able to relieve your distress? But if my eloquence persuades you, the problem reappears; for each of them can also justifiably ask, "Why me?" Entirely unsurprisingly, collective assumption of the responsibility to guarantee a minimum welfare level emerges as the preferred solution. Every project pursuer requires noninterference from all others. Therefore, an appropriately universalized duty to relieve the indigent satisfies principles of formal justice. Efficiency considerations also support this result.[40] A system of welfare rights is thereby derivable from an individuated theory of practical reason.

The analogy between justifiable rights infringements and welfare rights would be tighter still if it could be shown that recipients of relief have a duty subsequently to compensate providers. No such conclusion follows, at least not in its fully generalized form. An extraction of transfer payments from those who subsist at or near the baseline would plunge them below the level at which a decent life is livable, a thoroughly unjustifiable outcome from their perspective. The closest approximation to mandatory compensation is this: those who emerge from indigence are now obliged to contribute to the collective pool from which welfare payments are made. If we wish to press the analogy, we can put it this way: those who are welfare recipients today can justifiably be called on to be providers tomorrow; those who are secure cabin owners today might be imperiled backpackers tomorrow.

VIII

Rights establish boundaries that others must not cross. The truth of that proposition seems to be threatened by examples such as that of Feinberg's backpacker. I have attempted to show that these cases speak not to the stringency of rights claims but rather to their scope. If we properly attend to scope, permissions to infringe rights will not present themselves as ad hoc exceptions to the moral demands entailed by rights. Rather, these permissions will be seen to flow from the same underlying theory out of which rights themselves emerge. Compensation, both for infringements that are wrongful and for those that are justified, is to be understood as a secondary, equilibrium-restoring move. Finally, I have tried to show that permissible infringements are not *sui generis* but rather are more closely akin to the rationale for welfare rights than might have been suspected. If I am successful, it follows that a regime of strong, independent rights is morally sturdy. It is not in need of consequentialist infusions, nor does it demand of individuals that they act contrary to those reasons that well and truly apply to them.[41]

NOTES

1. Joel Feinberg, "Voluntary Euthanasia and the Inalienable Right to Life," *Philosophy & Public Affairs* 7 (1978): 93–123 at p. 102.

2. The case would be less difficult for strict constructionists if the conflict were between right and right such that the infringement of someone's rights were inescapable. That is not the case here. If the backpacker allows himself to perish in the blizzard, the outcome is terribly unfortunate, but no rights have thereby been infringed.

3. See, for example, J. J. C. Smart, "Extreme and Restricted Utilitarianism," *Philosophical Quarterly* 6 (1956): 344–54.

4. Judith Jarvis Thomson, "Some Ruminations on Rights," *University of Arizona Law Review* 19 (1977); reprinted in Thomson, *Rights,*

Restitutions and Risk (Cambridge: Harvard University Press, 1986), 49–65 at p. 56. Emphasis in original.

5. Feinberg, "Voluntary Euthanasia," 102. Emphasis in original.

6. They may, of course, also leave themselves liable to *punishment*. To speak crudely, individuals are properly punishable only if compensation is inadequate to restore the moral balance of the status quo ante. See section IV for a brief discussion of the triggering conditions for punishment. The problem confronted in the present case, however, is not some putative inadequacy of compensation but rather the identification of a wrongful act that might justify *any* steps to restore the moral equilibrium.

7. Philip Montague in "Rights and Duties of Compensation," *Philosophy & Public Affairs* 13 (1984): 79–88, argues that only wrongful actions generate duties to compensate and, therefore, that the backpacker owes nothing to the cabin owner. Montague's argument is criticized by Nancy Davis, "Rights, Permission, and Compensation," *Philosophy & Public Affairs* 14 (1985): 374–84; and Peter Westen, "Comment on Montague's 'Rights and Duties of Compensation,'" *Philosophy & Public Affairs* 14 (1985): 385–89. Montague responds in "Davis and Westen on Rights and Compensation," *Philosophy & Public Affairs* 14 (1985): 390–96. I take up Montague's arguments in section VI.

8. Why that should be so is complex. I believe that at least part of the answer is because individuals have reason generally to value not only what *comes to obtain* but also what they *act to bring about*. When you consent to a particular transaction, you are one of the parties instrumental in acting to produce that state of affairs, but when I impute your assent and act accordingly, you are a passive recipient of my action. It is our interest in being *agents* that renders actual consent crucial. A useful comparison is to Nozick's "experience machine" which will provide you any experience you crave, the illusion of having achieved whatever you might have wished to accomplish. It would certainly be pleasant to pass some time in this way. But would it be irrational of you to decline to spend the rest of your life hooked up to the experience machine? Most people, Nozick included, would say no. What matters to us is not only how things *feel* but how they *are*. See Robert Nozick *Anarchy, State, and Utopia* (New York: Basic Books, 1974), 42–45. Being the passive recipient of others' actions is, in certain relevant ways, like being an appendage of the experience machine. That which you want may be done, but the crucial point is that you are not the one who is doing it.

That is not, however, to maintain that it is always better from the perspective of an individual to be active rather than passive, nor that one is never justified in interposing one's own judgment of what an individual would want for the person's actual determination. So, to cite one prosaic example, you do not necessarily act wrongly in buying a friend a present rather than giving her cash so that she can pick out what she wants for herself.

9. Judith Jarvis Thomson, "Rights and Compensation," *Nous* 14 (1980); reprinted in William Parent ed., *Rights, Restitution and Risk*, 66–77 at p. 68.

10. I owe this version to David Cole.

11. I do not mean to imply that this is the only disqualifying condition. An additional one might be: one may not act to secure what is needed by infringing the rights of someone else when so to act places the other in a situation of comparably grave or graver need. Doubtlessly, a complete theory of needs and rights will require yet further clauses, but it is not my ambition here to develop that theory.

12. Indirectly utilitarian theorists may agree that a direct appeal to utility is misplaced but nonetheless maintain that the *ultimate* explanation of the wrongness of violating the cabin owner's rights is consequentialist in form. I shall not, on this occasion, take up the consequentialist challenge, but see L. Lomasky, "A Refutation of Utilitarianism," *Journal of Value Inquiry* 17 (1983): 259–79.

13. For example, when one otherwise would subject a loved one to comparable misery; see section V.

14. *Paternalism* also typically involves an attempt to make people better off by infringing their rights. The present case does not qualify as an instance of paternalism because the backpacker is not motivated to break into the cabin to enhance the welfare of its owner. Given the difference in motive, whatever arguments hold against paternalism would seem to apply with even greater force against the overcompensating backpacker.

15. For that fuller analysis, see L. Lomasky, *Persons, Rights, and the Moral Community* (New York: Oxford University Press, 1987).

16. See Nozick, *Anarchy, State, and Utopia*, 28–35.

17. Ronald Dworkin, *Taking Rights Seriously* (Cambridge: Harvard University Press, 1977), xi.

18. Notably Joseph Raz in *The Morality of Freedom* (Oxford: Clarendon Press, 1986). See esp. pp. 186–88 and 279–80.

19. See the reference in n. 15. The abbreviated account largely follows that of L. Lomasky, "Rights without Stilts," *Harvard Journal of Law & Public Policy* 12 (1989): 775–812.

20. Lomasky, *Persons, Rights, and the Moral Community*, 83.

21. Jules Coleman, "Corrective Justice and Wrongful Gain," in his

Markets, Morals and the Law (Cambridge: Cambridge University Press, 1988), 184–201 at pp. 187–88.

22. Considerations of economic efficiency may, as Coleman observes, be an important factor in choosing among alternative compensation schemes.

23. I believe that there is a morally significant distinction between rectification and compensation but will not pursue that point here. See Lomasky, *Persons, Rights, and the Moral Community*, 142–46.

24. Or, to avoid begging an important question, no harm is done to *A* above and beyond that constituted by the fact of *B's* encroachment on *A's* protected moral space.

25. Randy Barnett recommends in "Restitution: A New Paradigm of Criminal Justice," *Ethics* 87 (1977): 279–301, that criminal justice be subsumed under rectificatory justice. Barnett is correct to note that the harms occasioned by crimes generate a specific moral debt between victim and victimizer but errs in failing to acknowledge the significance of breaches in the overall moral order.

26. I have in mind not only strictly labeled "deterrence theories of punishment" but also theories in which considerations of deterrence are not primary but may be admitted just so long as we adequately retribute, reform, or whatever.

27. Thomas Hobbes, *Leviathan,* ed. Michael Oakeshott (New York: Macmillan, 1962), 100, 103.

28. The relevant contrast is with the backpacker of the third story in section II.

29. Nozick, *Anarchy, State, and Utopia,* 30n.

30. Nonetheless, it might appear that considerations of rights have given way to a purely consequentialist analysis. I believe this appraisal to be mistaken. See Lomasky, "Rights without Stilts," for an extended argument to the effect that these sorts of cases are more tractable within a theory of strong, independent rights than when fed into the consequentialist calculus.

31. Montague, "Rights and Duties of Compensation," 84.

32. See Jules Coleman, "The Morality of Strict Tort Liability,"in his *Markets, Morals and the Law,* 166–83.

33. But then why just *these* two innocent parties? The world is *filled with people* who are guiltless in the affair of the imperiled backpacker. Should they not all equally share in the costs? Perhaps some such consideration lies behind Coleman's contention in "Corrective Justice and Wrongful Gain" that corrective justice can be well served by a policy of compensating losses out of a social insurance fund. But see section IV above.

34. This assumption is developed in Roderick Firth, "Ethical Absolutism and the Ideal Observer," *Philosophy & Phenomenological Research* 12 (1952): 317–45. It is characterized as the highest level of moral appraisal in R. M. Hare, *Moral Thinking* (Oxford: Clarendon Press, 1981).

35. Moreover, it is the *primary* interest that the backpacker has in his own well-being from which the *secondary* interest that others may have derives; their concerns are not symmetrical. See Lomasky, *Persons, Rights, and the Moral Community*, 63–65.

36. This argument is developed more extensively in Lomasky, *Persons, Rights, and the Moral Community*, 84–100.

37. One additional qualification is that the quantity of resources extracted from an individual not seriously impinge on his prospects for project pursuit. There may be yet additional complications to be addressed by a full-fledged theory of welfare rights. It is not my ambition here to display such a theory but merely to sketch out a rationale for welfare rights that is premised on no impersonal standard of distributive justice.

38. For an elaboration of the argument, see my *Persons, Rights, and the Moral Community*, 125–29.

39. Inattention to this ambiguity vitiates, I believe, much of the argument of Thomson's "Rights and Compensation."

40. See L. Lomasky, "Response to Four Critics," *Reason Papers* 14 (1989) 110–29, esp. pp. 124–28.

41. I have benefited from conversations with David Cole and Robert Evans. I am especially grateful to Gerald Gaus for penetrating consideration and criticism of almost every aspect of this paper.

2

DOES COMPENSATION
RESTORE EQUALITY?

GERALD F. GAUS

1. Introductory

What does compensatory justice seek to accomplish?* A formal
answer, of course, is that, like all justice, it seeks to assure each
his due. Aristotle's analysis of "corrective" or "rectificatory" justice, however, proffers a more specific answer:

> What the judge aims at doing is to make the parts equal by the
> penalty he imposes, whereby he takes from the aggressor any
> gain he may have secured. The equal, then is a mean between
> the more and the less. But gain and loss are each of them more
> or less in opposite ways, more good and less evil being gains, the
> more evil and the less good being loss. The equal, which we hold
> to be just, is now seen to be intermediate between them. Hence
> we conclude that corrective justice must be the mean between
> loss and gain. This explains why the disputants have recourse to
> a judge; for to go to a judge is to go to justice. . . . What the judge
> does is to restore equality.[1]

*In thinking about these matters, I have greatly benefited from discussions with
Bob Evans and Loren Lomasky. I also benefited from the comments of Sharon
Beattie, John Chapman, Eve Cole, Jim Fetzer and Doc Mayo. My thanks to
Linda Hatten for her research assistance.

In this chapter I consider whether compensatory justice can be understood in this Aristotelian fashion, as somehow restoring equality between parties. In contemporary ethics and political philosophy this notion of compensation as a return to equality has had two very different manifestations. The first is "the principle of redress," according to which the fundamental aim of social justice is to redress undeserved inequalities. Section 2 argues that this principle is based on a strongly egalitarian ethic hostile to the fundamental claim of liberalism. I then turn in sections 3 and 4 to a more modest understanding of the "return to equality." It is sometimes argued that a rights violator who fully compensates a victim for her losses thereby restores his condition of moral equality with the victim. Here also, I shall argue, the Aristotelian account fails. However, I contend in section 5 that in one case compensatory justice does restore equality: justified rights violations.

2. Restoring Equality (I): The Principle of Redress

2.1. Social Justice and Moral Balance

Compensatory justice seems necessarily a second-level principle of justice insofar as it operates on other, more basic principles. Compensatory justice apparently tells us what to do when people do not live up to their first-level duties or when they fail to respect first-level rights. So understood, it is a part of what Rawls calls "nonideal" theory, that is, "principles for meeting injustice."[2] But Rawls seeks to assign an altogether more basic role to compensatory justice: he seems attracted to the view that it forms the foundation for much of ideal theory. Rawls explains the egalitarian character of the difference principle by saying that it achieves "some of the intent" of the principle of redress. "This is the principle that undeserved inequalities call for redress; and since inequalities of birth and natural endowment are undeserved, these inequalities are somewhat to be compensated for."[3] My point here is not simply that Rawls's theory of social justice is built upon a commitment to compensatory justice. As John Passmore points out, "From a certain point of view, facilitatory social justice can be thought of as reparative."[4]

But to conceive of social justice as reparative is typically still to view it as a response to past injustices: social justice as compensatory justice would still be a nonideal, second-level principle. But if we take the principle of redress as the foundation of social justice—or as one of the foundational principles[5]—the very notion of ideal social justice becomes essentially compensatory.

Rawls is more than a little reluctant fully to commit himself to the principle of redress; the "difference principle," we are told, is "not the same as that of redress," although "it does achieve some of the intent of the latter principle."[6] However, Rawls's discussion draws on an essay by Herbert Spiegelberg that provides an unabashed defense of the principle of redress. Writes Spiegelberg:

> The argument for the demand of universal equality . . . rests on two premises: (1) *undeserved discriminations call for redress,* (2) *all inequalities of birth constitute undeserved discriminations.* I shall conclude that (3) *all inequalities of birth call for redress.* Such redress implies, at least in principle, the cancellation of all inequalities of birth by equalization. In this sense it follows, that (4) *equality is a fundamental ethical demand.*[7]

In defense of (1) Spiegelberg refers to the legal notion of "unjust enrichment"; any special benefit that cannot be justified, it seems, constitutes an unjust enrichment. And in accord with Aristotle's analysis, Spiegelberg holds that this enrichment brings about a "moral disequilibrium"; compensatory justice calls for reestablishing the moral balance by equalization.[8] And since natural talents are undeserved discriminations, redress is called for.

David Gauthier has pointed out a fatal flaw in the case for the principle of redress. If we take seriously Spiegelberg's reference to unjust enrichment, the argument is that since the discriminations are undeserved, that is, they are contrary to desert, being enriched by them is unjust. But this does not provide the foundation for step (2). For "it is surely mistaken to hold that natural inequalities are undeserved. They are not deserved, they do not accord with desert, but equally they are not undeserved, they are not contrary to desert."[9] If (1) means that all discriminations contrary to desert require redress, it seems that nothing follows regarding discriminations based on natural talents. As Gauthier points out, though these inequalities are not sanctioned by desert, neither are they contrary to it. Indeed, as Rawls himself acknowledges, the upshot is that "[t]he notion of desert does not apply to such cases."[10] At this point it seems that the argument for the principle of redress depends on an equivocation between "not deserved" (not sanctioned by desert) and "undeserved" (violating the principle of desert).[11]

2.2 A Reformulated Argument for Redress

We can reformulate the argument for the principle of redress in a way that saves it from equivocation by substituting for step (1), principle E:

> E: Any discriminatory act—any action that provides differential advantages or burdens—stands in need of justification; any unjustified discriminatory act calls for redress.

Spiegelberg actually seems to have something akin to principle E in mind. "The premise that undeserved discriminations call for redress," he affirms, "thus implies that only morally deserved inequalities justify unequal lots: *without such special justification all persons, whether equal or unequal, ought to have equal shares.*"[12] The crucial claim here is not that these advantages are undeserved, but that they are unjustified (say, by the claim that they are deserved), and in the absence of such a justification they are unjust. For E it is enough that natural talents are not deserved (that is, not sanctioned by desert); there is no need to make the (false) claim that they are undeserved (that is, contrary to desert).

Building upon E, one could argue:

1. Any discriminatory act—any action that provides differential advantages or burdens—stands in need of justification; any unjustified discriminatory act calls for redress.
2. All social and economic inequalities are based on discriminatory acts—differential benefits and burdens are generated by social systems and institutions.

3. These inequalities thus demand justification.
4. They cannot be justified on the grounds that people deserve their differential talents and, so, deserve the differential benefits or burdens that flow from them.
5. Consequently, in lieu of some other justification for these social and economic inequalities, redress is called for.

Two comments are required here. First, I have framed the revised argument for redress not in terms of the unjustness of nature—for example, what natural endowments a person has received in the lottery of birth—but rather in terms of actions that are based on these. As Rawls says, "The natural distribution is neither just nor unjust; nor is it unjust that persons are born into society at some particular position. These are simply natural facts. What is just and unjust is the way that institutions deal with these facts."[13] Secondly, the revised argument provides only a presumption in favor of redress. As step 5 explicitly allows, there may be some other justification for these inequalities. All the revised argument maintains is that unjustified discriminations call for redress, and that desert is not available as a justification.

2.3 The Principle of Redress as Antiliberal

E is an egalitarian principle. It asserts a blanket moral presumption in favor of equality; it is incumbent on he who is talented to show that his talents are justified or, I suppose, to show that any advantages that accrue to him (say, the admiration of his fellows) can be justified. If he cannot provide a justification, his advantages have upset the moral balance and require redress. And, presumably, because Spiegelberg does not think one can justify such talents and advantages, we are led to a notion of social justice that seeks to restore the moral balance by somehow compensating for their unequalizing effects.

Principles that place the onus of justification on one party rather than another are substantive moral principles: they state that some condition is the moral status quo in the sense that it requires no further justification whereas departures from it do.[14] They present us with a moral asymmetry. Now liberal political philosophy typically offers a competing presumptive principle:

> L: Interference with another's activity requires justification; un-justified interference is unjust.

Certainly this is fundamental to liberal political and legal theory. As Joel Feinberg says, "most writers . . . have endorsed a kind of 'presumption in favor of liberty' requiring that whenever a legislator is faced with a choice between imposing a legal duty on citizens or leaving them at liberty, other things being equal, he should leave individuals free to make their own choices. Liberty should be the norm; coercion always requires some special justification."[15] Extending this presumption from liberal legal theory to liberal ethics seems straightforward.[16]

Now L and E are competing principles. If L holds, then Alf is free to praise Betty for her wonderful talents, and to shower gifts upon her, unless Charlie can justify interfering with Alf. Perhaps Charlie can provide some justification: all that the Liberal Principle says is that Alf is free to do as he wishes until Charlie can produce a justification for interfering with Alf by making him refrain from rewarding Betty as he sees fit, with his praise or his goods. But E holds that Alf or Betty must justify Alf's actions. According to the Egalitarian Principle Charlie need not say anything: unless Alf and/or Betty can justify their actions, they have upset the moral balance and so redress is in order.

Let me put my point in a less formal way. It is often argued that liberals suppose that each person is free to do as he wishes until some justification is presented for limiting his liberty. As Locke said, all men are naturally in "a *State of perfect Freedom* to order their actions . . . as they see fit . . . without asking leave, or depending upon the Will of any other Man."[17] To these liberals, the right to natural liberty determines the point of departure for all subsequent ethical and political justifications: all henceforth are concerned with liberty-limiting principles. Now the Egalitarian Principle postulates a very different starting point for normative theory: all successful justificatory argument establishes permissible inequalities. And in the absence of successful arguments, the fallback position is always a moral demand for equality. The formulated case for the principle of redress supposes precisely this: in the absence of some good reason, morality demands equality. And when we have departed from equality without justification, restoring equality is morally required. Hence the fundamental role of the principle of redress.

2.4. Liberalism and Formal Equality

Principle *E*, I have argued, is illiberally egalitarian. It may seem that this must be wrong. Many philosophers—indeed liberal philosophers—see *E*'s presumption in favor of equality as a demand of reason itself. Benn and Peters, for instance, defend the principle that *"none shall be held to have a claim to better treatment than another, in advance of good grounds being produced."*[18] They continue:

> Understood in this way, the principle of equality does not prescribe positively that all humans be treated alike; it is a presumption against treating them differently, in any respect, until grounds for distinction have been shewn. It does not assume, therefore, a quality which all men have to the same degree, which is the ground of the presumption, for to say that there is a presumption means that no grounds need be shewn. The onus of justification rests on whoever would make distinctions.
>   . . . Presume equality until there is a reason to presume otherwise.[19]

This is an immensely popular position; Richard Flatham, Isaiah Berlin and William Frankena, to name just a few, endorse it.[20] The consensus is that so understood the presumption in favor of equality is (1) a demand of reason or logic and (2) only weakly egalitarian in its implications. Both, I think, are wrong.

Consider first the claim that the presumption in favor of equality is a demand of rationality or nonarbitrariness. According to J. R. Lucas—certainly no radical egalitarian—"formal equality" is simply a statement of the universality of reason. "It requires that if two people are being treated, or are treated, differently, there should be some relevant difference between them."[21] So if Alf gives a present to Betty but not to Doris then nonarbitrariness demands that Alf have some reason that differentiates Betty from Doris. If he does not, if, as far as he is concerned, Betty and Doris are equally deserving of his attention and affections, then he is being arbitrary, illogical or irrational to shower gifts on Betty. This example already shows that the principle is not as intuitively obvious as some of its exponents would have us believe. Some philosophers insist that in this sort of case Alf's action simply resists any universalization: even if Betty and Doris are *exactly alike,* it has been argued, it is perfectly understandable, and not at all crazy, for Alf to love Betty and not Doris.[22] But suppose (as I think is correct)[23] we take a more traditional view, and hold that even here Alf is committed to some conception of universalizable reasons. If he is rational, something about Betty attracts him to her rather than to Doris (perhaps simply their shared history—Alf saw Betty first). If Betty and Doris were really exactly alike in every way, Alf's preference really would be irrational. But surely, even granting this, Alf need not *justify* his preference to Doris or anyone else. It is one thing to acknowledge that a rational Alf will have his reasons (though he may not be cognizant of them); it is quite another to say that he must justify his preference. Yet advocates of presumptions of equality typically assert, as do Benn and Peters, an "onus of justification." As Benn claims in a later essay, "discrimination in treatment between persons requires *moral* justification: it is not enough simply to *prefer* one to another since that involves regarding another person from the point of view of one's own satisfaction; respect for a person involves a right to be considered from his *own* standpoint."[24]

As Benn recognizes, a justification must provide others with what are reasons from their perspectives.[25] Principle *E,* Benn and Peters's egalitarianism, as well as Benn's later principle, places on each of us a moral requirement to provide reasons to others—justifications—whenever our actions lead to differential treatment. So far from being a simple and uncontroversial demand of reason, this principle would wreak havoc on our lives. One would need to justify to potential spouses whom one did not choose—provide reasons from their perspectives—why one didn't choose them. If one chose to buy a house in one neighborhood rather than another, and both need new residents, one would have to justify one's choice to those disadvantaged by it. But why must I justify to others my choice to live in East rather than West Duluth? It hardly is a demand of rationality itself that I do so. Indeed, such a pervasive requirement to justify oneself is terribly intrusive, and quite at odds with the liberal presumption in favor of noninterference.[26]

To be sure, in political, legal and administrative contexts the presumption in favor of equal treatment is explicable and important.[27] In these contexts officials are properly required to justify their differential treatment of citizens. In the absence of justification we certainly are apt to conclude that an injustice has been committed. But two features of these settings render them unhelpful in showing that E is a basic principle of morality.[28] First, citizens come before judges and administrators with rights and duties. The egalitarian principle is thereby transformed into the requirement that those with equal legal rights and duties be treated alike. This is clearly neither foundational, because it supposes an independently defined set of rights and duties, nor is it strongly egalitarian. Second, public officials differ from private citizens in a crucial respect. Whereas we suppose that private individuals are free to act as they see fit until, as it were, they run into the rights of others or some duty, *this* presumption does not hold for public officials. We presume that what one does in an official capacity always stands in need of justification, say, to a superior. If Alf is acting in his private capacity, it is entirely reasonable for him to respond to a request to justify his discriminatory actions with the retort that it is his own business why he acts as he does. Admittedly, if Alf has violated the rights of another we will insist on justification, but he is under no standing obligation to justify his actions to others. Public officials are. They must be able to provide publicly accessible reasons justifying what they do in their official capacity.[29] But we ask much less of private agents. And that is why the principle of formal equality before the law—so central to liberal political and legal theory—becomes illiberal when transplanted into ethical theory.

3. Restoring Equality (II): The Debt Model

3.1. What Is a Return to Equality?

So far I have argued that compensatory justice *qua* the principle of redress cannot provide the foundation for social justice in liberal theory. The principle of redress is most plausibly interpreted as relying on the presumption in favor of equality (*E*); and this presumption is inconsistent with the liberal presumption of noninterference (*L*). Now if we reject principle *E*, if equality is not the moral baseline, it follows that not every de-equalizing act must be either justified or redressed. We have now two types of actions that produce inequalities: those that call for either justification or redress and those that do not. What distinguishes them? The most obvious answer is that the former are *wrongful*, or *rights-violating*, deequalizing acts while the latter are not. It thus might seem that we are led to something like the following principle:

> Any discriminatory action that provides differential benefits to Betty, or burdens on Alf, when Alf has a right to equality, must be either justified or compensated.

But now that we have rejected the strongly egalitarian notion of compensatory justice articulated in the principle of redress, this revision of the egalitarian conception looks manifestly strange. It cannot be only rights to equality that ground compensation. Consider the following possibility: Alf has lots of property, Betty very little. Betty violates Alf's property rights by stealing. Would the above principle require compensation be paid to Alf? Not obviously. Perhaps it could be argued that although Alf and Betty have unequal *property*, they have equal property *rights*, and that is the condition of equality, to which we seek a return. But that will not do. Say Betty promises to buy Alf lunch: he has a right against her, but she has no corresponding right against him. Now suppose she breaks her promise. If Alf is entitled to some form of compensation the aim cannot be to restore an equality of rights.

What, then, is meant when it is said that compensatory justice restores equality? William Blackstone provides the following interpretation of Aristotelian corrective justice:

> Corrective justice . . . involves a rectifying or reparatory transaction between one person or party and another. Here there is an attempt to restore the equality which existed prior to the injury of one party by the other. The penalty imposed on the party who inflicted the injury and the corresponding benefit bestowed on the injured party should be proportional to the difference created by the injury.[30]

Unfortunately, this explication is not pellucid. But the account seems to involve two elements: (1) redistribution that allows for (2) a return to moral equality.

3.2. The Redistributive Claim

A claim of an unjust distribution of resources is fundamental to compensatory justice. Some wrongful action by Betty against Alf leads to an unjust distribution of resources between them.[31] The most obvious case is where Betty steals some of Alf's property, and quite literally transfers resources. Unlike penal sanctions, which follow from the mere act of wrongdoing, compensatory justice focuses on wrongdoing with redistributional consequences.[32] Compensatory justice, then, is premised on some just distribution, and seeks to return to that distribution after unjustified departures from it.[33] Compensation thus aims at the "elimination of unjustifiable *gains and losses* owing to human action."[34] To be sure, sometimes questions of compensatory justice do not appear to involve distributive issues. If Betty attacks Alf, he may reasonably claim compensation for his pain. But, of course, here too we confront a distributive issue: Betty's unjust action inflicts costs on Alf, and he seeks to recover these costs.

Compensation is usefully seen as a repayment.[35] This is the basis for the familiar notion that compensation is a sort of *debt*. Judith Thomson, for instance, says that the notion of a debt of compensation is familiar: "if we have wronged A, we owe him something; we should make amends, we should compensate him for the wrong done."[36] A special moral relation exists, then, between victim and aggressor: the aggressor is indebted to the victim, she owes him something because of what she has done.[37] The idea of a debt points to a distribution of resources to which we have a moral reason to return: until a transfer is made from aggressor to victim, the victim does not have that to which he is entitled while the aggressor has more than she is entitled to.

The notion of debt indicates that some amount, or some particular thing, is owed by the aggressor to the victim.[38] Let us, then, say that the debt has been completely repaid if the victim receives *full compensation*. According to Robert Nozick, "[s]omething fully compensates a person for a loss if and only if it makes him no worse off than he would otherwise have been; it compensates person X for person Y's action A if X is no worse off receiving it, Y having done A, than X would have been without receiving it if Y had not done A."[39] So we can say that by one's wrongful act one inflicts costs on another. Fully to compensate a person is to redistribute resources to him so that all these costs are, in a sense, repaid.

Blackstone points to a more modest notion of compensation. To determine the amount of compensation to repay a wronged party fully, Blackstone says, would require something like omniscience. His Aristotelian conception calls only for "proportional" compensation: "equal claims be given equal compensation."[40] However, for now let us pursue the demands of compensation as full repayment. Let us say, following Nozick and Gauthier, that full compensation demands that a victim receives the same utility from the two sets of actions: {being wronged, being compensated}, {not being wronged, not being compensated}.[41]

3.3. A Challenge to the Debt Model

The debt repayment model suggests a transaction between the victim and aggressor. And it does seem intuitively right that the aggressor owes the victim compensation. That is, the debt model suggests that if Betty has wronged Alf in a way that causes him loss, then (1) Alf has a claim to be compensated and (2) Betty

has an obligation to repay. Jules Coleman, however, has repeatedly argued against this fairly standard view. He writes:

> If there is wrongful loss, it ought to be annulled; the same goes
> for wrongful or unwarranted gains. Nevertheless, the principle
> of corrective justice which enables us to identify compensable
> losses and unjust enrichments does not commit us to adopting
> any particular mode of rectification. The principle that deter-
> mines which gains and losses are to be eliminated does not by
> itself specify a means for doing so. Presumably there is more
> than one way of rectifying undeserved gains and losses.[42]

At this point two aspects of compensatory justice to which I
have pointed diverge. If compensatory justice is taken as concerned with protecting a certain distribution of resources, then
what is essential is that wrongful losses and wrongful gains are
eliminated, and the just pattern restored. It does not greatly
matter who compensates the victim and how wrongful gains are
annulled: what matters is that somehow this is done in a way
that restores the just pattern.[43] But this proposal undermines
the debt model. For the debt model *adds* to the redistributional
requirement a moral relation between aggressor and victim: the
aggressor *owes* the victim. And until compensation occurs the
victim has a complaint *against the aggressor*. Not against others,
or society at large, but against the aggressor.

Coleman's proposal can be interpreted in both a radical and
a moderate sense. The radical interpretation is that the question
(1) "who has agressed against Alf?" is entirely independent of
(2) "who has an obligation to compensate Alf?" Now on the face
of it, Coleman misses a crucial moral fact: the victim's complaint
is against the aggressor, and not against society at large. If he is
not compensated, it is the aggressor who has not repaid her
debt. It is hard to believe that our two questions are really
independent. Coleman, however, would insist that they are—at
least in the case where, although the victim has incurred wrongful losses, the aggressor has not accrued wrongful gains. He
writes:

> So when I claim that if an injurer who through his fault imposes
> a wrongful loss on another but who does not thereby gain has an
> obligation to repair, his obligation cannot derive directly from

the principle of corrective justice, I mean only to be emphasizing
the obvious fact that he has secured no gain which would be the
concern of corrective justice to rectify. His victim's claim to recompense is on the other hand a matter of corrective justice. And
if we feel that the injurer should rectify his victim's loss, it must
be for reasons other than the fact that so doing is required to
annul his gain.[44]

This is not quite so obvious. The victim, as Coleman says, has
incurred a wrongful loss—the aggressor has brought about a
maldistribution of holdings. Resources, then, must be redistributed to return to a just pattern. Coleman's claim, then, is
that compensatory justice does not tell us where these resources
are to come from. But this seems mistaken. From the perspective of distributive justice, it can hardly be irrelevant who pays.
Unless the transfer of resources to victims comes from aggressors, new injustices will have replaced the old. This is a real
enough problem. Consider, for example, Judith Thomson's justification of preferential hiring:

> Lastly, it should be stressed that to opt for such a policy is not to
> make the young white male applicants themselves make amends
> for any wrongs done to blacks and women. Under such a policy,
> no one is asked to give up a job which is already his; the job for
> which the white male competes isn't his, *but is the community's,* and
> it is the hiring officer who gives it to the black or woman in the
> community's name. Of course the white male is asked to give up
> his equal chance at the job. But that is not something he pays to
> the black or women by way of making amends; it is something
> that the community takes away from him in order that *it* may
> makes amends.
>
> Still, the community does impose a burden on him: it is able
> to make amends for its wrongs only by taking away from him,
> something which, after all, we are supposing he has a right to.
> And why should *he* pay the costs of the community's making
> amends?[45]

Thomson clearly wants to avoid arguing that white males owe
blacks and women some of their ill-gained opportunities. Instead of telling us that opportunities are to be transferred from
the aggressors, that is, white males, to women and blacks, she
argues the community is giving some of its opportunities to

those who have been the victims of injustice. This is the crux of Coleman's simple redistributive theory: the important thing is that wrongful losses are annulled, and "the community" does this. So the aim is to annul wrongful losses. But eventually Thomson is forced to confront the fact that these opportunities will come from somewhere; and they will, in effect, be transferred from the white males, who (in the first quoted paragraph) did not seem to owe women and blacks anything. In the end, despite all she says here, Thomson is forced back into the position that many of the opportunities and advantages of white males have been the result of prior wrongs, and therefore constitute a sort of wrongful gain.[46]

My point, then, is that the aim of returning to a just distribution cannot totally separate the questions (1) who is the aggressor? and (2) who is going to pay? Resources to pay victims have to come from somewhere, and simply to transfer them from the innocent is not, prima facie, just.[47]

This, however, brings us to the moderate interpretation of Coleman's proposal. Admit that the aggressors owe victims something; but let us also acknowledge that discovering who is an aggressor against what victim may be costly, perhaps impossible. Consider the case of compensation for road injury. Many aggressors, that is, those who drive dangerously, do not cause actual physical harm. They expose others to risk of injury, a cost on others, and the aggressor gets where she wants to go faster. But only sometimes does this aggression result in an accident. And, as Coleman points out, although the accident imposes additional costs on the victim, the aggressor does not accrue additional wrongful gains.[48] Now who is to pay? Just those who have caused the accident? But if so, the aim cannot be to transfer wrongful gains to compensate for wrongful losses. For the accident-causing aggressor has accrued no more benefits than the lucky aggressor, who has exposed others to risk without causing an accident.

Certainly we can see here good reasons for treating all aggressors as collectively owing all victims compensation. If some aggressors are simply lucky they did not cause accidents, it is reasonable enough to say that they should not be able to gain from their dangerous activity. So a policy that creates a pool contributed to by all aggressors—and perhaps all drivers are aggressors sometimes—to compensate victims of accidents would be justified. No doubt better proposals can be formulated. But for now, I wish only to stress that insofar as we are concerned with compensatory justice (as opposed to some utilitarian scheme to maximize total happiness by paying accident victims) we cannot totally separate the issue of who is an aggressor from who is to pay. But that does not mean that we must adopt a simplistic model of aggressor and victim—say, the layman's model of tort law. The debt model of compensatory justice has room for cost and risk-spreading schemes.

3.4. The Return to Moral Equality

Up to this point I have been concerned with explicating, and defending, the first element of Blackstone's proposal: the idea that compensatory justice is essentially redistributive. The debt model, I have argued, captures a good deal of our thinking about compensatory justice.

Blackstone's second claim is fundamental to his neo-Aristotelianism: once the debt has been paid, victim and aggressor have returned to a sort of moral equality. Compensatory justice, he says, "is an attempt to restore the equality which existed prior to the injury of one party by the other." Once the debt is paid, moral parity between debtor and creditor is restored. The moral slate, as it were, is wiped clean. This is the sense in which, according to the debt model, compensatory justice restores equality.

Here, I think, the debt model fails as an account of compensation for wrongful violation of rights. No redistribution of *resources* can by itself restore moral parity between victim and aggressor.[49] Full compensation, in the sense I define it above, does not achieve so grand a result.

4. Two Models Of Rights And Wrongs

4.1. The Purely Instrumental Theory of Rights

To see why this is so, compare two models of rights. I shall call the first the purely instrumental theory of rights. The best examples of this instrumental theory are neo-Hobbesian accounts of rights. According to neo-Hobbesians, it is in the self-interest of everyone alike to accept a system of morality that restrains pursuit of self-interest. As Kurt Baier concludes, the "Hobbesian argument is sound. Moralities are systems of principles whose acceptance by everyone as overruling the dictates of self-interest is in the interest of everyone alike."[50] In this sort of theory, to justify some claim right R to X is just to show that each gains more through having her claim right to X respected than it costs her in having to acknowledge and respect others' claim rights to X.[51] To call such rights "instrumental" is just to emphasize that they are purely instruments for advancing one's interests. Rational utility maximizers would see that each can best achieve his goals if everyone acknowledges certain claims of others to act and to control resources. These rights have no point other than as instruments that further the goals of individuals. The system of rights is a *modus vivendi* among individuals devoted to their own ends: for each best to promote his ends, each agrees to honor limits on what may be done.

I take it that nothing is mysterious about an instrumental conception of rights—in one form or another it is probably the most popular understanding of rights. Now violation of instrumental rights can be compensated in a way that *does* return victim and aggressor to a condition of moral equality. Say that Betty wrongfully appropriates Alf's property, X. In order to remedy the resulting unjust distribution, Betty must, according to the debt model, compensate Alf. And I have said that full compensation would be paid if Alf received the same utility from, or his interests were equally well served by, the two sets of actions: {not have X stolen, not have compensation paid}, {have X stolen, have compensation paid}. Full compensation, of course, is apt to require much more than just the market value of X.[52] Betty will need to make a payment that takes into account Alf's pain at having his property taken, his fear that the social order is breaking down, and so forth. But let us say that, whatever the necessary payment is, Betty has made it. Alf now is just as well off as before Betty invaded his rights. He has no further complaint against her. His rights are tools to advance his interests, and Betty has acted so that his interests are not in any way harmed by her violations. So on what basis could Alf still feel aggrieved? To keep complaining seems peevish.

But something seems amiss with this analysis (and so, I shall argue, with the instrumental conception of rights). We do, I think, have reason to doubt that full compensation returns Alf and Betty to moral equality. If this account of rights and compensation holds, Betty can always convert any property right of Alf's into a liability right by paying full compensation. A property right, let us say, gives Alf a claim to X that excludes Betty from using it without his consent, unless she buys it from him; in contrast, a liability rule precludes Betty from using Alf's X unless she renders him compensation, after the fact, for using it. The crucial difference is that under property rules Betty must secure Alf's consent prior to her use of his X but she does not under liability rules.[53] Now the account I have given of Betty's compensating Alf shows that his property right was transformed into a liability right. Given adequate compensation made *after the fact,* Betty wipes clean the moral slate, and has rightful possession of X.

However, it might be said that even if Betty fully compensates Alf, she still has not restored her moral status with the community:

> The thief not only harms the victim, he undermines rules and distinctions beyond the specific case. . . . [W]e must add to each case an undefinable kicker which represents society's need to keep all property rules from being changed at will into liability rules.[54]

I shall not deal with the debate between proponents of the economic theory of the law and their critics as to whether this "kicker" explains why Betty, despite her compensation to Alf, remains open to criticism.[55] I wish to focus on a different question: putting aside the social kicker, is it true that Alf no longer has any complaint against Betty? If he does not have any remaining complaint, it follows that a sufficiently rich Betty can declare to anyone: "I can take whatever I want of yours—for a high enough price. Admittedly, I will have to pay you for your aggravation, perhaps rather extravagantly. But if I offer you enough, I can take it. And you will have no reason to complain."

Betty may have trouble with the rest of society—she may have to pay out mountains in compensation to the rest—but at least she is squared away with the victim. Is she? It seems quite clear to me that she is not, and that the instrumental account of rights is unable to explain why she is not.

4.2. Lomasky's Instrumentalism

Loren Lomasky, an advocate of the instrumental view of rights, seeks to explain why Betty is not squared away with Alf. In reference to Nozick's compensation argument, Lomasky writes:

> It assumes that an infringement of a right can be made good through compensation, the moral balance restored to what it was *ex ante*. No such general assumption is justifiable. Compensation is inevitably a second-best response that comes into play when full rectification is impossible.[56]

Lomasky depends here on a distinction between rectification and compensation. " 'Compensation' carries with it the connotation of providing something *equivalent* in value to that which has been lost, while 'rectification' has the sense of *restoring precisely* that which has been removed."[57] This distinction is important for Lomasky because he advances a strong *incommensurability* thesis that makes five claims.[58]

1. First, Lomasky affirms that any individual has certain ends or projects. Commitment to these projects or ends is the source of their value for an agent. Value is thus *personal* in the sense that what a person values depends on his ends; someone with different ends may quite properly value very different things.[59]

2. On this basis, Lomasky says that "individuals assign personal value to their own projects and not to a welfare measure consequent upon their acting in pursuit of particular projects. What A[lf] wishes to realize is specifically E1, not the attainment of whatever level of utility is associated with the realization of E1."

3. "A[lf] will therefore not be rationally indifferent between the necessary means to go about the pursuit of his project E1 and having the necessary means to pursue E2, even if it were somehow demonstrable that the attainment of E2 by A[lf] would

have the same welfare measure as does the attainment of E1 by
A[lf]."

4. And this is so, according to Lomasky, because Alf is not
obligated to accept some impersonal standard of value that
renders E1 and E2 commensurable. E1 and E2 need not be
commensurable; indeed, it seems typically they will not be.

5. Lomasky concludes compensation is a second-best response to rights violations. Compensation depends upon providing the victim with something of equivalent value. But if
values are not commensurable, this is not possible. In contrast,
rectification aims to give back the specific thing that was lost and
so is not undermined by the incommensurability of values.[60]

Lomasky, then, sides with philosophers such as Isaiah Berlin,
Stuart Hampshire and Bernard Williams in holding that values
are often incommensurable. Claims about incommensurability
are often puzzling. But one thing is certain: it cannot generally
be the case that Alf sees his own values as incommensurable. To
see why, suppose that Alf really has no way to trade off his
values against each other. When confronted with a choice between, say, advancing his project of securing Betty's love and
working to compete for tenure, Alf is unable to choose. Fundamental to our conception of a rational valuer-agent is that one
can decide which values to promote in particular choice situations. Alf may rationally forgo an opportunity to secure Betty's
affections in order to work on his book; if so he has selected
between his values. They are commensurable. If they were not,
Alf would be at a loss when, as is always the case, he is confronted with decisions about which to promote.

So Lomasky certainly would not want to claim that, as a
matter of course, Alf is unable to tell us whether advancing his
end E1 to a certain degree is to be preferred to advancing E2 to
some extent.[61] It cannot be the case that in Alf's valuational
economy there are no trade-off rates between ends. That would
lead to practical paralysis. What, then, do proponents of incommensurability such as Lomasky have in mind? They seem to
have at least two worries.

The first is real enough, but it is a special case rather than the
general rule. Sometimes one's values have been harmed in such
a way that one simply cannot be fully compensated. "No satisfac-

tory rectification or compensation can be made to the athlete who becomes a paraplegic as the result of an automobile accident."[62] This is true and important. In this person's valuational economy he has no end he would ever choose to promote at such a cost.[63] So we must admit that sometimes a person suffers a loss for which full compensation is impossible. But that is a long way from saying that as a rule full compensation is not possible. Say we put the following proposal to Alf the athlete: agree to laboratory tests that will leave his athletic ability impaired for one month (but he will recover thereafter) and we will pay one hundred thousand dollars. Alf may find it easy to weigh the two conflicting goals. And of course we don't need fantastic stories to make the point. Real athletes do it all the time: some even decide to pursue academic courses at some cost to their training. Only a monomaniac would never trade off any opportunity to pursue some end for opportunities greatly to advance other ends.

What, then, is the other worry? Here I think Lomasky's concerns are much like those of Bernard Williams and Stuart Hampshire: commensurability, they believe, supposes the existence of some third value in terms of which the two competing values are appraised.[64] In this vein Bernard Williams proffers three incommensurability claims:

(1). No currency exists in terms of which each conflict of values can be resolved.

(2). It is not true that for each conflict of values some value, independent of any of the conflicting values, can be appealed to in order to resolve that conflict.

(3). It is not true that for each conflict of values some value can be appealed to (independent or not) in order to resolve that conflict rationally.[65]

Claims (2) and (3) are very much akin to Lomasky's assertion that what Alf "wishes to realize is specifically E1, not the attainment of whatever level of utility is associated with the realization of E1." It is, I think, quite right to deny that some third value is always employed to adjudicate the competing claims of E1 and E2. Lomasky, Williams and Hampshire are right to reject claims (2) and (3). Should we reject claim (1) too? Much depends here

on just what we mean by "a common currency." Writes Stanley
Benn:

> To trade one value against another one must see them as in a
> sense substitutable—more of one *compensating* for less of an-
> other. The options open to us meet our competing commitments
> in varying degrees, and to reach a rational decision—to do the
> best we can in difficult circumstances—we have to be able to set
> a rate of substitution between them over the relevant range.
> Unlike a market price, which is also a rate of substitution, this is,
> in one sense, a subjective rate, the rate at which I am prepared to
> trade off commitments of one kind against commitments of an-
> other. That can be done without having to express the force of
> each in some common currency, such as utility or money; there
> can be a foreign exchange market without a gold standard.[66]

We need an exchange rate between ends and commitments;
without it, action is impossible. It must be the case that Alf is
able to decide whether advancing E1 to degree x compensates
him for the loss of an opportunity to advance E2 to degree y.
But if Alf can make that judgment, Betty can learn about Alf's
character and conclude that he has a stable disposition to make
this choice.[67] So she can compensate him according to his own
subjective exchange rate. But, perhaps, Alf does not simply
value that E1 be advanced to degree x, but that *he advances* it to
that degree. But this would only seem to increase the costs of
compensation to Betty: now she must compensate him for two
losses: (i) that E1 was not advanced and (ii) that he was not able
to act to advance his ends, but rather someone did it for him.
Lomasky sometimes suggests that it is (ii) that is beyond compensation. So perhaps the problem isn't simply that one's ends
are set back: perhaps the problem with a rights violation, as
Lomasky suggests, is that one's ability to pursue projects is undermined.[68] But if, like Lomasky, we see this in terms of what a
person values, compensation will still usually be possible. People
certainly are willing to impair their ability to pursue projects—
say, by endangering their health or even their lives—to attain
some important goals. So even if, for example, when Betty steals
Alf's car she impairs his ability to pursue projects, she probably
will be able to compensate him. Suppose Betty says: "How about
a hundred thousand dollars, that will allow you to achieve your

dream of going to college? Will that compensate you for what I did yesterday, that is, stole your 1978 Pinto?" It probably will. To be sure, if Alf was interfered with so regularly that he never got a chance to act for himself, the loss would become so grave that compensation would become impossible (we are thus back to the first worry discussed above). But, putting aside this sort of massive interference, I see no reason why the loss of (ii) cannot also be compensated for.

4.3. Respect-Based Theories of Rights

I have examined Lomasky's instrumentalism in some detail as he is alive to the challenge full compensation poses to a theory of rights. If rights are simply a means to secure our values, and if (as we must) we have a trade-off rate between values,[69] then full compensation for rights violations restores moral equality between victim and aggressor—it wipes the moral slate clean. As long as they are willing to pay the appropriate "fee" (that is, compensation) instrumentalism gives a license to aggressors to override the rights of victims. But the instrumentalist must be wrong about this: it permits aggressors to turn our property rights into liability rights when they so choose (at least to the extent that they are squared away with the victim). And, of course, the problem does not simply concern property rights in the narrow sense of "property" as control over external things. All rights—except perhaps the right to life and some rights to bodily integrity—are subject to being bought out in this way. The instrumental theory of rights is unable to explain just why the aggressor wrongs the victim when he overrides rights but compensates afterwards (remember, I am leaving aside here the "social kicker"). The problem, I want to suggest, is that the aggressor not only causes the victim a loss of *value;* in addition, he has acted in a way that is *unjustifiable* and so shows a lack of respect.

It may help to focus on a case in which violation of your rights is a boon to your values. Suppose that a colleague is known for not respecting your privacy. You have let it be known that you do not welcome visitors at night to your house. Indeed, you have made something of a point of it. Unfortunately, your colleague walks by your house on her way home from work, and often—all too often—she knocks on the door, looks through the window, you answer the door (it is hard to leave her outside knocking, especially tonight as it is twenty-five degrees below zero and she is obviously getting frostbite). When that happens it is almost impossible to keep her out; she stays for ten minutes, like clockwork. As usual, this all occurs one night; but tonight you have an appointment to tutor a really bad student. You promised his father (an old friend of yours) to tutor him in philosophy, so you are obligated to help. This, I should stress, really is a pretty awful student: he is the sort who, after two hours of discussing Kant, asks whether Kant was the same person as Hegel. It is all very trying. Now your colleague makes her nightly appearance at your window, and she barges in once again. Not even this student can withstand her, and this burdensome discussion ends. You feel a distinct relief; no, it is more than that—you are happy.

Does your colleague owe you compensation for violating your privacy?[70] It seems hard to see why: she has advanced your values. (Maybe you should pay her?) But, one may say, because of her you have failed to fulfill your obligation. Well, you have tried your best, and she is, after all, the one who ended the torture session, so you are blameless. So, then, should you thank her? Hardly. Indeed, you still have a complaint against her: she violated your rights (and so benefited you) by wrongfully interfering with your activity. Is, then, the complaint that she has set back your interest by undermining your ability to pursue projects? Surely not: you are now much freer than ten minutes ago to pursue projects (your colleague, after all, only stays for ten minutes or so.)

A defender of the instrumental interpretation may try to account for this by appealing to an act/rule distinction.[71] The *rules* that justify rights are instrumentally justified as a way for an agent to advance his values; but not every action that accords with rights advances interests, and not all rights violations set back interests. True enough. But the question remains: do you still have a complaint against your colleague who violated the rule and so benefited you? Aren't you lucky she didn't let the rule guide her? As Mill said, it is the pedant "who goes by rules rather than their reasons."[72] If in this case your rights are respected "we should employ the means and the end will not follow."[73] Consequently, Mill cautions against relying on "even the most plausible . . . absolute maxims of right and wrong" in such a way that one loses sight of the "paramount good they are intended to promote."[74] For you now to complain because your rights were violated (and, so, your interests were advanced) seems to be just the sort of rule worship Mill criticized.[75]

Perhaps *society* has an interest that the rule be kept; but we are now back to the social kicker. One might say: your colleague has shown once again that she does not respect your rights, and that is what you are complaining about. Your complaint is directed at her continuing disposition to violate your rights. But, surely, if she is moving to Australia tomorrow, wouldn't that make it all better? In that case (i) she has benefited you and (ii) you don't have to worry that her disposition will ever lead to her violating your rights again.

I want to suggest that your complaint has nothing whatsoever to do with your values being set back, your projects being thwarted or your ends being hurt. Rather, the complaint is that whatever good consequences that came from the intervention, your colleague acted in a way that could not be justified to you. According to the Liberal Principle *(L)*, interference with another's action requires justification; unjustified interference is unjust. Your colleague violated this principle: as always, she interfered with your activity in a way that could not be justified to you. And I take it that her violation was indeed unjustified. Despite its irksome character, you would have carried on with your tutorial duties—not because you wanted to, or because your interests were advanced, but because you understood it to be your duty. The fact that you were relieved that you were unable to fulfill that duty does not show you would have agreed to her interference. This does not seem mere rule worship. By interfering with your liberty in a way that was not justified, your colleague supplanted *you* as the source of decisions about what *you* should do. To an agent who conceives himself as self-directing, any attempt to subvert the natural tie between *his* practical decisions and *his* activity will be seen as a threat to his status as a person.

That is why one has a residue complaint even when one has not been harmed, or even when the harm has been undone. In our example you have not been harmed, but you have been wronged. Consequently, you can still properly *resent,* or be indignant about, your colleague's interference; the moral emotions of resentment and indignation,[76] as distinguished from simple anger, are responses to wrongs. As J. R. Lucas writes:

> We are angry when we are hurt, but indignant when we are treated unjustly. . . . Indignation, which is the conceptually appropriate response to injustice, expresses, as its etymology shows, a sense of not being regarded as worthy of consideration. Injustice betokens a lack of respect, and manifests a lack of concern.[77]

You can quite properly be resentful and indignant at your colleague's interventions; but, because you have not been in any way harmed, no compensation is owed. Nevertheless, you and your colleague are by no means on a moral par.

4.4. *Property Rights and Respect*

This account—I shall not say more here in defense of it[78]—provides the basis for a noninstrumental conception of the right to liberty, that is, the right that flows from Principle *L*. The claim, then, is that the Liberal Principle of noninterference is more than just valuable for promoting our aims. Often it is—although sometimes paternalist interference will promote our aims even better.[79] Rather, the idea is that the Liberal Principle articulates a basic demand of a self-directing person; by ignoring that demand your colleague did not respect your status as a self-directing agent. Wrongful violation of the Liberal Principle is always a sign of disrespect.

Charles Fried argues that this respect-based analysis carries over to property rights. The right to be free from violent intervention, he says, "is firmly rooted in moral notions of respect for persons and the physical basis of personality." This respect, according to Fried, extends also to a person's right to control the disposal of his labor and talents. "To deny him the right to dispose of his labor and talent is to assert that . . . [others] have

rights to them also. . . . But a person's right to his own person is
a fundamental tenet of liberal individualism."[80] Property rights,
Fried maintains, extend this relation. "By casting the relation
between a person and a thing in this form of a right, we with-
draw it *pro tanto* from the domain of collective imposition. To
say that the collector's 'penny Black' is *his* assimilates that relation to the relation between a man and what is quintessentially
his, namely, his person, his effort, his talents."[81] The core idea
is that property extends one's person: and so one who ignores
property rights shows disrespect for personality.[82]

We need not, however, embrace Fried's extension thesis. The
crucial point is that property rights are not rights simply to
some flow of benefits; they give the owner control.[83] Like other
liberal rights, property rights provide a morally protected sphere
in which a person may act according to his own values and aims
as he understands them.[84] Consequently the agent must have
discretion over how these rights are to be employed. Now if
these are the sorts of rights that are justified in a community of
self-directing agents, aggressors act unjustifiably when they seek
to convert property rights to liability rights. The aggressor en-
deavors to supplant Betty as the source of decisions about the
disposition of her resources: this usurpation betokens a lack of
respect. In this manner, violation of any of one's rights constitutes an unwarranted interference with one's activity, and so
runs afoul of the Liberal Principle.

A word of caution, however, is in order. Although, like all
rights property rights give scope to the agency of the right
holder, it must also be kept in mind that much of our practical
interest in property is precisely in the benefits—especially the
income—that flow to us from property rights. We readily trade
property if doing so increases our benefits. Consequently, we
should expect that a justified system of holdings will have a
place for "takings" or liability rights—cases in which property
can be taken without prior consent provided compensation is
paid.[85]

We all might benefit in some cases from decreasing certain
transaction costs, from public goods, or from the liberty to use
another's property in cases of dire need (see section 5). Given

these practical interests, we all may concur full compensation for taking one's property will, in some sorts of cases, wipe clean the moral slate.

4.5. What Can and What Cannot Be Compensated

Say Alf steals a "penny Black" from Betty. Lomasky is right that the best remedy would be rectification: for Alf to return it. If it has been lost, however, compensation in some other form is due. So let us suppose that in some way, Alf redistributes: he transfers resources to Betty such that, all things considered, her values and projects are at least as well off as before. But even if he returned the stolen property he has not wiped clean the moral slate: it remains the case that he acted without justification. Can he, then, increase the payment to make up for that too? Well, he can make up for the pain of being affronted. But repayment can only give back what was lost, the value the victim lost through the aggression. But I have tried to show that wronging is not simply harming; consequently, undoing the harm does not undo the wrong. One cannot undo wrongs in the way one can repay debts.[86]

Is poor Alf doomed forever, and can he never return to moral equality with Betty? At this point we come to questions of penal justice, and the place for mercy and forgiveness. All I wish to insist upon is that redistribution of resources does not allow Alf to recover his moral equality.[87] For in addition to the maldistribution he has brought about (which does require compensation), Alf has also wronged Betty by unjustifiably interfering with her. If Betty has a property right to X, Alf is not justified in expropriating it subject to compensation: if that was justified, Betty would have only a liability right. So when Alf unilaterally seeks to transform Betty's rights in this way, he is interfering without justification, and so, according to Principle L, wrongs Betty.

The Aristotelian model does not capture this continuing inequality. But some argue that this is misleading, because compensatory justice, properly understood, includes penal justice: a transfer of resources to the victim *and* the punishment of the aggressor would then both be parts of compensatory justice.[88]

Understood in this sense we can say that compensatory justice entails a return to equality (although we may want to say in some cases that even after punishment the aggressor is not fully squared away with the victim). But if so, compensatory justice only restores equality because we include in it penal justice. I think it doubtful that punishment is usefully understood as annulling wrongful gains, and in this way part of compensatory justice.[89] The important point, however, is not how we use the term "compensatory justice." What is crucial is that no mere redistribution of resources, no matter how generous, can restore moral equality between victim and aggressor.

5. JUSTIFIED RIGHTS VIOLATIONS AND PAYING DEBTS

The debt model misdescribes the aim of compensation for unjustified violations of rights. In contrast to Coleman I do not reject the debt model because it links the questions of who has aggressed and who is obligated to pay; rather, I object to the claim that payment of compensation restores moral equality between victim and aggressor. Once a debtor transfers the resources back to the owner, the debt is paid. Not so with unjustified rights violations. But the debt model does seem to capture at least some *justified rights violations*. Consider an example introduced by Joel Feinberg, and since the subject of extensive discussion:

> Suppose that you are on a backpacking trip in the high mountain country when an unanticipated blizzard strikes the area with such ferocity that your life is imperiled. Fortunately, you stumble onto an unoccupied cabin, locked and boarded up for the winter, clearly someone's private property. You smash the window, enter, and huddle in a corner for three days until the storm abates. During this period you help yourself to your unknown benefactor's food supply and burn his wooden furniture in the fireplace to keep warm.[90]

Feinberg holds that you would surely be justified to infringe the person's property rights in this way. However, "almost everyone would agree that you owe *compensation* to the homeowner for the depletion of his larder, the breaking of his window, and the destruction of his furniture."[91] Most philosophers have indeed agreed that what you did was justified, but you still owe compensation.[92] Yet some have questioned this: if you were actually justified in burning the furniture, Philip Montague holds, then you owe no compensation. If, says Montague, you were a vandal, simply destroying a person's property for the fun of it, you certainly would owe compensation. To say that the backpacker owes compensation too is to treat the backpacker as morally on par with the vandal and that, maintains Montague, is "extremely implausible."[93]

A respect-based account of rights provides a rationale for Feinberg's position and a reply to Montague. Here, the debt model really does apply. The backpacker owes the owner for what has been destroyed and used: until resources are redistributed back to the owner the backpacker is, quite literally, in the owner's debt. But once the debt has been paid, moral equality has been restored. Why? Presumably because this infringement of one's property rights can be *justified* to the owner. A justified system of property rights will presumably allow for others in dire and unexpected need sometimes to treat your property right as a liability right. Even the owner can see the point of allowing such action in special cases. So when the backpacker breaks the windows, she displays no disrespect. But the vandal does: his violation of the property right cannot be justified to the owner. Consequently, even if the vandal should compensate the owner, the moral slate is not wiped clean, equality is not restored. Hence, *pace* Montague, to follow Feinberg does not require treating the backpacker and the vandal as moral equals.

6. Conclusion: A Liberal Theory of Compensatory Justice

In this chapter I have sketched some of the main elements of a liberal theory of compensatory justice. First, we have seen that such a theory will not include the principle of redress, which is based upon an egalitarian presumption that conflicts with the Liberal Principle of noninterference. If we understand the Liberal Principle as the fundamental requirement of respect among self-directing moral agents, we reach a somewhat surprising conclusion: compensatory justice, understood as transfer of resources, cannot fully compensate for wrongdoing in the sense of returning aggressor and victim to moral equality. In cases of wrongful violations of rights, compensatory justice has a more modest, albeit important, task: to rectify the maldistribution of resources that results from wrongdoing. Although this may be a surprising conclusion, it nevertheless is attractive, for it shows why our rights so stubbornly resist being bought out, regardless of the size of the payment. Purely instrumental accounts of rights permit a complete return to equality after wrongful violation. And for that reason they are objectionable.

A "return to equality" is possible only when rights have been justifiably infringed. Although aggressors can repay victims for the harm done, transfer of resources cannot right a wrong.

NOTES

1. Aristotle, *The Ethics*, trans. J. A. K. Thomson (Harmondsworth, Middlesex: Penguin, 1955), 148–149.

2. John Rawls, *A Theory of Justice* (Cambridge: Harvard University Press, 1971), 246.

3. Ibid., 100.

4. John Passmore, "Civil Justice and its Rivals," in Eugene Kamenka and Alice Ehr-Soon Tay, eds., *Justice* (London: Edward Arnold, 1979): 25–49 at p. 42.

5. "Now the principle of redress has not to my knowledge been proposed as the sole criterion of justice, as the single aim of the social order. . . . It is thought to represent one of the elements in our conception of justice." Rawls, *A Theory of Justice*, 101.

6. Ibid. Nevertheless, I think William T. Blackstone is right to interpret Rawls as essentially endorsing the principle of redress. "Reverse Discrimination and Compensatory Justice," *Social Theory and Practice* 3 (Spring 1975): 253–88 at p. 281.

7. Herbert Spiegelberg, "A Defense of Human Equality," *Philosophical Review* 53 (March 1944): 101–24 at p. 111. Emphasis in original.

8. Ibid., 114. Cf. Blackstone, "Compensatory Justice," 281.

9. David Gauthier, "Justice and Natural Endowment: Toward a Critique of Rawls' Ideological Framework," *Social Theory and Practice* 3 (Spring 1974): 3–26 at pp. 15–16.

10. Rawls, *A Theory of Justice,* 104.

11. I am leaving aside here Rawls's controversial claim that we do not deserve the fruits of our talents because we do not deserve those talents. *A Theory of Justice,* 103–4.

12. Spiegelberg, "Human Equality," 114. Emphasis added.

13. Rawls, *A Theory of Justice,* 102.

14. For a criticism of presumptive principles, see Joseph Raz, *The Morality of Freedom* (Oxford: Clarendon Press, 1986), 8–12.

15. Joel Feinberg, *Harm to Others* (New York: Oxford University Press, 1984), 14–16. See also his *Social Philosophy* (Englewood Cliffs. N.J.: Prentice-Hall, 1973), 21.

16. I have tried to do so elsewhere. See my *Value and Justification: The Foundations of Liberal Theory* (Cambridge: Cambridge University Press, 1990), sec. 24; see also my "Contractual Justification of Redistributive Capitalism," in John W. Chapman and J. Roland Pennock, eds., *NOMOS XXXI: Markets and Justice,* (New York: New York University Press, 1989), 89–121 at pp. 97–101.

17. John Locke, *Second Treatise of Government,* in *Two Treatises of Government,* ed. Laslett Peter (Cambridge University Press 1960), 287 (sec. 4). Emphasis in original.

18. S. I. Benn and R. S. Peters, *Social Principles and the Democratic State* (London: George Allen & Unwin, 1959), 110. Emphasis in original.

19. Ibid., 111.

20. See Richard E. Flathman, "Equality and Generalization: A Formal Analysis," in J. Roland Pennock and John W. Chapman, eds., *NOMOS IX: Equality,* (New York: Atherton Press, 1967), 38–60; Isaiah Berlin, "Equality as an Ideal," in Frederick A. Olafson, ed., *Justice and Social Policy,* (Englewood Cliffs, N.J.: Prentice-Hall, 1962), 128–50; and William K. Frankena, "The Concept of Social Justice," in R. B. Brandt, ed., *Social Justice,* (Englewood Cliffs, N.J.: Prentice-Hall, 1962), 1–29. For a dissenting view see Richard Norman, *Free and Equal* (Oxford: Oxford University Press, 1987), 57–58.

21. J. R. Lucas, "Against Equality," in Hugo A. Bedau, ed., *Justice and Equality,* (Englewood Cliffs, N.J.: Prentice-Hall, 1971), 138–51 at p. 139. See also Raz, *The Morality of Freedom,* chap. 9.

22. See Robert Brown, *Analyzing Love* (Cambridge: Cambridge University Press, 1987).

23. See my *Value and Justification,* sec. 14.

24. Stanley I. Benn, "Human Rights—for whom and for what?" in Eugene Kamenka and Alice Erh-Soon Tay, eds., *Human Rights* (New York: St. Martin's Press, 1978, 57–73 at p. 67. Emphasis in original.

See also Flathman, "Equality and Generalization," 39; Berlin, "Equality as an Ideal," 131, 133.

25. See my "Subjective Value and Justificatory Political Theory," in J. Roland Pennock and John W. Chapman, eds., *NOMOS XXVIII: Justification* (New York: New York University Press, 1986), 241–69 at pp. 255–58.

26. For such a criticism of Benn's egalitarianism, see Les Holborow, "Benn, Mackie, and Basic Rights," *Australasian Journal of Philosophy* 63 (March 1985): 11–25. In his final work, Been weakens his Egalitarian Principle so as not to undermine the Liberal Principle. See *A Theory of Freedom* (Cambridge: Cambridge University Press, 1988), 117–21.

27. See Albert Weale, *Equality and Social Policy* (London: Routledge & Kegan Paul, 1978), 19; and Robert Nozick, *Anarchy, State and Utopia* (New York: Basic Books, 1974), 223.

28. It seems, then, that both *E* and *L* migrated from legal and political to moral contexts. I argue here that in the case of *E* this migration took a distinctly illiberal turn.

29. Stanley Benn and I have considered these issues more thoroughly in our "Public and Private: Concepts and Action," in S. I. Benn and G. F. Gaus, eds., *Public and Private in Social Life*, (New York: St. Martin's Press, 1983), 3–27, esp. pp. 9–10.

30. Blackstone, "Compensatory Justice," 255.

31. Compensatory justice thus presupposes a theory of distributive justice. Blackstone, I think, rather suggests this. Ibid.

32. See here Jules Coleman, "Justice and the Argument for No-Fault," *Social Theory and Practice* 3 (Fall 1974): 161–80, esp. pp. 174ff. I consider penal sanctions briefly in section 4.5.

33. See Jules Coleman, "The Morality of Strict Tort Liability," in his *Markets, Morals and the Law* (Cambridge: Cambridge University Press, 1988), 169.

34. Coleman, "Justice and No-Fault," 175. Emphasis in original.

35. Ibid., 176.

36. Judith Jarvis Thomson, "Preferential Hiring," in William Parent, ed., *Rights, Restitution and Risk*, (Cambridge: Harvard University Press, 1986), 149.

37. See here Robert K. Fullinwider, "Preferential Hiring and Compensation," *Social Theory and Practice* (Spring 1975): 307–20, esp. pp. 310–11.

38. I return to this problem below, section 4.2.

39. Nozick, *Anarchy, State and Utopia*, 57.

40. Blackstone, "Compensatory Justice," 268. For an analysis of some practical implications of the "proportionality principle," see Rob-

ert Simon, "Preferential Hiring," *Philosophy & Public Affairs* 3 (Spring 1974): 312–20.

41. Nozick, *Anarchy, State and Utopia,* 57; and David Gauthier, *Morals by Agreement* (Oxford: Clarendon Press, 1986), 211.

42. Jules Coleman, "Corrective Justice and Wrongful Gain," in his *Markets, Morals and the Law,* 187–88.

43. In this connection notice that Nozick's account of compensation does identify who is to do the compensating.

44. Coleman, "Corrective Justice and Wrongful Gain," 188.

45. Thomson, "Preferential Hiring," 151.

46. Ibid., 152. See also Bernard R. Boxill, "The Morality of Preferential Hiring," *Philosophy & Public Affairs* 7 (Spring 1978): 246–68.

47. It could be maintained that we all have a duty to rectify all injustices, perhaps individually or *qua* members of the polity. I shall not pursue here the implications of this strong principle.

48. Jules Coleman, "Corrective Justice and Wrongful Gain," 187–88.

49. Note that I focus here on the redistribution of resources, and so exclude penal sanctions; see section 4.5.

50. Kurt Baier, *The Moral Point of View,* abridged ed. (New York: Random House, 1965), 154. For other neo-Hobbesian justifications of morality, see Gregory S. Kavka, *Hobbesian Moral and Political Theory* (Princeton: Princeton University Press, 1986); and James M. Buchanan, *The Limits of Liberty* (Chicago: University of Chicago Press, 1975).

51. I shall not defend characterization of rights in terms of claim rights. For a standard account, see Feinberg, *Social Philosophy,* chap. 4. For sustained criticism of this view, see Alan R. White, *Rights* (Oxford: Clarendon Press, 1984).

52. See Gauthier, *Morals by Agreement,* 211.

53. On this distinction, see Guido Calabresi and A. Douglas Melamed, "Property Rules, Liability Rules and Inalienability: One View of the Cathedral," *Harvard Law Review* 85 (April 1972): 1089–1128.

54. Ibid., 1126.

55. For criticism of the economic analysis, see Alvin K. Klevorick, "On the Economic Theory of Crime," in J. Roland Pennock and John W. Chapman, eds., *NOMOS XXVII: Criminal Justice,* (New York: New York University Press, 1985), 289–309. See also the commentaries that follow by Richard Posner and Jules Coleman.

56. Loren E. Lomasky, *Persons, Rights, and the Moral Community* (New York: Oxford University Press, 1987), 143.

57. Ibid., 142. Emphasis in original.

58. The following discussion, and all quotations, draw on Lomasky, *Persons, Rights,* 142–46.

59. From this, it would seem that Lomasky presents an agent-relative account of value and value-based reasons to act. His position, however, is somewhat more complicated. See ibid., 159. For a discussion, see Eric Mack, "Against Agent-Neutral Value," *Reason Papers* (Spring 1989): 82–92.

60. Lomasky puts great emphasis on this incommensurability thesis, providing the basis for criticism of the use of indifference curves in moral theory. Although he does not say that they are useless, he thinks that indifference curves imply a commensurability Lomasky seeks to deny. *Persons, Rights,* 143–44.

61. Although it adds complications, it is important to stress that the choice is not simply between whether end E1 is to be preferred to E2 or *vice versa.* Rather, in any given situation Alf will be able to do more or less to advance an end; in one case it may be rational for Alf to forgo an opportunity to advance E1 to a low degree in order to advance E2 to a high degree, even though generally Alf cares more for the former than the latter. Stanley Benn examines the implications of this point. In *A Theory of Freedom,* chap. 3.

62. Lomasky, *Persons, Rights,* 144.

63. In terms of indifference analysis, we can say that such a person has a preference threshold: no trade-offs that take him below a certain level of physical fitness are acceptable, For an extensive analysis of thresholds, see Benn, *A Theory of Freedom,* 56ff.

64. Bernard Williams, "Conflicts of Values," in his *Moral Luck* (Cambridge: Cambridge University Press, 1988), chap. 5 and Stuart Hampshire, "Public and Private Morality," in his *Morality and Conflict* (Oxford: Basil Blackwell, 1983), chap. 5.

65. Williams, "Conflicts of Values," 77.

66. Benn, *A Theory of Freedom,* 48–49. Emphasis added.

67. On knowing the evaluative comparisons of others, see David Milligan, *Reasoning and the Explanation of Action* (Brighton, Sussex: Harvester Press, 1980), chap. 6.

68. Lomasky, *Person, Rights,* 144.

69. As I said above, in some cases we may have no trade-off rates for grave harms to a central value.

70. It has been put to me that she did not violate your privacy since, after all, you *let* her in; you could have just let her freeze. But this seems to me too simple a view of our rights to privacy. Someone who puts you in a position in which you can enjoy your privacy only by allowing her to incur injury is making the option of enjoying your right

too costly; it seems tantamount to a threat. And it seems the same holds true on less bitterly cold nights, when your colleague is seeking to increase the costs of your enjoyment of privacy in other, somewhat more subtle, ways. If you refuse to let her in, you know you are apt to have an unpleasant day at work tomorrow.

71. See Kavka's discussion of "rule egoism" in *Hobbesian Moral and Political Theory*, chap. 9.

72. J. S. Mill, *A System of Logic*, (London: Longman's Green, 1947), bk. VI, chap. xii, sec. 2. I consider Mill's view in more depth in "Mill's Theory of Moral Rules," *Australasian Journal of Philosophy* 58 (September 1980): 265–79.

73. Mill, *Logic*, bk. VI, ch. xii, sec. 3.

74. J. S. Mill, "Thornton on Labour and its Claims," in *The Collected Works of John Stuart Mill*, ed. J. M. Robson, (Toronto: University of Toronto Press, 1963), 5: 659.

75. Gregory Kavka tries to reply to a rather different charge of rule worship in *Hobbesian Moral and Political Theory*, 378–84.

76. According to David A. J. Richards, resentment is appropriate if you have been wronged, while indignation is the appropriate response to a wrong to others. See his *Theory of Reasons for Action* (Oxford: Clarendon Press, 1971), 253.

77. J. R. Lucas, *On Justice* (Oxford: Clarendon Press, 1980), 7. For further consideration of the moral emotions, see my "Commitment to the Common Good," in Paul Harris, ed., *On Political Obligation*, (London: Routledge, 1990), 26–64, esp. pp. 36–46.

78. I develop this argument more fully elsewhere. See my *Value and Justification*, section 24.

79. See Dan Brock, "Paternalism and Promoting the Good" in Rolf Sartorius, ed., *Paternalism* (Minneapolis: University of Minnesota Press, 1983): 237–60.

80. Charles Fried, *Contract as Promise: A Theory of Contractual Obligation* (Cambridge: Harvard University Press, 1981), 99.

81. Ibid., 101. This again points to the illiberal nature of the principle of redress, which seems to give others rights to our talents and what we make of them.

82. This relates to the claim by natural law thinkers that one's *summ* can be extended. See Stephen Buckle, *Natural Law and the Theory of Property* (Oxford: Clarendon Press, 1991).

83. I have argued for this notion of ownership in my "Contractual Justification of Redistributive Capitalism," 106–8. Cf. C. B. Macpherson, "Human Rights as Property Rights," in his *Rise and Fall of Economic Justice* (Oxford: Oxford University Press, 1987), 82.

84. See further Gerald F. Gaus and Loren E. Lomasky, "Are Property Rights Problematic?" in *The Monist* 3, 4.

85. Cf. Richard A. Epstein, *Takings: Private Property and the Power of Eminent Domain* (Cambridge: Harvard University Press, 1985).

86. A temptation here is to assume that if a person is wronged, then somewhere there *must* be a sort of harm that can be compensated. We would do well to follow Wittgenstein's advice. "Don't say: 'There *must* be . . .' . . . look and see. . . ." *Philosophical Investigations*, trans. G. E. M. Anscombe, (London: Macmillan, 1953), section 66.

87. Hence the inadequacy with proposals to base criminal justice simply on the provision of restitution. See Randy E. Barnett, "Restitution: A New Paradigm of Criminal Justice," *Ethics* 87 (July 1977): 279–301. For a more adequate view, see Roger Pilon, "Criminal Remedies: Restitution, Punishment, or Both?" *Ethics* 88 (July 1978): 348–57. Barnett replies in the "The Justice of Restitution," in Jan Narveson, ed., *Moral Issues* (New York: Oxford University Press, 1983), 140–53.

88. It is unclear whether this is Blackstone's view. See "Compensatory Justice," 254.

89. C. L. Ten criticizes this view of punishment in his *Crime, Guilt and Punishment* (Oxford: Clarendon Press, 1987), 38–42.

90. Joel Feinberg, "Voluntary Euthanasia and the Inalienable Right to Life," *Philosophy & Public Affairs* 7 (Winter 1978): 93–123 at p. 102.

91. Ibid.

92. Most famously, Judith Jarvis Thomson in "Rights and Compensation," in William Parent, ed., *Rights, Restitution and Risk,* chap. 5. See also Coleman, "Corrective Justice and Wrongful Gain," 186.

93. Philip Montague, "Rights and Duties of Compensation," *Philosophy & Public Affairs* 13 (Winter 1984): 79–88 at p. 84. See also the comments by Nancy Davis and Peter Westin, and Montague's reply in *Philosophy & Public Affairs* 14 (Fall 1985).

PART II

HISTORICAL
CONSIDERATIONS

3

JUSTICE BETWEEN GENERATIONS: COMPENSATION, IDENTITY, AND GROUP MEMBERSHIP

JAMES S. FISHKIN

Justice between generations confronts us with the issue of how to think about the interests of possible people. When we think of future generations, the interests in question are those of future possible people. When we think of compensation for past injustice, the interests in question, for purposes of determining compensation, are those of counterfactual, possible people—the people who would have existed had an injustice not occurred. The difficulty, of course, is that any people who receive compensation are not, themselves, counterfactual. To receive compensation, they must actually exist. Yet some consideration of what would have happened, had the injustice not occurred, is necessary if we are to evaluate any claim to compensation.

Consideration of the interests of possible people has produced a large literature on future generations.[1] My initial strategy is to take a position on that literature in the future persons case and then to apply my analysis to compensation for past injustice.

A common assumption is that a person X can be harmed if

and only if X is worse off than X otherwise would have been. Let us call this the identity-specific notion of harm. However, when dealing with possible people, this leads to bizarre implications. Consider an individual choice and then a social choice version of the same problem. Imagine a woman who is under medication or has a medical condition such that if she conceives a child during a specific period that child will have serious disabilities. However, if she were to wait until after the specified period, the child would, in all likelihood, be normal. Many of us would object to her conceiving a child during that period and we would do so on grounds of harm to the child. But we cannot do so according to the identity-specific conception of harm. For if a child were conceived under those conditions, it would not be worse off than it otherwise would have been. If the other alternative were chosen (if the woman were to wait) that child would not have existed at all. Another child, as differentiable from the first as one sibling is from another, would have been born instead. If there are harms to the child in conceiving someone disabled rather than someone normal, they cannot be conceptualized within the identity-specific understanding of harm.

Consider a social choice parallel. Imagine a third world country faced with the prospect of overwhelming population growth. Suppose that demographers and economists establish that if nothing is done, mass misery and malnutrition will result in several generations. However, if population growth were somehow sharply curtailed, a prosperous new society could be built. Once again, if we were to object to a laissez-faire population policy on the grounds that it would eventually produce the miseries of overpopulation, our objection could not be developed within the confines of the identity-specific analysis of harm. Once one takes account of all the factors that determine the identities of a given cohort—who marries whom, when their children are conceived, whom those children marry—it quickly becomes apparent that the identities of all those who would live under a policy of laissez-faire, several generations from now, have virtually no overlap with the identities of all those who would live under a policy of population control.

We have, however, an alternative view of human interests that might be dubbed the identity-independent notion of interests, harm included. In this perspective we would simply evaluate two states of affairs according to the interests satisfied or not, regardless of the identities of the individuals in those states of affairs being compared. The most well-developed version of identity-independent interests is utilitarianism in any of its familiar forms. If we are utilitarians, we simply compare the disutility of having a disabled child versus the utility of having a normal one, or we compare the disutility that results from over population versus the utility that results from population restriction. In none of these cases are we concerned with whether the people are the same or different.

Worth noting is that while utilitarianism is the most familiar example of an identity-independent theory, it is not the only possible one. Suppose we compared states of affairs in terms of an impartial distribution of Rawlsian primary goods or of some other metric for measuring benefits and harms that did not make reference to preference satisfaction. We can call these theories, utilitarianism included, *identity-independent* criteria for the assessment of interests. Derek Parfit is the most prominent theorist who has argued for some variant of utilitarianism precisely on the grounds that it is identity-independent and so avoids the difficulties of the identity-specific view.[2]

The problem with identity-independent theories is replaceability. The point can be made most dramatically with a science fiction scenario. Suppose that I could painlessly and instantaneously *replace* all the readers of this chapter with others who will appreciate it more. Furthermore, as a general matter, the new readers, let us call them replacements, will get more out of life. On whatever identity-independent dimension of value we are talking about, they will achieve higher scores. To simplify matters, if we assume that the criterion of value is utilitarianism, then they will add more utiles to life each day than did their predecessors.

I have not said anything about *how* this transition takes place. Perhaps, as in the movie *Invasion of the Body Snatchers*, it occurs through creatures from outer space taking on your appearances and incorporating your roles and memories. Perhaps I have a machine that simply fabricates new copies. Or perhaps a new, miniature technology is in the book that you are reading, a technology that will go into effect as soon as you reach a certain page. In any case, the reason for posing the issue in a science fiction scenario is that is clarifies the vulnerability of identity-independent views to replaceability arguments without raising empirical complications about the fear and disutility experienced by those who are eventually replaced. (For this reason you will have to consider my example hypothetical or assume that you have already passed the crucial page.)

Of course, replaceability arguments are not limited to science fiction. Consider this dialogue about the collectivization of Soviet agriculture from Arthur Koestler's novel, *Darkness at Noon*. The Commissar Ivanov is addressing the prisoner Rubashov:

> Yes, we liquidated the parasitic part of the peasantry and let it die of starvation. It was a surgical operation which had to be done once and for all; but in the good old days before the Revolution just as many died in any dry year—only senselessly and pointlessly. The victims of the Yellow River floods in China amount sometimes to hundreds of thousands. Nature is generous in her senseless experiments on mankind. Why should mankind not have the rights to experiment on itself.
>
> He paused: Rubashov did not answer. He went on: "Have you ever read brochures of an anti-vivisectionist society? They are shattering and heartbreaking; when one reads how some poor cur which has had its liver cut out, whines and licks his tormentor's hands, one is just as nauseated as you were tonight. But if these people had their say, we would have no serums against cholera, typhoid, or diphtheria . . ."[3]

The general problem is that for any identity-independent conception of interests, so long as the abstract structure of distribution, the payoffs to positions, is at least as good under the replacement scenario, there are no grounds for objecting on the basis of this kind of theory. In fact, if we are utilitarians and the replacement scenario would increase utility, we can be obligated to kill everyone and replace them with a new population of better utility maximizers. On the identity-independent view, people are simply vessels for holding so much utility, or whatever else is our metric of value. It is the utility that matters, not the vessels. If a vessel breaks, that has no importance provided that another can be found, or created that will hold as much or more.

The very merit of the identity-independent principles in dealing with the earlier counterexamples to the identity-specific view—namely, that they *disconnect* the assessment of interests from the identities of the people affected—renders them vulnerable to this replaceability scenario. Because the interests are viewed anonymously, these theories will permit us to object to production of the deformed child or to the miseries of overpopulation without worrying about whether the better-off people envisioned under the alternative choice are the same people. But the same anonymous consideration of interests leads these theories to neglect the question of whether the people under the replacement scenario are the same as the people in the original population. The general dilemma is that if we tie interests consistently to personal identity we face the identity-specific counterexamples, but if we untie them consistently from personal identity, we face the replaceability scenario.

It may be objected that "preference utilitarianism," unlike the sensate classical version, escapes this horn of my dilemma. I will argue, however, that the escape is illusory. Consider Singer's presentation of preference utilitarianism: "This other version of utilitarianism judges actions, not by their tendency to maximize pleasure or avoid pain, but by the extent to which they accord with the preferences of any beings affected by the action or its consequences." From this property of preference utilitarianism Singer concludes: "Killing a person who prefers to continue living is therefore wrong, other things being equal. That the victims are not around to lament the fact that their preferences have been disregarded is irrelevant."[4]

Singer's notion is that some beings, for example, animals, fetuses and infants, experience utility only in the primitive sensate sense. He believes replaceability arguments still apply in their case and he explores implications of this fact for the eating of meat, and the permissibility of abortion and even infanticide. However, he believes that the applicability of utility in this second higher sense of preference utilitarianism to more developed children and adults would block replaceability scenarios

applied to such persons. In this way his distinction between
preference and sensate utilitarianism might be taken to get us
out of our dilemma when applied, at least, to older children and
adults.

I believe that Singer's escape is only chimerical. Preference
utilitarianism is, at bottom, identity-independent and so vulnerable to some versions of replaceability. This becomes apparent
if one thinks carefully about what the "other things being equal"
clause might mean in Singer's solution. Recall that in our various scenarios, the replacements can *also* be imagined to have
preferences in a self-conscious and reflective sense. Satisfaction
of those preferences may easily turn out to balance the frustra-
tion of the life plans of the previously existing population.

More specifically, if we imagine, as Singer seems to, a special
disutility in an ongoing life being interrupted, whether or not
the person is around to regret the interruption, we might, sym-
metrically, imagine a special utility experienced by each replacement, for example, utility from the miracle of being brought
into existence. The new person may well experience an "existence bonus" that counterbalances the disutility from the previous person's existence interruption. Any reader of Walt Whit-
man's *Song of Myself* will have a vivid sense of such an existence
bonus. There is no reason, in principle, why one of these must
be greater than another. The theoretical vulnerability to replaceability remains.

The vulnerability is built into the foundations of utilitarianism. It is unavoidably identity-independent because it is what
might be called a purely structural principle. It defines the
sufficient conditions for approving a change based entirely on
information available from a listing of payoffs to positions under one alternative as compared to another.[5] If the total (or
average, for some versions) is higher under one alternative,
then it must be chosen. No reason exists for utilitarianism, or
any other purely structural principle, to concern itself with the
issue of whether the identities of the replacements are different
from the identities of the originals. Because utilitarianism completely divorces human interests from personal identities, it avoids
the counterexamples with which we started, but only by creating
a vulnerability to replaceability arguments.

Turn now to the questions of justice between past and present generations to see if parallel issues arise. Take the case of Alex Haley and the history of his family documented in *Roots*. His ancestors were subjected to terrible injustices in being kidnapped from West Africa and enslaved. Suppose compensation were to be paid now to their descendant, Alex Haley, whose case is distinct from that of many other African Americans only in that its history has been thoroughly investigated. Setting aside a host of particular legal questions such as statutes of limitations and questions of who should be held liable, and setting aside any factual controversies about the empirical claims Haley has made, the bare notion of compensation would have us consider the position Alex Haley would have been in had the injustices to his ancestors not occurred. If we are to make up for an injustice, we must return the world to the state of affairs it would have been in had the injustice not occurred. The difficulty, of course, is that we immediately confront the same problem we encountered with the identity-specific notions of harm in the future generations case. The notion of compensation, as commonly employed, simply presumes some variation of an identity-specific conception of interests. X is fully compensated for event E when X is as well off as X would have been, had E not occurred. Our problem is that had event E not occurred, X would not exist. If his ancestors had not been kidnapped and enslaved, Alex Haley would not exist today. His existence depends on the fact that the genealogical chain was not broken at any point. Hence the initial kidnapping to America and the slavery of his ancestors can all be taken as necessary conditions for there being such a person as Alex Haley, on whose behalf we make the claim for compensatory justice. The trouble is that we cannot employ this notion of compensation to correct injustices from a past generation, because the required state of affairs would entail the nonexistence of those who would have to be compensated.

Suppose we tried to apply an identity-independent notion, such as utilitarianism, to the problem of making up, in some sense, for injustices from the distant past? In this conception of human interests, the very idea of compensation dissolves. We have no longer a matter of rectifying an injustice for identifiable individuals. Rather, we are trying to achieve the best distribution of benefits and harms disconnected from any consideration of individual identities. Recall that our objection to this sort of theory, in the future generations case, is that population X could be replaced by another composed of better utility maximizers or composed of those who score better on whatever identity-independent criterion one wants to specify. The same problem recurs when we turn to the past. Rather than compensate group X, if a better overall distribution would result from benefits to some other group, we should, guided by identity-independent considerations, do that instead. Or indeed, group X, which is the subject of various historical injustices, has no special claim based on its history. If a better overall distribution would result from its being replaced by others, that should also be done.

However, under special assumptions, a prescription similar to that advocated in compensatory arguments could emerge. Consider an underclass produced by a history of discrimination. Suppose that underclass would, in fact, receive the most utility from redistribution because of declining marginal utility of income. Suppose further that it is the most in need of certain kinds of special consideration, otherwise horrendous social problems will create disutility for everyone. Then public policies directed primarily at this group could be advocated using this kind of identity-independent framework. Furthermore, these public policies would be an explicit response to the legacy of discrimination. The difference, of course, is that if it were to turn out that other problems were more susceptible to progress, those would have a greater claim on identity-independent grounds, even if those other problems were in no way the outcome of historical injustice. Application of identity-independent theories would require a kind of ahistorical diagnosis of what should be done. This ahistorical diagnosis might happen to address historical injustices, but nothing guarantees that this will be the case. The underclass formed by historical injustices might, for example, pose a nearly intractable problem. Or addressing its claim might produce less benefit, in terms of marginal utility, than attending to the claims of victims of a recent natural disaster for whom no claims of injustice arise.

In both the future-regarding and the past-regarding cases,

the problem is that, on the one hand, identity-specific claims to compensation suffer from the fact that the people who are putatively harmed or compensated may not be the same. On the other hand, identity-independent approaches suffer from an insensitivity to the separateness of persons and their particular claims. The most extreme version of this second problem is the replaceability argument, but less extreme versions will commonly arise because this kind of theory has no basis for awarding benefits to people with specific identities.

So far, I have considered only individualized compensation. Suppose we think of the original injustice as committed against a group and the claim to compensation as made on behalf of that group's present descendants. The same theoretical issues arise, but perhaps not in the same intractable form. To begin with, none of the individuals in the group would likely have existed had the injustice in the distant past not occurred. Were it not for slavery, the present-day African Americans would not be here. Furthermore, the very factors that make African Americans a group in the strongly psychological sense—they have interdependent preferences and a strong feeling of collective identity—are to some considerable degree a consequence of the history of discrimination and injustice for which compensation is being considered.[6] Hence, it is conceivable, that if America had had a different history, in which racial differences had not played a major role, then we might well have a society that was not race conscious, a society in which members of various races did not constitute distinctive groups in any strong sense. If that quasi-empirical hypothesis were true, then an analogue to the identity problem at the individual level presents itself. We cannot, it appears, demand compensation on behalf of the group, because were it not for the injustices in the distant past, the group would not exist, that is, it would not constitute a group in any strong sense. Rather, it would just be a collection of individuals having certain characteristics.

However, nonexistence of the group provides a conceptual benchmark for possible compensation in a way that nonexistence of an individual does not. A society in which races did not consider themselves to be distinct groups is precisely one that would not have suffered a history of racial injustice and oppression. To compensate group X for not living in such a society is to imagine the lives people who would have been identified as in that group would live, were they not members of the group, but were merely individuals in such a society. Group nonexistence provides a possible compensable benchmark in a way that individual nonexistence does not. It requires that we consider the hypothetical nongroup of individuated African Americans in the alternative nonracist world as the collection of individuals who define the benchmark. These individuals are not the same, of course, as the individuals for whom compensation is now being demanded. But any advocate of group compensation will face cases where the individual members differ but the claim can still be made on behalf of the group. The difficulty is the claim that the alternative benchmark for the group is not some other condition of the group, but rather, its nonexistence. Provided there are individuals who would have been identified as group members had the injustice occurred and others who would not be so identified in our imaginary just world, there is a viable benchmark. This is nonmembership in the group for the kinds of individuals who would have been members of the group if the injustice had occurred, but would not be, if it had not.

While this conception of compensation might surmount the identity issue, it still would have to deal with the question of *distribution* of compensation in the group. For example, among African Americans, a gap is growing between an underclass and the middle class. Some benefits that are sometimes justified on compensatory grounds will be mistargeted, in the sense that they go predominantly to the middle class leaving the drastic problems of the underclass untouched. Unless a principle of group compensation specifies criteria for distribution within the group, it would hardly seem defensible.

Suppose the German government had paid compensation for Nazi atrocities, not mainly to those who had actually suffered in the Holocaust, but to American and other Jews who escaped it. Even if far more intense interdependent preferences among American Jews were, in fact, causally a product of the Holocaust, because those benefiting from compensation would not be the prime (surviving) victims of the injustice, this policy would seem a travesty of compensation. Distribution in the group must conform to some criterion of severity of treatment. Hence, if there were to be a compensatory policy directed at blacks in this country, its primary beneficiaries ought to be the underclass and not the middle class. A further necessary condition for a valid case for intergenerational group compensation would have to be some criterion for distribution in the compensated group. This would direct compensation primarily to those most needy on the assumption that needfulness is historically connected to the injustice in question. In circumstances of highly salient group membership and racial sensitivities, the most disadvantaged have such a case at the present time.

A second necessary condition for group compensation would be an account of who pays in the present for injustices in the remote past. It hardly seems appropriate to hold people responsible for acts committed by their ancestors. But some principle that holds contemporary institutions responsible for previous acts by those same institutions might be acceptable. Governments would fit this bill as would private institutions with sufficient longevity.

These points are offered as a kind of prolegomenon to the possibility of a valid case for compensation. I am trying only to remove obstacles including ones I previously regarded as decisive.[7] How compensatory considerations are to be balanced against considerations of social justice viewed ahistorically is a matter that awaits systematic analysis. We need a concept of justice that incorporates the past as one component of its theory of second-best so that ideal principles can relate to actual, nonideal practices. Historical claims may be less urgent, and less amenable to treatment, than more immediate problems. To introduce the past may simply introduce another incommensurable consideration that adds to the moral complexity of what a Rawlsian would call nonideal theory—and that also adds to the plausibility of what a non-Rawlsian would embrace as intuitionism.

NOTES

1. My discussion of the future persons case builds on arguments I made in "Justice between Generations: The Dilemma of Future Inter-

ests," in Michael Bradie and David Braybrooke, eds., *Social Justice* (Bowling Green, Ohio: Bowling Green State University, 1982), *Bowling Green Studies in Applied Philosophy*, 24–33.

2. See Derek Parfit, *Reasons and Persons* (Oxford: Oxford University Press, 1984), pt. 4.

3. Arthur Koestler, *Darkness at Noon* (New York: Macmillan, 1941), 161–62. I was reminded of Koestler's treatment of this issue by Joel Feinberg's excellent essay "Rawls and Intuitionism," in Norman Daniels, ed., *Reading Rawls: Critical Studies of A Theory of Justice* (New York: Basic Books, 1975).

4. Peter Singer, *Practical Ethics* (Cambridge: Cambridge University Press, 1979), 80–81.

5. For an extended consideration of the character and limitations of purely structural principles, see my *Tyranny and Legitimacy* (Baltimore and London: Johns Hopkins University Press, 1979), chapters 10 and 11.

6. See Owen Fiss, "Groups and the Equal Protection Clause," in Marshall Cohen, Thomas Nagel and Thomas Scanlon, eds., *Equality and Preferential Treatment* (Princeton: Princeton University Press, 1977), 84–154, esp. pp. 125–26.

7. In my *Justice, Equal Opportunity and the Family* (New Haven: Yale University Press, 1984), I took the position that these identity issues posed an obstacle to both individual and group compensation arguments. See pp. 117–18.

4

SET-ASIDES, REPARATIONS, AND COMPENSATORY JUSTICE

ELLEN FRANKEL PAUL

Compensatory justice has, in recent years, surpassed distributive justice as a highly contentious moral concept, debated in both the political arena and philosophical discourse.* Ideological adversaries surely still argue about whether or not more redistribution would be a socially advantageous or a morally mandatory goal, but the really heated controversies have shifted elsewhere. Since the late 1960s—especially after the advent of affirmative action under President Lyndon Johnson's Executive Order No. 112462[1]—programs of a putatively compensatory nature have proven highly divisive, with the "winners" claiming their preferences as a right and the "losers" denouncing their impediments as reverse discrimination and a violation of *their* rights.

Recent racial incidents, particularly those of an exceedingly unpleasant nature at some of America's leading universities,

*I wish to thank Larry May and Marilyn Friedman of Purdue University for suggesting some useful bibliographical material on compensatory justice for groups, Kenn Cust of the graduate program in philosophy at Bowling Green State University for his tireless efforts in tracking down sources for this chapter, and Kory Tilgner and Tamara Sharp of the Social Philosophy and Policy Center for ancillary assistance of various sorts.

underscore the extent to which such policies have proven socially divisive. Youths raised entirely in the more enlightened racial atmosphere of post–Civil Rights Act America, graduates of integrated public schools, suddenly and unexpectedly manifest overt signs of antagonism toward blacks. Ugly racial incidents at Stanford University, Dartmouth College, and the University of Michigan, to name only the most conspicuous, are troubling, indeed. Even more disconcerting to civil rights proponents is the spate of cases decided by the Supreme Court in its 1988 Term, cases which in their collective impact signaled a less expansive interpretation of the equal protection clause of the Fourteenth Amendment and a heavier burden on plaintiffs to prove actual discrimination under Title VII of the Civil Rights Act of 1964.[2]

This is an opportune time to reexamine preferential programs, not with the intent of retreading well-worn philosophical ground,[3] but rather with the purpose of reflecting on the cogency and coherence of the concept of compensatory justice itself. *City of Richmond v. Croson,*[4] one of the most contentious of the Supreme Court's recent forays into the civil rights arena, will serve as the focal point for this reexamination, with other programs of a rectificatory nature functioning as illuminating analogies: United States policy toward the Japanese interned in camps during World War II; German reparations after that war to surviving victims of Nazi concentration camps; and, more speculatively, possible future acts of reparation toward the victims of Soviet-style regimes. These real-world experiments in compensatory justice will highlight the limitations in applicability of the concept and its complexities—indeed, its near breakdown—when one attempts to use it to rectify injustices to generations long dead, to diffuse and not easily identified victims and perpetrators, and to the acts of regimes that take as their raison d'être the wholesale violation of human rights.

I. Compensatory Justice Defined

In book V of the *Nicomachean Ethics,* Aristotle discusses what he terms "partial justice," and he distinguishes between two types of just action that fall within that rubric. The first, what we now call distributive justice, deals with the "distribution of honors, or material goods, or of anything else that can be divided among those who have a share in the political system."[5] Aristotle describes this type of justice as a "geometrical proportion": the individuals stand to each other as the things to be distributed related to each other, that is, "the ratio between the shares will be the same as that between the persons."[6] The root moral concept that Aristotle adduces for this type of justice is desert. As he succinctly puts it, "To each according to his deserts."[7] Those who contribute equally to the common welfare or the society's particular project ought to receive whatever benefits are to be distributed. Correspondingly, those who contribute unequally should receive unequal rewards in the same proportion as their contributions differ. Aristotle wisely observes that people's criteria of desert differ, adding his customary breakdown of criteria by the nature of regimes: democrats favor free birth; oligarchs, wealth or noble birth; and aristocrats name excellence.

Defenders of race-conscious remedies for perceived societal injustices often invoke some type of forward-looking justification that relies on this concept of distributive justice. Affirmative action in higher education, corporate hiring and promotion policies, and in federal contracting, they argue, will assist those at the bottom of the socioeconomic pyramid to advance, ameliorating the effects of the unequal distribution of rewards and benefits in a capitalist society. Thomas Nagel, for one, goes even further along the distributive justice path by contending that affirmative action, while better than nothing, is a mere palliative; his preferred course would be the wholesale, egalitarian redistribution of wealth.[8] Others are less radical, electing to justify remedial policies in our existing system on the grounds of promoting "equality of opportunity," whether narrowly or expansively understood, for competition in the marketplace to be fair, or fairer, for everyone. This too would fall within the purview of our modern conception of distributive justice that in its liberal guise demands, at the least, that all "positions" in society ought to be open to everyone, with talent winning out, or at the most, that competitors suffering some disadvantage in the competition be brought up to an even level before the competition begins. While the latter, more expansive version of "equality of opportunity" might be phrased in a backward-looking, compensatory way, this need not be done, and the argument could be put entirely in a forward-looking manner, couched in terms of distributive justice. The promotion of racial harmony and the creation of a color-blind society in which race will become irrelevant are typical ways in which forward-looking arguments are cast.

Here, however, I will not be concerned with forward-looking arguments for preferential policies, but rather with contentions arising from the past, from history. For these historical claims serve as the foundation that buttresses the demand for redress for *particular* groups. A problem with forward-looking arguments is that they tend to be overinclusive. If blacks, Orientals, Eskimos, Aleuts, Hispanics, women, etc. are to be given preferential treatment to enable them to compete on an equal basis with white males, without any historical claims about their exploitation or injury suffered from discrimination, then why not others who are similarly situated, who are likewise children of poverty and disadvantage? Whether acknowledged or not, forward-looking arguments rely on the backward-looking, compensatory arguments, if only to identify the desired beneficiaries. Preferential policies, just to add a sociological observation, would garner scant approval in our society if not for their reliance on past grievances. That explains why support is stronger for relief for blacks than for women, and for blacks in preference to other minority groups whose claims to be victims of discrimination, although real, are much less compelling.

Claims for preferential treatment for one group or another must rely on historical contentions that members of the group suffered unjust abridgments of their rights in the past, suffered under discriminatory practices of a political, economic, or social nature, and may still suffer from these same practices or else from the lingering effects of these practices. It is, then, Aristotle's second component of "particular justice," rectificatory justice, that encompasses these sorts of complaints. Rectificatory justice, as distinguished from distributive justice, does not look to the goodness or badness of the person, but to the damage: "it treats the parties as equals and asks only whether one has done and the other has suffered wrong, and whether one has done and the other has suffered damage."[9] Aristotle continues:

> As the unjust in this sense is inequality, the judge tries to restore the equilibrium. When one man had inflicted and another received a wound, or when one man has killed and the other has been killed, the doing and suffering are unequally divided; by inflicting a loss on the offender, the judge tries to take away his gain and restore the equilibrium.[10]

In involuntary transactions of this sort, Aristotle says, the just occupies a median between a gain and a loss: each ought to have an equal amount before and after the event.[11]

The essential features of rectificatory justice (or, interchangeably for us, compensatory justice) are these: (1) it treats the parties as equal; (2) it looks to the damage suffered by one party and inflicted by the other; (3) it is restorative, that is, it attempts to restore the victim to the condition he was in before the unjust activity occurred.

Now, moving beyond Aristotle, obviously restoration cannot always be to exactly the same state that the victim was in prior to the transgression—the murdered man cannot be restored to life and the wounded man may be so severely injured that medical science cannot restore him to his previous condition. And these are the relatively simple cases. Usually, courts in tort cases presume that the victim can be compensated in monetary terms, with compensation for actual injuries and pain and suffering, and when the injury was inflicted as a result of wanton disregard for the rights or safety of others, an additional award of punitive damages. There are much more difficult cases for a compensatory theory to handle. What about the person, *A*, whose real property is illegitimately seized by another, *B*, and before *A* can get it back he dies and *B* dies. Four generations later *A*'s heirs sue to get the land back from *B*'s heirs who are, with the passage of time, totally unaware of the original transgression. What does rectificatory justice tell us then?

Aristotle's rectificatory justice pertains to acts between individuals, not to unjust acts committed by individuals against groups, or one group against another, or "society" against a group, or a government against a group. Can the principle stretch enough to encompass these kinds of claims? For those who endorse preferential policies based on group victimization it had better, and we will examine in section III some of the attempts offered by philosophers to apply the concept to group injustices. However, before we proceed, I would like to refine Aristotle's rectificatory justice by placing it in a larger theory that tells us what kinds of acts are unjust and so trigger at least in theory, if not in practice,[12] a right to compensation.

The moral theory that I will rely upon is one that would have been acceptable to most pre-affirmative action liberals, whether they were of a classical or modern welfare-state proclivity. To a considerable extent, we were all Lockeans then, even if some added a bit more in the way of "rights-to" various goods, to the distaste of the purists. In recent years, this consensus has been seriously eroded by a belief that results override principle, that it is permissible to violate some people's rights in order to achieve a system in which all people's rights will eventually be respected. However, even for those who embrace this view, considerable agreement exists that rights of some sort are important, if only in the distant future.

The theory holds that individuals have rights—calling them "human rights" or "natural rights" really makes no difference —and others ought to respect these rights by not crossing the boundaries of the protected sphere surrounding each individual. These rights include—and here, welfare liberals would say "but are not limited to"—life, liberty, and property.[13] Compensation is due whenever a person infringes my right and, thereby, causes me harm. Trivial rights violations may occur that cause no harm beyond the infraction itself, and redress typically is not pursued by the victim because it is simply too much effort for the insult. An example of a trivial boundary infraction occurs when someone casually trespasses on my land in crossing over to a neighbor's yard, thereby causing no damage other than my slight discomfiture, if that. It would be a rather unpleasant world in which to live if people sought recompense for such minor infractions, and they usually do not.

Recent attempts at defining compensatory justice are compatible with Aristotle's tripartite criteria for rectificatory justice. James W. Nickel describes the concept in the following way:

> Compensatory justice requires that counterbalancing benefits be
> provided to those individuals who have been wrongfully injured
> which will serve to bring them up to the level of wealth and
> welfare that they would now have if they had not been disadvan-
> taged. Compensatory programs differ from redistributive pro-
> grams mainly in regard to their concern for the past.[14]

Nickel's definition explicitly mentions as a criterion that compensatory justice regards the past, an important addition that
was implicit in Aristotle. Bringing victims "up to the level of
wealth and welfare that they would now have if they had not
been disadvantaged" is a more expansive notion of compensation than Aristotle's of simply restoring the victim to the condition that he was in prior to the unjust act. Nickel's broader view
is more harmonious with our modern tort law version of compensation in which the victim is compensated for the actual
injury, pain and suffering, loss of earnings, sometimes psychic
losses, etc. Especially with the passage of much time between
the injury and the recompense, restoring the individual to his
ex ante position will not fully erase the injurious event, and the
modern tort law reflects a more adequate attempt to make the
victim whole once again or, as economists would put it, to make
him indifferent between his having never suffered the injury
and having suffered the injury, but with full compensation for
all damages.

A more complete set of criteria for compensatory justice,
then, is the following: (1) it is backward-looking, in the sense
that what is relevant is an act or acts in the past that transpired
between the contesting parties (i.e., the victim and the perpetrator)[15] that violated the victim's right(s); (2) it looks to the injury
suffered by the victim and inflicted by the perpetrator; (3) in
effecting a remedy it treats the parties as equals in the sense
intended by the idea of "equality before the law," that is, that
the rights of each party must be respected; (4) it attempts,
through compensation of one sort or another,[16] to bring the
victim to the condition he would have been in, or its equivalent,[17] had the injurious event never occurred.

The modified definition has several advantages over Aristotle's: it covers cases that cannot be described as resulting from
unjust acts, for example, injuries resulting from negligence; it

expands on Aristotle's notion of treating the parties as equals by maintaining that the rights of each party must be respected, which carries the implication that in rectifying the initial injury, no further rights violations ought to be inflicted on the victim or the perpetrator; and it incorporates the more expansive, modern view of compensation.

We now have a working set of criteria for compensatory justice combined with an underlying moral theory about when compensatory justice would come into play, when rights violations of a nontrivial sort have occurred.

II. Set-Asides: The Legal Morass

City of Richmond v. Croson (1989) sent shockwaves through the civil rights community as well as the state governments, some thirty-six of them, and the 190 local governments that have over the years adopted set-aside programs to devote a percentage of their public works contracts to firms owned by minorities or women.[18] Modeled on federal programs legislated by Congress and operating throughout the country, states, counties, and cities had assumed that once a federal program had passed constitutional muster in 1980, their programs, framed in similar terms, would be likewise insulated.

In *Fullilove v. Klutznick*,[19] a badly fragmented Court[20] upheld 6–3 the "minority business enterprise" (MBE) provision of the Public Works Employment Act of 1977 against constitutional challenge on grounds of the equal protection component of the due process clause of the Fifth Amendment.[21] The MBE provision mandated that grants to local public works projects by the federal Economic Development Administration must be made contingent upon assurance that at least 10 percent of the funds be expended for MBEs. Minority businesses were defined in the Act as those owned at least 50 percent, 51 percent in the case of publicly owned companies, by minority group members. Qualifying minority groups were designated as Negroes, Hispanics, Orientals, Indians, Eskimos, and Aleuts. Chief Justice Burger, joined by Justices White and Powell, reprised the legislative history of the set-aside amendment, which had been introduced into the House by Representative Mitchell, who stated that only

1 percent of federal contracts went to minorities while they constituted 15–18 percent of the population. He and others spoke of the intricate bidding process that, they alleged, discouraged minorities from competing for contracts and the need for economic stimulation to minority businesses hard-hit by the then prevailing recession. Although no hearings were held on the amendment by congressional committees, Burger found sufficient legislative rationale in the scanty floor discussion and in several reports on the condition of minorities prepared by various committees.[22]

The Chief Justice argued that it was clearly Congress's intent to insure that grantees would not employ procurement practices that "might result in perpetuation of the effects of prior discrimination."[23] Curiously, he added, "The MBE program does not mandate the allocation of federal funds according to inflexible percentages solely based on race or ethnicity."[24] This contention is dubious at best, given the 10 percent set-aside mandated in the act. He handily dispensed with the contention that, in fashioning remedies, Congress must act in a wholly "color-blind" fashion. Much is heard from all of the justices in preferential treatment cases that the color-blind society is still the ultimate goal, but in upholding such measures the justices routinely argue that means that do take race into account are necessary in the short run to eviscerate the effects of past discrimination. These measures will hasten the day when Hubert Humphrey's goal, expressed during the debates on the Civil Rights Act of 1964, of a society in which race becomes irrelevant, will be achieved.[25]

The Chief Justice declined to articulate a definitive test for review of racial preferences challenged under the equal protection clause, remarking that in either of the tests developed in the opinions in *University of California v. Bakke* (1978),[26] the set-aside program would "survive judicial review." The justices have been disputing for a decade now about the proper standard of review for such cases. Some contend that nothing less than strict scrutiny will do. Usually but not always, challenged preferential measures will not survive such heightened judicial examination. Others more sympathetic to preferential policies argue for what is termed an "intermediate standard of review" that is more deferential to Congress, and hence a standard under which preferences are more likely to survive.[27] Justices Marshall, Brennan, and Blackmun in their concurrence in *Fullilove* employed this more lenient standard of review, as is their wont. Overriding all quibbles about standards of review, it is clear from Chief Justice Burger's opinion that he was reluctant to abrogate Congress's scheme for achieving its "constitutional mandate for equality of economic opportunity."[28]

Before departing *Fullilove*, Justice Stevens' dissent is worth noting because it is one of the few occasions in which a more than cursory attempt is made to plumb the philosophical justification for set-asides. It is also remarkable for a particularly acerbic footnote.

> The very attempt to define with precision a beneficiary's qualifying racial characteristics is repugnant to our constitutional ideals. ... If the National Government is to make a serious effort to define racial classes by criteria that can be administered objectively, it must study precedents such as the First Regulation to the Reich's Citizenship Law of November 14, 1935 . . .[29]

Justice Stevens discerned four separate justifications advanced for set-asides, only two of which are immediately relevant for our compensatory-justice analysis: (1) that the set-aside is a form of reparation for injuries suffered in the past to all members of the designated class; and (2) that it is an appropriate remedy for past discrimination suffered by minority businesses that have been denied federal contracts.[30] Citing the congressional program to recompense Indian tribes for unjust treatment by the government, Stevens argued that in a plan for recompensing classwide victims of governmental injury, the government has an obligation to "distribute that recovery among the members of the injured class in an evenhanded way." Furthermore, he contended, the award should bear "some rational relationship to the extent of the harm it is intended to cure."[31] While wrongs committed against Negroes as a class would justify classwide recovery of an equal sum for every member of the injured class, set-asides operate as a "perverse" form of reparations. They benefit most those least disadvantaged in the class, and leave the most disadvantaged and, hence, the most likely to be still suffering from the effects of past wrongs, with no benefits. In addition, the history of discrimination against blacks cannot count as an argument for special privileges for Eskimos or Indians. They too suffered, but not in the same magnitude.

More fundamentally, Stevens contended that if no attempt were made to measure the recovery by the wrong suffered or to distribute reparations on an evenhanded basis within the class, almost any group in America could argue based on its history that it deserved reparations, and shape a remedial program for itself so long as it could muster the political muscle.

On the second justification, Justice Stevens found it unlikely that in recent years minority businesses have been discriminated against in federal contracting, a conclusion he surmised from the dearth of litigated claims on behalf of such businesses since the enactment of the Civil Rights Act's Title VI, which bars discrimination in any program receiving federal money. Even assuming that some firms were the victims of discrimination, the set-aside program, he continued, sweeps too broadly to right any past wrong by covering firms that never applied for federal contracts, ones that successfully applied, firms formed after the passage of the act, unsuccessful bidders due to reasons other than discrimination, and actual victims of discrimination. And the latter already have their judicial remedy. Hence, he found it impossible to characterize the set-aside as "narrowly tailored."

Turning, now, to *City of Richmond v. Croson*, the Court was even more fragmented in its opinions than in *Fullilove*, but this time the tide turned against a set-aside program.[32] The Richmond City Council's Minority Business Utilization Plan, challenged by a contractor on Fourteenth Amendment equal protection grounds, was modeled closely on the federal program approved in *Fullilove*, but this was not sufficient to insulate it from a declaration of unconstitutionality by the Court. Prime contractors were required to subcontract 30 percent, more generous than the 10 percent allotted in the federal program, of the value of their contracts to at least 51 percent minority-controlled businesses. Even the definition of favored minority groups echoed the federal classifications: "[c]itizens of the United States who are Blacks, Spanish-speaking, Orientals, Indians, Eskimos, or Aleuts."[33] The Richmond plan was described as remedial in nature and designed to encourage wider participation of minorities businesses in the construction of public works, and it was not geographically bound, allowing minorities from anywhere in the country to participate. Proponents of the plan before the city council, and there were only two from the public, cited a study showing that while Richmond was populated 50 percent by blacks, only .67 percent of the city's prime construction contracts had been awarded to blacks. Contractors' associations, whose spokesmen opposed the set-aside, had virtually no minority contractors on their rosters. In her opinion, Justice O'Connor pointed out that there was no direct evidence given at the city council meeting prior to the adoption of the plan that the city had practiced racial discrimination in its contracting nor that the city's prime contractors had discriminated.

Croson instigated its suit when it was denied a contract to install urinals in the city jail after it was unable to find an MBE able to supply the fixtures at a price that had been built into its bid. The city refused either to grant the company a waiver or raise the contract price and denied Croson the contract even though it had been the sole bidder.[34]

Justice O'Connor's opinion emphasized the personal nature of the rights created by the equal protection clause of the Fourteenth Amendment, which reads: "[N]o State shall . . . deny to any person within its jurisdiction the equal protection of the laws." The Richmond plan, she opined, denies to certain individuals, solely on the basis of race, the right to compete for a fixed share of public contracts. Their personal rights "to be treated with equal dignity and respect are implicated by a rigid rule erecting race as the sole criterion in an aspect of public decision making."[35] Searching judicial scrutiny, she and three of her colleagues think, is necessary when examining such plans in order to determine whether race-based measures are "benign" and "remedial," or rather, unlawful because they are motivated by "illegitimate notions of racial inferiority or *simple racial politics*" (emphasis added). For Justice O'Connor, as her opinion unfolds, was concerned about the dominance of the Richmond City Council by blacks who held five out of the nine positions. That strict scrutiny test has two components: a showing of compelling governmental interest; and once that is demonstrated, proof that the means chosen are narrowly tailored to achieve the compelling state interest.

She contended that the standard of review under the equal protection clause should not differ depending on the race of those burdened or benefited. Justice Marshall's advocacy, in his dissent, of a "relaxed standard of review" for race-conscious classifications designed for a remedial purpose, she finds unacceptable. Without strict judicial scrutiny of legislative determinations of remedial purpose, she thinks that the goal of creating a color-blind society, in which irrelevant factors of a person's race are eliminated entirely from governmental decision making, will be forever impossible.[36]

For Justice O'Connor, the Richmond scheme could not survive strict judicial scrutiny. Generalized assertions about discrimination in the past in an industry will not suffice to demonstrate a compelling state interest in remediation. Absent more specific findings, legislative remedies cannot be tailored to the "precise scope of the injury" and there would be "no logical stopping point" for the "ill-defined wrong": "an amorphous claim that there has been past discrimination in a particular industry cannot justify the use of an unyielding racial quota."[37] Statistical comparisons between the number of blacks in the city and the percentage of city contracts awarded to blacks will not lead to a presumption of discrimination—although the Court accepts such statistical measures in other cases, such as allegations of discrimination in entry-level employment—because special qualifications are necessary. The relevant pool must be the number of minorities qualified to undertake the work. Likewise, racial discrimination in the Richmond construction industry cannot be inferred from the absence of minorities in local construction associations, without some showing that there are MBEs in the area eligible for membership. Only then, could it be inferred that racial discrimination barred these firms from entry. Findings of nationwide discrimination by Congress or inferences from a history of school desegregation in Richmond, relied on by Justice Marshall and the dissenters, are not sufficient because such factors "could justify a preference of any size or duration."[38] Hence, the majority held that the city had failed to demonstrate a "compelling interest in apportioning public contracting opportunities on the basis of race."[39] The inclusion of other groups in the Richmond set-aside plan, particularly Eskimos and Aleuts, drew judicial notice, as Justice O'Connor noted that their "random inclusion" casts doubt on the city's true purpose in enacting it. This "gross overinclusiveness" of groups in all likelihood never discriminated against in Richmond "impugns the city's claim of remedial motivation."[40]

As for the second prong of the strict-scrutiny test, Justice O'Connor found it virtually impossible to assess whether the Richmond plan was narrowly tailored to remedy past discrimination, since it lacked any link to particular findings of discrimination. She did suggest, however, that if minority firms lacked capital or had difficulty meeting bonding requirements, a race-neutral program of city financing for small firms would accomplish greater minority participation. The majority saw a distinction between Richmond's plan and that upheld in *Fullilove* in regard to the waiver provision that in the latter allowed a waiver when the MBE's higher price was not the result of prior discrimination, while the former did not. Mere administrative convenience will not justify the imposition of a quota system when cases can be appraised on an individual basis.[41]

Justice O'Connor concluded by suggesting that cities have plenty of perfectly legitimate means of eradicating discrimination in the construction industry, and she urged that when they do choose to invoke racial classification to provide proper findings

> Such findings also serve to assure all citizens that the deviation from the norm of equal treatment of all racial and ethnic groups is a temporary matter, *a measure taken in the service of the goal of equality itself*. Absent such findings, there is a danger that a racial classification is merely the product of unthinking stereotypes or a form of racial politics.[42] (Emphasis added)

Justice Marshall, in his impassioned dissent, could discern nothing to distinguish between the Court-approved set-aside scheme in *Fullilove* and the one deemed anathema by the majority in *Croson*. He found it ironic that Richmond should be condemned now for benefiting blacks when a long history of judicial procedures established Richmond's discriminatory obstinacy in the past. Invoking an intermediate test, which he has supported throughout the Court's affirmative action decisions, Justice Marshall found "important governmental interests" served by Richmond's set-aside plan: in eradicating the effects of past racial discrimination; and in prospectively insuring that its present contracting policies do not "perpetuate the exclusionary effects of past discrimination."[43] On the second prong of his intermediate standard of scrutiny, he found the set-aside plan "substantially related to the interests it seeks to serve," for it was limited in duration and it had only a minimal impact on innocent third parties.[44] Given the failure of race-neutral measures to eradicate the effects of past discrimination, Justice Marshall concluded that, in the words of Justice Blackmun in *University of California v. Bakke,* "[i]n order to get beyond racism, we must first take account of race."[45]

The Court has not distinguished itself by its opinions in *Croson.* As with earlier attempts at grappling with affirmative action remedies, the Court was almost comically fragmented in its opinion and the majority less than forthcoming in its reasoning when it came to distinguishing *Croson* from a nearly identical federal set-aside program approved in *Fullilove.* Rather than explicitly repudiating *Fullilove,* a bitter pill that the Court is always reluctant to swallow, they chose instead to find hairsplitting distinctions. One of these set the unfortunate precedent of arguing that equal protection means one thing when applied to the federal government and another when applied to the states and their subdivisions.

III. Set-Asides and Compensatory Justice

Leaving the legal quagmire, I wish, now, to examine set-asides from the perspective of the theory of rights and particularly the criteria established in Section I for compensatory justice attendant upon rights violations.

A. The First Criterion

The first criterion of compensatory justice is: that it is backward looking, in the sense that what is relevant is an act or acts in the past that transpired between the contesting parties, the victim and the perpetrator, that violated the victim's right(s). On first reflection, a set-aside program might meet Criterion I if it were designed to remedy a violation of rights committed by one party, the government, against the other party, the person whose rights were violated. Criterion I has three components and it is necessary to examine each one separately before we can assess this initial impression. They are: (1) the act(s) requirement; (2) the identification of a victim and a perpetrator; and (3) a showing that the act is a rights violation. I shall examine (3) first, for it will be impossible to identify (1) until we know what kinds of discriminatory acts count as rights violations.

(3)Discriminatory Acts as Rights Violations. What kinds of acts committed in the past are rights violations triggering a valid claim for compensatory justice? On a rights theory, as elaborated in Section I, an individual would have no right to dictate how other people regard him, or how they react to him in their private social and economic relations. Title VII of the Civil Rights Act of 1964 notwithstanding,[46] I would argue that in private employment decisions, as in other more anonymous economic relations, individuals are free to make any decisions they like, regardless of whether they choose to hire the most highly qualified individual, their Aunt Nellie, a member of their church, a black because they are black, or a white because they do not wish to associate with blacks. This, undoubtedly, offends prevailing sensibilities, but I can discern nothing in rights theory that can entitle one person to dictate to another how that person ought to dispose of his legitimately acquired assets. And it is precisely such dictation that is involved in maintaining that *A* must spend his money in hiring *B* rather than *C* whom *A* prefers for *any* reason, no matter how disconcerting or disgraceful others may find that reason to be. To maintain otherwise, is to claim that *B* has the right to abrogate *A*'s rights, when *A* has not transgressed against any right of *B*'s. Since rights are the same for everyone—you ought not violate mine, I ought not violate yours—this claim is unfounded.

The act requirement cannot be met by citing instances of private discrimination, no matter how obnoxious or widespread.

That private contractors refused in the past to hire minorities as construction workers or to contract with minority business as subcontractors is irrelevant from a rights perspective. One would undoubtedly wish to condemn such private acts as unvirtuous or uncharitable, but not as rights violations.

What about acts of governments and their officials? Can discriminatory laws and practices count as acts of rights violation? They certainly can. Governments, unlike individuals, have an obligation to protect their citizens from rights violations; individuals are only obligated not to violate others' rights, but they have no further obligation to see that others remain rights-abiding. Governments—and this is captured wonderfully in the Fourteenth Amendment's equal protection clause—have an obligation to enact laws that treat all people equally, to enforce those laws in an evenhanded manner, and to provide impartial courts to judge individual claims of rights violations by private individuals and the government. If a government violates this principle of "equality before the law," by failing to meet these desiderata, it has committed an act that counts as a rights violation.

(1) The Act(s) Requirement. It is governmental acts, then, for which we must search to justify a compensatory remedy, of a sort yet unidentified. To take the City of Richmond as a concrete example: did the city commit acts that violated the rights of minority contractors; did the city enact laws or execute its laws in a manner that violated the principle of "equality before the law"? These are the relevant questions. If the city barred blacks from bidding for public-works contracts, or passed over their bids even though they were the lowest submitted, or imposed different standards on blacks than on other bidders, then it committed an illegitimate act that would meet the act requirement of Criterion I. On this account, Justice Scalia got it exactly right when he maintained that governments are allowed to take race into account in fashioning a remedy only when they act to rectify a past violation of the equal protection principle that they themselves committed.[47]

To justify a remedial program that benefits minority contractors, one would have to show that the government committed

an act that violated the rights of the victim. General societal
discrimination perpetrated by individuals in their private social
and economic relations will not suffice, and neither will a statistical comparison of the number of minorities employed as city
contractors with the number of minorities in the city, nor a
comparison of the minority city contractors with the available
minority contractors in the city.[48]

(2) *Identification of a Victim and a Perpetrator.* To meet this criterion, a set-aside program would have to be buttressed by a
showing that the municipality or federal government, the perpetrator, committed its rights-violating act against a victim. Now,
it is perfectly clear who counts as a perpetrator. It is the government. But who counts as a victim?

Here, typically, legal commentators, moral philosophers, and
judges invoke the history of black slavery, Jim Crow legislation
in the South that barred blacks from enjoying full legal rights
and instituted segregation in schools and places of public accommodation, and the recent, more subtle, societal discrimination that serves to perpetuate the effects of slavery and state-
mandated segregation. Surely, this sweeps too broadly, for it
would count every black person as a victim. In addition, other
racial, ethnic, or religious minorities could claim victim status—
Jews, Orientals, Hispanics, Eskimos, the Irish, Catholics, even
women—for all at one time or another in this country suffered
under societal discrimination and, in the case of women, discriminatory laws that, for example, barred them from voting,[49]
practicing certain professions, and enjoying the same rights
over property as men.

What we need to identify are *actual* victims of governmental
acts that violated their rights. This is a much more confined
investigation. Who was victimized by Richmond's or the United
States government's enactment of laws barring minority contractors from bidding or of practices that had the same effect?
This is the relevant question. If there were no such laws or
practices, then there were no victims.

In the case of Richmond, it stands beyond dispute that when
blacks were enslaved they could not bid for public construction
contracts, for they could not contract for *anything*. After slavery

—despite the passage of the 1866 Civil Rights Act,[50] which was designed to guarantee to the emancipated slaves contractual freedom among other rights, and despite the subsequent constitutionalization of its principles in the Fourteenth Amendment —blacks were routinely denied these rights and treated unfairly by government officials prejudiced against them. During slavery and the prevalence of Jim Crow laws in the South, it is reasonable to assume that blacks in Richmond were routinely denied access to public contracts.

Unfortunately, this does not get us very far. Among all the blacks then living, who are the ones who would have chosen to become the owners of construction companies? And who among these owners would have bid on public contracts? These counterfactual historical queries are simply impossible to answer. Furthermore, even if these individual victims could be identified, we have one more complexity: they are virtually all dead. All the slaves are long dead, as are many of the blacks who suffered under Jim Crow, if one dates its demise from *Brown v. Board of Education*,[51] at least de jure if certainly not de facto, or the Civil Rights Act of 1964, or somewhat later.

Compensatory justice, formulated in Aristotle's individualistic manner that I modified, requires identifiable individuals as victims. It cannot count victims long dead, nor counterfactual victims, that is, but-for-victims: but for governmental discrimination I would have been the low bidder on a city construction contract.

Some advocates of preferential policies try to overcome this problem by arguing that blacks are the heirs of slaves who had their rights massively violated under the protection of state laws, and the U.S. Constitution, and they ought to be compensated. Still others argue that the theory of compensatory justice must be given a *group* dimension, so that actual victims do not have to be identified and members of the group can be offered preferential programs of various sorts as compensation. This latter argument I will examine in due course. As for the former, I find it difficult to resolve. Clearly, in some instances of rights violations, heirs do have a legitimate claim to restitution or recompense, for example, someone steals your father's land or personal property. However, even here matters get messy when the rights violation has not been redressed for generations. Does the grandchild, the great-grandchild . . . the n-th grandchild have the right to reclaim the stolen property? This is why our laws, both criminal and civil, have statutes of limitations that render claims stale with the passage of time. These limitations seem perfectly sensible, for they insist that if a person does not act to claim his lost possession within a reasonable amount of time, he and his heirs are forever barred from complaining. Intervening events, and the reliance of innocent third parties on legitimate transactions involving the stolen property, make it likely that others' rights will be violated if we attempt to repair damages that are of ancient lineage.

As perplexing as these property rights violations are, they are the easy cases. What about claims to inherit the right to compensation for rights violations of the life and liberty sort. If slave A was killed by his master, does his heir unto the third, fifth, or n-th generation have a claim against the heirs of the master? The slave's right to liberty was breached in almost every way imaginable, but can his great-great-granddaughter claim recompense from the heirs of the master, or more pertinently for our set-aside problem, from the government whose policies permitted and enforced slavery? I doubt that anyone can resolve these questions, other than by adopting the sensible solution devised by the common law judges: some rights violations lapse with time and, therefore, are uncompensable. It is impossible to right all the wrongs of the past, and to attempt to do so would surely mean that resources would not be available to compensate the victims of the present.

Criterion I in Retrospect. A set-aside program of the Richmond variant would flounder on component (2), identifying the perpetrator and the victim, because it does not point to specific victims. Rather, it dispenses its compensation to anyone who can claim membership in six named, but no more closely defined, groups. Given the problems foreshadowed above with respect to blacks, seemingly the easiest group among whom victims could be found, it goes without saying that the problems are infinitely compounded when a group is identified only as Spanish-speaking. Why should Ricardo Montalban's construction company receive a set-aside from the City of Richmond?

A genuine victim would be a black contractor denied a contract even though the lowest bidder. However, to rectify this injustice one does not need to resort to a set-aside program, which may reward not the victim but another black contractor down the street or in Alaska. The aggrieved black contractor, just like an aggrieved white contractor, should repair to the courts and demand that the law be obeyed by the city.

The first and third components, the act and rights-violation requirements, limited compensable acts to those committed by governments acting in violation of the "equality before the law" principle. Set-asides of the Richmond type aimed at rectifying a myriad of societal ills and private acts of discrimination cannot satisfy these components. An act that requires compensation would be one committed by the government against the rights of a victim. Such violations could be more appropriately dealt with in the courts where victim-plaintiffs would vindicate their rights and be awarded compensation.

B. The Second Criterion

Criterion II calls for identification of an injury suffered by the victim and inflicted by the perpetrator. A set-aside program has difficulty with this requirement, too. Injury cannot be claimed by Ricardo Montalban who established his construction company after the passage of the set-aside program in Richmond with the express purpose of taking advantage of it. The city never did him any damage, indeed he may never have entered the city. Nor can injury be claimed by Joe Smith, a black man, who never owned a construction company, nor by Mike Brown, an Eskimo, who owns a construction company but never bothered to bid for a contract in Richmond.

Once again, what would count as an injury is an act of discrimination by the city that denied a contract to the lowest bidder, who could then bring the city to court to redress the rights violation perpetrated against him.

C. The Third Criterion

Criterion III requires that, in effecting a remedy, the parties be treated as equals in the sense intended by the principle of "equality before the law," that is, that the rights of each be respected. Set-asides present one more complicating factor because they make individuals other than the perpetrator and the victim parties to the remedy. The remedy, apportioning a fixed percentage of public works dollars for designated minority group members, bars from competition nonminority contractors solely on the basis of their race. Thus, individuals who never themselves contributed to slavery, nor to Jim Crow laws, and may never have themselves engaged in discriminatory activities amounting to rights violations,[52] must bear the burden of the remedy. What a set-aside accomplishes as a remedy, then, is to create a new generation of victims. They would have claims to recompense for having their right to be treated equally before the law transgressed. This leads to an infinite regress: whoever is called upon to redress the assault on these people's rights, will again have a claim to compensation . . .

One more point deserves mention: what sense does it make to demand compensatory sacrifices for the heirs of slaves from the heirs of immigrants who came to the United States after the manumission? These heirs of immigrants who arrived in the post–Civil War period comprise most of the population of the United States.[53] Many of their ancestors came to this country to escape oppression in other parts of the world: Armenians, Soviets, Vietnamese, Haitians . . . The list is almost endless. Even thinking about how they might get redress for the injuries suffered by their ancestors under a theory of compensatory justice is extremely disconcerting. Do we look to the Tsars' heirs to compensate the serfs or the victims of pogroms in Russia? Do the Tsars' heirs look to the Soviets for compensation for their ancestors' murders? A theory of compensatory justice of the Aristotelian, individualistic sort seems to break down under the burden of enormous, multifarious, sometimes even mutually negating injuries suffered in the past.

D. The Fourth Criterion

The victim, according to Criterion IV, must be recompensed in some manner that brings him to the condition he would have occupied, or its equivalent, had the injurious event never occurred. How might this apply to the current black population, most of whom are the heirs of slaves forcibly brought to this country? [54]

Onora O'Neill raises an intriguing point in the context of discussing the wrongs committed by European nations in the era of their colonial conquests:

> Precisely because the results of those wrongs are so immeasurable, complex, and intricate we cannot easily identify their present victims or quantify the harms they have suffered. Indeed, we may be reasonably sure that no present person would exist had the massive movements of population and transformations of ways of life of the European expansion not taken place. [55]

How do we restore to the position they would have occupied individuals who would not be alive today but for their ancestors' forcible enslavement?

Leaving aside this metaphysical speculation, what about real people, actually existing descendants of slaves who are here now? How can they be restored to the positions they would have occupied but for slavery? If not for the slave trade, most of the descendants of the slaves would now be living in Africa under regimes known neither for their respect for human rights, indeed for human life, nor for the economic well-being of their citizens. The typical denizen of one of these states, I dare speculate, would envy the condition of the black teenage mother on welfare in one of this country's worst inner cities. Starvation, war, tribal depredations, infant mortality, disease, and hopelessness are the standard condition of many regions of Africa, for example, Ethiopia and Somalia.

It seems, then, that if we take the restorative element of compensatory justice literally, blacks in America would be owed worse lives than the ones that they currently live: a not terribly satisfactory conclusion. While Criterion IV works well enough in assessing damages in a medical malpractice case, for example, where it makes sense to try to restore the victim to his condition ex ante, the criterion leads to bizarre conclusions in the case of recompensing descendants for massive rights violations sustained by their ancestors.

Additionally, it defies imagination how set-asides can be justified as an appropriate means of compensation when they reward "victims" so haphazardly and with no attempt to equate compensation to the extent of the injury sustained, if any.

E. Compensatory Justice for Groups

An Aristotelian, individualistic theory of compensatory justice, as we have seen, collapses under the weight of demands for compensation for rights violations sustained by members of groups who may be long dead and for their descendants. It even has difficulty dealing with recompense for rights violations that those descendants may have themselves directly suffered at the hands of their government, because to favor them now with special privileges engenders more rights violations inflicted on other, innocent third parties.

Some philosophers who support preferential treatment have tried to surmount these difficulties by either explicitly refashioning the theory of compensatory justice in order to add a group dimension or simply employing an undefined concept of group compensation. Bernard Boxill does the latter. Compensation, he contends, is owed to blacks as a group "because they have been wronged and disadvantaged by slavery and discrimination."[56] Had it not been for these wrongs, blacks would be more equal to other groups in income, education, and well-being. Compensating blacks as a group "requires making them, as a group, more nearly equal to those other groups."[57] If blacks were more nearly equal, he continues, then some of them would be occupying desirable positions, and thus a policy of placing the presently most qualified blacks in those desirable positions would be justified as compensation to the group.

Boxill's argument, despite his ineffectual protest to the contrary, falls victim to Alan Goldman's argument that those benefited by such a program are likely to be the least discriminated against members of the minority group. Consequently, preferential policies would "invert the ratio of degree of harm to degree of benefit."[58] Boxill's rejoinder, that even qualified blacks have suffered from discrimination, really misses the point, because surely the victims of the most egregious rights violations should receive recompense first, not last or never. However, Boxill really does not look to rights violations but to all sorts of ancillary harms suffered by blacks as the result of societal discrimination. To have these sorts of claims count as compensable, a *theory* of compensatory justice distinct from Aristotle's needs to be elaborated for groups and Boxill has not given us one.[59]

Another attempt at arguing for a group compensation principle has been made by Paul Taylor. "The principle of compensatory justice," he writes, "is that, in order to restore the balance of justice when an injustice has been committed to a group of persons, some form of compensation or reparation must be made to that group."[60] Even if a member of the discriminated-against group was not himself discriminated against, he has a right to compensation simply because he is a member of the group. Society in general owes an obligation to compensate and, through affirmative action programs, anyone who is in the affected group can rightfully claim the benefit. Furthermore, it is not sufficient for the society to compensate "each member of the group, not qua member of the group but qua person who has been unjustly treated . . . , it is leaving justice undone. For it is denying the specific obligation it owes to, and the specific right it has created in the group as such."[61]

Taylor's concluding remark, I must confess, I find completely unintelligible. If every victim of an unjust act were compensated, where is the remainder of injustice that is owed to the group? What is the group other than its members, or is Taylor conceiving of the group as a superorganic whole that is more than its parts? In addition, it is difficult to see how such haphazard programs as set-asides and affirmative action, which benefit victims and nonvictims, some victims and not others on a seemingly random basis, can be said to compensate "the group."[62] Taylor, like Boxill, has not developed a *theory* of compensatory justice for groups, one that would tell us, as Aristotle's theory did for individuals, the criteria for when a group deserves recompense.

IV. REPARATIONS

In order to refine the theory of compensatory justice adumbrated earlier and to discover whether there is a way of recompensing victims of rights violations when they are both of a serious nature and the victims widely diffused, it will be helpful to examine two reparations programs enacted by governments.

In 1988 the United States Congress promulgated a long overdue measure to recompense citizens and permanent residents of Japanese ancestry who were rounded up on the West Coast and interned in camps for the duration of the Second World War.[63] Of the approximately 120,000 people who suffered this fate, 60,000 are still alive, and it is only these individuals who are each entitled to the sum of $20,000 allotted as recompense by Congress. Descendants of the original internees are not eligible; only those who die after the enactment of the measure and before the payout occurs can have heirs claim their allotment.[64]

Budgetary constraints on the U.S. Treasury, one suspects, had more to do with the shaping of the policy than any clear notion of compensatory justice. The amount of the compensation is arbitrary, as not all victims suffered the same duration of incarceration or the same extent of other ancillary losses. Most victims will have to wait additional years as Congress parsimoniously doles out shares to the oldest victims first, many now well into their nineties and dying at the rate of two hundred per month. Nevertheless, there are some aspects of the program worth noting. First, only actual victims who had their right to liberty violated will receive compensation. The sole exception is that the heirs of victims who die after the passage of the act can claim a share, but this seems sensible because the elders so close to death would have a pretty strong likelihood of passing the money on to their heirs as an inheritance had they lived to collect. Second, the compensatory program came with an apology from the President and an admission from Congress that a "fundamental injustice" had been committed against them, an apology that seemed to assuage the feelings of some of the victims. Third, even though over forty years had passed since the rights violations had occurred, the victims were easily identifiable and many of them were still alive. While far from ideal, this reparation scheme, when combined with compensation for property losses approved by Congress in 1948, provides one example of a scheme of reparations that is both theoretically sound and practically manageable.

The Federal Republic of Germany, in September of 1952, consummated an agreement with Israel and the Conference on Jewish Material Claims against Germany for the payment of reparations to living Jewish victims of the Nazi concentration camps, survivors of the victims, Jewish groups working to resettle the survivors, and the State of Israel to accommodate them. The Federal Republic enacted a series of laws to implement the program of reparations for victims of the Nazis under which 1.2 million people received compensation, and by 1965 approximately $4.4 billion had been paid.[65]

The 1952 Reparation Agreement provided that Israel would receive DM 3 billion and an additional DM 450 million would go to Jewish philanthropic groups, with payment spread out over twelve years and made in the form of commodities rather than specie. Under a protocol that the Federal Republic signed with the Claims Conference, the Germans promised to extend existing legislation for compensating individual victims of the Nazis. This protocol provided that compensation would be paid to victims who suffered loss of liberty (adding new categories to the existing program for forced labor and life underground), to professionals and businessmen for loss of the opportunity to earn a livelihood (up to DM 25,000 or a pension), to stateless victims who would receive compensation for deprivation of liberty and damage to health and limb, and to those who sustained property damage. Restitution programs, then already in place to return identifiable property, were to continue. A second protocol provided for payment to the Claims Conference organizations as spiritual heirs of the exterminated Jewish victims, the funds to be used to assist in the aid, rehabilitation, and resettle-ment of the survivors. This is the DM 450 million mentioned above.[66]

What distinguishes these two programs from set-asides, and the German reparations scheme is much more sophisticated and complete in the rights violations it seeks to recompense, is that they are aimed at a group, surely, but a group of *actual* victims who are alive and can still suffer lingering and traumatic injury from the massive rights violations they sustained. The victims are identifiable, more easily in the case of the Japanese internees since the U.S. government kept excellent records and less so in the German case where victims were required to give proof of their eligibility. Heirs of the victims, except in narrowly defined instances, were not considered victims in either program. The German reparations to Israel and the Jewish philanthropies are a step removed from actual victims, but due to the enormity of the catastrophe that befell the Jews, the millions killed, it seems appropriate not to leave their property or its value in the hands of individuals who may have contributed to their demise.

All reparation programs share a common feature of extract-ing compensation for the victims from all taxpayers in the coun-try, mulcting indifferently both those who are completely inno-cent of any wrongdoing and those who may have committed atrocities. Governments create no wealth of their own, and they possess only what they manage to extract from their citizens. There is inevitably some injustice in extracting money from the innocent to compensate the victims, but in instances of such massive rights violations to identifiable victims as the Japanese and Jews, this exaction seems as justifiable as taxation can ever be. Otherwise, monstrous rights violations would simply be un-compensable, which hardly accords with a scheme for protect-ing rights.

V. Reparations *IN EXTREMIS*

Let us suppose that the Soviet Union, a regime that from its inception in 1917 set out massively to violate the rights of vir-tually everyone under its governance, dramatically altered its essential character and wished to recompense its victims.

Could a theory of compensatory justice, even one modified to cover extensive rights violations to groups, as in the cases of the Japanese internees and the Jewish victims of the Nazis, encompass such a desire on the part of the Soviet government? What are the rights violations it inflicted? Just a cursory review of Soviet history will serve to unmask rights violations committed on a scale inconceivable in prior epochs and unmatched even by the Nazis. A few scant weeks after the Bolshevik seizure of power, Lenin established the Cheka, his secret police that he called the "sword and the shield of the party," and Revolutionary Tribunals to terrorize all those who resisted his coup d'état. The purpose of both institutions was to practice extra-legal terror, murder anyone who resisted, seize property from the bourgeoisie and grain from the peasants: in short, War Communism. As good Marxists, Lenin and his cohorts proceeded to liquidate the bourgeoisie as a class, which meant shooting many of them and terrorizing the rest. Throughout the Lenin-Stalin period one's class origins, going back to one's grandparents, became one's destiny.

During Stalin's reign of terror, land was seized from the peasants and they were forcibly herded into collective and state farms with millions, designated as *kulaks* or rich peasants, deported to death camps in the East or to starvation out in the frozen wilds of Siberia, and millions more perished in the forced famine of 1932. Estimates vary between 7 and 15 million deaths as a result of collectivization and the state-terror famine that the party inflicted on the recalcitrant peasantry to starve them into submission. In the late 1930s at the height of the great purge, 10–15 million people inhabited the Gulag, accused of the murder of Kirov, the Leningrad party leader, spying for the West or Nazi Germany, or industrial sabotage.[67] All charges were "proved" by confessions extracted from the victims by terror and torture. From Poland, both in 1940 and when the Soviet Red Army recaptured the country, 1.75 million people were deported to the camps, with many perishing, to say nothing of the Polish officers murdered in Katyn and elsewhere.[68] Similar deportations occurred in other occupied countries of Eastern Europe. Deaths attributable to Communism throughout the world, the results of a system exported at the direction of the

Soviets, are estimated at between 85 and 160 million, and those in the Soviet Union alone at 50–70 million. Secret-police terror has persisted throughout the post-Stalin period, waxing and waning as the party decrees, operating under more strictures and on a lesser scale to be sure.

Of those not sent to the camps during the Stalin period, lives were marred by witnessing the seizures of their relatives. Women whose husbands were arrested as "enemies of the people," if not incarcerated themselves, became pariahs, lost their apartments and jobs, and even their closest relatives were terrorized into abandoning them. Workers in the "workers' state" were frozen in their jobs by state decree to prevent them from fleeing in search of subsistence, and those late by more than 20 minutes were subject to arrest and a tour of the camps. A system of internal passports made travel, except with the approval of the Chekists, unlawful, and peasants, who were denied such passports, became virtual serfs on the collective and state farms to which they had been forcibly consigned.

How could a regime repair such rights violations, murder, property seizures, and disruptions of lives and liberty, the extent of which almost defies the human imagination? Victims are everywhere and almost everyone is a victim. Who are the perpetrators who must pay? Stalin liquidated many of them, including virtually all of the old-Bolsheviks who comprised his pre-Kirov Central Committee and Politburo, and the purge extended to party cadres throughout the country. At various times in the 1930s, he liquidated the liquidators, purging twice the leaders and their henchmen in the NKVD (as the secret police was known at that time), the NKVD purging the GRU (Soviet military intelligence) and vice versa, and the NKVD murdering the high-ranking officers of the Red Army. Of the murdered old-Bolsheviks and those that followed them to their deaths from the NKVD and the Red Army, virtually all had blood on their hands, for the party cadres with the able assistance of the others had carried out the war on the peasants, both under Lenin's War Communism and more brutally and effectively under Stalin's collectivization. Thus, in a certain twisted, perverted sense of justice, some of the guilty have paid, and paid with their lives, but of course their successors have not, nor have their innocent victims been recompensed, nor their heirs restored to the property seized from their grandparents and parents.

A theory of compensatory justice seems utterly to collapse under the weight of this history. Everyone now living, even the KGB and party cadres,[69] can claim parents or grandparents who were victims of murder, property seizures, and, at the very least, violations of their liberty, for these acts were the very essence and raison d'être of the Bolshevik regime from its inception.

Then, to quote Lenin: "What is to be done?" Recreating each person's history and ancestry of brutalization by the regime seems a nearly impossible enterprise, and who is to pay the compensation when virtually everyone is a victim to some degree? I might add that the very nature of the Soviet regime makes accomplices of many of its victims to varying extents, for example, the millions of informants, party members enjoying the fruits of theft and the privileges of the nomenklatura, and Red Army and KGB officers doing likewise. The perpetrators, as well as the victims, are legion.

Perhaps compensatory justice can give us some guidance even *in extremis*. Here, where civilization disintegrated under Lenin and Stalin, there were still degrees of rights violations suffered by their victims. Those who survived the camps or psychiatric torture as political prisoners in any era up to and including the present,* have rights claims exceeding in dimension anything suffered by the "free" population, or the population of the "Big Zone," as some dissidents would say. A regime of a new order, one that sincerely wishes to compensate for past injustice, would certainly choose these victims as the claimants with the greatest entitlement to recompense, even if everyone else, victims, too, must pay a tithe to accomplish this. It would be far better to extract compensation from party members, Red Army officers, and secret policemen who enjoyed the perks of the regime. Although as Solidarity realized, in practice this may be impossible, and these perpetrators may have to be bought off in order to move the country toward democracy without the tanks and troops decamping. As for the millions of dead, nothing can be

* Excluded, of course, would be those prisoners who themselves have blood on their hands, which would need to be determined on a case-by-case basis.

done, they are beyond worldly concerns.[70] And virtually every living person in the Soviet Union is their first- or second-generation heir.

A new order would certainly wish to restore land and property rights to its people, but with the passage of time, and the murder of millions, restitution of exactly what each person would have had but for the Bolsheviks would be impossible. Even more inconceivable would be an attempt to meet the more rigorous standard of Criterion IV. In such extraordinary circumstances, the best that can be done in the name of compensatory justice is first, to cease committing property and liberty infringements, and, second, to start anew by creating an order of equality before the law, with laws that protect, rather than depredate, the rights of all. This would be a tall enough order without attempting the impossible, that is, righting all the wrongs of a barbarous regime.

VI. Conclusion

Compensatory justice, as conceived by Aristotle as repairing the effects of injustices by one individual against another, can only serve as a rough indicator of a solution to injustices inflicted by governments against large numbers of victims. In many instances, as we have just seen, the rights violations are so omnipresent as to constitute the essence of the regime, with perpetrators and victims intermingled to such an extent that individuals are often both. Compensatory justice can only tell us that, *in extremis,* the victims who suffered the most and survived are the first claimants and the rest must, more than likely, be satisfied with a state dedicated to rights-protecting.

Certainly worth noting, in addition, is that only in liberal, democratic regimes does it makes sense, in the real world, to even speak about a government compensating victims of its past rights violations. Compensatory justice means nothing, say, to a victorious Nazi regime or to a Soviet state in its period of hegemony.

Set-asides, and *mutatis mutandis*[71] other preferential-treatment programs that fall under the rubric of affirmative action, do not satisfy the requirements of compensatory justice. They reward an ill-defined class of victims, indiscriminately favor some in that class and leave others totally uncompensated, benefit groups whose members were never the victims of state-imposed discrimination, and, most importantly, do not concentrate recompense on those whose rights were most flagrantly violated, namely, the black *slaves,* now long dead. Upon emancipation, certainly, the slaves should have received compensation along the lines of that given by the Federal Republic of Germany to the victims of the Nazis. That this was not done, and perhaps it could have been best done by dividing up the masters' plantations among the former slaves, is an omission that compounds the historical injustice committed against those enslaved. Under a theory of compensatory justice to groups of actual victims of heinous state acts, slavery as practiced in the South is archetypically the kind of rights violation that requires recompense, like that against the surviving Japanese internees, the surviving Jewish victims of the Nazis, and the survivors of the Soviet Gulags.

Blacks of this era, however, fall into the category of those sustaining rights violations of a lesser order, for example, those blacks who suffered under Jim Crow and the separate but unequal practices that persisted at that time and well into recent years. These are the types of injuries that a compensatory justice theory must leave to vicarious and indirect recompense. That is, the victims should be guaranteed that they shall live henceforth under a government that no longer perpetrates such acts, that ensures to everyone equality before the law, with laws that are fashioned to apply equally to everyone,[72] and a government that lives up to Justice Harlan's declaration that our "Constitution is color-blind, and neither knows nor tolerates classes among citizens."[73]

This is not an entirely satisfying resolution for those who take rights violations "seriously." Many who suffered grave rights violations throughout the post–Civil War period will not have their rights vindicated. Compensatory justice certainly has its limitations.

NOTES

1. This Executive Order, of September 24, 1965, mandated "affirmative action" by all companies dealing with the federal government as private contractors. Overseen by the Office of Federal Contract Compliance Programs (OFCCP) in the Department of Labor, affirmative action in the Nixon administration took on a more precise meaning with such devices as the Philadelphia Plan and its mandate that construction contractors in that city meet numerical hiring goals. By 1980, 325,000 companies nationwide were subject to such federally mandated plans. See Gary L. McDowell, "Affirmative Inaction: The Brock-Meese Standoff on Federal Racial Quotas," *Policy Review* 48 (1989): 32–37.

2. *Richmond v. Croson*, 57 LW 4132 (1989); *Wards Cove Packing Co. v. Atonio*, 57 LW 4583 (1989); *Price Waterhouse v. Hopkins*, 57 LW 4469 (1989); *Patterson v. McLean Credit Union*, 57 LW 4705 (1989); *Martin v. Wilks*, 57 LW 4616 (1989).

3. For supporters, see Judith Jarvis Thomson, "Preferential Hiring," in M. Cohen, T. Nagel, and T. Scanlon, eds., *Equality and Preferential Treatment* (Princeton: Princeton University Press, 1977), 19–39; and George Sher, "Justifying Reverse Discrimination in Employment," in *Equality and Preferential Treatment*, 49–60. For opponents, see Robert Hoffman, "Justice, Merit, and the Good," in Barry Gross, ed., *Reverse Discrimination* (Buffalo: Prometheus, 1977), 359–72; and William A. Nunn III, "Reverse Discrimination," in *Reverse Discrimination*, 306–9.

4. *Richmond v. Croson*, 57 LW 4132 (1989).

5. Aristotle, *Nicomachean Ethics*, trans. Martin Ostwald (Indianapolis: Bobbs-Merrill, 1962), 1130b, 31–33.

6. Ibid., 1131a, 23–24.

7. Ibid., 1131a, 24–25.

8. Thomas Nagel, "Equal Treatment and Compensatory Justice," in Cohen, Nagel, and Scanlon, *Equality and Preferential Treatment*, 3–18. Nagel argues that our entire system is unjust because of unequal rewards to individuals resulting from the unequal and undeserved distribution of talents, primarily intelligence. Policies of preferential treatment, for him, are not "seriously unjust," and ought to be pursued since they are not incompatible with justice and do have some social utility. A much more radical reordering of society, however, is what he has in mind to address the far more fundamental and intrinsic weaknesses of our system that go beyond the injustice caused by racial and sexual discrimination.

9. Aristotle, *Nicomachean Ethics*, 1132a, 4–7.

10. Ibid., 1132a, 7–13.

11. Ibid., 1132b, 18–20.

12. I added "if not in practice" because, as the argument progresses, I will argue, somewhat reluctantly, I might add, that with the passage of time some rights to compensation simply cannot be enforced, even though in theory the person still has that right. For now, a simple example will suffice: *X* cannot receive compensation from *Y* for a personal injury suffered if *Y* has died and left no estate.

13. I have insufficient space to defend these rights, although I and others have attempted a defense elsewhere: see my *Property Rights and Eminent Domain* (New Brunswick, N.J.: Transaction, 1987), chap. 3; Samuel C. Wheeler III, "Natural Property Rights and Body Rights," *Nous* 14 (1980): 171–93; Murray Rothbard, *For a New Liberty: The Libertarian Manifesto* (New York: Collier Books, 1978); and Israel Kirzner, "Entrepreneurship, Entitlement and Economic Justice," in Jeffrey Paul, ed., *Reading Nozick* (Totowa, N.J.: Rowman & Littlefield, 1981).

14. James W. Nickel, "Preferential Policies in Hiring and Admissions: A Jurisprudential Approach," in Gross, *Reverse Discrimination*, 327. In the literature on affirmative action, definitions of compensatory justice tend to be less complete and more intuitive than Nickel's. This one is fairly representative:

> The principle of compensatory justice is that, in order to restore the balance of justice when an injustice has been committed to a group of persons, some form of compensation or reparation must be made to that group.

Paul W. Taylor, "Reverse Discrimination and Compensatory Justice," in Gross, *Reverse Discrimination*, 298.

15. "Perpetrator" is not the most felicitous term, for it does not describe well the agent who injures another through negligence, but I do mean to include all agents of injury except those who cause injury through mere accident ("acts of God").

16. Here, I mean either monetary compensation, compensation-in-kind, or some less tangible recompense such as a social program directed exclusively at the victims.

17. The phrase "or its equivalent" is intended to cover those cases where it is impossible to restore the individual to health, but we try to give him enough money to make his life functional and as happy as it can reasonably be.

18. The figures on the number of set-aside programs are from Diane Bast, Mayer Freed, Daniel Polsby, and Thomas Ulen, "Disadvan-

taged Business Set-Aside Programs: An Evaluation," in Heartland Policy Study series, Heartland Institute (1989).

19. *Fullilove v. Klutznick*, 448 U.S. 448, 65 L. Ed. 2d 902, 100 S. Ct 2758 (1980).

20. Burger announced the judgment of the Court, but his opinion was joined only by White and Powell, the latter of whom also wrote a separate concurrence. Marshall, for Brennan and Blackmun too, wrote another concurring opinion, and Stewart was joined by Rehnquist in one dissent, while Stevens wrote his own dissent.

21. Programs to benefit minority businesses date back much earlier than this. President Nixon's Executive Order No. 11458 instituted a federal policy to direct government contracts to disadvantaged businesses. The Small Business Adminstration, through its Section 8(a) program, aids disadvantaged businesses. It attempts by preferential treatment to garner federal contracts and other devices to aid in the development of viable minority businesses. Similarly, the Department of Transportation administers a highway building and repair program that contains a set-aside provision, under the Surface Transportation Assistance Act of 1983. See Bast et al., "Disadvantaged Business Set-Aside Programs."

22. This exiguous legislative trail will become significant when we come to *Richmond v. Croson*. There the plurality insisted that the Richmond plan failed constitutional standards because no direct evidence was adduced by the city for prior discrimination by the city that would justify a rectificatory program, unlike, they wrote, the situation in *Fullilove*. But, ironically, or tragically, depending on one's perspective, the federal program was upheld *despite* the absence of direct legislative findings.

23. Ibid., 448 U.S. 448, 473.

24. Ibid.

25. Justice Harlan's famous dissent in *Plessey v. Ferguson*, 163 U.S. 537, 559 (1896) invoked the color-blind imagery: the "Constitution is color-blind," he wrote.

26. *University of California v. Bakke*, 438 U.S. 265 (1978).

27. Nevertheless, C. J. Burger did employ a test of sorts, for he examined, first, whether the objectives of this legislation were within the powers of Congress, and, second, whether the means employed to achieve that purpose violated the equal protection component of the due process clause of the Fifth Amendment. I might add for clarification, that if one repairs to the Constitutional text, there is no equal protection clause in the Fifth Amendment; it was read into the Amendment's due process clause by judicial construction to mirror the Four-

teenth Amendment's due process plus equal protection language. This was significant because the Fourteenth Amendment only applies to the states.

Some members of the Court have repeatedly stated that racial classifications must be subjected to the strictest judicial scrutiny—to the "most stringent level of review," as Powell states in his concurrence in *Fullilove*—because "immutable characteristics which bear no relation to individual merit or need are irrelevant to almost every governmental decision" (p. 496). In a model of judicial muddle, Powell proceeded in the next two sentences to display the bind that the justices have gotten themselves into with so-called *benign* preferences:

> In this case, however, I believe that [the set-aside program] is justified as a remedy that serves the compelling governmental interest in eradicating the continuing effects of past discrimination identified by Congress.
>
> Racial preference never can constitute a compelling state interest. (Pp. 496–97)

One more clarification. The strict scrutiny test as usually phrased by its adherents involves a two-pronged approach: (1) that the policy serve a *compelling* state purpose; and (2) that it do so by a narrowly drawn means to fulfill that governmental purpose (*Fullilove*, Powell concurrence, 935–36). Advocates of a looser standard of review, such as Justices Brennan, Marshall, and Blackmun, put forth the following test: (1) is the racial classification designed to further an important governmental objective; and (2) is it substantially related to achievement of that objective (*Fullilove*, Marshall concurrence, 519).

28. *Fullilove*, 489.

29. *Fullilove* (Stevens, J., dissent), 534, n. 5.

30. The other two arguments are: that the class members have a special entitlement to "a piece of the action" when government distributes benefits; that the program fosters greater minority participation in our competitive economy (*Fullilove*, Stevens dissent, 536).

31. Ibid., 537.

32. In *Croson*, Justice O'Connor delivered the opinion of the Court in part, with her colleagues carving up sections of the opinion that they could join: Rehnquist, White, Stevens, and Kennedy partook of Parts I, III-B, and IV; Rehnquist and White came in on part II; Parts III-A and V garnered the approval of Rehnquist, White, and Kennedy. Justice Stevens and Kennedy filed concurring opinion in part and concurred in the judgment. Justice Scalia filed a concurrence in the judgment. Justice Marshall was joined in dissent by Brennan and Blackmun, and Justice Blackmun filed a separate dissent in which Brennan joined. Thus, Justice O'Connor delivered the opinion of the

Court, commanding a majority vote, only in Parts I, III-B, and IV, and merely an opinion for the other sections. I suppose it is superfluous to add that this is no way to go about rendering judicial decisions.

33. *Croson*, 4134.

34. *Croson* had a checkered history in the lower courts. The District Court upheld the plan, as did the Fourth Circuit Court of Appeals. However, on remand from the Supreme Court, with instructions to reconsider in light of the Court's intervening decision in *Wygant v. Jackson Board of Education*, 476 U.S. 267 (1986), the appeals court reversed. The Fourth Circuit majority read *Wygant* to impose a strict-scrutiny standard in which the city would have to show a compelling governmental interest in order to invoke racial preferences, and that it cannot rest on "broad-brush assumptions of historical discrimination" (*Croson*, 4136, quoting the appeals court decision). To make this showing, societal discrimination of a general nature will not be sufficient, and the municipality would have to show findings of its own prior discrimination. The appeals court majority concluded that no such specific findings had been made by the city, and hence the set-aside program would not withstand constitutional challenge. On the second prong of the strict-scrutiny test, the court determined that the 30 percent set-aside program was not narrowly tailored.

35. Ibid., 4139, from Section III-A of her opinion, thus commanding the assent of only three other justices: the Chief Justice, and Justices White and Kennedy.

36. Ibid., 4139.

37. Ibid., 4140, from Section III-B, which commanded majority assent.

38. Ibid., 4142, Section III-B.

39. Ibid. Justice O'Connor concludes her analysis of the first prong of the strict-scrutiny standard by again invoking the color-blind vision:

> To accept Richmond's claim that past societal discrimination alone can serve as the basis for rigid racial preferences would be to open the door to competing claims for "remedial relief" for every disadvantaged group. The dream of a Nation of equal citizens in a society where race is irrelevant to personal opportunity and achievement would be lost in a mosaic of shifting preferences based on inherently unmeasurable claims of past wrongs. (P. 4142)

40. Ibid.

41. Ibid., 4143, Section IV. Indeed, distinctions between *Croson* and *Fullilove* are difficult to discern, and thus I suppose, the majority ought to be commended for finding any, but this is really stretching. One more weighty distinction was discerned by Justice O'Connor in Section

II, joined by the Chief Justice and Justice White, namely that the Fourteenth Amendment grants Congress unique enforcement powers (in Sec. 5) that give it wide latitude while, conversely, the equal protection clause is a constraint on states and their political subdivisions. The three justices seem to be implying that the equal protection component of the Fifth Amendment has different standards from the equal protection clause of the Fourteenth Amendment, a rather novel claim.

42. Ibid., 4143, Section V, commanding the allegiance of four justices.

Justice Scalia, in his concurring opinion, was even less sympathetic to schemes of racial preference. Agreeing that strict scrutiny is the proper standard for examining race-based classifications, he went on to argue that the Fourteenth Amendment prohibits governments from employing race to redress past discrimination, with only one exception: where the remedy would redress its own past racial classification of an unlawful nature.

43. Ibid., Marshall dissent, 4151.

44. Ibid.

45. Ibid., 4154, quoting *University of California v. Bakke*, 438 U.S., at 407.

46. Title VII bars employment discrimination on the basis of race, sex, or national origin in hiring, salaries, and promotion. See: Civil Rights Act of 1964 (42 U.S.C. Sec. 2000e, 78 Stat. 253).

47. *Croson*, Scalia concurrence at 4147:

> In my opinion there is only one circumstance in which the States may act *by race* to "undo the effects of past discrimination," where that is necessary to eliminate their own maintenance of a system of unlawful racial classification.

48. The latter is the more narrow statistical standard that Justice O'Connor finds appropriate in her opinion in *Croson*.

49. I should note that under a rights theory voting does not count as a fundamental right.

50. 1866 Civil Rights Act, 42 U.S.C. 1981.

51. *Brown v. Board of Education*, 347 U.S. 483 (1954).

52. Although, as argued earlier, private acts of discrimination in employment situations are not rights violations, and hence, not compensable.

53. *Historical Statistics of the United States: Colonial Times to 1970* (Washington, D.C.: U.S. Department of Commerce, Bureau of the Census, 1975).

54. Bernard Boxill argues that, ideally, compensating blacks requires placing them in positions they would have occupied had they

not been wronged. He does not discern the problems with this that I discuss in the text, but he does find another difficulty with it, that is, that it is impossible to tell how any particular individual would have fared absent slavery and discrimination. Thus, he endorses a group compensation principle that I shall discuss later in the text. See Bernard Boxill, *Blacks and Social Justice* (Totowa, N.J.: Rowman & Allanheld, 1984), 154–55.

He does not really see the problem, abumbrated below in the text, of restoring blacks to the condition in which they would have been without slavery:

> We can form some estimate of the assets blacks as a group had before slavery and discrimination. Consequently, we can apply the ideal conception of compensation, and reasonably propose to place blacks as a group in the position they would have occupied had there been no slavery and discrimination. (P. 155)

55. Onora O'Neill, "Rights to Compensation," *Social Philosophy & Policy* 5 (1987): 81.

56. Boxill, *Blacks and Social Justice*, 153.

57. Ibid.

58. Alan Goldman, *Justice and Reverse Discrimination* (Princeton: Princeton University Press, 1979), 91–92.

59. Elsewhere, Boxill has argued that the present white population ought to be considered as members of a company that incurred debts before they joined, and that they ought to bear such debts to blacks. This formulation is replete with problems: why just debts to blacks; where is the limit to groups claiming to be owed a debt; why should people who did not choose to join the "company" of the United States assume its "debts"? See Bernard Boxill, "The Morality of Reparation," in Gross, *Reverse Discrimination*, 277.

60. Taylor, "Reverse Discrimination," 298.

61. Ibid., 301–2.

62. For other critics of Taylor, see Nickel, "Preferential Policies in Hiring and Admissioins," 328–29; and Robert Hoffman, "Justice, Merit, and the Good," in Gross, *Reverse Discrimination*, 367–70. Boris I. Bittker raises another serious problem with preferential policies as usually framed, namely, that they make it imperative to identify members of the favored group, with the implication that the government would have to come up with racial codes to define membership in the group. He finds this extremely distasteful, in much the way Justice Stevens did in his footnote in *Fullilove*. Bittker's solution is to pay reparations to all individuals forced to attend segregated schools in the South. See Boris

I. Bittker, *The Case for Black Reparations* (New York: Random House, 1973).

63. Restitution for World War II Internment of Japanese-Americans and Aleuts, Pub. L. 100–383, Aug. 10, 1988, 1–2 Stat. 903. The Supreme Court of the United States on several occasions upheld the various orders resulting from Executive Order 9066, of Feb. 19, 1942, restricting Japanese during the war: see *Toyosaburo Korematsu v. United States*, 324 U.S. 885 (1945) (upholding conviction for remaining in a military area contrary to the Civilian Exclusion Order); and *Kiyoshi Hirabayashi v. United States*, 320 U.S. 81 (1943) (upholding conviction for violation of a curfew order). It is worth noting that in *Korematsu* the Court said that "all legal restrictions which curtail the civil rights of a single racial group are immediately suspect. . . . It is to say that courts must subject them to the most rigid scrutiny."

The 1988 Act was not the first designed to in some measure compensate the Japanese internees. The American-Japanese Evacuation Claims Act of 1948 provided for compensation for lost or damaged personal or real property when not otherwise covered by insurance. Specifically excluded from compensation were damage or loss "on account of death or personal injury, personal inconvenience, physical hardship or mental suffering" (July 2, 1948, C. 814, 62 Stat. 1231). The act also established a Commission on Wartime Relocation and Internment of Civilians to investigate the "facts and circumstances" surrounding Executive Order 9066.

64. As of the end of 1990 only a handful of people have received monetary compensation for their detention.

65. Bittker, *The Case for Black Reparations*, 141, n. 7 (for the amount of compensation) and 183 (for the number of people compensated). The reparations to Israel and the Claims Conference ended in 1966.

66. Nana Sagi, *German Reparations: A History of the Negotiations* (New York: St. Martin's Press, 1986), chap. 11; and Ronald W. Zweig, *German Reparations and the Jewish World: A History of the Claims Conference* (Boulder and London: Westview Press, 1987).

67. Robert Conquest, *The Great Terror* (London and New York: Macmillan 1968), 525–35.

68. Teresa Toranska, *"Them": Stalin's Polish Puppets* (New York: Harper & Row, 1987), 216.

69. In Soviet regimes, perpetrators are themselves often victims. To mention just one conspicuous and recent example, General, later President, Jaruzelski of Poland was himself as a child deported to a Soviet camp along with his father, who died in the camps. This is the same man who did the Soviet's bidding throughout his career in the army

138 ELLEN FRANKEL PAUL

and party and imposed martial law in 1981, arresting Solidarity's leaders. See Michael T. Kaufman, *Mad Dreams, Saving Graces: Poland: A Nation in Conspiracy* (New York: Random House, 1989), chap. 8. Examples of this phenomenon from the Soviet Union itself are legion.

70. The Soviet regime has its own rather touching way of acknowledging past "mistakes," known as "rehabilitation." The principal party victims of the purges of the 1930s have now in the late 1980s undergone this transformation in the status of the dead, Bukharin, Kamanev, and Zinoviev included. It seems possible that even Trotsky might enjoy a similar destiny, for a few of his works have been recently (1989) republished in an obscure Soviet journal.

71. A wonderful Latin weasel-phrase.

72. This position was eloquently expressed by Justice Scalia in his concurrence in *Croson:*

> The relevant proposition is not that it was blacks, or Jews, or Irish who were discriminated against, but that it was individual men and women, "created equal," who were discriminated against. And the relevant resolve is that should never happen again. (P. 4148)

73. *Plessey v. Ferguson,* 163 U.S. at 559 (Harlan, J., dissenting).

Some may argue that on a theory of compensatory justice as applied to large groups of victims, the current generation of blacks should be screened to discover those who suffered most under Jim Crow and the so-called "separate but equal" standard of education in the South. Boris Bittker, indeed, makes this argument. Given that the United States now has no victims of the order of Gulag or Nazi concentration camp survivors, the country could focus on a class of claimants sustaining lesser wrongs. However, Bittker himself finds distressing the prospect of identifying the victims by racial characteristics, preferring to assign victim status indiscriminately to all those who attended segregated schools. See Bittker, *The Case for Black Reparations.* This seems a rather arbitrary distinction. In principle, one might argue this way on my compensatory justice theory. These people do have legitimate claims because they did suffer wrongs from violations of their right to liberty. But, I think, such an investigation might prove more socially divisive than it would be worth to the victims who receive reparations. Glenn Loury casts doubt on the wisdom of policies of recompense that require an exercise in "comparative victimology," and he makes a good point. See "Why Should We Care about Group Inequality?" *Social Philosophy & Policy* 5 (1987): 2261–63.

Those blacks who can prove that they were convicted of crimes unjustly as a result of discrimination certainly deserve recompense, as do others who can prove similarly grave acts of injustice against them by the government. It is the diffuse rights violations that fell on millions of blacks that seem uncompensable in any direct way on a compensatory justice principle.

PART III

COMPENSATORY AND DISTRIBUTIVE JUSTICE

5

COMPENSATION AND REDISTRIBUTION

ROBERT E. GOODIN

Compensatory justice is profoundly conservative. Across its diverse range of applications, it usually serves to restore some status quo ante. That is characterized in various different ways: as the same position people were in before others wronged them (compensatory damages, in the law of torts); as the same position people were in before public takings of their private property (just compensation, in the law of eminent domain); as the same position people were in before changes in public policy put them out of work (compensation provisions in legislation liberalizing trade, deregulating airlines, and extending the boundaries of national parks); as the same position people were in before an accident or injury or other misfortune befell them (workmen's compensation, unemployment compensation, accidental injuries compensation, criminal injuries compensation).[1] Characterize it as you will, the notion of some preexisting state that is to be recreated virtually always seems to lie at the core of compensatory justice.[2]

That emphasis upon restoring the preexisting state obviously flies in the face of ideals of redistributive justice. There, the whole point is to alter those antecedent distributions that compensatory justice is at such pains to recreate.[3] The two notions seem unalterably at odds. Compensation strives to preserve what redistribution strives to change. Redistribution alters what compensation seeks to preserve.

It seems to follow that it would be incoherent to pursue at one and the same time both compensatory and redistributive justice.[4] For any given situation we must choose one or the other. Rarely will it be compensatory justice that we abandon. We would rarely be prepared to let wrongs go unrighted, merely on the ground that the wronged are far richer than those wronging them;[5] we would rarely be prepared to deny workers compensation for accidental injuries at work, merely because they were being overpaid anyway.[6] Insofar as principles of compensatory justice have us firmly in their hold, principles of redistributive justice can apparently get no grip at all. Or so it seems, if compensation and redistribution are seen as polar opposites.

That point has come to assume particular importance among contemporary contractarians. If the permissibility of interventions were predicated upon the agreement (real or hypothetical) of everyone affected, and if people's agreement were in turn predicated on compensation (direct or indirect, explicit or implicit) for any losses, then genuinely redistributive interventions would be decisively blocked. That, in stylized form, is the theme of the tradition running from Nozick's *Anarchy, State and Utopia* through Epstein's *Takings*.[7] But note well that the positive arguments of that lineage are primarily arguments in favor of compensation. Antiredistributivist conclusions follow only on the further supposition that redistribution is necessarily the antithesis of compensation.[8]

The burden of this chapter is to argue that that is not true. Compensation and redistribution are not necessarily incompatible. It all depends upon how you set about justifying compensation in the first place. Some of the arguments that might be offered would indeed make compensatory justice an implacable foe of redistributive justice. But those turn out to be the least defensible rationales for compensation. The rationale for compensation that I deem most defensible is broadly compatible with a certain measure of redistribution, practiced in a certain way; it may even demand a certain measure of redistribution.

Here I shall be making a weak claim strongly and a strong claim weakly. My major thesis, for which I shall be arguing strongly, is a compatibilist thesis. Properly conceived, compensation is perfectly compatible with redistribution of a certain sort. More formally, the moral goal that is served by compensation does not imply that we must not redistribute at all. Establishing that claim involves a two-step argument, first showing what the true goal of compensation is (section I), and then showing that that goal is perfectly consistent with redistribution of a certain sort (section II).

My minor theme, which I offer in a more speculative spirit, is an entailment thesis. Perhaps compensation actually entails or is entailed by redistribution in certain respects. More formally: the moral goal that is served by compensation might actually imply that we must redistribute, under certain circumstances and to some extent; or the moral goal that is served by redistribution might actually imply that we should compensate, again, under certain circumstances and to some extent. I offer some thoughts along these lines in section III.

I should emphasize at the outset that the major purposes of this chapter will have been served by the compatibilist thesis alone. The principal aim is to block one apparently powerful argument against redistribution. If that blocking move also creates an opening for further advancing the positive case for redistribution, that is merely a bonus.

I. RATIONALES FOR COMPENSATION

Compensation is supposed to provide the "full and perfect equivalent" of what was lost, and so to restore completely the status quo ante.[9] Possible reasons for wanting to do so are of three different sorts. The first has to do with the substantive rightness of the status quo ante to be restored. The second has to do, conversely, with the wrongness of the process by which that status quo ante was upset. The third has to do with something more formal about the status quo ante, wholly apart from its content or the process by which it was disturbed.

I shall explore each possibility in turn. To foreshadow: arguing against substance-based rationales for restoring the status quo ante eliminates those rationales for compensation that would indeed set it necessarily in opposition to redistribution, which clears the ground in turn for the compatibilist thesis to be developed in section II.

A. Restoring Right Outcomes

The first and most natural hypothesis is that the reason for wanting compensation is to restore a status quo ante that embodied a distribution that was, in some sense, *substantively right*. On this hypothesis, the rightness of that distribution wholly explains why we should want compensation to restore it.

Following Nozick, we can further decompose claims about the rightness of the distribution being restored. One class of claims traces its rightness to some special features of the *pattern* or *end-state* embodied in that distribution. A second class of claims traces its rightness to some special features of the *history* or *process* by which it came about.[10] Typical of the former class are claims of egalitarians, who maintain that a distribution is just insofar as it displays a pattern of equal holdings. Typical of the latter are claims of so-called "entitlement theorists," who maintain that a distribution of property is just so long as the history of its creation conforms to certain rules of justice in original acquisition and subsequent transfer.[11]

Representing as they do structure and process arguments respectively, end-state and historical analyses seem to exhaust all the logically possible ways of arguing for the rightness of distributions. Neither form of argument, however, is capable of rationalizing the practice of compensation as we know it.[12] Those arguments only privilege *certain* sorts of distributions—those displaying the favored characteristics picked out by each kind of argument. Compensation, in contrast, restores *any* status quo ante, regardless of whether or not it displayed any such characteristics.

Consider, first, end-state theories. They assert that we should provide compensation because the pattern embodied in the antecedent distribution was the right one. For it to have been upset was wrong and for it to be restored would be right. Compensation would do that. Hence we should compensate.

Notice, however, that in practice the payment of compensation is independent of any judgment about the justice of the antecedent pattern of distribution. People claiming compensation for damage done to them need not prove, to win their case, that relative deprivation was exacerbated by the wrong done to them. They need prove only that they were harmed.

The law of torts protects rich and poor alike. People may claim compensatory damages whenever they can prove that they were harmed by another's tortious conduct. To win their case, they do not have to prove they need the money. Those making ostentatious displays of donating their damage awards to charity were no less entitled to receive them than were those who have to use the money to buy basic necessities.[13] By the same token, those accused of committing torts cannot say, in their defense, that they took only from those richer than themselves.[14] Current tax laws may imply that a transfer of something like 10 percent of the income of those in high tax brackets to those in low tax brackets would be required for an ideally just pattern of distribution. But the moral superiority of that pattern does not excuse the poor in stealing from the rich, provided they take only the 10 percent ideally coming to them.

In the law of eminent domain, likewise, the government is obliged to compensate property owners whenever it takes their property. That obligation is independent of any judgment about the justice of their holding that much property in the first place. Indeed, inheritance tax laws may imply that it is unjust for property to be concentrated in so few hands.[15] We would nonetheless be required to compensate a landowner for property seized during his life, even if we had intended to take the property without compensation upon his death.

Or, again, social security benefits are characteristically earnings related. Workmen's compensation, unemployment compensation, accidental injuries compensation, criminal injuries compensation, and the like all aim to compensate people, inter alia, for whatever earnings they have actually lost.[16] In consequence, those programs all pay people more the more they earned.[17] That is independent of, and in certain ways flatly contrary to, public judgments made in other contexts about the justice of income differentials.[18] The results may be paradoxical, but the practice of paying compensation in this fashion is well-nigh universal.[19]

None of this, of course, is to say that we refuse ever to countenance enquiries about the justice of patterns of holdings. Those enquiries must merely proceed along a separate track. The duty to pay compensation for damage done is independent of whether people have relatively too much or relatively too little by way of present endowments. That, in turn, implies that the reason we insist upon compensation does not have crucially to do with the correctness of the pattern of the distribution that the compensation would restore.

Consider, next, historical entitlement theories. They assert that we should compensate because people have been deprived of what is, by historical entitlement, rightfully theirs. To upset that distribution was wrong and it should be restored. Compensation would do that. Hence we should compensate.

But that is not the way compensation works in practice. Consider the paradigm of tort law. It does not contain any provision insisting that courts mount a title search to ensure that people have historically clear claims to their property before requiring tortfeasors to compensate them for damage to it.[20] As the Reporters for the American Law Institute's *Second Restatement of the Law of Torts* comment, "The important thing in the law of torts is the possession [of property], and not whether it is not rightful as between the possessor and some third party."[21]

The tortfeasor's duty to compensate is not defeasible, even upon production of clear evidence of force or fraud in the history of the plaintiff's acquisition of the damaged property.[22] J. D. Rockefeller may have engaged in some pretty dubious practices, legally as well as morally, in building the Standard Oil empire. That fact does not make it any less of a tort for me to spraypaint graffiti on that company's gas pumps, nor does it do anything to reduce the damages I have to pay in compensation for cleaning them up.

This insensitivity to historical titles in awarding compensation is no peculiarity of tort law.[23] Just compensation, under the law of eminent domain, is owed to those who possess and hence have an interest in property, whatever the strength of their legal title.[24] Or, again, my entitlement to compensation under various social insurance schemes (workmen's compensation, etc.) is contingent merely upon the requisite contributions having been made. How I or my employer came by the money used to fund those contributions is irrelevant to my entitlement. Likewise, my entitlement to unemployment compensation is contingent merely upon having lost my job. Whether that job was rightfully mine, or whether I bribed someone to get it, is irrelevant.[25]

None of this is to say that we refuse to look into the historical basis of people's titles to their property. It is simply to say that those enquiries, too, must proceed along a separate track. The duty to compensate for damage done is independent of those other enquiries. That, in turn, suggests that the reason we insist upon compensation does not have crucially to do with the historical rightness of the distribution that compensation would serve to restore.

The postulate that compensation is justified on the grounds that it restores a substantively right distribution cannot therefore be sustained. Different theories exist as to what makes distributions right. But all would sensitize us to particular right-making characteristics that defensible distributions must have, whereas compensation is in practice almost systematically insensitive to such considerations.[26]

B. Righting Wrongs

The above arguments justified compensation in terms of claims about the substantive rightness of the status quo ante that it would restore. A second set of arguments justified compensation in terms of the wrongness of the process by which that antecedent distribution was upset.

This analysis has a certain appeal. Even if we are unsure which outcome is substantively right, we can say with confidence that certain ways of altering outcomes are definitely wrong. Without necessarily joining historical entitlement theorists in claiming that outcomes are substantively right if produced through certain processes, we can nonetheless agree that outcomes are procedurally wrong if produced in certain ways—through force or fraud, for example. Righting procedural wrongs may be justifiable independently of any theory of the substantive rightness of the outcomes thereby produced.

This analysis comes naturally to those approaching compensation by way of torts. Those, by definition, are wrongs. Their wrongfulness lies not in the substantive wrongness of the outcomes that they produce but rather in the wrongness of producing outcomes in those ways. Compensatory damages right wrongs, in tort law, not in the sense of restoring substantively right distributions but rather in the sense of cancelling the effects of wrongful styles of intervention in others' affairs.[27]

That characterization places compensatory damages in torts, and among compensation schemes torts enjoy undoubted historical primacy. But it would be mistaken to take the primordial for the paradigmatic.[28] Nowadays, compensation arises in many different forms. And true though that analysis of "righting wrongs" may be of tort damages, it is simply untrue of various other modes of compensation equally important in today's world. Consider especially no-fault compensation systems. Both worker's compensation and New Zealand's more general accidental injuries compensation are paid to victims, independently of any inquiry into fault or blame or wrong on the part of the victims or of anyone else. Those modes of compensation right not so much wrongs as mere bads.[29]

Compensation, then, is a mixed bag. In some cases (notably, tort damages and criminal injuries compensation) it is clearly designed to right procedural wrongs. In others (notably, workmen's compensation and accidental injury compensation), clearly it is not. And still other cases fall between these two poles.[30]

To save the analysis of compensation as justifiable righting of procedural wrongs, we must at this point argue that one or the other of these cases was somehow paradigmatic. An argument along these lines might be mounted. Historically, worker's compensation became no-fault less for reasons of high moral principle than for pragmatic reasons: establishing fault often proved prohibitively expensive, thereby blocking otherwise meritorious claims. Contemporary concerns for extending the no-fault principle are often similarly motivated pragmatic concerns.[31] These no-fault schemes of compensation might therefore really be designed to right *presumptive* wrongs that would cost more than it is worth to prove conclusively.

Such an analysis, though possible, would always be a little suspect. Essentially what we would be doing, in holding some cases of compensation to be paradigmatic and others deviant, would be excusing our failure to explain half the cases the theory is supposed to cover. Instead of giving a rationale for compensation, we would be rationalizing our failure to provide a rationale for a great deal of compensatory practice.

If that were the best we could do it might be good enough, provided the rationalization for the inadequacy of the rationale were really convincing. We can do better, though. As I hope to show in section C below, an alternative rationale for compensation is both more complete and more convincing.

C. Underwriting Reasonable Expectations

Having forsaken rationales for compensation based on the substantive rightness of the previous situation or on the wrongness of the way in which it was upset, we are left looking for its justification in some more formal feature of the status quo ante. The substantive content, historical background, and distributional pattern of the status quo ante are all apparently irrelevant to our decision to provide compensation to restore it. What we apparently need is an argument to the effect that we should restore it, merely because the previous state was the status quo ante.

No simple argument along those lines is going to work. The familiar flaws of the naturalistic fallacy warn us against any easy slide from propositions about what *is* to assertions about what *should be* the case. The mere fact that "*x* existed" is no reason for supposing that it should have existed. It provides still less of a reason for supposing that it should be recreated once it has *ceased* to exist.[32] That the status quo ante was the status quo ante cannot justify a policy of restoring it.

There might, however, be a way to derive the requisite justification from a more complex set of facts, all connected some-

how to the fact that the state being restored was indeed the
status quo ante. The further propositions that we need to complete this more complex version of the nonsubstantive, nonpro-
cedural rationale for compensation, are three:

1. People reasonably rely upon a settled state of affairs persisting (or, anyway, not being interrupted in the ways against
   which compensation protects them) when framing their life
   plans.
2. That people should be able to plan their lives is morally
   desirable.
3. Compensation, if sufficiently swift, full, and certain, would
   restore the conditions that people were relying upon when
   framing their plans, and so allow them to carry on with their
   plans with minimal interruption.[33]

I need not belabor the central ethical premise of this analysis,
namely proposition 2. The moral desirability of people being
able to frame and follow through on their life plans can be
defended in a variety of familiar ways. One points to the value
of autonomy. Another points to unity and coherence as a source
of value in people's lives. Yet another points, in indirect, rule-
utilitarian fashion, to the value that we all derive from being
able to anticipate what others are going to do.[34]

All I need add here to those standard accounts is the further
proposition that, however important it may be that people should
be able to frame life plans for themselves, it is all the more
important that they be able to follow through with those plans
once they have embarked upon them. The point of planning is
not the act of planning per se, but seeing those plans come to
fruition. Whether you tell an autonomy-based story in terms of
sunk psychological costs or an indirect-utilitarian story in terms
of reliance upon established patterns in others' behavior, it proves
to be especially important that people be able to follow through
with their plans once they have set off down some particular
path.

Not much elaboration is required on the third proposition,
either. The function of compensation is straightforwardly to
restore the status quo ante. It will serve its expectation-preserv-
ing purposes, however, only if certain further conditions are

satisfied. The compensation must be *complete*, giving people back the full and perfect equivalents of what they lost, if they are to be able to carry on as before. It must be *swift*, restoring them promptly to avoid damaging interruptions to their ongoing projects.[35] And it must be *certain*, allowing no doubt that compensation will be forthcoming, so they can plan with confidence. Should any of these conditions fail to be satisfied, people's plans would be at risk of irremediable harm.

The first proposition will presumably be the most contentious. All kinds of objections are raised against theories tracing entitlements to "reliance" or "expectations" more generally. Hume's theory of property rights and the reliance theory of contractual obligation are both criticized on the ground that people can form completely baseless expectations and rely upon utterly unreasonable assumptions. That someone expects or has relied on something is not conclusive, morally, in the absence of some reason for supposing that good grounds exist for the reasonableness of that expectation or reliance.

One response to such an objection is this. Nothing is unreasonable, statistically, in predicting that a settled state of affairs will persist in much the same form. Induction is not *that* unwarranted. The future is indeed only marginally different from the present, very much more often than not. But suppose the status quo embodies a pattern of systematic and entrenched injustice. We would have good ground, statistically, for predicting it to persist. We would have no ground, morally, for expecting—still less, for demanding—that it do so. We must therefore say something further about *what sorts* of interruptions to people's plans we propose to remedy through compensation.

We do not try to reverse all changes in people's plight. We compensate only in certain, well-defined situations: accident, crime, disability, unemployment, tortious wrong, and so forth. That catalogue seems to suggest that we compensate to restore the status quo ante only if it has been upset either (a) in ways people had no reason to expect or (b) in ways people had a reason to expect not to occur.[36]

As usual in moral and legal philosophy, that formulation intentionally straddles the statistically unpredictable and the morally unacceptable.[37] The advantage is that we can thereby

deem "reasonable"—and hence, by my formula, compensable
—expectations that are well-founded morally but not statistically. It would be perfectly reasonable, morally, for people to
expect crime not to happen, even if they knew, statistically, that
it often did.[38]

It also follows from my analysis that certain sorts of altera-
tions to the status quo should not be compensable. It would be
unreasonable for people to frame their plans on the assumption
that certain things would go on as they are. One case has to do
with righting moral wrongs. It is unreasonable, in a moral (if
not, alas, in any statistical) sense, for thieves to expect to retain
their booty or for monopolists to expect to continue enjoying
the fruits of their privileged market position. No compensation
is due them to make up for any interruption to their life plans
when those things are taken from them by due process of law.[39]

Another has to do with risky ventures and unsettled situations. As a matter of policy, we guarantee the security of bank
deposits, but we do not underwrite the value of stock portfolios.
The reason—consistent with the explanation I offer for compensation generally—is that people have no good ground, of a
statistical or still less a moral sort, for expecting high business
profits over the long run, in a way they did (even before the
advent of the Federal Deposit Insurance Corporation) have
good statistical grounds for expecting banks usually not to fail.

Still another has to do with situations that never actually were
the status quo ante. The standard reductio ad absurdum of the
reliance theory of contractual obligations is that it would allow
me to write H. Ross Perot, saying that I was relying upon the
expectation that he would send me ten thousand dollars to
prevent foreclosure on my mortgage. So long as the purported
reliance is genuine, the reliance theory would seem to imply
that Perot has an obligation to send the money, even though he
had made no prior commitment to do so and even though my
reliance upon his doing so was baseless.[40] That may or may not
be a good reductio of the reliance theory of contract law. But it
cannot be used as a counterexample against the expectation-
based theory I am developing for compensation. Expectations
in my theory must be tied to some status quo ante, in a way that
that expectation about Perot's benefaction clearly was not.

Despite all I have said about what we need not compensate people for, the point remains that we do not always pay everyone all the compensation that on my account they truly deserve. People's life plans can be interrupted in ways that they had no reason to expect, or good reason to expect not to happen, but for which they receive no compensation.

Sometimes that happens because no compensation is possible or because the only possible form would be so grossly inadequate that compensation would constitute a travesty. Where harms are truly irreparable, and the loss truly irreplaceable, little more than token compensation is offered. That seems reasonable enough.[41]

But that is not the whole story. People are not always compensated for losses they had no reason to expect, even when their losses are in principle perfectly replaceable. The reason is not one of principle, though. It is not as if we think that they ought not, or even that they need not, be compensated. We merely have trouble figuring out who should pay the compensation in question. This interpretation accords well with the history of compensation schemes. Tort damages came first, because it was clear who should pay. Workmen's compensation and the like came next, once we had devised principles of insurance allowing us to charge everyone involved in risky enterprises premiums proportional to their contributions to the risk of accident. The next steps are presumably to extend the same insurance concepts to embrace compensation for disease, economic dislocation, and so forth.[42].

The ease with which compensation schemes worldwide tended to evolve in these directions suggests that the reason for beginning where we did, and pausing where we have, was only ever pragmatic. It is not as if we ever thought that, on principle, to deserve compensation you had to have been injured in some particular way. We merely found it easier saying from whom people injured in those ways should recover. The ethical defense of compensation was always couched in terms of stabilizing expectations, and only purely pragmatic considerations ever stopped us from going the whole way toward that ideal.

D. Interim Conclusion

In summary: The true justification for compensation lies not in the substantive content of the status quo ante that it restores. Nor does it lie in the wrongfulness of the process by which that status quo ante was upset. Nor does it lie in the fact that the situation that compensation would restore was, indeed, a status quo ante. The justification lies instead in a complex set of facts about the way in which people had been reasonably relying upon the settled status quo ante persisting in much the same shape into the future when framing their life plans.

It bears emphasizing, in light of what is to come, that this analysis presents no more than a prima facie justification for compensation. It certainly does provide one reason for compensation restoring the status quo ante, but that reason is not necessarily conclusive. Countervailing reasons, which may well prove stronger from time to time, may well argue, for altering the status quo in certain respects—even at the cost of upsetting some people's expectations. The argument I give for compensation does not say that that must never be done, merely that there will always be some moral cost in doing so.

My case for compensation also implies, however, that that cost is variable rather than constant. The status quo can often be altered at little cost, and sometimes at no cost at all, in terms of upsetting people's expectations. Insofar as one of these less-cost strategies is pursued, we have less reason (in the limiting case, no reason at all) in favor of compensation or against redistribution.

II. The Compatibility of Redistribution
and Compensation

My principal concern in this section lies not in arguing for redistribution but in blocking certain sorts of arguments against it. Principles of compensatory justice have a powerful hold. We feel that people should be compensated for certain sorts of harms, and we feel that that compensation is due them whether they be rich or poor. Compensatory justice—restoring as it does

the status quo ante—thus seems systematically to trump principles of redistributive justice.

How powerful that trump is, however, depends upon how
principles of compensatory justice are justified. If the reason
for restoring the status quo ante had to do with its substantive
rightness either because of its pattern or of its history, then any
redistribution (which necessarily deviates from that right distribution, also) would be condemned. But redistributivists need
not fear. Compensation, as I have shown, cannot find justification in any such facts about the substantive content of the status
quo ante.[43]

The evil that the fallacious, substance-based rationales would
ask compensation to rectify is the evil of upsetting a substantively just distribution. The evil that my rationale would ask
compensation to rectify is the evil of a "bolt from the blue" that
people had no reason to expect and that threatens to make a
mockery of their life plans. On my theory of compensation,
what is sacrosanct is not the preexisting distribution but rather
preexisting expectations and the plans and projects that people
have built around them. The point of compensation is not so
much to undo changes in the status quo ante as to undo the
effects of unanticipated changes to it.

The differences between these cases for compensation matter
enormously when it comes to the justifiability of redistribution.
Redistribution necessarily alters the status quo. If the reason we
should compensate were that it was wrong to alter the status
quo, because the distribution being altered was substantively
just by some standard, then redistribution would be wrong for
precisely the same reason that compensation would be right.
But if the reason we should compensate is not that it is wrong
for the status quo to have been altered, but merely wrong for it
to have been altered in certain sorts of unanticipatable ways,
then the conflict between redistribution and compensation is
erased.

On the expectations-based argument, what is wrong is not
altering the status quo but rather altering it unpredictably.
Therefore redistribution that alters the status quo would be
perfectly permissible, just so long as it was done in a predictable
manner. This is just to say that redistributions ought to abide by

something akin to rules of natural justice. In economic policy, just as in criminal law, public affairs ought as far as possible to be conducted according to known rules.[44] So long as people know well in advance when and how redistributive policies will affect them, redistributions cannot come as a "bolt out of the blue" wreaking unreasonable (because unanticipatable) havoc on their lives.

Standing rules of distribution of precisely that sort are written into our tax codes. The progressive income tax has long been on the books. Its rates change marginally from time to time, but everyone has had more than adequate warning of the government's general intention to tax higher incomes more heavily than lower; indeed, given how little the real rate of tax paid varies from year to year, people have even had adequate warning of the rough magnitudes involved. Since those laws predate any of us entering the workforce, we all ought reasonably be expected to have framed our life plans taking those redistributive measures into account. We would have no grounds for complaining about an unanticipatable interruption in our plans when those tax bills fall due, had we failed to do so.

My argument on that score presupposes, first, that people can reasonably be expected to take the previously announced policies of their government into account when forming their plans. That seems minimally contentious, at least insofar as those policies constitute "settled intentions" of the government and, we might want to add, insofar as those policies are not actually immoral. Whether that latter proviso is strictly necessary is something of an open question.[45] But in practice it hardly matters.[46] My case further presupposes that governments can make and stick to redistributive policies that stretch well beyond any individual's planning horizon. Governments surely do so; they engage in long-term economic planning, investment in basic research and development and so forth on a far longer time horizon than that of the typical individual or firm. True, periodic elections mean that democratic governments have a higher mortality rate and shorter life expectancy than do citizens themselves. Still, one government's plans and projects are much more often than not retained by its successors, and so a government's redistributive policies ought reasonably be expected to persist even if that particular government falls.[47]

The main thrust of my compatibilist claim has to do with an *ongoing* system of redistribution. Where redistribution is conducted according to settled principles of long standing, we have no reason to fear that it will do any real violence to the sorts of moral values that compensation is designed to serve. That of course leaves the problem of transitions. How are we to institute those rules of redistribution in the first place?

Problems of transitions are genuinely difficult in practical terms and genuinely fascinating intellectually. They have, accordingly, generated a large literature and much discussion.[48] While I have no compelling solution to the problem of transitions, neither is that as much of an omission as it might seem. Transitions, after all, are merely transitional—short-lived, episodic, and hence relatively inconsequential—compared to the more protracted regimes on either side of them. I am, therefore, much more concerned to give a proper account of those settled states than I am to give a good account of transitions.

Still, my analysis does offer some potential solutions to the problem of how to shift from less to more redistributive regimes with minimal interruption to people's life plans. One solution is simply advance notice. Gordon Tullock commends the example of nineteenth-century reforms abolishing various sinecures in the British civil service only upon the death of their incumbents; others offer more modest suggestions along similar lines.[49] Delayed implementation of this sort might help to cushion redistribution's blow to your life plans.[50] The problem, from the redistributivist's perspective, is that it does so by reducing the redistributive effect of the policy, at least in the short term.

Another alternative would be to redistribute without warning, but then to compensate losers straightaway in some other currency. So long as their compensation leaves them as well off as before—understood here as able to pursue the same life plans as before—they will have no grounds for complaint. That compensation might come at little cost to our larger redistributive intentions, if we think that the distribution of the commodities offered in compensation matters very much less, morally,

than the distribution of the commodities that were redistributed. Economists, anthropologists, and political theorists alike
observe that we tend to be "specific egalitarians" in this way,
worrying more about the distribution of some commodities than
of others or of money in general.[51] Insofar as we can take
advantage of this curious fact to redistribute what matters and
to compensate with what does not, redistribution might once
again be squared readily with the deeper values that compensation is supposed to serve.

In short, there are solutions to the problem of how to institute redistributivist measures de novo without upsetting reasonable expectations too badly. I would not want the argument to
stand or fall on the strength of those proposals. Neither do I
think that it should have to do so. It should be more than
enough to have shown that my compatibilist thesis is true for
the more standard case of an ongoing system of redistribution
according to settled rules of long standing. There redistribution
clearly can proceed with little cost to the deeper moral values
that compensation is supposed to serve.

Bringing about redistributions in the ways I propose, either ·
in the transitional case or in an ongoing system of redistribution, carries costs of various other sorts. I would not want to
deny that. I merely say that if you are worried about the sorts
of moral considerations that motivate compensation—things
like protecting reasonable expectations and life plans built around
them—then there are ways to arrange your redistributive scheme
to protect those values. That may or may not be the optimal
mode of redistribution, all things considered.

Just as at the end of section I.D I said that my argument for
compensation provided only one not necessarily decisive reason
for compensating, so too by the same token must I here say that
those same concerns provide one reason, though not necessarily
a decisive one, for arranging redistribution in one way rather
than another. There may be powerful countervailing reasons
for not following that advice. Consider, for example, the familiar argument of economists that if we want to redistribute we
should do it through unanticipatable, once-and-for-all, lump-
sum transfers in order to minimize the disincentive effects and
consequent efficiency losses.[52] The redistributive "bolt from the

blue" that Pigou and his followers recommend on efficiency grounds would wreak havoc with people's lives: indeed, it is crucial to the success of his efficiency-protecting scheme that the redistribution be utterly unpredictable. Whether the efficiency gain would be worth the cost in terms of disruption to people's lives is an open question.[53] Happily, though, it is a question that I do not have to answer here.

My compatibilist thesis does not hold that redistribution of the form I suggest is compatible with *every* value that we may wish public policy to promote. My claim is merely that, perhaps surprisingly, such redistribution is thoroughly consistent with the purposes that compensation should serve. So long as that is true, arguing for compensation is not necessarily arguing against redistribution.

III. THE MUTUAL ENTAILMENT OF COMPENSATION AND REDISTRIBUTION

The point of my previous argument is that redistribution is consistent with compensation. That is to say, it does not necessarily offend against compensation's underlying moral principle, properly understood. Perhaps we can go further and say that redistribution actually implies or is implied by compensation in certain circumstances. Maybe the same moral principle that demands compensation sometimes also demands redistribution, or vice versa.

I offer these speculations more tentatively. The central argument of the chapter is the compatibilist thesis already established; and that argument is perfectly capable of standing on its own, without any support from the ones I am about to embark upon. Still, if these further extensions also go through, I will have succeeded not only in blocking an apparently powerful argument against redistribution but in actually advancing the positive case for it.

A. Redistribution Implies Compensation

The thought with which this chapter began is that compensation and redistribution are implacable foes. That thought has been undermined by the demonstration that the two can be reconciled. But showing that the two are not necessarily enemies is still far short of showing, as I shall now attempt, that they are necessarily friends.

The first leg of that argument proceeds by a reductio. Suppose we harbor egalitarian ideals. Suppose, further, that some rich person suffers accidental or even tortious damage, of the sort for which we think people ordinarily should be compensated. If we are egalitarians, why bother? Under our redistributive program, rich people are scheduled to have a certain amount taken away from them anyway. Dame Fortune or tortfeasors have simply spared us the trouble.[54]

That way of thinking is plainly crazy. No one supposes that insurance companies should refuse to pay out on policies just because the house that burned down was a rich person's; no one even thinks that, as a matter of public policy, large houses of the rich should be uninsurable.[55] And the same seems true of all the other hazards that face us in contemporary life and of all the other mechanisms that we have for compensating people when they strike.

What is fundamentally wrong with such propositions is just this. We do not redistribute by accident. Redistribution is a matter of policy, not of happenstance. Those who hold redistributivist ideals invariably demand *intentional* redistribution. They want to produce a certain pattern of holdings, or they want to rectify certain historical wrongs. But they wish to do so systematically, not randomly.[56]

In the same way that redistributivists think it unjust for some people to get rich by sheer luck, so too must they agree that it would be unjust for some but not others to be relieved of their undeserved riches by the sheer bad luck of their being the uncompensated victims of accidents or injuries. No one is in favor of "capricious redistribution."[57] The upshot is that redistribution-in-the-large seems to imply compensation-in-the-small.

The compensation thereby endorsed by redistributivist ideals is highly qualified. Money given to the rich person whose house burned down may well be subsequently taxed away in the course of a larger redistributivist program. And the losses intentionally inflicted upon the rich by a scheme of redistribution can themselves hardly be compensable. So the sort of compensation implied by redistribution is both provisional and partial. What is surprising is not that it is shaky in these ways but, rather, that the implication is there at all.

B. *Compensation Implies Redistribution*

In similar fashion, the goals that compensation is supposed to serve might actually imply a certain measure of redistribution. Once again, the implication will certainly be partial and may well be weak, but the surprise is simply that it should be there at all.

In section I, it was shown that compensation standardly strives to restore some status quo ante. That general rule has one conspicuous exception, though. We run programs of "disability compensation" of various sorts—invalid pensions, attendance allowances or invalid care allowances, mobility allowances, and the like.[58] Furthermore, we offer those benefits even to the congenitally handicapped. In providing mobility assistance to the congenitally handicapped, however, we are not restoring them to some status quo ante in which they were able to walk: if their handicaps are congenital, their impaired mobility has been lifelong. That makes this case very unlike the ordinary practice of compensation.

What we are doing here is not restoring the congenitally handicapped to some status quo ante. Rather we are bringing them up to a standard that, while normal for the species, is one that those particular individuals never actually enjoyed.[59] Worthy though that practice may be, it cannot be justified in the same way as ordinary compensation. Bringing up to some minimal norm of human existence people who never previously enjoyed it certainly does not "restore" anything to them. In terms of the rationale for compensation developed in section I.C above, their life plans have not been interrupted by any dramatic changes.

These people might, however, suffer a closely related problem. Without that "minimal baseline norm" secured, these people may be unable to frame and to follow life plans at all. If it is morally desirable that people should do so—as one crucial step in my argument for compensation asserts it to be—then perhaps redistributive transfers to underwrite that "minimal baseline norm of human existence" are themselves morally mandated by the selfsame principle. It may be confusing to call it "compensation." But the confusion is minor, since redistribution of that sort serves the same moral goal as compensation itself.

Exactly where the "minimal baseline norms" should be set for what goods should probably be left open. In general, this "preconditions of agency" style of argument implies that those norms should guarantee everyone enough of what they need to be able to plan their lives at all. What that amounts to is an empirical matter. It seems empirically likely, however, that the gravest forms of deprivation remedied by the redistributive transfers of the welfare state—gross poverty, protracted unemployment, persistent illness, and homelessness—would all qualify as major interferences with any planning at all. They therefore qualify for relief under my principle.[60]

The "preconditions of agency" argument is most persuasive when the resources involved are, literally, preconditions. That is to say, the move is most persuasive when it is literally impossible to frame and follow any lifeplans at all unless those resource needs have been met. But that is a limiting case that will rarely occur. The handicaps for which programs to aid the disabled compensate (impaired mobility and the like) reduce one's options. But they hardly preclude one from conceptualizing plans, nor do they usually even reduce one's options down to a single possibility. The same is arguably true of poverty and most of its corollaries.[61]

If "preconditions" is too strong, "preoccupations" may serve almost as well. The reason we should redistribute resources to meet people's basic needs is that without those resources the psychological prerequisites of planning one's life are lacking. Almost inevitably, people who do not know where their next meal will come from or where they will sleep tonight will find those concerns completely absorbing.[62] Preoccupied with how to satisfy their immediate needs, they are incapable of thinking much beyond that. If we regard it as desirable for people to frame and follow plans of a larger sort for their lives, we ought therefore do what we can to remove those barriers to such longer-term planning.

This argument claims that redistribution may be needed to enable some people to plan in the first place, whereas the previous arguments maintained that we need to compensate people to allow them to carry on reasonable life plans once embarked upon them. The difference between facilitating the framing of plans and facilitating follow-through on projects in progress may well matter enormously, morally. Logically, perhaps, making plans comes before carrying them out. But the disruption of projects in progress matters far more, both phenomenologically and consequently morally, at least for any morality that takes people's self-respect seriously. That blunts the force of preconditions-of-planning style arguments for redistribution, which is one reason I prefer to emphasize the arguments of previous sections and to put these propositions more tentatively.

Another reason is that admitting a connection between autonomy and resources is a double-edged sword. That connection having been made, when resources are redistributed away from the rich, they can then complain of a loss of autonomy to them that is strictly analogous to the gains in the autonomy of the poor that they experience from the resources being redistributed toward them.[63]

I do not think that that complaint is compelling. Assuming resources yield diminishing marginal autonomy just as they do diminishing marginal utility, redistribution will do more to promote the autonomy of the poor than to decrease autonomy of the rich. Moreover, there is a world of difference, in autonomy terms, between not being able to plan at all and not being able to carry out fancy plans for some highly luxurious existence. But those are larger arguments than can be pursued here. And the arguments of the first two sections are, for the purposes of this chapter, more than enough anyway.

IV. Conclusion

My analysis explains the apparent paradox of running compensatory side-by-side with redistributive policies. Paying some relatively rich victim compensation that redistributive measures will claw back may seem to amount to giving with one hand and taking back with the other. But there is method in that seeming madness.

If we think it is morally desirable to ensure that people are able to plan and organize their lives in a sensible fashion, we must be systematic about both compensation and redistribution. Just as people must be able to count on compensation whenever harmed in certain ways, so too must they be able to count on redistributive policies working in a similarly relentless fashion, no matter whether they are on the giving or the receiving end of those policies. Erratic compensation would be profoundly unsatisfactory. For the same reason, we should be profoundly unsatisfied with redistribution erratically taking only from those unlucky enough to suffer harms and rewarding only those lucky enough to benefit from their misfortunes. Both compensatory and redistributive policies can in this way be seen as manifestations of broadly the same principle, a principle of subjecting the contingencies that buffet individuals' lives to some sort of rational public control.[64]

NOTES

1. For comprehensive surveys, see P. S. Atiyah and Peter Cane, *Atiyah's Accidents, Compensation and the Law*, 4th ed. (London: Weidenfeld & Nicolson, 1987); and Donald R. Harris et al., *Compensation and Support for Illness and Injury* (Oxford: Clarendon Press, 1984). On eminent domain, see Frank I. Michelman, "Property, Utility, and Fairness: Comments on the Ethical Foundations of 'Just Compensation' Law," *Harvard Law Review* 80 (1967): 1165–1258; and Richard A. Epstein, *Takings: Private Property and the Power of Eminent Domain* (Cambridge: Harvard University Press, 1985). On displaced workers, see Robert S. Goldfarb, "Compensating Victims of Policy Change," *Regulation* (September/October 1980): 22–30; and Joseph J. Cordes and Robert S. Goldfarb, "Alternative Rationales for Severance Pay Compensation under Airline Deregulation," *Public Choice* 41 (1983); 351–69.

2. "Virtually always," because we sometimes speak of "disability compensation" even for congenital handicaps. My remarks in section III.*B* below build on that example.

3. One way of making sense of this would be to say that compensa-

tion invariably restores a "post-fisc" status quo ante that already incorporates redistributivist state transfers. Then there would be no conflict between compensation and the (redistributivist) status quo ante that it restores. Alas, that is not an accurate characterization of compensation as presently practiced. Compensation payments are usually taxable, which suggests that compensation recreates a status quo ante that is pre-fisc (that is, one that we would still want to tax) rather than post-fisc.

4. Simultaneous pursuit would indeed be incoherent: if logically incompatible, they cannot both be achieved simultaneously. Sequential pursuit would not be incoherent in this strong logical sense. Still, since each reverses the accomplishments of the other, something must be said to justify the peculiar practice of giving with one hand and taking back with the other.

5. The doctrine of "deep pockets" in torts might seem to tend in that direction. But notice that that doctrine is used only to decide which among multiple tortfeasors should bear the costs. It never dictates leaving a wrong unrighted merely on the ground that the victim, though wholly blameless, nonetheless has the deepest pockets in town.

6. Unless, perhaps, that better pay incorporated a "risk premium" compensating them ex ante for the risk of such accidents, in which case it might be argued that the injured worker has already been compensated once and to compensate him again would constitute double-dipping. Cf. John Broome, "Trying to Value a Life," *Journal of Public Economics* 9 (1978): 91–100; and Robert E. Goodin, *Political Theory and Public Policy* (Chicago: University of Chicago Press, 1982), chap. 8.

7. Robert Nozick, *Anarchy, State and Utopia* (Oxford: Blackwell, 1974), chap. 7; and Epstein, *Takings*, esp. p. II.

8. That is the aspect of that tradition upon which I shall concentrate, anyway. It is also true, and is perhaps more damning, that by demanding compensation for takings of private property that tradition assumes what it needs to prove, which is the justifiability of property rights as presently construed and distributed.

9. The phrase, coined by Justice Brewer in *Monongahela Navigation Co. v. U.S.*, 148 U.S. 312, 326 (1893), has been echoed in legal texts ever since.

10. Nozick, *Anarchy, State and Utopia*, chap. 7.

11. This is the line of latter-day Lockeans such as Nozick, *Anarchy, State and Utopia*; and Epstein, *Takings*.

12. By that, I mean the practice of providing compensation— understood as the full and perfect equivalent of what was lost—to right any and all wrongful damage to persons and property. Although

that ideal is rarely realized perfectly, it is the ideal practice rule rather than the inevitably imperfect implementation of it that a theory of compensatory justice must strive to rationalize.

The practice of compensation is often intertwined with various other practices, such as deterrence of harm-causing activities, via liability rules in torts. Many of the peculiarities of notionally compensatory practices, inexplicable on my account, might be explained by reference to those other, competing considerations. Still, I trust that there are enough "clean" cases of compensation to build a theory around those paradigmatic instances.

13. Certainly they were no less entitled to win judgment in the tort suit, at least. How much they win in damages may be another matter. Traditionally, those were also independent of any reflection upon need or distributive justice, merely reflecting how much people had lost through the tort against them. In recent times this has changed only at the margins, despite calls for tort damages to be more redistributive; see, for example, Richard Abel, "Torts," in David Kairys, ed., *The Politics of Law* (New York: Pantheon, 1982), 185–200.

14. The same is true in contract law. For distributional reasons we refuse to countenance certain sorts of contract, for example those entailing usurious interest rates or slave wages. See Anthony Kronman, "Contract Law and Distributive Justice," *Yale Law Journal* 89 (1980): 472–511. But distributional considerations primarily constrain what sorts of contracts will be considered valid in the first place. They would not excuse the breach of an otherwise valid contract. Poor debtors are not excused, by reason of their relative poverty alone, from repaying debts owed to the rich.

15. Indeed, in terms of end-state theories, that is what inheritance tax rates must imply. Process-based, historical entitlement might allow a more nuanced interpretation of inheritance tax policies, for example, that it is not wrong for the rich to enjoy their riches, it is merely wrong for them to pass them on to others. In the end-state terms here under discussion, though, the pattern of holdings is all that can matter. There is no place for considerations about how people came by their riches— through their own efforts or through bequests—to enter these calculations.

16. Often these benefits replace up to 90 percent of lost earnings, occasionally tax free. See U.S. Department of Health, Education and Welfare, *Social Security Programs throughout the World 1972* (Washington, D.C.: Government Printing Office, 1978).

17. That correlates, in a rough-and-ready way, with paying people more the less they now need it, for high earners on average have

higher savings to tide them over emergencies. Unemployment benefits, and social insurance benefits more generally, are virtually never means-tested; consequently, compensation of these sorts can hardly be represented as a response to "need."

18. We know, from their tax policies, that many governments themselves think that a more equal pattern of income distribution would be preferable and that it is government's job to promote it. Yet the very same governments, through their compensation policies, set systematically about reproducing the same nonideal pattern of income distribution they try to correct through their tax policies.

19. For elaboration, see Robert E. Goodin, "Stabilizing Expectations: The Role of Earnings-Related Benefits in Social Welfare Policy," *Ethics* 100 (1991), forthcoming.

20. That is not to say that questions of title are wholly irrelevant. Thieves brash enough to sue for damage to automobiles they have stolen are unlikely to persuade many juries to decide in their favor, whatever tort law may say on the matter. For present purposes, I do not need to claim that questions of title never enter. It is enough to say that questions of title do not always enter; that is, tort law does not require any systematic checking of titles, and hence it responds to issues of historical entitlement only in really blatant cases like the stolen car.

21. American Law Institute, *Second Restatement of the Law of Torts* (St. Paul, Minn.: West, for the American Law Institute, 1965), sec. 328E, comment. Similarly, section 821E specifies "who can recover for private nuisance," naming first and foremost "possessors of the land"; and in comment c on that section, the Reporters pointedly add that "the term [possessors of land] applies to adverse possessors [i.e., those who have no title to it] as well as those rightfully in possession."

22. The *Second Restatement of the Law of Torts*, sec 889, again specifies: "One is not barred from recovery . . . merely because at the time of the interference he was committing a tort or a crime or, in the case of an interference with his title to or possession of lands or chattels, because it was tortious or illegal for him to have the title or possession."

23. It is even an open question whether those injured in the course of committing a crime should be entitled to criminal injuries compensation. Note that the New Zealand accidental injuries compensation scheme, subsuming the criminal injuries compensation scheme there, made no exclusion for injuries incurred in the commission of a crime. See Terence G. Ison, *Accident Compensation* (London: Croom Helm, 1980): 37–38.

24. In the American Law Institute's Model Eminent Domain Code, *Uniform Laws Annotated*, vol. 13 (St. Paul, Minn.: West, for the American Law Institute, 1986), sec. 609, similar protections are offered to the person on record as owner of property and the person in actual possession of it.

25. Unless, perhaps, the reason I lost the job was in penalty for having obtained the job improperly in the first place.

26. "Almost," because occasionally we refuse compensation on account of egregious immorality in the history of acquisition. Middle Eastern governments often took that attitude in confiscating oil fields without compensating their multinational corporate owners. In Britain, the Labour left urged, unsuccessfully, a similar policy of "no speculative gain" when renationalizing industries privatized under Prime Minister Thatcher. But those really do represent the exceptions rather than the rule.

27. Similarly, the obligation to pay just compensation for takings of private property under powers of eminent domain, has historically been analyzed as part and parcel of "due process" even where it was not constitutionally mandated; see Edward S. Corwin, "The Doctrine of Due Process of Law before the Civil War," *Harvard Law Review* 24 (1911): 366–85, 460–79 at p. 378; and J. A. C. Grant, "The 'Higher Law' Background of the Law of Eminent Domain," *Wisconsin Law Review* 6 (1931): 67–85.

28. In deciding which harms are compensatable and what are not, we have historically been most ready to compensate given some clear agent to blame. We were prepared to compensate for torts, where tortfeasors are readily identifiable, long before we were prepared to compensate for accidents, where agency may be clear but blame is not. We are now prepared to compensate for the consequences of accidents, where at least human agency is clear; but we remain reluctant to compensate for the strictly analogous consequences of disease, where human agency presumably is typically absent. See Atiyah and Cane, *Atiyah's Accidents, Compensation and the Law,* chap. 20; and Jane Stapleton, *Disease and the Compensation Debate* (Oxford: Clarendon Press, 1986). All of that seems to fit the model of compensation as righting procedural wrongs: wrongs imply agency, and compensation in practice has historically been biased in favor of cases in which agency is clear. In reply, I merely note that we have now moved well beyond compensating only where blame is clear. That, in turn, suggests that the search for an agent committing a wrong was always more pragmatic than principled: it never was the case that we thought only those harmed by others' wrongs deserved compensation, on principle. It was always

merely a matter of figuring out who, in practice, should pay. I return to these themes toward the end of section I.C.

29. In other cases, like eminent domain, compensation prevents an intervention from being wrong at all. Such cases are importantly different from crimes or torts, which would hardly be permissible provided only compensation were paid. But I take it that extending the basic formula to embrace the subjunctive as well—"compensation is justifiable to right what is or would have been a wrong"—does no real violence to the basic logic of that position.

30. Unemployment compensation is nearer the latter pole. Claiming unemployment benefit is importantly different from mounting a claim for wrongful dismissal; but there is a tinge of fault-based logic in the fact that a claim for unemployment compensation might, in many places, be denied if the claimant were himself responsible for his own unemployment, having voluntarily resigned his post or having given an employer good grounds for dismissal. While unemployment compensation is not compensation to right a wrong, therefore, claims for it are defeasible on the basis of a wrong of a certain sort on the claimant's part.

31. Michael Freeden, *The New Liberalism* (Oxford: Clarendon Press, 1978); and Cane and Atiyah, *Atiyah's Accidents, Compensation and the Law*, chap. 21.

32. One problem is that multiple candidates appear for the role of status quo ante, each corresponding to a different past period. We have no reason for favoring any one over the others. Another problem is that arguments for protecting the status quo ante often illicitly turn on arguments for protecting the status quo; yet once the status quo ante has been upset, there will have been established a new status quo, itself deserving of protection under that principle.

33. Martin Feldstein, "Compensating in Tax Reform," *National Tax Journal* 29 (1976): 123–30 at p. 124, rests his case for compensating those who would lose from closing tax loopholes and ending tax subsidies on the proposition that "individuals make commitments based on existing tax laws" at least some of which "may be irreversible or reversible only slowly or with substantial loss." Or, again, the report of the Senate committee recommending the compensation provisions of the Airline Deregulation Act of 1978 argued, "Airline employees have relied on the present regulatory system through their reliance on the conditions that have resulted from that system. . . . Many airline employees have given most of their working lives to the air transportation industry and have too much invested to leave it now. . . . Since employees will not be able to adjust in the sense their employers can, the

Committee believes that a reasonable program of transition assistance should be provided" (quoted in Cirdes and Goldfarb, "Alternative Rationales," 356). In a more theoretical vein, Michelman, "Property, Utility, and Fairness," 1211–13 and throughout, traces the case for just compensation for public takings in eminent domain cases to Benthamite arguments about the need for stable and secure expectations to maximize social utility.

34. These themes are adapted to debates about compensation in Robert E. Goodin, "Stabilizing Expectations" and his "Theories of Compensation," *Oxford Journal of Legal Studies* 9 (1989): 56–75.

35. This analysis is perfectly consistent with, and borne out by, the practice of compensation. On the one hand, we think it important that compensation should be paid promptly, and we regard it a scandal that the average time between injury and tort judgment is three years (Atiyah and Cane, *Atiyah's Accidents, Compensation and the Law,* 272). On the other hand, we also seem to think that after a certain period of time, no compensation need be paid at all. On tort claims, the statute of limitations specifies a few years, typically; on social security claims, such as for workmen's compensation, the time limit for claiming is usually a few weeks or months. Various reasons can be given for that practice. The most standard has to do with problems of amassing reliable evidence long after the event, which may be a powerful reason in some cases (for example, torts) but is weak in others (for example, workmen's compensation, where the factory safety officer's log or hospital's records are utterly reliable long after the event). The most satisfactory reason for the practice seems to be that compensation is supposed to avoid interruptions to people's life plans; and such compensation would have no point long after the event, because by then that interruption would already have occurred (Goodin, "Stabilizing Expectations," sec. 3).

36. Notice that clause (b) in this formulation goes some substantial way toward subsuming the model of righting wrongs analyzed in section I.*B*. That is acceptable, since the arguments offered against that model merely served to suggest that it is at least a partial account, true of some but not all cases of compensation. If clause (b) here is taken as subsuming that model, clause (a) can be taken as providing the rest of the story needed for a complete account.

37. See, for example: H. L. A. Hart and Tony Honoré, *Causation in the Law,* 2nd ed. (Oxford: Clarendon Press, 1985), chaps. 2 and 3; J. L. Mackie, "Responsibility and Language," *Australasian Journal of Philosophy* 33 (1955): 143–59; and Robert Nozick, "Coercion," in P. Laslett,

W. G. Runciman, and Q. Skinner, eds., *Philosophy, Politics and Society,* 4th series (Oxford: Blackwell, 1972), 110–35 at p. 112.

38. Whether that expectation is *so* reasonable, morally, that we should compensate victims for crimes that they "bring on themselves" (by walking after dark in Central Park, or by going out without locking their house doors) is another question. I would not therefore wish to press clause (b) all that hard. Specifically, I would not care to rely upon it alone to establish links between compensation and redistribution. Those who suppose that egalitarian outcomes are morally required, for example, might use clause (b) to argue that equality is a "morally reasonable expectation" that ought to be underwritten by compensation when it is disappointed, just as should be the absence of crime; then redistribution would indeed be nothing more than a species of compensatory policy, using clause (b). I suspect many things are wrong with that move, primarily among them that clause (b) is not strong enough to sustain the weight of so large an argument.

39. Michelman, "Property, Utility, and Fairness," 1235–39 and Cordes and Goldfarb, "Alternative Rationales," 364–65.

40. Charles Fried, *Contract as Promise* (Cambridge: Harvard University Press, 1981), 10. Even if Perot had done something to arouse this expectation in me, there is a world of difference between "arousing expectations" and "inducing reliance," as Neil MacCormick points out in *Legal Right and Social Democracy* (Oxford: Clarendon Press, 1982), chap. 10. But under the doctrine of "estoppel," Perot and his ilk would be liable if he knowingly let others rely to their cost upon such expectations without attempting to warn them. See Robert E. Goodin, *Protecting the Vulnerable* (Chicago: University of Chicago Press, 1985), 42–52, for analysis of these issues.

41. Harris et al., *Compensation and Support,* 90; and Goodin, "Theories of Compensation," sec. 2.

42. Given the overwhelming importance of larger social sources of disease and economic dislocation, it is only right that society as a whole should there pay the bulk of the premium, through tax revenues. Such factors explain why "social insurance," so called, should deviate so systematically from the standard actuarial principles of ordinary private insurance. In terms of note 23, these schemes imply a notion of "collective agency" both in causing the harm and compensating for it; that we need not fear this notion is the theme of Robert E. Goodin, "The State as Moral Agent," Alan Hamlin and Philip Pettit, eds., *The Good Polity* (Oxford: Blackwell, 1989), 123–39.

43. I might add "or the procedural wrongess of upsetting it." But

as I say in note 32, model I.*C* subsumes and provides a proper rationale for model I.*B*, so there is no further need to comment separately upon that latter model.

44. Lon Fuller, *The Morality of Law* (New Haven: Yale University Press, 1964). Finance ministers regularly argue the need for a certain measure of confidentiality in the conduct of economic affairs. They cannot let news of a currency devaluation dribble out, without undermining the goals that that policy is meant to serve, for example. One suspects Treasury officials, in their penchant for secrecy, of offering exceptional cases as if they were the rule, however.

45. It seems unreasonable, at least in the nonmoralized statistical sense, for people to proceed with their life plans in the expectation that the government's settled redistributivist intention, however immoral, will not be acted upon. The unreasonableness involved seems akin to that displayed by people who persist in their long-standing practice of strolling around Central Park after dark, as though it has not become a den of thieves. The mugged stroller, like the unjustly treated citizen, may well have a point when protesting that "you simply shouldn't have to take any notice of such immoralities in leading a decent life." But he can hardly profess *surprise*, as distinct from outrage, when pulled aside by the thief or the sheriff.

46. It is only reasonable that advocates of redistribution should be expected to say something persuasive in its moral defense. By the same token, if the only way opponents of redistribution can enlist the support of compensatory justice is by showing that there are some other grounds, independent of that, for thinking redistribution immoral, then it is not the notion of compensatory justice but rather those "other grounds" for thinking redistribution immoral that does all the work in their argument, too.

47. That is true even in cases of dramatic regime changes, and not just ordinary electoral turnover. De Gaulle's constitution for the Fifth Republic "did not repudiate spending commitments embodied in the social security legislation of previous French regimes; . . . the Federal Republic of Germany still pays benefits to the families of soldiers who fought for the Third Reich"; Richard Rose and B. Guy Peters, *Can Government Go Bankrupt?* (London: Macmillan, 1979), 115, 263.

48. See, most especially, Harold M. Hochman, "Rule Change and Transitional Equity," in H. M. Hochman and George E. Peterson, eds., *Redistribution through Public Choice* (New York: Columbia University Press, 1974), 320–41; and Louis Kaplow, "An Economic Analysis of Legal Transitions," *Harvard Law Review* 99 (1986): 509–618.

49. Gordon Tullock, "Achieving Deregulation—A Public Choice

Perspective," *Regulation* (November/December 1978): 50–54 at p. 53; and Martin Feldstein, "On the Theory of Tax Reform," *Journal of Public Economics* 6 (1976): 77–104 at pp. 98–99. Cf. Goldfarb, "Compensating Victims of Policy Change," 29–30.

50. "Cushion," because a typical consequence—produced through the operation of the market on the value of the thing scheduled to be taken from you—would be to make the effects of the proposed changes felt gradually and increasingly strongly as the implementation date nears. A freehold scheduled to be confiscated in fifty years' time becomes, in effect, a fifty-year leasehold, suffering a certain immediate loss in value in consequence and a steady decrease in value as each of those fifty years ticks by. Cushions are important though: small changes are presumably less damaging than large ones to planning.

51. James Tobin, "On Limiting the Domain of Inequality," *Journal of Law and Economics* 13 (1970): 368–78; Mary Douglas and Brian Isherwood, *The World of Goods* (London: Allen Lane, 1979); and Michael Walzer, *Spheres of Justice* (Oxford: Martin Robertson, 1983).

52. A. C. Pigou, *The Economics of Welfare*, 4th ed. (London: Macmillan, 1932), pt. 1, chap. 9.

53. For some estimate of the magnitude of the effects, consider the calculations of Sheldon Danziger, Robert Haveman, and Robert Plotnick, "How Income Transfer Programs Affect Work, Savings and Income Distribution," *Journal of Economic Literature* 19 (1981): 975–1028 at p. 1019: contemporary U.S. transfer payments, practiced in a markedly anti-Pigouvian way, seem to produce a 4.8 percent reduction in labor supply due to disincentive effects, in exchange for a reduction of 75 percent in poverty and a 19 percent reduction in the Gini coefficient of income inequality.

54. Perhaps the most explicit expression of this thought comes from the "new welfare economists." They made the possibility of "hypothetical compensation" the measure of a permissible alteration in economic affairs: if gainers could, in principle, compensate losers and still have something left over, then the change was potentially a Pareto improvement. They left it as "hypothetical" compensation, rather than insisting upon the payment of actual compensation, on the ground that that would unjustifiably lock in the existing distribution and arbitrarily preclude the possibility of redistribution. Nicholas Kaldor, "Welfare Propositions of Economics and Interpersonal Comparisons of Utility," *Economic Journal* 49 (1939): 549–52 at pp. 550–51 and his "Community Indifference: A Comment," *Review of Economic Studies* 14 (1946–47); John R. Hicks, "The Foundations of Welfare Economics," *Economic Journal* 49 (1939): 696–712 at pp. 711–12; and Tibor Scitovsky, "A

Note on Welfare Propositions in Economics," *Review of Economic Studies* 9 (1941): 77–88.

55. What is at work here is not a general prejudice against ever preventing people from insuring against whatever they want. Some things, such as punitive damages in torts, are already uninsurable.

56. Consistent with (but neither implying nor implied by) that thought is the proposition that we want to compensate systematically for harms done, whether by rich to poor or vice versa, as embodiment of the value of "equality before the law." To say that the poor need not compensate rich people they have harmed is to imply, unacceptably, that the rich are from their perspective simply not "morally considerable."

57. Michelman, "Property, Utility, and Fairness," 1217–18. A similar analysis can be given as to why we insist upon just compensation for those whose property is taken under the power of eminent domain. Some, such as Epstein, *Takings*, see this as akin to a problem in contracts or torts: if you want to use another's property, you must pay for the privilege; and this applies as strongly to public agencies as to private ones. My counterproposal builds on Justice Black's comment, in *Armstrong v. U.S.*, 364 U.S. 40, 49 (1960) that, "The Fifth Amendment's guarantee that private property shall not be taken for a public use without just compensation was designed to bar the Government from forcing some people alone to bear public burdens which, in all fairness and justice, should be borne by the public as a whole." Following that logic, the takings issue is akin to a problem in just taxation, where the relevant principle is one of "horizontal equity." In the taxation case it would be wrong because inequitable to impose differential taxes on people in the same income class. In the takings case, it would be similarly wrong because similarly inequitable to impose differential sacrifices on people in the same income class merely because they happen to own something that the public requires. Here again, it is equity rather than the arbitrary sharing of burdens to provide public goods and services that obliges us to provide just compensation to those whose property we take for public uses.

58. Atiyah and Cane, *Atiyah's Accidents, Compensation and the Law*, chap. 16; and Harris et al., *Compensation and Support*, 4–12.

59. A. J. Culyer, "Economics, Social Policy and Disability," in Dennis Lees and Stella Shaw, eds., *Impairment, Disability and Handicap* (London: Heinemann for the SSRC, 1974), 17–29 at pp. 22–23.

60. For a defense of welfare rights along this general line, see Raymond Plant, "Needs, Agency, and Welfare Rights," in J. Donald

Moon, ed., *Responsibility, Rights and Welfare* (Boulder: Westview, 1988), 55–75.

61. It may well be that food, clothing, and shelter—and the basic income required, in market societies like our own, to secure them— are "primary goods," necessary for whatever else one wants to do. Still, one can always cast one's plans in contingent terms, stipulating what one would do were one's basic needs satisfied. Such primary goods may be preconditions of efficacious acting, but they are not preconditions of planning per se.

62. Likewise, disabilities might be similarly absorbing, even when they do not literally preclude planning one's life.

63. Peter Jones, "Freedom and the Redistribution of Resources," *Journal of Social Policy* 11 (1982): 217–38, offers a parallel move in the context of the positive/negative liberty debate: if liberty is what the rich lose when money is taken from them through redistributive taxes as champions of negative freedom contend, then it must be liberty that the poor gain when money is given to them in the course of that redistribution, as champions of positive freedom proclaim.

64. Earlier versions of this chapter were discussed in London, Norwich, and New Orleans. I am particularly grateful for the comments, then and later, of Elizabeth Anderson, Brian Barry, Debbie Fitzmaurice, Martin Hollis, Sheldon Leader, Saul Levmore, Onora O'Neill, Morris Perlman, and Albert Weale.

6

COMPENSATION WITHIN THE LIMITS OF RELIANCE ALONE

ELIZABETH ANDERSON

Robert Goodin's chapter, "Compensation and Redistribution," makes three central claims. First, the true justification for compensation lies in the fact that people have reasonably relied on the continuation of a state of affairs. Second, if we justify compensatory schemes by appealing to the substantive justice of the status quo that compensation seeks to restore, then we could not justify measures to redistribute property holdings. Third, the same considerations that make reasonable reliance morally relevant for compensation may also justify redistribution. I shall argue that while the first two claims are doubtful, Goodin provides us with the resources to construct a stronger argument for the last claim than he thinks is available. His arguments are thwarted, however, by a commitment to parsimony as a fundamental aim of moral theory. Reliance is not the one true justification for compensation, but just one justification among others that are equally valid even if less able to account for the full range of compensation practices.[1] And these other justifications for compensation sometimes justify redistribution as well.

Parsimony demands that a moral theory accept the fewest moral principles required to account for our considered judgments about morality or our actual practices, in Goodin's case. If a single moral principle can generate all of the outcomes we consider just in the area in question, compensatory practices, then we should not invoke other moral principles that merely generate redundant recommendations for a subset of the practices we wish to justify. At least, we should not regard the other principles as fundamental. Goodin appears to accept the ideal of parsimony in holding that reliance is the single real justification for compensation.

If reliance is the only justification for compensation, then Goodin can say that the justifications for redistribution and compensation are closely related, but not that they are the same. On his account, compensation is justified because it enables people to live out the plans they have already made, whereas redistribution is justified because it enables people to frame life plans in the first place. But surely many compensation plans, such as federal deposit insurance and unemployment insurance, are better justified by the latter than by the former consideration. Goodin suggests that we insure bank deposits and not stock investments because we have no good grounds, either statistical or moral, for expecting that the value of stock investments will not fall. However, before federal deposit insurance, we had no better reasons, statistical or moral, for expecting that banks would not fail. Similarly, we have every reason to expect that jobs with marginal firms will and can only be temporary, since marginal firms are not in a position to guarantee stable employment. *Before* deposit and unemployment insurance were established, plans framed in expectation of being able to draw on income from these sources were unreasonable. Hence reliance cannot justify these compensation schemes. But the fact that they establish stable expectations that enable people to form reasonable plans in the first place does justify these schemes. The justifications for compensation and redistribution in these cases turn out to be exactly the same.

Of course, there is another sense of reliance in which workers' reliance on their jobs does justify unemployment insurance. They rely on their jobs in the sense that they need the income from their jobs to survive—they have nothing else to rely on. But from this it does not follow that they have actually framed the kinds of long-term plans that are of concern in Goodin's sense of reliance. They may merely have "planned" to cope with their misfortunes, come what may, or to deal with life day by day. Considerations of need are distinct from considerations of reliance in Goodin's sense, and also help to justify some compensation schemes.

Some compensation programs are actually redistributive. They distribute income more equally than market forces operating alone. Unemployment compensation redistributes income from the employed to the unemployed; workmen's compensation redistributes income from firms to the disabled. This redistributive function is not removed by the fact that compensation itself is positively correlated with the individuals' incomes prior to loss. In cases such as these, reliance, autonomy, and need considerations all support the same programs. People need a steady income not just to live out their plans, and to plan out their lives, but also simply to survive.

These observations show that Goodin tries to make the concept of reliance do too much work, and in the process prevents his case for the mutual entailment of compensation and redistribution from being as forceful as it could. Compensatory schemes are justified not just because they enable people to carry out plans they have already made, but because they provide people with some of their basic needs and because they promote autonomy, the opportunity to frame long-term plans of life that is secured by creating institutions that make justified reliance possible. The same considerations that justify compensation also justify redistribution in some cases, and in other cases, compensation itself serves redistributive aims. The parsimonious temptation to try to make do with but one moral consideration to account for compensatory practices may thus have weakened Goodin's case.

Let us now turn to Goodin's second claim. Parsimony is not the only reason why Goodin argues that reliance is the sole true principle of compensatory justice. He also believes that if we justify compensatory justice on another ground, that it restores a substantively just situation, then it seems that the very justice of the status quo ante would rule out any redistributive policies. For the ultimate purpose of redistributive justice seems to be precisely to change the prior distributions that compensatory justice attempts to recreate. How can we be justified in changing the status quo ante through redistribution, if what justifies compensation is that it restores a just status quo ante?

Goodin's concern would be warranted if the status quo in terms of which we calculate compensations is the same as the situation in terms of which we measure redistributions. But this is usually not the case. Redistribution is measured against the distributions of property that real markets actually generate, or, in contractarian theory, against the distributions of property that markets would generate, if they were allowed to operate according to some system of laissez-faire founded on natural property rights. In this latter sense, redistribution is not defined against a status quo at all, since a complete system of unregulated markets based on natural property rights has never existed. Redistribution, in the sense important to such contractarian theorists as Nozick, is defined against a purely hypothetical state of affairs. But our practices of compensation generally aim to restore an actual status quo ante, not a hypothetical state of affairs that never existed. Nor do our practices of compensation generally aim to restore the status quo prior to government measures that change the distributions of actually existing markets. Compensation is calculated on the basis of a state of affairs to be restored that already includes the results of, and provisions for, redistributive measures. For example, compensatory damages for lost income in the law of torts are subject to income taxes. And a person can claim compensation for damaged property in the law of torts even if the property was obtained through redistribution. The status quo that actual practices of compensation seek to restore is a situation that already incorporates the effects of redistribution undertaken for the sake of justice, not the status quo prior to any redistribution, much less some hypothetical laissez-faire state.

Since the situation that redistributive measures seek to change is not the same as the situation that compensatory measures seek to restore, no incompatibility arises between compensatory and distributive justice even where we justify compensation on the ground that it restores a substantively just situation. Indeed, once a just system of property holdings and redistributive policies is in place, one of the reasons why we would want to attend to compensatory justice is that it restores a substantively just pattern of holdings. The good of providing people with their basic needs may simultaneously justify a pattern of holdings achieved through redistribution and a compensatory scheme designed to restore this pattern when it is disrupted. Unemployment insurance helps to fulfill this latter function.

But Goodin claims that our present practices of compensation can't in fact be rationalized in terms of the justice of the status quo ante, even if hypothetical compensatory practices could be. For our compensatory practices restore the status quo without investigating whether it is substantively justified. A poor person is still liable for damages in the law of torts, even if the plaintiff is wealthier than she and even if compensating the plaintiff would restore a pattern of inequality that is substantively unjust. Goodin suggests that if compensation were to be justified by the claim that it restores a substantively just status quo ante, and if substantial inequalities in income were unjust, then tort law should not protect the rich and the poor equally. A person would be entitled to claim damages from another only if compensation would move us closer to an equal pattern of holdings.

But surely this suggestion is mistaken. Only a parsimonious view of moral theory would tempt one to this assertion. On a parsimonious view of moral theory, a moral rule or principle accounts for a practice or particular judgment just so long as it would recommend the practice or yield the judgment given the relevant moral facts. Moral rules conceived in this way are nothing more than input-output devices. If moral rules are conceived of parsimoniously, and if justice concerns patterns of property holdings, then perhaps a person should only be able to collect damages from another if this would move us closer to a just pattern of property holdings. But the rules of justice are more than devices for generating independently desirable outcomes. They also express moral principles. The rules of tort law express the moral principles that inflicting certain kinds of harm on others constitutes a wrongful act, and that people are entitled to equal moral consideration. The law of torts could not express these principles if it were also used to redistribute income more equally. If the rich could not claim tortious damages from the poor, this would be tantamount to expressing the principle that moral consideration is not owed to those wealthier than oneself, that people are not morally equal. It follows that tort law is no place to practice egalitarian redistribution, even if such redistribution is independently justified. If our rules of justice are to express sound moral principles and not just generate outcomes deemed acceptable on independent grounds, then we must accept a division of labor between the principles of compensatory and redistributive justice. This means that the rules of compensatory justice may be justified because they help to restore a substantively just status quo, even if these rules are not based on inquiry into the justice of the status quo. For justice itself demands that these inquiries take place in a different forum.[2]

Goodin offers us some provocative thoughts about the relation between compensatory and redistributive justice. He also presents some modest lessons about the dangers of allowing the ideal of parsimony to influence moral theory. I cannot agree that reliance is the one true justification for compensation. In practice, we recognize many different kinds of claims as relevant compensations of justice: need, consent, fair gambles, equality, reciprocity, and reliance are all valid considerations when justice is the concern. Each type of consideration needs distinct rules that express it, for we care not just about outcomes but about the principles that generated them. This helps explain how compensation can be justified because it helps to restore a just state of affairs, even if it does not attempt directly to perform the redistributive functions that justify the status quo. If we resist the temptation to theorize too parsimoniously, we will be in a better position to defend Goodin's claim that some of the same considerations that justify compensation also justify redistribution.

Given these problems with Goodin's commitment to parsimony, why does he pursue this ideal of theorizing? Why is the ideal so pervasive in normative theory generally? At least three reasons come to mind. One is a belief in foundationalism. Many people hold that the vast diversity of moral claims we make *must* in principle be justified by only one fundamental moral idea.

Any theory that accepts a diversity of justifying principles simply hasn't dug deeply enough into the "real" ground of our practices. A second reason for parsimony comes from an instrumental conception of moral theory as an input-output device for making decisions. A moral theory with but one principle avoids the difficulties that can arise when two or more principles conflict. It promises the instrumental advantages to decision making of yielding answers relatively quickly and straightforwardly, without anguish, at least so long as the principle itself is clearly stated. Third, analogies with scientific theory seem to compel parsimony in normative theory as well: if we should not postulate entities in science that are not needed to explain observations, why should we postulate values in morality that are not needed to guide our decisions?

The antiparsimonious view of normative theory is motivated by the following thoughts. First, the diversity of principles we actually accept in justifying actions is no illusion, if, as I believe, this diversity is rooted in the diversity of the practices and experiences we find worthwhile. We need no unitary foundation to support these practices and experiences.[3] Second, the principles we use to guide our decisions are not merely instrumentally valuable for getting us the right answers. We also want to get these answers for the right reasons, and to express these reasons in our practices. Since the reasons we find compelling are diverse, we can secure the public, expressive function of decision-making principles only by admitting more than one, and so only by accepting some of the instrumental costs of pluralism mentioned above. Finally, we should recognize a distinction between moral and scientific theories. Our moral theories should fit our conception of a suitable moral life, of what ought to be, even if this does not conform to the austere picture of what science prefers to draw. A parsimonious moral theory is suitable only to a lean and barren moral life. And even in scientific theory, the virtue of simplicity must be weighed against that of fruitfulness. The postulation of unobserved causal forces is not strictly necessary to predict the occurrence of any empirical observations, but it does generate new hypotheses that promote scientific progress. Similarly, even if only one or a few moral principles are needed to yield all of the decisions we *presently* think right, the presently "redundant" or latent principles may play a crucial role in shaping our future moral practices for the better. We might be better off thinking of such principles as like unused rainforest trees, worthy of preservation for their own sake and for their potential for future human development. Just as we have grown beyond viewing rainforest trees merely as candidates for the chainsaw, we should grow beyond viewing many moral principles merely as candidates for Occam's razor.

NOTES

1. Goodin acknowledges the complexity of justifications for compensation where he claims that the practice of compensation is a mixed bag. This claim stands in tension with his more ambitious aim, to show that reliance is the real justification for compensation.

2. Further reasons explain why mechanisms of compensation should not be used to achieve redistributive aims. As Goodin says, they could achieve these aims only in a haphazard, piecemeal fashion. But the reason why the haphazard achievement of aims is undesirable is not, as Goodin claims, because we think that it is unjust for people to gain or lose property through sheer luck. State-run lotteries are widely accepted as just in this country, even though they redistribute income by sheer luck. Rather, we reject haphazard mechanisms of redistribution because they fail to express appropriate principles of justice, among which is equality before the law. Fully to express the principle that the distribution of holdings should reflect a certain pattern of equality, we much choose rules of justice that will achieve these patterns for everyone, not merely between those individuals who have happened to meet in court. And once the appropriate redistributive rules are in place, say through a progressive income tax, then to exact proportionate redistributions through mechanisms of compensatory justice is redundant.

3. For an antifoundationalist account of political justification along the lines of this suggestion, see Don Herzog, *Without Foundations* (Ithaca, N.Y.: Cornell University Press, 1985).

7

ON COMPENSATION AND DISTRIBUTION

SAUL LEVMORE

My comments on and objections to Goodin's "Compensation and Redistribution" grow in large part out of a perspective that insists that the roles of compensation and deterrence, or even of incentive effects in general, cannot easily be separated from one another. This is true in the law of torts, in eminent domain, and perhaps elsewhere as well. And if liability rules are meant to serve a deterrence purpose, or even a combined deterrence and compensation function, then the question of the "compatibility" of efforts to preserve the status quo, and attempts to change it, largely dissolves because liability rules and redistribution rules serve not opposite but different functions. Liability rules deter certain activities, and the law must use *other* tools to redistribute, or its deterrence aim will not be accomplished.

Two examples of the importance of including incentive effects in any positive theory of liability rules, or of the availability of compensation, will make this point within the framework adopted by Goodin. Consider first the popularity of negligence rules, or fault-based liability, in tort law. The law-and-economics literature suggests that strict liability rules and negligence rules have much the same effect on minimizing the costs of accidents.[1] One might, however, choose between these rules on the basis of their "activity level" effects, administrative costs (under one rule negligence must be established while under the other a large number of losses must be measured), or fairly subtle influences on risk taking.[2] With some notable subject-matter exceptions, most legal systems have chosen the negligence, rather than the strict liability, principle as their mainstay.[3] But the key features of compensation employed in Goodin's argument for "compatibility," that reasonably relied upon expectations ought to be and are protected and that "bolts from the blue," as Goodin calls them, are undesirable, suggest strongly that the system not stop with negligently caused losses but that *all* bolts inflicted on some parties by others be compensated. Without belaboring the matter, my point is that the choice of negligence rather than strict liability indicates that it will not do for a positive theory to focus on the unfairness or on the impact of sudden and unexpected losses that burden the innocent. That many victims of "bolts" were able to purchase insurance to protect their "reasonable expectations," and that most legal systems do not rush to use tax monies to compensate victims of crimes reinforces this point: one would be at a loss to explain the contours of our legal system with Goodin's central theme, that unexpectedly inflicted losses should be compensated. Moreover, given the harsh redistributive effects of strict liability rules, which raise prices for all consumers, it will not do to retreat to normative theorizing and suggest that, indeed, we *ought* to compensate for all bolts.[4] There are, of course, respectable arguments to be made for using a strict liability rather than a negligence rule, but these arguments cannot, I think, simply be based on sympathy for those who are hit by "bolts from the blue."

I think it useful to examine some concrete details of our liability rules to see, from another angle, the pitfalls of highlighting compensation features to the exclusion of the incentive aspects of these rules. Goodin's conviction, that recovery by surprised, innocent victims must be complete, swift, and certain, as opposed to the view that recovery serves a complex combination of deterrence and intuitively defined moral goals—is at odds with much in the law's treatment of losses caused by minors, economic losses caused by tortfeasors, changes in tax law, and governmental takings of services and other expectations, to name just a few items on a long list of sources of surprise to the average citizen. I turn now to explore two of these subjects.

The observer who focuses exclusively on compensation must find puzzling the long-standing and, I might add, cross-cultural rule that, when a wartime government takes a farmer's corn or an entrepreneur's factory, it must pay fair compensation, but when it drafts soldiers and "takes" away their opportunity to earn civilian salaries it need not compensate. None of the circumstances thought appropriate for compensation in "Compensation and Redistribution" or in other writings distinguishes services from property. In contrast, the observer who concentrates on *incentive* effects will note quite readily that powerful activity-level effects encourage governments to precommit to compensating victims in some settings more than others. A government that does not pay for the food it takes will soon find itself without food because private citizens will cease planting and harvesting. On the other hand, a government that does not pay the fair market value of the human services it inducts is *un*likely to find itself without these services because citizens are unlikely to leave the jurisdiction or underinvest in education unless the government is engaged in a remarkably long and harsh war effort.

Somewhat similarly, and more unfortunately, an area of law that is only weakly understood through incentive effects is often even less explicable when viewed through the lens of compensatory considerations. Consider the fact that typical tortfeasors pay for the property they destroy, the medical expenses they generate, and even the earning streams they disrupt, but not for the "pure economic losses," or once-removed burdens they inflict.[5] Thus, if a stranger negligently runs me over with his motor vehicle, he will *not* be made to reimburse my employer for the cost of hiring a substitute lecturer while I recuperate. Satisfactory normative and positive theories regarding this question are scarce. My own view is that recovery is available under the law only when there is a substantial *net* social loss *or* when no other damages are readily available with which to deter an obvious wrong. But whether or not this modification of an existing theory works as a predictive matter, or is defensible as a normative enterprise, it is surely the case that thoughts of compensation, rather than deterrence, lead one astray. There is, after all, nothing more compelling and deserving about the property or economic losses of the directly injured party than the losses of an indirectly injured person. Moreover, there are numerous exceptional situations in which indirect economic losses *are* recoverable, and these cases can be explained more readily with deterrence than with compensation considerations. In the well-known case of *Union Oil v. Oppen*,[6] for instance, fishermen successfully sued for their lost profits after a negligent oil spill polluted the waters they normally fished. There is nothing more or less compelling about the compensatory arguments in this setting than in most where lost profits are not recoverable. If, for example, one fisherman is disabled by a negligent stranger, the fisherman's partner, who may be unable to handle a boat alone, is *not* able to collect for lost profits caused by the tort, even though his losses are as real and as sudden as are those caused by an oil spill. The more useful way to think about the matter, from a positive and perhaps even from a normative perspective, is to note that in the latter case the driver who runs over one fisherman is deterred by the suit for medical expenses and lost earnings that will be brought by the victim or his family. In the *Union Oil* situation, however, if the fishermen do not recover for their economic losses there will be no deterrence working against oil spillage because no other obvious plaintiff exists. The legal system thus appears to allow suits for economic losses, even where it is apparent that it is not a great *net* loss because other fishermen gain and so forth, when to fail to do so would be to allow a tortfeasor to go substantially undeterred.

In short, in numerous areas, both broad and specific, the legal system appears chaotic when viewed through the lens of compensation, but relatively sensible when approached from a perspective that is dominated by or at least includes deterrence considerations. That this is true not only in Anglo-American law, but also in a wide range of legal systems, as I have discussed elsewhere,[7] emphasizes, I think, the grave error of ever focusing on compensation alone.

Turning briefly to a somewhat different aspect of "Compensation and Redistribution," Goodin's work encourages us to think

of compensation and redistribution as compatible because to
deny compensation and to allow torts, takings, and the like to
visit the few unlucky victims who happen in their paths is to
redistribute from a few victims to a few tortfeasors or other
causal agents. This sort of redistribution among a few lucky and
unlucky persons is just the opposite of what a good redistribution policy is said to do, namely *broadly* redistributing to less
fortunate persons. I quite agree with this observation and I
think it a fair launching point for a small argument of my own
about the relation between compensation, deterrence, and redistribution. Consider the all-too-familiar situation in which fifty
thousand factories or five million drivers contribute to the acid
rain or to the smog that envelopes twelve million citizens in Los
Angeles. We *might* use private law to allow examination of how
many of these polluters could cut back on their activities at
reasonable cost. We could, in other words, allow the reality of
mass tort suits to extend to everyday but complex and large-
scale interactions.

But we do *not* normally allow tort law to migrate in this
manner. And, once again, other legal systems also do not control behavior on this scale with tort, injunctive, and similar tools.
The obstacle even rises or sinks to the explicit, doctrinal level,
as it is often said that individuals can seek injunctive relief from
"private" but not "public nuisances."[8] A factory emitting noise
or particles that interfere with residential life on my block is the
sort of polluter I can challenge in court; in contrast, all the
factories in the Ohio Valley represent the sort of defendants no
one can challenge in a private way.

A fair explanation of this distinction builds on the idea that
the law operates in the shadow of, and as a catalyst for, bargains.
If several homeowners are successful in convincing a court to
block the construction of a factory on nearby land, the losing
defendant can always try to buy out the homeowners and then
build the factory as he or she pleases. It is therefore said that
the parties can "bargain around" an "incorrect" judicial decision.[9] But it is clear that if there are very many homeowners,
such bargaining is far more imaginary than practical. In such
circumstances, to assemble the various parties and to reach a
result that is not sabotaged by free riders and holdouts will be

impossible.[10] After all, the factory owner will need to bargain successfully with every homeowner, and unanimity is difficult to achieve. This difficulty of bargaining fairly explains the underlying disinclination to allow private parties to proceed prospectively against "public" nuisances. It goes without saying that the legal system does not then ignore all such nuisances but rather uses administrative agencies, fines, licensing requirements, and other tools to deal with these problems.

Goodin draws attention to another aspect of this institutional switch from private to public avenues of relief. One might say that we do not use tort suits to handle smog problems because with so many involved parties in mass lawsuits, there would "only" be mass compensation—and mass compensation may as well be done with truly mass redistribution policy tools. Private law, in this view, links together deterrence of some behavior, compensation for some unexpected losses, and inevitable wealth transfers among the parties who are affected by the very rules that take aim at deterrence and compensation goals. In contrast, public, or mass, problems are better resolved with administrative orders and other nontort rules, in part because to do otherwise would create so much of the by-product of wealth transfers as to threaten whatever good might be accomplished by the incentive effects of tort suits. With so much wealth redistribution at stake, one must take wealth effects seriously. Put differently, a combination of (a) careful income tax and welfare policy and (b) separate regulatory attention to, and fines and licenses regarding, pollution and other large-scale problems may be preferable to tort suits that deter wrongdoing but deliver compensation and, therefore, wealth transfers as part of the same package.

In sum, the choice between traditional, common law, essentially private regulation and public, bureaucratic mechanisms as alternative forms of social control can be seen not only as a decision about the relative efficiency and administrability of different systems, each of which almost surely has spheres of superiority, but also as a decision about wealth distribution. That a large component of tort damages, such as lost earnings and lost property values, is a function of wealth emphasizes this point that the actual and the ideal size of the regulatory state is a question about wealth distribution as much as it is a question about the relative advantages of different incentive systems.

NOTES

1. Richard A. Posner, *Economic Analysis of Law*, 3rd ed. (Boston: Little, Brown, 1986), 160–61. See also Steven Shavell, "Strict Liability versus Negligence," *Journal of Legal Studies* 9 (1980): 1.

2. See Posner, *Economic Analysis of Law*, 160–65; Steven Shavell, *Economic Analysis of Accident Law* (Cambridge: Harvard University Press, 1987), 79–83; and John E. Calfee and Richard Craswell, "Some Effects of Uncertainty on Compliance with Legal Standards," *Virginia Law Review* 70 (1984): 965.

3. See Saul Levmore, "Rethinking Comparative Law: Variety and Uniformity in Ancient and Modern Tort Law," *Tulane Law Review* 61 (1986): 235.

4. See George Priest, "The Current Insurance Crisis and Modern Tort Law," *Yale Law Journal* 96 (1987): 1521, 1553–60. Priest explores the regressive distributional effect of expanded liability and third-party insurance in the tort system, which serve to force low-income consumers to subsidize high-income consumers who, when injured, collect relatively large amounts in place of their lost earnings.

5. See *Prosser & Keeton on Torts*, 5th ed. (St. Paul, Minn.: West Publishing, 1984), 997–1002; and William Bishop, "Economic Loss in Tort," *Oxford Journal of Legal Studies* 2 (1982): 1.

6. *Union Oil v. Oppen*, 501 F.2d 588 (9th Cir. 1974).

7. See note 3 above.

8. *Prosser & Keeton on Torts*, 646–50. See also A. Mitchell Polinsky, "Resolving Nuisance Disputes: The Simple Economics of Injunctive and Damage Remedies," *Stanford Law Review* 32 (1980): 1075.

9. See Guido Calabresi and A. Douglas Melamed, "Property Rules, Liability Rules, and Inalienability: One View of the Cathedral," *Harvard Law Review* 85 (1972): 1089, 1115–24.

10. For some discussion of the free rider and holdout problem when there is one tortfeasor and many victims, see ibid., 1106–7, 1115–24.

PART IV

THE TAKINGS ISSUE

8

COMPENSATION AND GOVERNMENT TAKINGS OF PRIVATE PROPERTY

STEPHEN R. MUNZER

I present here an account of when compensation is due for government takings of private property. The main idea is that a pluralist theory of property rights yields the soundest approach to takings and compensation. However, I provide few legal details and I only outline, rather than justify, a trio of underlying principles.

The structure of this chapter is as follows. Section 1 explains the problem. Section 2 outlines a pluralist theory that will be used to solve it. The theory contains principles of utility and efficiency, justice and equality, and desert based on labor. Section 3 articulates some fundamental background judgments about government action and private property. Section 4 then applies the principle of utility and efficiency, in light of these background judgments, to the moral and political problem of takings. Section 5 expands this interim solution by bringing in the principles of justice and equality and of desert based on labor. Finally, Section 6 summarizes the analysis.

The topic of this volume is compensatory justice, and some words on the relation of this chapter to that topic are in order. I deal mainly with what some lawyer-economists call compensation ex post rather than compensation ex ante. If someone buys a lottery ticket and fails to win the lottery, he loses the price of the ticket. Yet, according to Richard A. Posner, he is compensated for the loss ex ante by the prospect of a large gain because he participates voluntarily in the lottery.[1] In contrast, if the government demolishes a person's house and does not pay for it, the homeowner loses its value. Almost always the government should be required to pay for it; payment is compensation ex post, for the owner neither explicitly nor tacitly agreed to its demolition.[2]

Does *justice* require compensation? It depends on the meaning of "justice." When I speak of the principle of justice and equality, I do not suppose that "justice" in this sense is the sole determinant of whether compensation is due. For the principle of utility and efficiency and the principle of desert based on labor also bear on compensation. Suppose that, in a particular case, these two principles override the principle of justice and equality and decree that no compensation be paid. Does this mean that the property owner is being treated *un*justly? It does if "justice" retains the sense that it has in the principle of justice and equality. But it is possible to use "justice" in a broader, all-things-considered sense, and in that sense no injustice has been done. To prevent ambiguity, I shall use "justice" in the first way. Justice in that sense is not the only factor in deciding whether to compensate.

Put broadly, I address whether, all things considered, the government should pay for takings of private property. The resolution of this issue can involve justice. Any payment that is required usually will be compensation ex post. Indeed, receipt of compensation ex ante—as may occur, for example, in some instances of zoning or mining regulation[3]—is a reason for making no further payment. I offer no systematic treatment of the relation of compensation to deterrence, distribution, or redistribution.

1. THE PROBLEM

One can understand *property* in two main ways. A popular conception views property as things, particularly tangible things such as land, houses, automobiles, tools, and factories. A more sophisticated conception sees property as relations among persons with respect to things, particularly legal relations involving rights, duties, powers, and immunities. Both are intelligible ways of thinking about property, though the sophisticated conception is more useful for most legal and philosophical purposes. I shall use the word *property* in both ways; the context will reveal how it is used in any given occurrence. If the holders of property are the state or city, we have *public property*. If the holders are identifiable entities distinguishable from some larger group, there is *private property*. The most common example of the latter is individual private property, where a person is the owner, in severalty, as lawyers say. Other sorts of private property exist when the owners are persons considered together, such as partnerships and cotenancies, or are artificial entities that represent the interests of persons, such as corporations.

Government takings of private property pose at least two problems. One is legal. How should the law deal with situations in which government adversely affects private holdings? In many countries, this is a problem mainly of constitutional law rather than statutory or common law. In the United States, it centers on the command of the Fifth Amendment, known as the takings clause, that "nor shall private property by taken for public use, without just compensation."[4] The other problem has to do with moral and political theory: How should a society deal with situations in which government adversely affects private holdings? A *taking*, in this context, is thus an adverse effect on private property caused by government action. To distinguish the two problems is important because the adoption of constitutional and other institutionalized legal norms can affect the applicability of any abstract solution offered by moral and political theory. To understand that the moral and political problem is more fundamental is also important because an answer to it should guide an answer, and if necessary correct an existing answer, to the legal problem.

I deal here only with the moral and political problem of takings. In addition, I place to one side a pair of issues that is at least adjacent to the problems of takings. One concerns government action that affects persons' freedom over their bodies.

Examples include laws requiring military service or restricting abortion. Some may find it bizarre that anyone would even imagine that such laws take private property. But if persons have property rights in their bodies, then government action adversely affecting these rights might be a taking. If there were a taking, then the government might have to pay compensation or even abandon its action. Space does not allow pursuit of these controversial issues. I shall deal only with government action that adversely affects property rights that people have in external things.

The other adjacent issue involves taxation. Some may find it astonishing that anyone would maintain that to tax is to take. Yet many libertarians contend that taxation is morally and politically legitimate to support only minimal functions of the state such as police protection and national defense. Other taxation unjustifiably takes private holdings without compensation. Indeed, those liberterians who assimilate property rights in external things to property rights in the body might say that unjustifiable taxation is not only a taking but also a kind of forced labor or slavery.

To clarify the difference between takings and taxings, it will help to distinguish between unfixed and fixed distributions of property. A distribution is unfixed if it is vulnerable to a legitimate tax on income or wealth, and is fixed if it is not so vulnerable. Assume, by way of illustration, that a society has legitimate taxes on income and decedents' estates. Then unadjusted gross earnings prior to withholding are unfixed; they become fixed once income tax is paid. Again, holdings fixed in an owner become unfixed on his or her death until estate tax is paid. The point of the distinction is this: the moral, political, and legal problems of takings arise only insofar as a distribution is fixed because there is no "private property" in a full sense to be taken except insofar as legitimate income and wealth taxes have been paid. The standard background for takings, then, presupposes that legitimate taxation is no longer in the picture.

The distinction between fixed and unfixed distributions suggests that legitimate taxings are not takings, but it does not resolve any substantive or every conceptual issue, for three reasons at least. First, the distinction does not determine which taxes, if any, are legitimate. Though a theory of property has implications for taxation, it is hardly a full-blown theory of taxation. The distinction functions as a set-aside rather than a dodge. Second, in some instances taxes on income and wealth may amount to a taking. Examples are a gross receipts tax set so high that it destroys a business or a property tax on Indian real estate that was exempted by treaty from land taxes.[5] It may be difficult to say whether these taxes are illegitimate, or, though legitimate, are takings. Anyway, there is not always a clear line between taxes and takings. Third, if one thinks that a legitimate tax can have a redistributive purpose, then one might allow that a taking could also have such a purpose. In fact, most takings that occur in the United States lack any clear redistributive purpose. And even if a taking were intended to redistribute, it would not follow that it would *be* a tax. But if redistribution is sometimes legitimate, and if takings can redistribute, then one cannot rule out certain takings simply on the ground that they aim to redistribute income or wealth. Contextual factors determine whether taxation is a less intrusive, more efficient, or morally better means of redistribution than takings. So even if as a general matter taxes on income and wealth are preferred means, this will not always be so. In a country with grossly unjust and disproportionate land holdings, land reform measures classifiable as takings may be in order,[6] and no moral or political justification may exist for providing full, or perhaps any, compensation.

I am, then, concerned with government action that adversely affects private property rights[7] in external things, prescinded from issues of taxation. Sometimes the government may acknowledge such impact, as when it condemns private land by eminent domain to build a school. At other times it may dispute the impact or at least any duty to compensate, as when it conserves wetlands or preserves architectural landmarks.

2. OUTLINE OF A THEORY

A theory of property rights sheds much light on the moral and political problem of takings. For reasons that I give elsewhere,[8] the most satisfactory theory of property is a pluralist theory that consists of three main principles and an account of how those principles are related. The theory is *pluralist* in the sense that it contains several principles that are irreducible and sometimes conflict; when conflicts occur, priority rules can resolve some, but not all, conflicts.[9] The principles are a principle of utility and efficiency, a principle of justice and equality, and a principle of desert based on labor. While these principles may not be the only principles that make up a satisfactory moral, political, and legal theory of property, they are by far the most important. The proposed theory justifies some private and some public property. When the principles are fully specified, and when sufficient empirical evidence is gathered about the situations in which one is to apply them, the theory illuminates many practical problems.

A satisfactory theory of property should, in the first place, include some principle that recognizes the moral import of actions that affect persons' happiness, welfare, preference-satisfaction, or the like. Suppose that, to have a candidate for analysis, one selects preferences. Then such a principle would rest on a conception of the equal moral worth of persons, namely that, assuming equal strength, the preferences of each person count equally with the preferences of others. This formulation helps to clarify some relations between *utility* and *efficiency*. Both of these words, as used here, involve the satisfaction of the preferences of individuals, but only *utility* assumes that one can make interpersonal comparisons of preference-satisfaction.

The combined principle of utility and efficiency is as follows: property rights should be allocated so as (1) to maximize utility regarding the use, possession, transfer, etc. of things and (2) to maximize efficiency regarding the use, possession, transfer, etc. of things. In this principle, the first clause has priority over the second in the following sense: if it is possible to rank alternatives in terms of both utility and efficiency, then one should use the ranking supplied by utility. If, however, it is possible to rank alternatives in terms of either utility or efficiency but not both, then one should use whichever ranking is available. This amalgamated principle is possible because utility and efficiency have in common the concept of individual preference-satisfaction. The principle is not redundant because utility, unlike efficiency, presupposes that interpersonal comparisons of preference-satisfaction are possible. As a result, utility supplies both ordinal and interpersonally comparable rankings of alternatives, whereas efficiency supplies only ordinal rankings.

A satisfactory theory should, moreover, include some principle that recognizes the rights of persons. Such a principle would also rest on a conception of the equal moral worth of persons. The conception would, however, differ from the utilitarian conception of equal worth as equal counting, for the latter is compatible with sacrificing the individual utility of some to promote overall utility. Any such sacrifice ignores or undervalues the separateness of persons, that is, the idea that persons have rights not to have certain of their interests traded for overall utility.

One can formulate the principle of justice and equality in this way: unequal property holdings are justifiable if (1) everyone has a minimum amount of property and (2) the inequalities do not undermine a fully human life in society. It recognizes, where feasible, rights to minimal property and to a fully human life. This principle is a standard of justice in that it regulates morally how benefits and burdens are to be shared among persons. Its minimum involves the things needed by almost everyone for a decent life. The principle is also a standard of equality in that it requires showing, in the event that persons have different property holdings, why the difference is morally and politically acceptable. In this principle, the first clause is concerned with the provision of a minimum and the second with the narrowing of inequalities once a minimum is satisfied.

Finally, a satisfactory theory should include some principle of desert or entitlement. This principle rests on a conception of persons as agents who, by their actions in the world, are responsible for changes in it and in consequence deserve or are entitled to something. Whereas the first two principles emphasize, in different ways, the equal worth of persons, this final principle attends to differences in merit.

A labor theory of property is the obvious source of such a principle, but at present no agreement exists on how the principle should be formulated. I argue that a qualified desert version is the best candidate. The labor-desert principle maintains that a person's work gives a qualified justification for private property rights. This justification of property rights for the laborer is qualified by the rights of others, limitations on the process of acquisition, post-acquisition changes in situation, restrictions on transfer, general scarcity, and the nature of work as a social activity. The principle sums up how labor and desert, with their traditional emphasis on the individual, can be translated into a modern social context.

My view of property rights locates their justification in a pluralist scheme that knits together utilitarian considerations, considerations of justice of a roughly Kantian or Rawlsian kind, and considerations of desert of a thoroughly un-Rawlsian kind. These considerations are independent and irreducible.

The pluralism of this theory will be unsatisfying to those who desire theories that rest on a single principle or at least one supreme principle. And some philosophers may see in the trio of principles only the academic lawyer's penchant for ransacking every available cupboard for a multicourse banquet of arguments, with little thought given to the integrity of the meal.

Yet the soundest theory of property is indeed pluralist in the sense explained. It is in fact a defect to press everything into a single mold. In speculating about property, many theorists attempt to reduce too much to a single perspective. Locke appeals to labor; Bentham rests his case on utility; Marx protests the evils of alienation. Each thinker, through the intensity of his partial vision, contributes much to thinking about property, but at the same time obscures the validity of other perspectives. My theory, in contrast, accommodates competing points of view. And, more successfully than other pluralist accounts, it combines these perspectives, not on an ad hoc basis or as a tedious compromise, but on a principled basis into a coherent framework. Indeed, only a pluralist theory appears competent to grapple with our considered judgments about property and the complexity and uncertainty of moral and political life.

3. BACKGROUND JUDGMENTS

These three principles—of utility and efficiency, of justice and equality, and of desert based on labor—form what will be called the basic theory of property.[10] If one accepts the basic theory, one should try to build a moral and political theory of takings on it.[11] One need not claim that it would be impossible to construct a portion of a theory of takings without the basic theory. Some legal scholars have in fact done much useful work on takings while attempting to remain uncommitted on the philosophical theory of property. The attempt may spring in part from doubts that there are suitable underpinnings. But since the basic theory provides these philosophical underpinnings, it would be a poor strategy to theorize about takings while remaining silent, or explicitly trying to keep options open, on the soundest general theory of property. Such a strategy would yield an account of takings that is, at best, incomplete.

With the basic theory in hand, one must first make some fundamental background judgments about government power and private property. The judgments rest on the finitude of government resources and the desirability of both some private property and some government action. Since, under the principle of utility and efficiency, some government projects advance preference-satisfaction, the government should at least be able to purchase private property on the open market to pursue those projects. Often market transactions are cheaper than forced transactions, that is, the use of eminent domain. In fact, about 80 percent of federal land acquisitions in the United States use the market.[12] But should the government have any power of eminent domain? Some will find tempting the suggestion that, since private land developers often assemble large parcels by using agents, options, and straw transactions, the government can do the same. The temptation should be resisted. As Thomas W. Merrill convincingly argues,[13] this suggestion is overly broad. Market mechanisms do not always yield optimal land assembly when very large tracts are needed or when only one or a few sites will do. Highways, wilderness areas, and urban renewal are cases in point. Furthermore, acquiring land through the market requires secrecy to prevent holdouts and strategic bargaining, and in an open society governments are less good than private developers at keeping secrets. The first background judgment, then, is that a power of eminent domain, carefully employed, is justified. This judgment holds even if one uses only the principle of utility and efficiency. It is even more secure if one recalls that the labor-desert principle and the principle of justice and equality may favor some government projects that utility and efficiency alone do not.

Next, one should reject two extreme positions on takings and compensation. On the one hand, it is implausible to hold that the government should *never compensate*. For takings, as defined in section 1, include government acquisition of private titles to land. A rule offering no compensation would undermine the stability of private holdings. It would thus conflict with the fact that some private property is justifiable under the basic theory. Indeed, from the standpoint of efficiency and utility alone, never to compensate is bound to be suboptimal, since at least sometimes the preference-dissatisfaction experienced by those whose land is condemned and by those who occupy similar positions will outweigh the gains from the government project.

On the other hand, it is implausible to maintain that the government should *always compensate*. Takings, as defined in section 1, include all adverse effects on private property caused by government action. Often the action takes such undramatic forms as closing a street for a week to make road repairs or taking several hours to make a safety or health inspection, which can cause minor losses in revenue to affected businesses. So, even from the perspective of utility and efficiency alone, to compensate in every case would be suboptimal. Of course, if the government action is Kaldor-Hicks efficient,[14] then gainers theoretically could compensate losers, and if it is not, then one can question the action. But Kaldor-Hicks efficiency does not require that gainers compensate losers, and indeed one point of this criterion of efficiency is that the transaction costs of compensation may be too high to make it worthwhile. More detailed arguments are required to establish conclusively that these two extreme positions are misguided. Still, the foregoing arguments strongly support the second background judgment, namely, the cautious conclusion that the government should *sometimes compensate*. One can now enlist the basic theory to show when it should do so.

4. UTILITY, EFFICIENCY, AND TAKINGS

Since it could be unwieldy to develop simultaneously all three principles as they relate to takings, one might elaborate first the component of utility and efficiency and see later what differences desert based on labor and justice and equality make. Fortunately, for the first stage of the inquiry, one has an excellent guide, a utilitarian approach offered by Frank I. Michelman.[15]

The basic utilitarian strategy is to maximize net gains and minimize net losses. To pursue this strategy, Michelman defines three special terms.[16] *Demoralization costs (D)* are the disutilities to uncompensated losers and their sympathizers and the lost future production from impaired incentives or social unrest that would arise if no compensation were paid. *Settlement costs (S)* are the costs, chiefly the administrative costs of operating a compensation program, that must be borne to avoid demoralization. *Efficiency gains (E)* are the excess of the gains produced by a government action over the losses inflicted by it, not including *D* or *S*. Michelman's term *efficiency gains* is somewhat misleading because the value of *E* involves interpersonal comparisons of gains and losses; *utility gains* would be more accurate. The relative magnitude of these three quantities can be determined empirically in any given situation.

Any time government action is proposed, it is vital to assess the costs and benefits of the action itself and the costs and benefits of paying compensation to demoralized losers. This assessment yields conclusions on two issues of public policy. First, if the costs of demoralization and of settlement both exceed the efficiency gains of government action, then the action is unjustifiable. It should not be undertaken at all because the efficiency gains of the measure will not be worth its costs. In other words, the proposed action should be rejected altogether if $D>S>E$ or $S>D>E$. Utility sets a limit to the defensible use of the power of eminent domain.[17] Second, if the government action is justifiable, that is, if the efficiency gains exceed the costs of either demoralization or settlement, then the utilitarian approach is to pay the lower of these two costs. Hence, the government should compensate if demoralization costs exceed settlement costs, that is, if $E>D>S$ or $D>E>S$. On the other hand, the government should not compensate if settlement costs exceed demoralization costs. It is not worthwhile to compensate if the costs of administering payment are higher than the demoralization to be avoided, namely, where $E>S>D$ or $S>E>D$. Given strict inequalities and a way of valuing gains and losses, Michelman's utilitarian approach seems to solve, for each of the six possible orderings of gains and costs, the problem of whether a proposed government action is justifiable and, if so, whether compensation should be paid.

It is, however, possible to refine and improve on this analysis. Michelman in effect defines S as the costs that must be borne to reduce D to zero. Given this definition, government action will be unjustifiable if both $D>E$ and $S>E$. However, it might still be the case that E would exceed the sum of the costs of allowing some demoralization to result by the use of a less expensive settlement program. Call the revised values D' and S' respectively. Government action will then be improper just in case $D>E$ and $S>E$ *and* there is no minimal sum of D' and S' such that $E> (D'+S')$. Hence Michelman's first conclusion, that the proposed action should be rejected where $D>S>E$ or $S>D>E$, is overly simple. It should be accepted nonetheless if $E>(D'+S')$. This observation has an effect on whether to compensate, and, if so, how much to compensate, when the government action is justifiable. Once again, demoralization and settlement may be related in such a way that $(D'+S')$ is lower than D taken alone or S taken alone. If this is the case, it makes sense to compensate by just that value of D' such that the sum of D' and S' is as low as possible. This is another way of saying that partial compensation is an eligible solution under the principle of utility and efficiency. In fact, it would appear to be the standard solution except where both $(D'+S')>D$ and $(D'+S')>S$.

The reality is more complicated than the appearance because much depends on how one elaborates the utility component of this principle. If one adopts an act-utilitarian strategy that even bars use of "rules of thumb," then partial compensation will indeed be the standard solution. Yet if one adopts a strategy derived from rule-utilitarianism, or from a version of act-utilitarianism that uses "rules of thumb,"[18] such as the rule that promises should be kept, then partial compensation will be an eligible, but not the standard, solution. In these last two cases, one must be able to state and apply a rule that promotes utility. Such a rule would have to specify actions, programs, and situations in which partial compensation maximizes net gains. To frame such a rule does not seem impossible. But it does not promise to be easy. One should regard partial compensation as only an eligible solution.

Another refinement clarifies the variables in Michelman's calculus. Some of his definitions are unclear or unduly narrow. The labeling, if not the definition, of *E* should be changed. Because *E* contemplates interpersonal comparisons of utility, and because these comparisons may not always be possible, it would be better to speak of *utility/efficiency gains (U/E)*. For *D* one substitutes *noncompensation costs (N)*, which are all costs incurred if no compensation is given. *N* includes *D*. But the new term frees the analysis from the unduly psychological overtones of the word "demoralization." Also, it includes all costs stemming from risk aversion, even if they are not part of *D*. For *S* one substitutes *compensation costs (C)*, which are all costs that are paid if full compensation is given. Full compensation is in turn defined as the amount needed to reduce *N* to zero. *C* includes the various administrative costs mentioned by Michelman. But the new term also includes costs that one does not usually consider administrative. Here are three examples: If the availability of full compensation induces persons to invest in risky property more than they would do otherwise, then the overinvestment retards the efficient allocation of resources *(incentive effect costs)*. Again, if the availability of full compensation induces persons to affect the probability or magnitude of an event that triggers compensation, as by lobbying or bribery, then their actions retard efficiency *(moral hazard costs)*. Yet again, if raising the revenue for full compensation causes economic distortion or evasion, then such effects retard efficiency *(revenue costs)*. Given strict inequalities and a way of valuing gains and costs, the six possible orderings of gains and costs described earlier still hold, substituting *U/E* for *E*, *N* for *D*, and *C* for *S* throughout. Similarly, one can construct revised values, called N' and C', which affect the justifiability of government action and the matter of partial compensation in the ways described above.

One may now introduce three further refinements that stem from the principle of utility and efficiency as elaborated elsewhere.[19] The first refinement observes that to maximize utility, in this context, is to maximize the satisfaction of preferences, especially those preferences that involve rational and institutionally legitimate expectations concerning material things.[20] One should not give equal weight to all expectations of equal strength or intensity in assessing utility/efficiency gains and costs of compensation or noncompensation. Instead, one should favor expectations that are part of a web of concordant expectations supported by social and legal institutions. More precisely, one should insist that, as a general matter, only expectations that are both rational and institutionally legitimate present a strong structural claim for protection. This insistence will reduce costs associated with incentive effects, moral hazard, and raising revenue for compensation. Hence, in determining values for U/E, N, C, and $(N' + C')$, one should look beyond the expectations held by an individual person to whether the expectations satisfy the criteria for rationality and institutional legitimacy.

Consider contrasting hypothetical illustrations that involve expectations and rezoning. Assume that the basic theory justifies government power to zone and, because land use needs can change, to change existing zoning classifications. In one community, unimproved land was rezoned from commercial to single-family residential. The owner claimed that the rezoning destroyed his expectations of a large profit from building a shopping center. However, he had not engaged an architect or contractor or applied for a building permit. In this case, if the zoning authority has done its work well, the new classification is sound. The utility/efficiency gains favor the rezoning. No compensation, or at least little, is in order. Noncompensation costs are apt to be low where an owner has taken no concrete steps to develop his property. If the government had to compensate in relatively similar situations, it would make sensible use of the power to rezone expensive and hence would retard utility. Such considerations should be built into legal or social rules on zoning. The owner of the rezoned property has, then, no rational and legitimate expectations that justify compensation.

Suppose, though, that in a similar community an owner claimed that rezoning from commercial to single-family residential destroyed her expectations of a large profit from a shopping center. In this case, she had engaged an architect two years earlier, obtained a building permit a year ago, and now her contractor has the shopping center half completed. Here one might well wonder if conditions have changed so radically as to make the rezoning wise. If they have not, the rezoning runs counter to utility and should be abandoned. But suppose that conditions are radically different and that utility/efficiency gains favor the rezoning. Then full compensation, or something close to it, is required. Noncompensation costs are likely to be high when the owner has taken several concrete steps over a two-year period to develop the property. The costs stem not merely from the keen disappointment and financial loss to the owner. They derive as well from the fact that, if no compensation is paid, similarly situated property owners will not develop their land in ways that would be useful (high costs from risk aversion). Moreover, if the government does not have to compensate, it may overuse the power to take and may not take into account the full consequences of its action (*fiscal illusion*). These deterrent considerations should be part of the legal and social order. Thus in this case the owner of the rezoned property does have rational and legitimate expectations that make compensation desirable.

The second refinement is that one should stress that takings policy must enlist the rational alteration of preferences, and hence must look to the long run. From the standpoint of utility, one should move to the set of preferences and expectations that it is possible to satisfy and that, if satisfied, will yield the most satisfaction. This thought, applied to takings, means that the government should adjust its practice of regulation and compensation to accommodate new conditions and to inhibit the entrenchment of preferences and expectations whose satisfaction would not maximize utility. In economic terms, the adjustment pays special attention to incentive effect costs over time. It seeks to restructure incentives.

Consider the introduction of zoning in the early decades of this century.[21] It may well have been the case that owners of newly zoned land expected compensation. To have compensated might have best promoted utility in the short run. But cities were becoming more crowded. Conflicting land uses were creating problems. So it made sense, in the long run, not to compensate certain owners of newly zoned land. Had their expectations of compensation been upheld, it would have been too expensive for most cities to do as much zoning as was desirable. It is true that cities could have borrowed and amortized the loans needed to compensate; in fact, cities sometimes issue bonds for one-shot projects such as sewers. Yet, in the case of initial zoning, this course of action would have been expensive because it would only have spread over time the costs of compensating for one instance of zoning, and might not have provided the flexibility necessary to rezone in the face of future changes in circumstances. To have postponed a change, for example, by saying that twenty years hence all loss in value from new zoning would go uncompensated, would have been unsatisfactory. That would probably have been too late. And postponement would have fostered the undesirable expectation that the government would regulate land use only when those favored by the existing system were not disturbed. Hence, a policy of uncompensated initial zonings for a certain range of situations, over time, altered what count as rational and legitimate expectations about land use regulation.[22]

The third refinement is that one should insist, to the consternation of some critics of utilitarianism, that room exists for both property *interests* and property *rights*. A *property interest* is an entitlement to property that is just as powerful in given circumstances as can be justified on grounds of utility and efficiency alone. A *property right* is a property entitlement that has some threshold capacity to withstand competing claims of utility and efficiency. The phrase "in given circumstances" signals that one is invoking a strategy derived from rule-utilitarianism or from a version of act-utilitarianism that allows rules of thumb.

This distinction between property interests and property rights applies to takings as follows. An anti-utilitarian may object that one can, in the utility component of the theory, recognize only property interests. One cannot support morally the enforcement of property rights against the government when, in given circumstances, it would advance utility not to enforce them. The concept of a right includes the power to trump some competing considerations of utility and efficiency. Here one should reply that sometimes a property interest falls under a rule that affects the calculation of utility. If one views the interest in the given circumstances only, as an extreme act-utilitarian would, no property right exists. But if one views it not merely in the actual circumstances given but as falling under some rule undergirded by utility, then a property right, as defined above, might well exist.

With these three refinements in hand, one can summarize the utility and efficiency component of the moral and political theory of takings in this way. First, make sure that the government action creates utility/efficiency gains that exceed the costs of either compensation, noncompensation, or some minimal sum of these costs. If it does not, then reject the action. If it does, approve the action and pay the lower of the two costs. In ascertaining these costs, pay special attention to incentive effects, moral hazard, revenue costs, fiscal illusion, rational and legitimate expectations, long-range rational alteration of preferences, and the desirability of some property rights as distinct from property interests. The impact of this theory cannot be determined without empirical information about the factors influencing the costs just listed. But it seems almost certain that, despite gains that are Kaldor-Hicks efficient, the costs of compensation sometimes will be high enough to rule out full compensation. It also seems likely that sometimes utility will favor no compensation for government actions that adversely affect private property.

A final note: one should be cautious, but not hidebound, about substituting private insurance for government compensation. Someone might argue that if persons are risk averse, if there is full information and markets are perfectly competitive, and if the cost of an insurance policy equals its expected value (actuarially fair insurance), then people will want to insure fully against the risk of government action adversely affecting their property. Even if there are departures from full information, perfect competition, and actuarially fair premiums, many people will want to buy some insurance, provided that the departures are not too great. If one assumes also that private markets are more efficient than government intervention, private insurance is better than government compensation.

One should neither flatly reject nor wholeheartedly endorse this argument. One possibility is that insurance companies have overlooked a new form of business. If they can do a better job than government compensation, delight is in order. At least this is so for the utility component of the theory; one should be skeptical that the private market can do better once nonutility components are introduced.

Another possibility, however, is that insurance companies have overlooked nothing. In fact, "takings" insurance is virtually unavailable in the United States. Although some writers have professed to know why this is so,[23] their explanations are not wholly convincing. Moral hazard is an unsatisfactory explanation. For insurance companies could use deductibles or coinsurance, exclude recovery in certain cases, or lower premiums for actions that reduce moral hazard, as with insurance for homes, automobiles, and medical care. Also unsatisfactory is the explanation that the practice of government compensation antedated private insurance and made it otiose. Many adverse effects of government action still go uncompensated. And antedating has not foreclosed private suppliers in other areas; the postal service has existed for centuries, yet companies like United Parcel Service and Federal Express do well. A more helpful, but still not wholly satisfactory explanation appeals to an asymmetry of information—that would-be insureds have a better idea of the risks than would-be insurers (*adverse selection*). This explanation helps, because in some situations would-be insureds actually may have better information than would-be insurers. Interestingly, there is some private and some government-sponsored insurance against expropriation for United States investors in foreign countries;[24] in this situation, insurers may have as good information as insureds. But the explanation is not wholly satisfactory. For even if there were an informational asymmetry, one needs more evidence and analysis to show that it is sufficiently great to preclude altogether a market for "takings" insurance. Also, the government could negate the asymmetry by requiring everyone to insure (compare mandatory automobile insurance). In sum, the argument is unconvincing that market failure explains the absence of private insurance against takings, or that government insurance would not be a possible substitute.

5. The Impact of Labor-Desert and Justice and Equality

At this point, one is at best halfway to a solution of the moral and political problem. One must now integrate the perspective of utility and efficiency on takings with the rest of the basic theory of property. That theory also includes a principle of desert based on labor and a principle of justice and equality. To apply the remaining principles, one should first ascertain whether the society to which the moral and political theory of takings will apply conforms, in its property arrangements, to the basic theory. Obviously, conformity is a matter of degree, and perfect conformity is quite unlikely. To simplify matters, assume that there are just two possibilities. Either the society conforms very well *(full conformity)*, or it fails to conform in a number of major respects *(partial conformity)*. The difference between full and partial conformity affects, first, the justification for exercising the power of eminent domain, and, second, the compensation offered, if any, to adversely affected property owners. The simplifying assumption elides no issue of principle. But it makes the following analysis less complicated than it would be otherwise.

Suppose that a society fully conforms to the basic theory. In that case, justification of the proposed government action turns solely on considerations of utility and efficiency. *Ex hypothesi* no corrective or backward-looking adjustment is needed. So the use of eminent domain rests on the forward-looking ground that reallocating resources will promote utility and efficiency. Only the principle of utility and efficiency is relevant. Hence, the utility/efficiency gains of the proposed action must exceed at least one of the following: the noncompensation costs, the compensation costs, or the minimal sum of such costs under a revised compensation program.

To handle issues of compensation under full conformity, one must ascertain the ground of the property entitlements adversely affected by the government action, and distinguish between degenerate and nondegenerate cases. *Degenerate cases* are those in which the entitlements rest on utility alone; on all three principles, but desert based on labor and the principle of justice and equality offset each other; or on a combination such that utility offsets any competing principles with force to spare. Identification of these cases is apt to be controversial. It may be hard to show, as in the first case, that only utility is in play. It may be harder to do the moral mathematics contemplated by the last two cases. Given these difficulties, identification will most likely have to proceed by social or legal rules classifying different situations. But if one can identify such cases, then the decision whether to compensate and, if so, how much, will turn solely on the utility component of the moral and political theory of takings. These cases are degenerate because they involve no moves beyond those described in the previous section.

The *nondegenerate cases* arise when utility and efficiency do not exhaust the force of or limitations on property entitlements. Utility and efficiency need not, but ordinarily still will, be in play. But here the principle of desert based on labor and the principle of justice and equality support, or limit, entitlements in a way not reducible to considerations of utility and efficiency. If they do, then the case for compensation is, respectively, stronger or weaker. For example, imagine that the government appropriates the right to manufacture and distribute a new vaccine from a person who discovered it after years of solitary research. The principle of desert based on labor strengthens the case for full compensation to the discoverer. No suggestion is made, in this example or in others, that a single scale or gradient exists for being entitled to compensation. The claim is only that one can appreciate, in some less precise way, how considerations other than utility can strengthen or weaken the case for compensation.

One may now shift attention to cases involving only partial conformity to the basic theory. The initial move is to ascertain the purpose of the government action. Does it aim to promote utility by reallocating resources, or to correct some shortcoming in existing property arrangements, or some combination of the two? Some may assume that if the existing arrangements are deficient, then the government's purpose must be to correct them. But one should not assume this. Nor should one assume that the government must be deemed to have a corrective purpose. The reason is that takings may not be a good corrective means. As pointed out in section 1, taxation is ordinarily better than takings as a method of redistribution. Takings are ordinarily too haphazard or ill-tailored to correct systematically. There are exceptions, as will emerge. And there would be something wrong with a society if it failed to conform to the basic theory in major respects and never tried to correct the deficiencies. Prolonged failure to come to grips with the deficiencies might justify ascribing a corrective purpose. At all events, one should first ascertain purpose. One need adopt no particular view of discovering or ascribing purpose. One can select whichever view best suits the task.

Suppose that one finds that the government action aims only to promote utility by reallocating resources. Suppose further that no aggravating circumstances exist; the government has not, for example, been ignoring departures from the basic theory for a long time. In this situation the use of eminent domain, subject to a proviso, is justified exactly as before, namely, if the efficiency gains exceed the costs of compensation, noncompensation, or some minimal sum of the two. The proviso is that the government action must not exacerbate the shortcomings of the existing property arrangements. One can resolve the issue of compensation in parallel fashion. Whether compensation is offered and, if it is, how much, will proceed in accordance with the degenerate and nondegenerate possibilities discussed under the heading of full conformity. But there is a proviso: the compensation paid or withheld must not exacerbate existing deficiencies. One makes these choices because, since no correction is sought, the pertinent considerations are, with one exception, the same as in the case of full conformity. The exception is that neither the government action nor the compensatory practice may exacerbate current departures from the basic theory. In fact, even the exception has an exception. Should the utility/efficiency gains be sufficiently great, they can override the proviso. But this is not likely and is not merely a matter of balancing.

Suppose, however, that the government action aims to correct some shortcoming in existing property arrangements. Variables abound. The corrective purpose may be avowed or ascribed. The need for correction may stem from past wrongdoing or from a change in circumstances that caused a formerly acceptable property arrangement to become unacceptable under the basic theory. The ground for correction may be utility or not.

Though even a schematic discussion of all the possibilities would be lengthy, the following general points stand out. First, the government action must be a better corrective mechanism than taxation. Otherwise one should opt to tax and redistribute. Second, it matters whether the need for correction proceeds from past wrongdoing in connection with the property at issue. If it does, then, other things being equal, action becomes more urgent. If the government takes such action, then, other things being equal, the case for compensation, or at least full compensation, diminishes in the event that those whose property is adversely affected are themselves wrongdoers or profited from past wrongdoing. Third, if the ground for correction is utility, this will affect prior calculations of utility. The problems are apt to be especially knotty when nonutility considerations undergird or limit the property entitlements in question. The treatment of nondegenerate cases under full conformity indicates some of the problems. Fourth, if the ground for correction is not utility, a different problem can arise, namely, conflict among the three principles of the basic theory. For the nonutility ground sometimes can justify exercises of eminent domain even though the utility/efficiency gains fail to offset the costs. And it can sometimes justify more, less, or no compensation in cases where a different amount of compensation would advance utility.

An illustration that involves the labor-desert principle may bring closer to earth this unavoidably abstract discussion of corrective action under partial conformity. Imagine that a century ago a small group of industrialists owned most of the productive resources in heavy manufacturing. They paid employees an extremely low wage, market conditions gave employees no effective opportunity to work elsewhere, and industrialist profit margins were high. With only minor changes, these conditions have prevailed down to the present day. Descendants of the original industrialists hold sway over heavy manufacturing, through either closed corporations or control of sufficient shares in corporations that have gone public. Descendants of former employees work in the plants. Wages are higher but still low. Employees have little control over conditions in the workplace. As a result of these and other factors, productivity sags.

Accordingly, the government proposes a compulsory buyout of the manufacturing plants. Ownership is to be transferred first to the government and gradually over the next fifty years to present and future employees. The program is ultimately to be self-funding. Initial capital for the purchase comes from the government. The government investment is to be gradually retired from anticipated increased productivity deriving from better incentives for employees. Current shareholders will receive compensation, some of it deferred, that amounts to about ninety cents on the dollar for the market value of their holdings.[25]

One would have to add many details to this rather stylized illustration before it would be possible to judge the proposal with confidence, but here is how to go about it. One should first decide whether this is an appropriate exercise of eminent domain. Not only must one determine whether some tax program that leaves ownership of the plants undisturbed is superior to the government proposal. One must also decide whether the plan has a good chance of success. Yet one's criterion of success is not that the efficiency gains must exceed the minimal sum of compensation and noncompensation costs. One must recognize that utility is not the sole aim of the proposal. It has also a corrective aim based on a nonutility consideration. The government is in part trying to adjust for past violations of desert based on labor that were involved in the low wages and high profits over the last century.[26]

Suppose one concludes that these and additional facts justify eminent domain. One must move next to judge the compensatory aspects of the plan. On the one hand, the lack of full compensation should be troubling, because the precedent, if not firmly cabined, may destabilize expectations regarding other forms of productive property. On the other hand, full compensation would exacerbate problems of funding and leave past wrongdoing uncorrected. The assessment will turn significantly on how well the political and social repercussions of the program can be controlled. One could add further details in many different ways. It seems plausible that, on some set of further details, less than full compensation would be justifiable.

A pair of warnings may forestall some misguided objections to this integrated moral and political theory of takings. First, the theory is not a formula or a calculus. It is a set of distinctions, together with reasons for them, that enables someone who accepts the basic theory to think more systematically and effectively about takings. Second, the theory can be developed. One method of development is to conjoin it with an account of institutional competence. Some judgments about takings may be better made by legislatures and others by courts. Another method is to elaborate subordinate rules that comport with the theory of takings but are easier to apply directly than is the theory itself.

6. CONCLUSION

The moral and political problem of takings is: How should a society deal with situations in which government action adversely affects private holdings? An acceptable solution requires a normative theory of property. The most satisfactory theory currently available is pluralist in character. It contains a principle of utility and efficiency, a principle of justice and equality, and a principle of desert based on labor. Under this theory, and in light of some plausible background judgments, the government should sometimes compensate for takings. More fully, the principle of utility and efficiency requires that government action should not go forward at all if its efficiency/utility gains fail to exceed the costs of either compensation, or noncompensation, or some minimal sum of these costs. If the gains do exceed them, the government should compensate only if doing so is cheaper than not compensating. The results derived from this principle are, however, importantly qualified by the principle of justice and equality and the principle of desert based on labor.[27]

NOTES

1. See Richard A. Posner, *The Economics of Justice* (Cambridge: Harvard University Press, 1981), 94.

2. Out of an abundance of caution, I would suggest that the concept of compensation ex post is clearer than that of compensation ex ante. Nor all lawyer-economists or philosophers would agree that every voluntary assumption of risk, every discount in price, or every offsetting benefit is "compensation" ex ante.

3. See, for example, *Penn Central Transportation Co. v. New York City*, 438 U.S. 104, 138–41 (1978) (Rehnquist, J., dissenting), contrasting landmark regulation unfavorably with zoning; and *Plymouth Coal Co. v. Pennsylvania*, 232 U.S. 531 (1914) (mining regulation). One can see a rough correspondence between compensation ex ante and what Justice Holmes called "average reciprocity of advantage" in *Pennsylvania Coal Co. v. Mahon*, 260 U.S. 393, 415 (1922).

4. U.S. Constitution, amendment V.

5. On whether taxings can ever amount to takings, see *A. Magnano Co. v. Hamilton*, 292 U.S. 40 (1934); *Alaska Fish Salting & By-Products Co. v. Smith*, 255 U.S. 44 (1921); and *Swimming Turtle v. Board of County Commissioners of Miami County*, 441 F. Supp. 374 (N.D. Ind. 1977). See also *City of Pittsburgh v. Alco Parking Corp.*, 417 U.S. 369 (1974) (combination of taxing and direct competition by taxing authority).

6. For an interesting examination of this issue, along republican lines, see Gia L. Cincone, "Land Reform and Corporate Redistribution: The Republican Legacy," *Stanford Law Review* 39 (1987): 1229–57 esp. at pp. 1235–46.

7. I ignore the infrequent cases where one government unit seeks to take or regulate the property of another government unit. See, for example, *City of Temple Terrace v. Hillsborough Association for Retarded Citizens, Inc.*, 322 So.2d 571 (Fla. Dist. Ct. App. 1975), aff'd, 332 So.2d 610 (Fla. 1976) (zoning). When the United States government condemns the property of other government units, issues of federalism arise. The justifications for compensating public condemnees may differ to some extent from the justifications for compensating private

condemnees. See Michael H. Schill, "Intergovernmental Takings and Just Compensation: A Question of Federalism," *University of Pennsylvania Law Review* 137 (1989): 829–901.

8. See Stephen R. Munzer, *A Theory of Property* (Cambridge: Cambridge University Press, 1990).

9. This variety of pluralism, sometimes called *intuitionism,* is defended in Stephen R. Munzer, "Intuition and Security in Moral Philosophy," *Michigan Law Review* 82 (1984): 740–54; Christine Swanton, "The Rationality of Ethical Intuitionism," *Australasian Journal of Philosophy* 65 (1987): 172–81; and J. O. Urmson, "A Defense of Intuitionism," *Proceedings of the Aristotelian Society* 75 (1974–75): 111–19. See also Thomas Nagel, "The Fragmentation of Value," in his *Mortal Questions* (Cambridge: Cambridge University Press, 1979), 128–41.

10. Munzer, *A Theory of Property,* 317, defines the "basic theory of property" more broadly, but the definition in the text will do for present purposes.

11. Unlike this chapter, the final chapter of the book deals also with the legal problem of takings.

12. See Comptroller General, *Federal Land Acquisitions by Condemnation: Opportunities to Reduce Delays and Costs* (Washington, D.C.: General Accounting Office, 1980), 81.

13. Thomas W. Merrill, "The Economics of Public Use," *Cornell Law Review* 72 (1986): 61–116 at pp. 81–82.

14. On Kaldor-Hicks efficiency, see Nicholas Kaldor, "Welfare Propositions of Economics and Interpersonal Comparisons of Utility," *Economic Journal* 49 (1939): 549–52; and J. R. Hicks, "The Foundations of Welfare Economics," *Economic Journal* 49 (1939): 696–712.

15. Frank I. Michelman, "Property, Utility, and Fairness: Comments on the Ethical Foundations of 'Just Compensation' Law," *Harvard Law Review* 80 (1967): 1165–1258 at pp. 1214–18. Michelman's efforts to develop a fairness theory of takings (ibid., 1218–24) based on Rawls's theory of justice are unsuccessful, for the reasons given in Stephen R. Munzer, "A Theory of Retroactive Legislation," *Texas Law Review* 61 (1982): 425–80 at pp. 477–80, and will not be pursued further here.

16. Michelman, "Property, Utility, and Fairness," 1214.

17. It is only *a* limit. Even if the proposed action is justifiable, the government should use the market when doing so is cheaper than using eminent domain. For the view that, under one model, the government in effect generally chooses the cheaper alternative, see Merrill, "The Economics of Public Use," 101.

18. See, for example, J. J. C. Smart, "An Outline of a System of

Utilitarian Ethics," in J. J. C. Smart and Bernard Williams, *Utilitarianism: For and Against* (Cambridge: Cambridge University Press, 1973), 3–74 at pp. 42–57.

19. Munzer, *A Theory of Property*, chap. 8.

20. See Munzer, "A Theory of Retroactive Legislation," 427–39.

21. Here the lawyer will think of the famous case of *Village of Euclid v. Ambler Realty Co.*, 272 U.S. 365 (1926).

22. This argument in terms of expectations overlaps, but is not identical with the argument that, because of imperfections in the market, zoning sometimes promotes efficiency better than other courses of action. For insightful criticisms of zoning, see Robert C. Ellickson, "Alternatives to Zoning: Covenants, Nuisance Rules, and Fines as Land Use Controls," *University of Chicago Law Review* 40 (1973): 681–781.

23. See Lawrence Blume and Daniel L. Rubinfeld, "Compensation for Takings: An Economic Analysis," *California Law Review* 72 (1984): 569–628 at pp. 592–97 (moral hazard and adverse selection); William A. Fischel and Perry Shapiro, "Takings, Insurance, and Michelman: Comments on Economic Interpretations of 'Just Compensation' Law," *Journal of Legal Studies* 17 (1988): 269–93 at p. 286 (adverse selection); Louis Kaplow, "An Economic Analysis of Legal Transitions," *Harvard Law Review* 99 (1986): 509–617 at p. 539 n. 84 (government compensation antedating private insurance markets); and Schill, "Intergovernmental Takings and Just Compensation," 855–56 (adverse selection and moral hazard).

24. See, for example, Joseph P. Griffin, "Transfer of OPIC's Investment Insurance Programs to Private Insurers: Prospects and Proposals," *Law and Policy in International Business* 8 (1976): 631–56; and Vance R. Koven, "Expropriation and the 'Jurisprudence' of OPIC," *Harvard International Law Journal* 22 (1981): 269–327.

25. For general discussion from a republican perspective, see Cincone, "Land Reform and Corporate Redistribution," 1247–56.

26. The text assumes that it is possible to elaborate the notion of a "group" such that the original employees and their descendants are members of the same group over time and that the buyout program is corrective rather than merely redistributive. No attempt is made to justify this assumption here, but it will be important to do so eventually in light of Christopher W. Morris, "Existential Limits to the Rectification of Past Wrongs," *American Philosophical Quarterly* 21 (1984): 175–82.

27. For helpful criticisms and suggestions I wish to thank Jules Coleman, Kenneth L. Karst, Christopher W. Morris, James W. Nickel,

John Shepard Wiley, Jr., and Stephen C. Yeazell. Special thanks go
to Margaret Jane Radin and Carol M. Rose, who commented extem-
poraneously on a version of this chapter presented to the American
Society for Political and Legal Philosophy in New Orleans, January
1989.

9

PROPERTY AS WEALTH, PROPERTY AS PROPRIETY

CAROL M. ROSE

Stephen Munzer's interesting and provocative chapter speaks of a "taking" of property as anything that "adversely affects" one's property rights, and he considers a variety of compensation devices that might offset governmental takings "fully" or something less than fully. But the concept of "taking" property does not really make sense unless we have some idea of what one's property right includes in the first place: without that underlying understanding, we couldn't really tell what measures might affect the right adversely, and certainly we couldn't tell what would be "full" compensation for adverse effects, or anything less than "full" compensation.

This is not an abstract or difficult point. In fact, it is amply illustrated in a number of examples from well-known "takings" law, particularly in some of the defenses that governmental bodies make when someone charges that a given regulation "takes" private property. For example, one governmental defense is nuisance prevention: your property is not "taken," the argument goes, if the regulation in question merely prevents you from perpetrating a nuisance.[1] The idea is that your property right never included nuisance activity in the first place, and

223

hence you have had nothing "taken" through the regulation. A second example is the antimonopoly defense: your property is not "taken" if a regulation simply imposes some restraints on the returns from your monopoly enterprise, and limits you to a reasonable return on your investment.[2] The theory of this defense is that your property right never included a right to charge monopoly prices, giving you unreasonably high returns at the consumers' expense, and your property right is thus not impaired by the rate regulation.

There are more takings defenses, and I will come back to some of them later. The specific ways that these defenses are used, followed, or rejected is not what matters. What matters is that these defenses show that "takings" jurisprudence depends on some underlying understanding of what your property right entitles you to do, and what it does not. You can only claim compensation for adverse effects to something that is within your property right. One might start, then, with the question, what "takes" your property; but one quickly arrives at a more general question, namely, what does your property right include?

But then, to answer this second question, we have to ask a third and even larger one: what is it that we are trying to accomplish with a property regime? If we know the answer to this most general question about property, we can begin to see what we include in property, and what we leave out, and so what kinds of governmental actions we deem to "take" property.

Munzer argues that three principles give direction to a property regime, namely, (a) preference-satisfaction (that is, a combined version of efficiency and utility);[3] (b) justice/fairness; and (c) desert. He further argues that these principles are pluralistic, because one principle cannot be reduced to another. My own position differs from Munzer's quite substantially. I do not think that he sets out a pluralistic system at all, because I think all three of his principles can be rolled into the first: preference-satisfaction.

Munzer's tilt toward preference-satisfaction is not really unusual, because some version of preference satisfaction has generally dominated the American vision of property. But there is also another and much older vision of property in our tradition, and Munzer does not really discuss this vision at all. This second, traditional understanding is that property is aimed at securing to each person what is "proper" to him or her.

I shall begin with the dominant, preference-satisfying view, and will attempt to show that the principles that Munzer describes as pluralistic can all really be subsumed under the same cluster of moral and political ideas. I will then go on to the older but weaker vision of property as "propriety." My argument is that our pluralistic understandings of property derive not from any inevitable clash of Munzer's principles, which I think can all be understood in a way that is compatible with preference-satisfaction, but rather from the system that we actually live with. Our system is pluralistic because our dominant, preference-satisfying understanding of property is subject to constant, albeit often ill-articulated intrusions from the traditional and very different understanding of property as "propriety."

I. PROPERTY-AS-PREFERENCE-SATISFACTION

Munzer sets out three principles for a property regime: utility/efficiency, fairness, and desert. Both parts of utility/efficiency, he says, aim at preference-satisfaction, and on his own presentation, that rolled-together principle clearly outweighs the other two principles. Quite noticeably, he gives preference-satisfaction precedence in location, as well as in the length and sophistication of his discussion. Indeed the structure of his argument suggests that a property regime is aimed primarily at utility/efficiency—that is to say, some version of preference-satisfaction—even though this dominant principle is subject to the constraints of two other principles, namely fairness and desert.

I certainly agree with Munzer that preference-satisfaction can be seen as a goal of a property regime; indeed, most modern theorists focus on that goal. But I think that he is too cryptic about the means by which a property regime is thought to maximize preference-satisfaction. When we look more closely at those means, we notice that Munzer's other principles—that is, fairness on the one hand and desert on the other—are not independent constraints at all, but rather fit neatly into the overall version of property as an institution that maximizes the satisfaction of preferences.

A. Maximizing Preference-Satisfactions

Munzer does not tell us much about how the maximization of preferences comes about through a property regime. It sometimes seems as if he envisions a finite number of good things in the world, a kind of big bag of resources, and he writes as if the way to maximize preferences would be to divvy up the contents of the bag in a way that most people would like. To extrapolate from his examples of public and private property, this would presumably mean that we would have public ownership of streets and wilderness areas (since, as he says without much explanation, some government projects advance preference-satisfaction), and presumably we would have private ownership of most other things, like clothes and dishes; one also supposes that there would be some disagreements about whether other items should be public or private. He seems to think that once we solve the issues about which things we prefer to have in which hands, our property regime should attempt to maximize preferences by getting those things in the relevant hands, although we modify this scheme by applying the constraining considerations of the other two principles, fairness and deservingness.

This analysis loses sight of the classic view of the role that property plays in maximizing preference-satisfaction. On that view, a property regime isn't just supposed to divvy up the contents of the bag; it is supposed to make the bag *bigger* and put more things in it.

How does a property regime do that? Well, to get some idea, we should compare a property regime to a nonpropertized commons. Let's suppose some berry patch is an unowned commons. According to the classical view, the patch will be all right so long as there are a lot of berries and only a few berry-eaters.[4] But once the berry-eaters get numerous enough, they start competing, and they are likely to get into conflicts about who gets how many berries; and in the meantime, while everyone is grabbing and fighting over the berries, nobody cultivates new berry bushes, the whole patch is depleted, and everybody is worse off.[5]

But let's suppose we institute a property regime for the patch: What happens now? Well, first of all, people stop fighting over the berries. The property regime has allocated the patch, or parts of the patch, to one person or another, so that everyone knows who has what, and stops wasting resources on grabbing and fighting, or *rentseeking,* as this sort of activity is now fashionably designated.[6] Second, individual owners are now secure in their little corners of the berry patch, and this security encourages each to labor on his or her corner to make it more productive. Finally, since everyone knows who has what, the various owners can trade berries, or even berry patches, so that the one who values the berries or the berry patches the most winds up with them. How does that person show that she wants the berries the most? The clearest signal she can give is that she offers the most for them, that is, the most in spuds, or hats, or tools, or whatever else her labor and foresight has allowed her to accumulate.

So the upshot of all this is that a property regime maximizes preference-satisfaction not just by divvying up resources, but by making resources *more valuable.* The property regime creates a bigger bag, because in a property regime, (a) we aren't wasting time and energy on fighting; (b) we are busily investing that time and energy in our own resources, and thus making them more valuable, knowing that we will get the rewards; and (c) we can trade the products of our efforts; that is, we can make a smooth set of Pareto-superior moves, whereby everybody is better off just because we all get the things we want the most. In a property regime, then, we are better off because we enhance resources instead of dissipating them, and because we can make gains sheerly from trading things we have, for things we want even more.

By the way, there are more public roads and other public goods in a property regime, too. Some resources are most economically produced and managed on a large scale, and because of these scale economies, they are best allocated to joint control rather than to individuals. In a well-oiled property machine, these kinds of products will wind up as joint property of some sort—perhaps family property, or corporate property, or perhaps municipal or state or even national property. But we should note that this joint or public allocation also expands the total bag of goodies, because these kinds of resources are most productive in some kind of multiple ownership.

The need for larger-scale management, incidentally, is a standard reason for the power of eminent domain that Munzer considers, and this need provides a well-known example of a limitation on individual property rights. Your property does not include the right to extort a holdout price for property that is most productively managed by the public; hence you may have to sell your property to the public at fair market value, and you don't get compensated for any monopoly price you might otherwise have charged.[7]

So in short, Munzer's discussion perhaps unduly abbreviates the standard but powerful story about property as a preference-satisfying institution. According to that story, a property regime satisfies preferences not by divvying up a finite bag of resources, but rather by encouraging behavior that enhances resources' value, making the total bag a whole lot bigger and more diverse.

With that, I will turn to the second and third principles that Munzer locates in a property regime, namely fairness and desert, which he sees as pluralistic constraints on preference-satisfaction. My own view is that these principles do not necessarily imply anything pluralistic at all, in the sense that they are in some way incompatible with a preference-satisfying understanding of a property regime. On the contrary, they fit quite handily with a property regime whose purpose is seen as the satisfaction of preferences.

B. Justice or Fairness

Munzer treats the principle of justice, or fairness, as a tenet that requires a minimum set of holdings. But this understanding of justice or fairness is fairly easy to justify on preference-satisfaction grounds, if one supposes a diminishing marginal utility of wealth. Now, this is a controversial supposition, but it is at least reasonably plausible that an additional dollar would be worth more to a poor person than to a wealthy one. Some of the classic economic thinkers, like Alfred Marshall, thought so, and the idea may be implicit in our graduated income tax as well.[8]

Again, this view is not uncontroversial, but if we accept it at least hypothetically, then some wealth transfers from the rich to the poor will maximize the total amount of preference-satisfaction, since the poor get more satisfaction than the rich out of the same resources. On the other hand, there is a preference-satisfaction limitation on such transfers: we wouldn't want to take so much from the rich that they get discouraged about investing, because if they do get discouraged, then the total bag of goodies shrinks too much, that is, it shrinks more than is warranted by the incremental satisfactions of the poor.

We should note that this point ties in with the idea of "demoralization costs" that Munzer takes from Frank Michelman, and that Michelman took from Jeremy Bentham.[9] If rich people have too many of their earnings taken, they will get discouraged, and ultimately they will quit working. Why will they get discouraged and quit? Munzer makes some interesting elaborations on this argument, but the basic reason is that their expectations are violated—that is, their expectations of keeping the things that they invested in and worked on.

But note that it is the property *regime* that gives them those expectations in the first place,[10] and it does so for utilitarian reasons. We call certain things "property rights," and foster the expectation that owners can control and enjoy the things they have worked for, in order to encourage both rich and poor to invest the labor, time, energy, and effort that will make resources more valuable and the total bag bigger. As Munzer notes in his interesting and valuable discussion, compensation is one tool we use to try to reduce the demoralization attendant upon "takings," and thus compensation has a utilitarian function.

But as Frank Michelman saw, our fairness and utilitarian considerations lead in the same direction.[11] It would be easy enough to imagine ourselves living under a different set of expectations. For example, we might expect that anytime an individual acquired a significant amount of anything, he or she would have to give it all up.[12] If we lived under such a system, nobody would have her expectations violated when her things were confiscated, and the system would not be unfair or unjust in the sense of bait-and-switch, or pulling the rug out from under the citizenry.

Individuals in such a system wouldn't get demoralized about the confiscation of their investments. They just wouldn't invest effort and energy in the first place, which of course would mean that the system would be likely to produce a considerably smaller total bag of resources and goods. But, according to the classic property theory, that runs directly contrary to the result we are trying to achieve with a property regime. And so, we have what we call "fair" or "just" compensation for takings of property, in order that more investments will be made, and more aggregate preferences will wind up being satisfied.

In short, it is pretty easy to see that our concepts of justice or fairness are not necessarily constraints on a preference-maximization version of property, but are rather part of the *very same* moral and political universe. We could easily look at these justice or fairness considerations as part of an overall design: the property regime is supposed to encourage investment and enterprise, and ultimately to get more preferences satisfied by encouraging the behavior that creates a bigger bag of more valuable things.

C. Desert

The third principle in Munzer's trio, desert, is even easier to justify on preference-satisfaction grounds. The reward to labor is an obvious corollary to a property regime that tries to increase the bag of goodies by encouraging the investment of effort and time. We should note, for example, that it is not just *any* old labor that gets rewarded, for example, sweeping sand into the ocean. On the contrary, the labor that gets rewarded is the labor that produces goods or services that people *want*. And so, the reward to "deserving" labor also falls into line with preference-satisfaction. The deservingness that counts is the labor that results in producing what people want.

In short, it seems entirely possible to construct a version of property, and of "takings" of property, that includes all three principles in Munzer's trio. The principles of preference-satisfaction, fairness, and desert can easily be cast as a smooth and seamless whole—a whole that is entirely dominated by maximizing preference-satisfaction. In fact, I think Munzer's examples illustrate this, even though he uses them to show an irreducible pluralism among his three principles.

He uses the example of a vaccine whose distribution rights are taken from the hard-working discoverer. But when we compensate the discoverer, we do not depart in the slightest from utilitarian considerations. This is someone whose labor produces something highly desirable, and we certainly would not want to discourage such a person, or others who might follow his or her example; and so it is quite in order to accord the discoverer a measure of compensation to encourage such behavior. You can call it fairness, you can call it desert, you can call it encouragement of preference-satisfying behavior: they amount to the same thing.

As to the rather fanciful example of the century-old plant—enjoying at once an inexplicable monopoly grip on some product as well as on its own labor force—utilitarian principles would be exceedingly unlikely to suggest a monopoly payoff upon appropriation of such an entity. Why not? Because it does nothing for preference-satisfaction to encourage monopoly, except, perhaps, as a limited way to encourage innovators like our vaccine producer. Monopolists generally only restrict supply and charge higher prices, and thus they restrain rather than expand total preference satisfaction. And so we try not to reward them. Instead, we regulate their earnings to some rate that would seem "reasonable" to a nonmonopolist, so that monopolistic ventures do not seem particularly attractive. This kind of regulation is of course built into our standard takings law; [13] and once again, desert and preference-satisfaction do not diverge. Instead, they are part of the same strategy. The dominating partner in the strategy is preference-satisfaction; the conception of "desert," like the conception of "fairness," is tailored to encourage the behavior that maximizes that goal.

II. Property-As-Propriety

I have gone through the ways in which property, viewed as a vehicle for preference-satisfaction, subsumes a set of principles of fairness on the one hand and desert on the other. What I want to do now is to describe a completely different understanding of a property regime. It is an understanding based on a quite different conception of what property is good for. This understanding of property can also include principles of fairness and desert, but they come out quite differently from the ideas of fairness and desert that are incorporated in a preference-satisfying understanding of property.

What is the purpose of property under this other understanding? The purpose is to accord to each person or entity what is "proper" or "appropriate" to him or her. Indeed, this understanding of property historically made no strong distinction between "property" and "propriety," and one finds the terminology mixed up to a very considerable degree in historical texts.[14] And what is "proper" or appropriate, on this vision of property, is that which is needed to keep good order in the commonwealth or body politic.

A. Property, Propriety, and Governance

That "property" was the mainstay of "propriety" was a quite common understanding before the seventeenth and eighteenth centuries; and this understanding continued, albeit in abated form, even after the great revolutions at the end of the eighteenth century. One earlier example is in the work of Jean Bodin, a sixteenth-century French political theorist, who was commonly regarded as a monarchist and spokesman for the able French king Henry IV, and who was much quoted on the subject of sovereignty. Bodin, for all his monarchist proclivities, nevertheless thought that property was a fundamental restraint on monarchic power. We need to have property, he said, for the maintenance and rightful ordering of families; families in turn were necessary as the constituent parts of the commonwealth itself.[15]

This version of property does *not* envision property as a set of tradable and ultimately interchangeable goods; instead, its proponents thought that different kinds of property were associated with different kinds of roles. The family property that Bodin was talking about was almost certainly land, and not just any land, but the specific landholdings associated with and "proper" to a specific family. The law itself acknowledged the "properness" of landholdings to specific families, and included a variety of restraints on alienation by individual family members, in effect treating those individuals as trustees for succeeding generations of their families.[16]

Moreover, in a European tradition at least as ancient as the Middle Ages, land was associated with males. Men might acquire control of property through their wives and female relatives, but women themselves generally lacked full control of land, and rather had property only in movables, which meant money and transient things; even their limited landholdings were treated metaphorically as "movable." In fact, Howard Bloch, speaking of medieval France, has made the point that females *were* money: they were transient beings, and the subject of family trades, as Bloch put it, "the kind of property which circulates between men."[17] But like money, women did not represent "immovable," "real" property. Property that was real was land, an attitude that continued well into the eighteenth century and beyond.[18]

What is perhaps most important, landownership and indeed property in general carried with it some measure of governing authority, and this authority had notably hierarchical characteristics.[19] Indeed, in the regime of property-as-propriety, property and entitlement formed the key element in what the modern Critical Legal Studies proponents might call the reproduction of hierarchy, though this phrase would not have seemed in any way damning to those who adhered to this traditional view of property.[20] Property "properly" consisted in whatever resources enabled one to do one's part in keeping good order; and the normal understanding of order was hierarchy—in the family,[21] in the immediate community,[22] in the larger society and commonwealth,[23] in the natural world,[24] and in the relation between the spiritual and the natural world.[25]

A person's property fixed his location in this hierarchy. Thus a monarch had his own property in the royal domains, and in theory, though much less in practice, he should not need to tax the subjects, since the income from those domains would enable him, as the traditional phrase put it, to "live of his own." That is, his royal property would provide him with the wherewithal to exercise his role of overall governance.[26] The members of the noble estate in turn had their own lands, on which *they* were subrulers or "co-governors"; and other subruling orders had the property they also needed to maintain proper order within their respective jurisdictions.[27] For example, municipalities had their own endowments, which were managed by the ruling corporations of the "burghers" or "citizens," a class that by no means included all the residents of a given community, but only its leading members.[28] One should note that this pattern was brought to the New World cities as well; Hendrik Hartog's history of New York centers on the city's endowed property and its management by the ruling "corporation," and his work illustrates the pattern associating property with governance into the early nineteenth century.[29]

Elsewhere in the areas colonized by Europeans, one finds this same association of property with authority. The American colonial enterprises, as well as the East India Company, were initially organized on this principle: the proprietors and charter holders acquired not only monopolistic property rights in their respective colonial enterprises, but also the right and duty to govern the colonial charges and keep them in proper order.[30] In a way, property merged with authority in American "republican" thinking as well, a subject to which I shall return shortly.

Before the advent of modern centralized fiscal and bureaucratic techniques, both Old Regime Europe and to a somewhat lesser extent its colonies had a political organization that amounted to a kind of farming-out system, a system that fused property with "proper" authority.[31] Monopolistic guild privileges governed large segments of the economy—textiles, shoes, metalwork, and on and on; and in justification of their exclusive privileges, the holders of these monopolies were charged with keeping their respective enterprises in "good order and rule."[32] In France, public offices, notably judicial magistracies, could be purchased as hereditable property; as such, these magistracies became the founding property for the so-called "nobility of the Robe," which came to dominate the French aristocracy in the eighteenth century.[33] In England too in the same era, some public offices were seen as freehold properties of the office-holders.[34] In short, in this tradition, all rights were in some measure seen as property, and property entailed some measure of "proper" authority, to be exercised ideally as a trust for those to whom one was responsible for governing.

Now let me come to a subject that touches on the theory of "takings": In the theory of governance in the Old Regime monarchies, when a ruler's ordinary revenues failed to cover the expenses of governance, the ruler had to *ask* his subjects for subsidies; even the king, it was said, could not just take their property as he wished.[35] But the reason was quite different from the reasons that are given by preference-satisfaction theories. It was not so much that confiscations from the subjects would discourage their industriousness, but rather that the things that were truly the subjects' property were things that were *proper* to them—proper because their property enabled them to take their appropriate roles, and to keep good order throughout each corner of the realm.[36]

Though royal practice deviated far from this theory by the eighteenth century, particularly on the Continent, a good deal of lip service was paid to the notion that the king could not simply appropriate the subjects' property. Certainly royal overreaching continued to be the subject of great bitterness and recrimination and even rebellion; the French Revolution itself was preceded by years of complaint by various propertied classes about royal inroads on their entitlements and "liberties."[37]

B. American "Republicanism" and Property

In America, a version of property-as-propriety can be located in a historic political mentality that is now much discussed, namely "civic republicanism." Republican property was not so hierarchical as monarchic property, because it was thought that in a republic, the people rule themselves, and as a consequence a much broader range of citizens needed to have property. Montesquieu's writing supported this position, and although he would never have advocated such a thing for monarchic/aristocratic France, he noted that democratic republics entailed a much wider and more equal dispersal of property.[38] The reason, repeated again and again in the early American republic, was that property lent independence to individuals, and that independence enabled them to exercise the autonomous judgment necessary for their common self-rule.[39]

As to the persons who had little property, or who—like married women or slaves or children or madmen—were excluded from property ownership on principle because of their purported incapacities and "dependency": republican theory had few qualms about excluding such persons from the franchise.[40] Republicanism had its own pyramid of hierarchy, although perhaps a more flattened one than monarchy or aristocracy. But the logic was everywhere the same: ruling authority entailed property, and vice versa. Republicanism too divided the populace into rulers and ruled, and the rulers were those citizens who had the property necessary to independence, and therewith the ability to participate in governance.

It should be noted that in this republican idea of property, as in monarchic or aristocratic versions, not all property was alike. Jefferson's agriculturalism stemmed from the view that landed property particularly fostered independence, and Jefferson was not alone in a certain republican uneasiness about manufacturing and commercial forms of property.[41] Commerce entailed *inter*dependence, since one manufacturer or trader had to depend on another, and another, and another; thus the property acquired from these interdependent activities was suspect, precisely because it was not autonomous. In a way, American agrarians were not so far removed from the medieval view that land was genuine and real, while money was merely transient, dependent, effiminate, and unsturdy.

Notice as well that the republican vision of property was more or less indifferent to encouraging accumulation or aggregate wealth. Republicanism, like other "proprietarian" visions, associated property with governance and good order, but republican good order specifically entailed a certain sturdy equality among those who counted as self-governing citizens; great differences of wealth might corrupt republican virtue, and were thus a special matter for republican alarm.[42]

Moreover, in republicanism as in all proprietarian under-standings, governance and good order always included a duty of liberality to the larger community, for the sake of the common good.[43] For any version of property-as-propriety, it was understood that the ill-fortune of others presented the proper-tied with a duty to assist, and not with an occasion to revile or shame those in need. Though the practice of generosity and contribution was certainly subject to the predictable limitations of personal cupidity, there was little question that generos-ity was a moral and political duty of the haves to the have-nots—which was the same as saying, of course, that generosity was a duty of those with authority, to those without it.[44] Al-though there were certainly contrary murmurings earlier, it was not until the nineteenth century, and the ascendancy of a preference-satisfying moral and political theory, that political thinkers systematically cultivated the notion that generosity might induce perverse—that is, non-wealth-maximizing—incentives in the recipients.[45]

C. Justice and Desert Under Property-as-Propriety

If we were to take propriety and good order as the objects of a property regime, it is quite clear that considerations of "justice/fairness" and of "desert" would have different meanings than they do where the goal of property is taken as the maximization of preference-satisfaction.

"Justice" on this older understanding meant having that which is appropriate to one's station, as well as giving that which one's station demands. Property-as-propriety entailed governing au-thority in some domain; but because of that authority, property was a kind of trust as well. On such an understanding, it would not be considered unjust or unfair to request a sacrifice for the sake of a larger community, especially from those whose prop-erty extends beyond their proper needs, or whose propertied role makes them responsible for good order in the commu-nity.[46]

"Desert" on this understanding would also be based not on useful labor, but on status or station: one deserves to have that which is appropriate to one's role and station, but not more and not less. Many kinds of goods might hardly be considered very firm property at all, since they had no connection with the holder's role in keeping proper order, and were thus merely "acquired" and accidental.[47] Perhaps connected with that ideal, aggrandizement beyond one's station routinely met with outrage in the era before the great revolutions, as for example in the harsh treatment to "regrators" and hoarders in Stuart England, and in colonial America as well.[48]

This set of attitudes now seems quite antiquarian, as indeed it is. But we still hear some echoes, perhaps most notably in connection with welfare law and policy. One example is of course in Charles Reich's famous argument about the status of governmental benefits as property: his argument, among other things, is that benefit recipients are a part of the body politic, and as such have a "rightful claim" to hold these benefits as property, so that they can maintain their "independence" and participate in the commonwealth.[49] Cass Sunstein is currently working some of these themes into his own considerations of welfare law and, not surprisingly, he is doing so with a nod to the republican theory of seventeenth-century England and the early American republic.[50]

An attractive feature of the older view, for Sunstein and for others, is no doubt the concept of trusteeship that permeated the idea of property-as-propriety. Property endowed the "haves" not only with rights, but also with responsibilities about the disposition of property; their property was "theirs" only in trust for family, community, and commonwealth. A much more problematic feature of this older view, for Sunstein and other "republican revivalists," is of course the profoundly hierarchical character of the older ways of thinking about property—a flavor perhaps best captured in the ambivalence of our contemporary response to the phrase "noblesse oblige."[51]

Despite that ambivalence, one might well suspect that a substantial motivation in our welfare laws stems not so much from sophisticated preference-maximizing theory—the supposed declining marginal utility of wealth and all the rest of it—as from the older conception of property-as-propriety. Many who support welfare may well do so out of a sense that poverty (and perhaps great wealth too) is a kind of disorder in the republic, that our poorer citizens should have the economic means to escape this disorder, and that our wealthier citizens have a duty to help out. In some measure the sense may be that the disorder of poverty brings scandal and disgrace to our community, and that the station of propertied persons obliges them to do something about it.

D. *"Propriety" in Modern Property Law*

At this point I will return to the "takings" issue, and to the question of which elements in "takings" law are pluralist and irreducible and which are not. It seems to me that the genuinely pluralistic character of our takings law stems from its reflection of two complete but different ideas about what property is good for. The first and dominating idea casts property as an engine for the maximization of preference-satisfactions; the second, now a weaker but still very stubborn idea, casts property as the vehicle for propriety and decent good order.

The preference-satisfying vision of property is so common that its arguments, and its "takings" applications, seem almost self-evident. Richard Epstein's book on *Takings* runs through these arguments with easy facility. The arguments really reduce to one: that uncompensated redistributions violate the very purpose of a property regime, namely, to increase the size of the bag of goods, or as Epstein puts it, the size of the pie.[52]

But property in the second sense, that is, property as "propriety," as the foundation of decency and good order, appears in our property law as well. Where does this occur? Some examples appear in commonly used judicial tests for governmental "takings" of private property. One test places special limitations on governmental actions that constitute "physical invasions" of individual property.[53] On a preference-satisfaction view, property is more or less all alike; a physical invasion is like any other adverse effect, raising only questions of dollar values and demoralization costs. But the matter looks different on a property-as-propriety view: a physical invasion is particularly reprehensible because it is a special affront to the owner of the property; it is a pointed violation of his or her understanding of decency and order.

An even more telling example lies in a kind of secondary test under the rubric of "diminution in value." Generally speaking, a regulation that drastically reduces the value of a property may be equated with a "taking" of that property, though the line-drawing on this issue is fraught with difficulty.[54] One subtest for "diminution in value" inquires whether the affected property can continue to produce a reasonable income after the regulation is in place; if so, on this test, the diminution has not crossed the line to a taking.[55]

This is a "test" that seems incomprehensible from a utilitarian or preference-satisfaction point of view, where the issue should be the effect on the proprietors' "demoralization" and future willingness to work and invest. But the underlying idea here is not preference-satisfaction at all. The presupposition is that the owner does not need more than a decent income, as opposed to a maximizing income, from his or her property; hence the legislature's imposition on the property may be treated as a legitimate demand on a citizen, so long as the citizen's decent and proper income is preserved.

Similarly, another common "takings" test balances the owner's private loss against the public's benefit, but this is incomprehensible from the point of view of maximizing preference-satisfaction. Large public benefits might justify a compensated taking through eminent domain, but not an uncompensated taking. Why should the private owner lose expected rights simply because the public gains greatly?[56] But from the angle of vision of property-as-propriety, this balancing of public gain against private loss suggests that citizens have a duty to give up that which their representatives think the community can use better than they. This balancing test harks back to the underlying idea of property-as-propriety, namely that property carries the authority, but also the responsibility, of a trust to the larger community.

CONCLUSION

My own view then, is roughly as follows: first, that we have two different conceptions of the goals of a property regime, namely property-for-preference-satisfaction, and property-for-propriety; second, that these different postures toward property are not compatible; and third, that we can see their incompatibility at a number of junctures in our extremely confused law of "takings." Thus I agree with Munzer that the principles of takings compensation may be pluralist, or even "incoherent" in the sense that the elements may be in potential conflict. Our own law reflects that fact.

But I do not think that the incompatible elements of our law are the principles that he is talking about. On the contrary, his trio of principles can easily be subsumed under the overall viewpoint of preference-satisfaction. My own position is that in our law, the incompatible elements arise from the mixture of this dominant preference satisfaction conception of property on the one hand, with a weaker but very different historical conception of property-as-propriety on the other. What we have, in short, is two quite different historical visions of the purposes for which we have a property regime in the first place, and our takings law muddles along with the consequences.

NOTES

1. See, for example, *Euclid v. Ambler Realty,* 272 U.S. 365 (1926); compare Richard Epstein, *Takings: Private Property and the Power of Eminent Domain* (Cambridge: Harvard University Press, 1985), 112–29, 132–33.

2. The classic case is *Munn v. Illinois,* 94 U.S. 113 (1877), discussed by Harry Scheiber, "The Road to Munn: Eminent Domain and the Concept of Public Purpose in the State Courts," in *Perspectives in American History* (Cambridge: Harvard University Press, 1971), 5:329, 356.

3. As Munzer points out, the difference between these two revolves around the possibility of interpersonal comparisons of utilities. I will follow his head in putting this issue to one side, though it is of course,

an important problem that can, for example, divide utilitarians from libertarians.

4. John Locke, *Second Treatise*, in *Two Treatises of Government*, ed. P. Laslett (Cambridge: Cambridge University Press, 1960), § 31.

5. Jeremy Bentham, *Principles of the Civil Code*, in *Theory of Legislation*, ed. R. Hildreth (Bombay: Tripathic, 1975), 67–77.

6. Bentham, *Principles of the Civil Code;* on "rentseeking," see James Buchanan, Robert Tollison, and Gordon Tullock, *Toward a Theory of the Rent-Seeking Society* (College Station, Tex.: Texas A&M University Press, 1980).

7. Thomas W. Merrill, "The Economics of Public Use," *Cornell Law Review* 72 (1986); 61, 74–78, 82–85, 101–2.

8. Alfred Marshall, *Principles of Economics* (Philadelphia: Porcupine Press, 1982 [reprint of 8th ed.; London: Macmillan, 1920]), 80–81. On the income tax, see Walter Blum and Harry Kalven, *The Uneasy Case for Progressive Taxation* (Chicago: University of Chicago Press, 1953), 56–62, for a skeptical view of the declining marginal utility of income. See also Richard Posner, *Economic Analysis of Law*, 3d ed. (Boston: Little, Brown, 1986), 434–36, suggesting that an increasing marginal utility of wealth is equally plausible.

9. Frank Michelman, "Property, Utility, and Fairness: Comments on the Ethical Foundations of 'Just Compensation,' " *Harvard Law Review* 80 (1967): 1165, 1211–14; Bentham, *Principles of the Civil Code*, 70–73, describing various "evils" of attacks on property, including "deadening of industry."

10. Bentham, *Principles of the Civil Code*, 67, stating that property is no more than a basis of expectation.

11. Michelman, "Property, Utility, and Fairness," 1222–24.

12. The potlatch may be an example, though this particular ceremony may have the function of preserving the peace among competing hunting groups; see D. Bruce Johnsen, "The Formation and Protection of Property Rights among the Southern Kwakiutl Indians," *Journal of Legal Studies* 15 (1986): 41–42.

13. See text at note 2 above.

14. J. G. A. Pocock, "The Mobility of Property and the Rise of Eighteenth Century Sociology," in Anthony Parel and Thomas Flanagan, eds., *Theories of Property, Aristotle to the Present* (Waterloo, Iowa: Laurier Press, 1979), 141–42. Forrest McDonald points out that even John Locke often exercised this usage: *Novus Ordo Seclorum. The Intellectual Origins of the Constitution* (Lawrence, Kans.: University of Kansas Press, 1985), 10–11. For the much-debated question whether Locke was a precapitalist preference maximizer rather than a "propriety"

advocate, see sources in McDonald, *Novus Ordo Seclorum,* 65–66, n. 22; and Carol Rose, " 'Enough and as Good'of What?" *Northwestern Law Review* 81 (1987): 417, 423–24, n. 30.

15. J. W. Allen, *Political Thought in the Sixteenth Century,* rev. ed. (London: Methuen, 1960), 424–25; see Bodin's *Six Bookes of a Commonweale* (Cambridge: Harvard, 1962 [facsimile University Press reprint of 1606 English translation]), 11–12, 110–11.

16. Ralph E. Giesey, "Rules of Inheritance and Strategies of Mobility in Prerevolutionary France," *American Historical Review* 82 (1977): 271–72, 275–77. Giesey discusses the lineage property *(propres)* of commoners; aristocratic land had different rules of succession but also kept landed property in the hands of the larger family.

17. Howard Bloch, "Women, Property, Poetry" (unpublished manuscript on file with this author, delivered at Conference on Property and Rhetoric, Northwestern University, 1986), 6–7; the paper is drawn in part from Bloch's *Etymologies and Genealogies: A Literary Anthropology of the French Middle Ages* (Chicago: University of Chicago Press, 1983).

18. Bloch, "Women, Property," 17; Pocock, "Mobility of Property," 153, notes that commerce was discussed in feminized terms in the eighteenth century, even by its proponents.

19. For some examples from the late Holy Roman Empire (Germany), see Carol Rose, "Empire and Territories at the End of the Old Reich," in James Vann and Steven Rowan, eds., *The Old Reich: Essays on German Political Institutions 1495–1806* (Brussells: Librairie Encyclopédique, 1974), 62–63, 67–70.

20. Robert Darnton, "What Was Revolutionary about the French Revolution?" *New York Review of Books,* Jan. 19, 1989, p. 4, notes our present difficulty in comprehending the pre-Revolutionary "mental world" in which "most people assumed that men were unequal, that inequality was a good thing, and that it conformed to the hierarchical order built into nature by God himself."

21. See William Blackstone, *Commentaries on the Laws of England* (Chicago: University of Chicago Press, 1979 [reprint of 1765 ed.]), 1: 416–20, 430–32, describing head of household's authority over servants, wife, and children. This is probably most dramatically represented by the principle of coverture, according to which the wife loses her separate legal identity during the time of marriage.

22. See Peter Laslett, *The World We Have Lost: England before the Industrial Age,* 2d ed. (New York: Scribners, 1971), 21, 62–66. Laslett compares the dominance of the English local gentry to the looser structure of the English colonies, but compare Rhys Isaac, *The Transfor-*

mation of Virginia 1740–1790 (Chapel Hill: University of North Carolina Press, 1982), 131–35, describing Virginia gentry.

23. Laslett, *The World We Have Lost,* 31–32, for seventeenth-century perceptions of English gradations. The "body politic," with a governing head as well as arms, feet, and so on, was a dominating metaphor for larger social and political organization; see, for example, Conrad Russell, *The Crisis of the Parliaments: English History 1509–1660* (London: Oxford University Press, 1971), 41–43; and J. R. Hale, *Renaissance Europe* (Berkeley and Los Angeles: University of California Press, 1977), 167–68.

24. Arthur O. Lovejoy, *The Great Chain of Being* (New York: Harper, 1936); on the eighteenth-century use of this naturalistic metaphor, see especially 183–207 et seq.

25. See John Calvin, *Institutes of Christian Religion,* in *On God and Political Duty,* 2d ed. (Indianapolis: Bobbs-Merrill, 1956), 47–49, referring to civil magistrates as God's viceregents, and opposing those who would dispense with political authority.

26. See Roger Lockyer, *Tudor and Stuart Britain, 1471–1714* (London: Longmans, 1964), 27–28; Allen, *Political Thought,* 418.

27. For the term "co-governor," see Dietrich Gerhard, "Problems of Representation and Delegation in the Eighteenth Century," in *Liber Memorialis Sir Maurice Powicke* (Louvain: Nauwelaerts, 1965), 123 (quoting Roland Mousnier).

28. See, for example, Gerald Strauss, *Nuremberg in the Sixteenth Century* (New York: Wiley, 1966), 50–51, 74–84, describing the city's property and the patriciate, respectively.

29. Hendrik Hartog, *Public Property and Private Power: The Corporation of the City of New York in American Law* (Chapel HIll: University of North Carolina Press, 1983), 21–22, 33–34, 40; see also Carol Rose, "Public Property, Old and New" (review), *Northwestern Law Review* 79 (1984): 216, 219–22.

30. J. H. Parry, *The Age of Reconnaissance* (New York: Mentor, 1964), 215, 284–85; Charles M. Andrews, *The Colonial Period in American History* (London: Oxford University Press, 1967), 28–45, 259. For an example of a proprietary charter, see "The Charter for the Provence of Pennsylvania, 1681," in Michael Kammen, *Deputyes and Libertyes* (New York: Knopf, 1969), 164–66. For the transformation of the chartered corporate analogy into a metaphor of political responsibility, see Akhil Amar, "Of Sovereignty and Federalism," *Yale Law Journal* 96 (1987): 1425, 1432–35.

31. See generally Rose, "Public Property," 219–21.

32. See E. M. Heckscher, *Mercantilism,* trans M. Shapiro (London:

Allen & Unwin, 1935), 1: 254, 285–86, quotation at p. 286 from a seventeenth-century English document concerning a guild lawsuit.

33. See generally Franklin L. Ford, *Robe and Sword. The Regrouping of the French Aristocracy after Louis XIV*, 2d ed. (New York: Harper, 1965).

34. J. H. Plumb, *The Growth of Political Stability in England 1675–1725* (Baltimore: Penguin, 1969), 38–39.

35. Allen, *Political Thought*, 418–19; Blackstone, *Commentaries*, 1:135–36.

36. Allen, *Political Thought*, 421. Montesquieu, in *Spirit of the Laws* (London: Gryphon, 1984 [facsimile reproduction of authorized 1751 edition]), generally argued against confiscation, and cited Bodin favorably to say that in criminal cases any confiscation should be limited to alienable "acquired" personal property (1:79); Bodin's discussion, *Six Bookes*, 581, had made very clear that this kind of property was not "proper" in the way that land was proper to particular families. Similarly, in discussing taxes Montesquieu favored taxation of salable things rather than inalienable family land (e.g., 1:260).

37. See Robert R. Palmer, *The Age of Democratic Revolution* (Princeton: Princeton University Press, 1959–64), 1: 448–65. For non-French examples, see 1: 341–48, 377–84, on the disturbances in Belgium and Hungary set off by the attempts of the Austrian emperor Joseph II to revoke, respectively, guild and aristocratic privileges.

38. Montesquieu, *Spirit of the Laws*, 50–53; cf. the inequalities inherent in monarchies, 1: 66–67, 88–89.

39. McDonald, *Novus Ordo Seclorum*, 74–75. McDonald makes the point that Southerners were more likely than New Englanders to favor wide distribution of landownership; see also Lacy K. Ford, Jr., *Origins of Southern Radicalism: The South Carolina Upcountry, 1800–1860* (New York: Oxford University Press, 1988), 50–51. Readers are also recommended to an extended discussion of the republican tradition of property in Gregory S. Alexander, "Time and Property in the American Republican Legal Culture," *New York University Law Review* 66 (April 1991).

40. See generally Robert Steinfeld, "Property and Suffrage in the Early American Republic," *Stanford Law Review* 41 (1989): 335–76. See also McDonald, *Novus Ordo Seclorum*, 25–27; Christopher Hill, "The Poor and the People in Seventeenth-Century England," in Frederick Krantz, ed., *History from Below: Studies in Popular Protest and Popular Ideology* (Oxford: Blackwell, 1988), 29ff. (Noting seventeenth-century republican view that excluded the poor from definition of the "people").

41. Alexander, "Time and Property"; L. Ford, *Origins of Southern Radicalism*, 52, 73–74. See also Montesquieu, *Spirit of the Laws*, 1: 56–57, noting that the republican spirit of frugality supported commerce, but that the resulting riches and inequalities of wealth might undermine that spirit; see also 1: 344, on the subject of money.

42. See Montesquieu, *Spirit of Laws*, 1: 52–57; Montesquieu gave some quite extreme examples of this concern, noting somewhat disapprovingly that some founders of republics redistributed all land for the sake of equality (1: 52), but speaking more favorably of other republican methods of preserving equal property (1: 53–58). He also argued that the greatest security for liberty and equality occurred where there was no money at all and hence no possibility of accumulation (1: 344). Some at least mildly leveling sentiments appeared in comments of the Antifederalists, for example the "Federal Farmer," Letter of October 13, 1787, in Herbert Storing, *The Complete Antifederalist* (Chicago: University of Chicago Press, 1981), 3: 251. See also Carol Rose, "The Ancient Constitution vs. the Federalist Empire: Antifederalism from the attack on 'Monarchism' to Modern Localism," *Northwestern University Law Review* 84 (1989):74, 92–93. For further ambiguities in the American republican attitudes to virtue and equality, see Gordon Wood, *The Creation of the American Republic* (New York: Norton, 1969), 65–75.

43. Montesquieu argued that republicans should vie in service to the common good (*Spirit of the Laws*, 1: 50), and claimed that it was relatively easy to increase tax levels in republics, since the citizens thought they were really only giving to themselves (1: 265).

44. See Roger Tawney, *Religion and the Rise of Capitalism*, 3d ed. (New York: Mentor, 1965), 216–19; for the example of one city-state, Strauss, *Nuremberg*, 195–99; for American republican attitudes, see Wood, *Creation of the American Republic*, 63–65, 68–70.

45. Tawney, *Religion and the Rise of Capitalism*, 219–25; see also, for example, David Ricardo, *Principles of Political Economy*, vol. 1 of *Complete Works*, ed. P. Sraffa (Cambridge: Cambridge University Press, 1951), 105–7 (arguing that poor relief impoverishes all, "invites imprudence" in the poor, and noting general hardening of view about poor relief since eighteenth century). For the shift from republican to preference-satisfaction theories in the United States, particularly with the experience of the War of 1812, see Steven Watts, *The Republic Reborn: War and the Making of Liberal America, 1790–1820* (Baltimore: Johns Hopkins University Press, 1987); see also the discussion of the thought of Noah Webster in Alexander, "Time and Property."

46. See, e.g., Tawney, *Religion and the Rise of Capitalism*, 216–17; Erasmus's advice to Charles V, urging light taxation on the poor and

heavy duties on the luxuries of the rich, cited in Hale, *Renaissance Europe,* 163; and William Tyndale's *Obedience of a Christian Man* (1535), cited in Russell, *Crisis of the Parliaments,* 43, exhorted agricultural landlords to restrain rents and fines and to "be as fathers to your tenants."

47. See note 36 above, concerning Bodin's and Montesquieu's acceptance of the uncompensated taking of "acquired" goods; see also Vivian Gruder, "A Mutation in Elite Political Culture: The French Notables and the Defense of Property and Participation, 1787," *Journal of Modern History* 56 (1984): 598, 611–12, on the French "Notables'" views on taxing rentier' profits.

48. McDonald, *Novus Ordo Seclorum,* 14.

49. Charles Reich, "The New Property," *Yale Law Journal* 73 (1964): 733, 785–86.

50. Cass Sunstein, "Beyond the Republican Revival," *Yale Law Journal* 97 (1988): 1539, 1551. See also Akhil Amar, "Republicanism and Minimal Entitlements," *George Mason University Law Review* 11 (1988): 47–51; and Frank Michelman, "The Supreme Court, 1985 Term—Forward: Traces of Self-Government," *Harvard Law Review* 100 (1986): 4, 40–41.

51. See Richard Epstein's criticism in his "Modern Republicanism —or The Flight from Substance," *Yale Law Journal* 97 (1988): 1633, 1635–36; Mark Tushnet, "The Concept of Tradition in Constitutional Historiography," *William and Mary Law Review* 29 (1987): 93, 96–97.

52. Epstein, *Takings,* 3–6. For further consideration of constitutional institutions promoting wealth-maximization, see *Symposium, The Constitution as an Economic Document, George Washington Law Review* 56 (1987): 1–186; particularly relevant is the article by Richard Posner, "The Constitution as an Economic Document," 4–38.

53. See, for example, *Nollan v. California Coastal Comm.,* 107 S.Ct. 3141 (1987); and *Loretto v. Teleprompter Manhattan CATV Corp.,* 458 U.S. 419 (1982).

54. For some of the writings on these difficulties, see Carol Rose, "Mahon Reconstructed: Why the Takings Issue Is Still a Muddle," *Southern California Law Review* 57 (1984): 562, nn. 5–6.

55. See, for example, *Penn Central Transportation Co. v. City of New York,* 438 U.S. 104 (1978).

56. See Robert Ellickson and A. Dan Tarlock, *Land-Use Controls* (Boston: Little Brown, 1982), 136, n. 3.

10

DIAGNOSING THE TAKINGS PROBLEM

MARGARET JANE RADIN

"The philosopher's treatment of a question is like the treatment of an illness," said Wittgenstein, in one of my favorite remarks of his.[1] Here I would like to reflect upon the malaise that afflicts what legal scholars call the taking issue. The taking issue requires a court to determine when government action that adversely affects someone's claimed property interest should be understood to "take" that person's property. Under the Constitution, government actions that "take" property are disallowed unless compensation is paid.[2] The malaise is that no one can tell with satisfactory certainty what government actions those are.

How should we decide when "property" has been "taken"? The taking issue is central and pervasive. It is central because private property is a central commitment of a liberal legal system, a commitment that demands immunity of private holdings from defeasance. The issue is pervasive because almost all government actions make some entitlement holders worse off relative to others, yet government could not exist if it were required to undo all of its own actions by compensating everyone adversely affected by any action with distributive effects.

The taking issue is also remarkably intractable. For reasons that I hope my investigations will make clear, it is not to be solved simply by formally defining "property" and then observ-

248

ing that it has been "taken." Judicial efforts to develop a coherent takings doctrine have met with consistently telling criticism.[3] Often it seems that courts have not been able to do better than to tell us that when government regulation "goes too far" they will deem it a taking, whereas otherwise they will deem it within the state's normal "police power."[4] This is no more than to repeat the question, because "going too far" is a synonym for "taking." The sight of such a pervasive and central field of law in apparent disarray has enticed many able theorists, but their critical commentary has been more convincing than their efforts to reconstruct.[5]

Why is the taking problem so hard? If we cannot solve the problem, at least we can learn something by trying to understand why the solution eludes us. In the diagnosis I offer I set out three problems that are intertwined in the taking issue, which I characterize as problems of corrective justice, of the personal/fungible continuum, and of political contextuality. The upshot of my diagnosis is that two central difficulties of liberal legal and political theory are reflected especially clearly and urgently in the taking issue because of the importance of the liberal commitment to protection of private property. One difficulty is that the normative basis of liberalism resists reduction to formal rules, while rules are required by the equally important liberal commitment to the traditional ideal of the Rule of Law. The other difficulty is that the core liberal concepts of liberty, personhood, and polity are endlessly contested, while liberal political theory at the same time requires at least a basic consensus about them. If we relinquish the search for a coherent master-rule that can decide takings cases, we may find that the disarray in takings jurisprudence is somewhat alleviated. I suggest, in other words, that its disarray is partly an artifact of the commitment to formal rules and to the notion of an uncontested conception of property. Finally I take another view by considering the role of nonideal and ideal theory in trying to resolve the taking issue.

I. Three Problems Embedded in the Takings Issue

A. The Problem of Corrective Justice

At first sight the takings issue appears to be a problem of compensatory justice: if private property is taken, then compensation is required. But concealed within the takings issue is a problem of corrective justice, and it forms an obverse to the compensatory justice problem. The heart of the concealed corrective justice problem is that a takings claim should, at least prima facie, be honored only if the property taken is rightfully held. If the property is wrongfully held, then corrective justice may require that the holder compensate the rightful holder or indeed return the property to her. It seems, at least prima facie, doubly wrong if instead the wrongful holder receives compensation for the taking. The theory of property that demands strong taking protection against the government also demands strong protection for individuals against theft, trespass, and nuisance, as well as any other wrongful arrogations of property rights.

The concealed corrective justice problem means that in every case where a taking is claimed, we must decide whether or not the interest the government infringes is in fact justly held as a property right by the claimant. Often this threshold issue is called the baseline problem.[6] Because of the baseline problem, even what looks like a paradigm case of taking can flip-flop. Suppose the government bars Susan from land she claims to own, transfers title to itself, and then grants title to John. Susan claims that this is an unconstitutional taking. Is the answer obvious? First we need to know whether Susan is merely a trespasser against John.[7] If she is, then even though "property" has been "taken," the government should not compensate Susan for her loss.

The concealed corrective justice problem causes the most difficulty not with identifying obvious cases of claimants' thievery from, or trespass against, other individuals, although there are many nonobvious cases. The deepest difficulties instead center around identifying activities of entitlement holders that should be analogized with nuisance, deciding what to do about cases in which the government itself bears responsibility for wrongful arrogations of property rights by entitlement holders, and deciding whether, and when, settled expectations and elapsed time should turn old wrongs into new rights. I shall elaborate briefly on these three aspects of the baseline problem.

1. The Nuisance Analogy. Suppose Susan is engaging in some activity on her land that has the effect of lowering the value of neighboring land in some way.[8] Then the government regulates land use in such a way as to deny Susan the right to engage in the activity, thereby lowering the value, at least to her, of her land. Can Susan claim that she is owed compensation for a taking of her property right? First we have to know whether Susan really possessed a property right to engage in the activity in question. If not, government regulation to prevent the activity is an action of corrective justice vis-à-vis the neighbors, and not a taking from Susan.

In the constitutional takings context, the nuisance concern is often raised by asking whether the government regulation merely prevents the claimant from inflicting a harm on the community, rather than forcing the claimant to confer a benefit. If the court decides that the activity is a harm, then compensation is not decreed; if the claimant must yield up a benefit, then compensation is proper. In the analogous tort-law context, it has become obvious that the nuisance issue involves a normative baseline problem that cannot yield to definitional analysis or sweeping general rules. The court must find a way to decide in each case whether the nuisance defendant's conduct was "unreasonable."[9] The decision involves a contextualized normative judgment about what level of self-restraint in light of the concerns of neighbors we think it appropriate to require of landowners.[10] It has not proved possible to formulate general rules that can either explain all past cases or predict the outcome of future ones. The only general principle is the standard of situated, case-by-case normative judgment expressed in the requirement that property owners be "reasonable."

In the takings context it has become equally clear that whether the claimant is inflicting a social harm or instead being required to confer a benefit cannot be decided by definition of "harm" and "benefit" or by general rules.[11] Situated moral judgment is required. In the famous case of *Miller v. Schoene*,[12] a government regulatory scheme ordered landowners whose land contained cedar trees infected with rust to cut down their trees to avoid infecting other landowners' apple trees, and the Supreme Court held that compensation was not required even though the land value of the cedar owners was substantially lowered. In the celebrated case of *Hadacheck v. Sebastian*,[13] a brickyard that was originally located far from any residences was ordered to cease operations when residential uses later gradually moved next to it, and the Supreme Court held that compensation was not required even though the land value of the brickyard owner was drastically diminished. More recently, in the famous case of *Just v. Marinette County*,[14] the Wisconsin Supreme Court denied that implementation of a wetlands ordinance required compensation of landowners who were prevented from building anything on their land, decreeing, or purporting to observe, that landowners have no right to change their land from its natural state.

These are all famous cases because the intuitions of many commentators run counter to the courts' decisions not to compensate. It may be easy in these "hard" cases to see that each of them requires a decision about whether the claimant landowner has a right to engage in the activity in question. *Miller* decided that there is no right to grow cedars where neighbors grow apples. *Hadacheck* decided there is no right to continue operating a brickyard when people want to live next to it. But that easy insight must be followed by the understanding that such a baseline decision is required in every case. It is only that the cases that appear "easy" (at a given time and place) fall more readily into widely shared and largely tacit conventional understandings about the scope of landowners' rightful control over decision making with respect to land use. (In some more environmentally conscious future, the *Just* case could come to appear easy.) So far no one has been able to reduce these conventional, intuitive, contextually contingent baseline judgments to a set of formal rules. Hence the concealed corrective justice issue tends to block any general solution to the takings problem, at least if we understand a general solution to be one that can be stated *a priori* in the form of a general rule.

2. *Wrongful Delineation of Property Rights.* Another aspect of the corrective justice problem further weakens the possibility of a general rule-like solution. How shall we treat the issue of government (and/or broadly social) responsibility for wrongful holding of property rights? Consider first the easy case in which we have all come to realize that previously recognized property rights were wrongful: slavery. It seems that it would be inappropriate to offer compensation to the dispossessed slave owners at the time of emancipation, even though their financial statements collectively showed considerably less net worth after emancipation. One reason it seems inappropriate is that abolishing property rights in human beings, and declaring that human beings simply cannot be property, seems inconsistent with paying compensation as if "property" has been taken. At least the symbolic message seems too morally mixed, in such an important case.[15] We should not accept for compensation purposes the very baseline that abolition recognizes as wrongful.

Can this reasoning be generalized to other cases? Curtailing of husbands' supposed property rights in wives comes to mind. More problematically, we can consider, for example, supposed property rights of employers to maintain an unsafe workplace, of landlords to rent uninhabitable and unsafe housing,[16] and of industrial producers to pollute air and water. Even if positive law has previously clearly recognized these supposed property rights of employers, landlords, and industries, once we decide that positive law has been wrong to do so, and that no such property rights do or should exist, it seems to contradict that recognition to turn around and grant compensation as if the property rights did exist after all. .

The preceding argument will perhaps make no sense to some traditional legal positivists. Property, they will perhaps say, simply is whatever the government says it is from time to time, and the notion of mistakes about property is just incoherent. People used to be property, and now they aren't; landlords used to have the right to rent uninhabitable housing, and now they don't. From the traditional positivist point of view, the issue of whether or not to compensate when property rules change may be complicated,[17] but it cannot turn on whether the previous property regime was wrongful. For those other than traditional positivists, however, the underlying moral vision of what a property scheme should be, as it unfolds through time, must have some effect on our decision whether to grant the legitimacy to wrongful property holding that compensation bespeaks.[18] And for all of us, since the contest between affirmation and denial of the separation of law and morals in property runs deep, and perhaps we all embrace aspects of both,[19] the hope of a general rule-like solution for the takings problem recedes.

3. Settled Expectations and the Problem of Vested Rights. Perhaps the most difficult corrective justice problem has to do with when we should ignore it. The institution of private property lives in both the past and the present. It lives in the past because rightful holding depends upon an acceptable history of acquisition. It lives in the present because the mechanisms of adverse possession and prescription continually change old wrongs into new rights. The main rationale for adverse possession has always been practical: without a way to cut off old claims, not even rightful titles would be safe against lawsuits out of their distant past.[20] In the institution of property, corrective justice has its day but fades, continually overshadowed by present realities. This is a vital pragmatic compromise. Without protection against trespass and dispossession, the institution of private property could not fulfill the liberal promise of security in holdings, but neither could it do so if all holders were continually vulnerable to the successors of rival claims out of the past. Why isn't it a taking for the government to promulgate statutes of limitation that deprive holders of their rightful claims? Only because if the government omitted these statutes, the omission would "take" more.

The issue of how much we should live in the present regarding claimants' holdings causes difficulty in the takings context. Of course, if a claimant wrongfully acquired property but has achieved title by adverse possession, government deprivation can be a taking just as much as if the claimant's title were otherwise acquired. The difficulty arises in cases that are not traditional adverse possession or prescription but in which we might see a similar fading of corrective justice in light of present realities. In other words, while corrective justice concerns can cause even a case that looks like a paradigmatic taking to flip-flop, after enough time has passed it can flip-flop back again. After enough time, the entrenched status quo can come to be treated as vested rights.

Outside the bailiwick of traditional adverse possession and prescription, we have no guidance about how much time is enough, nor even whether a case is one in which the fading of corrective justice in favor of the status quo is morally appropriate. We can distinguish two kinds of cases. In the first kind the government moves to defease rights the holders thought they had (the vested rights problem). In the second kind the government must decide whether to pay off claimants for takings long past. (The second case may also pose a vested rights problem if successors to the original claimant stand to lose if the earlier claim is recognized.)

In the first kind of case, we would not want to say that settled expectations should validate ownership of slaves after we come to understand that ownership to be wrongful, even though slave-holding was a part of ordinary life for a long time. The social and legal entrenchment of slavery could not make slave-ownership a vested right. On the other hand, perhaps we might think that a claimant whose long-continued activity (for example, brickmaking or pig farming)[21] eventually comes to be seen as socially "unreasonable"—nuisance-like—should nevertheless have the right to continue the activity.

In the second kind of case, we might want to honor some Indian land claims even though the takings occurred long ago.[22] On the other hand, we could not hold the government liable for all of (what we now see as) its mistakes in changing property regimes. Even if we now think the Supreme Court was wrong in 1887 to deny compensation to breweries whose business was completely destroyed by prohibition,[23] that does not mean we should seek out and compensate their successors.

What are the considerations that would go into the decision whether to allow settled expectations to override the prima facie demands of corrective justice and be treated as vested rights?

No one has achieved a general theory that can answer this question, and here I only sketch a few concerns. Much more will be relevant than an observation of the length of time the claimant has mistakenly thought she enjoyed a property right. It will matter just how harmful the wrongful holding is in its present context. (Harm to how many people? To interests how central? Is their social situation favored or disfavored? Is the harm irrevocable?) It will also matter whether we think that the claimant knew or should have known that the holding was wrongful even before the government moved to defease it, and whether we can sympathize with the claimant's attachment to the holding even though we now see it as wrongful.

Similarly, what are the considerations that would go into the decision whether the government must now compensate for its old wrongs? Again, much more will be relevant than an observation of how long ago the wrong occurred. It will matter just how deep was the wrong. (Harm to how many people? etc.) The historical significance of the wrong will matter too. How important is the continuing sense of this past wrong to today's polity? If the harm has no continuing significance we can choose to live in the present. But if the harm is *too* significant, compensation may be politically impossible. Why did we compensate the victims of Manzanar but not the victims of segregation?

B. The Problem of the Personal/Fungible Continuum

The primary liberal theories of property find property to be necessary for the proper flourishing of individuals. They find —and forge—a link between private property and the differentiation, maintenance, and development of the self. Different strands of liberal thought emphasize different aspects of such a connection. Some theories emphasize a positive aspect: proper self-development and flourishing are linked to proper connection with the external world, and private property is necessary to this connection.[24] Other theories emphasize a negative aspect: proper self-maintenance and flourishing are linked to proper protection from the external world, and private property is necessary to this protection.[25] Marx declared that "bourgeois property" had abolished the connection between property and individual personhood,[26] by which he meant that private property in the context of the full-blown market society did not serve this function. But I believe that neither a complete acceptance of the liberal story about property, nor a complete acceptance of the Maxist critique, can do justice to the place of property in our form of life.

I believe, in other words, that our practice of private property, in a complex way, can validate both some aspects of the liberal conception of property and some aspects of the critique of that conception. I have attached the label "personal" to property that is connected, and is understood morally as rightly connected to the proper development and flourishing of persons, understood primarily in its positive aspect, and I have attached the label "fungible" to property that is not connected to persons in this way but instead is understood as representing interchangeable units of exchange value.[27] I believe that in our practice of property we do not attach equal moral weight to all interests that we accept as property, because we do understand, though almost always tacitly, that property interests are morally ordered on a continuum from personal to fungible, and that the personal interests are deserving of greater legal protection. Home-ownership carries greater moral weight in the legal system than does ownership of vacant land held for investment. The differing strength of holders' claims greatly complicates the takings issue. Exactly what has been taken, and from whom, matters. Even where legal doctrines do not take account of this, the pattern of decisions does.[28]

1. Tests for Taking and the Personal/Fungible Continuum. Market-oriented tests for whether a taking has occurred, and if so, what compensation is due, respond to the taking of fungible but not personal property. One prevalent market-oriented test for whether a taking has occurred is whether government action has lowered the market value of the claimant's holding by a large enough margin, typically more than 75 percent.[29] If property is personal, the claimant could experience a grievous loss even if market value decreased little, or indeed increased.

Market value need not track—is incommensurate with—justifiable personal connection.[30] Suppose Jack redesigns his tract house and rebuilds it into an idiosyncratic but deep architectural expression of his personality, and in doing so he violates zoning regulations mandating uniformity. Suppose further that uniformity increases market value. If we recognize Jack's interest as properly personal, then we may find the regulations to "take" property from him in a way that is unrelated to market value.[31]

Assuming we are clear that a taking has occurred, the market-oriented test for what compensation is due is the fair market value of the property interest taken. This is the dominant legal standard for determining compensation,[32] but it can seem quite wrong in cases where property interests are apprehended as personal and incommensurate with money.[33] In such cases it may be difficult to decide whether compensatory justice requires higher compensation or whether no compensation should be paid because the problem is outside the scope of compensatory justice.

A prevalent nonmarket test for whether a taking has occurred asks instead whether government action amounts to a physical invasion or occupation of the claimant's property. Analogously with a dignitary interpretation of the meaning of trespass, the physical invasion test can be understood as responsive to the central commitment in liberal theory, primarily in its negative aspect, of connection between property and personhood. Who diminishes my property, diminishes me. Instead of inquiring about how much fungible wealth the claimant may have lost, this test speaks in terms of invasion and insult.

Although this test seems central to the underlying concern about persons and their connection to the external world, or persons and their cloak of protection against the external world, it cannot appropriately be treated as a systematic rule.[34] For one thing, it misses the mark when the claimant is a business entity. All property is fungible for business entities; they have nothing to lose but their wealth. So a loss that would count as trespassory, a dignitary invasion, against a person, cannot be *that* kind of loss for a corporation.

Moreover, even when the claimant is a person, if her holding is fungible then the invasion test also misses the mark. In *Loretto v. Teleprompter Manhattan CATV Corp.*,[35] a majority of the U.S.

Supreme Court held, on the basis of the physical invasion test, that it is a taking for a statute to permit a cable television operator to install a cable on a building without the owner's consent, even with provision for payment of a nominal fee to the owner. Once we accept that the strength of property claims varies depending upon whether they are personal or fungible, that is, depending upon the closeness of their fit with the core concerns of the liberal ideal of property, and once we understand, therefore, that the physical invasion test in itself responds only to government threats to personal property, the result in *Loretto* seems to push the liberal ideal way beyond its bounds. A cable on the roof of a building the owner rents out as a fungible investment no more invades her personhood than does a tax or a utility assessment.

So far in this section I have outlined how the complexity attendant upon the personal/fungible continuum renders prevalent tests for takings partial rather than general. To this observation we should add another. Unless decisions about whether to consider property personal are susceptible to predetermination by *a priori* rules, that complexity also means that even when the takings tests are stated as rules, like the rule against physical invasion, those rules cannot function in the way rules are traditionally thought to. Some judgments about personal property may be rule-like, though not immutably so; for example, the judgment that in this time and place the home should be treated as personal. Other judgments about personal property may be irreducibly case-specific.

2. Further Ramifications: Limits on Eminent Domain and on Fungible Property. I also want to suggest that if we recognize the personal/fungible continuum, as I believe we do, albeit tacitly and incompletely, we might find a moral limit on the power of eminent domain. We might find, moreover, that even an otherwise clear taking of a fungible interest might not require compensation if its defeasance is required to maintain interests, even nonproperty interests, closely connected to personhood.

The broad power of eminent domain, with the requirement of monetary compensation at market value, seems, by implicitly understanding all property to be fungible, paradoxically to ex-

clude the moral core of the liberal rationale for property.[36] To
the extent that we recognize personal property, we might think
that some property should not be taken at all. We might think
that for some things no compensation can be "just." We might
find some things to be inalienable, if they are closely connected
with personhood, or at least inalienable involuntarily to the
government.[37] If we conceive of the body as property, can kid-
neys be condemned for public use?[38] While some cases may
appear easy, which things ought to be inalienable on grounds of
inseparability from personhood cannot be distinguished by a
bright-line theoretical rule.

Recognition of the personal/fungible continuum should also
lead us to conceive of conflicts between property and nonproperty personal interests, like freedom of noncommercial speech,
differently depending upon whether the property is personal
or fungible.[39] The concern here is connected with the corrective
justice aspect of the takings problem considered in the preceding section. In any given case we might find under the circumstances that a claimed fungible property interest is wrongly
held, such that it cannot prevail against nonproperty interests
that appear more closely connected with personhood. If property is fungible (for example, a large shopping center), we might
find that a statute permitting political speech on the claimant's
property is not a taking, even though it appears to be literally a
government action permitting a physical incursion into the
claimant's space and a limit on the claimant's right to exclude.[40]
On the other hand, a similar statute directed against homeowners might more readily be understood as a taking.

C. The Problem of Political Contextuality

The takings issue is at first sight a problem of classifying a
particular statute or a particular transaction: Does government
action X take the private property of claimant Y? Yet the takings
issue is deeply dependent upon political context; and how we
construe the political context depends upon the political theory
we accept.[41] We are deceived if we think that solving the takings
problem involves scrutinizing individual statutes or transactions
outside the context of political theory and political reality. The

title of this section is itself deceptive if it suggests that the complexity of contextual judgment becomes apparent for the first time when we consider takings and politics. The largely tacit problems revealed so far, of corrective justice and the personal/fungible continuum, undermine the hope of a general solution to the takings issue just because they place each decision in a variegated moral context.

Many who tend toward traditional legal positivism, who tend to think of law as a body of rules laid down, and who tend to think of legal decision making, at least for some majority of core cases, as uncomplicated rule-application, will also tend to think that the problems of corrective justice and the personal/fungible continuum can be solved with appropriate rules that will delineate the relevant moral distinctions.[42] I do not deny that partial, contingent rules are possible, such as the rule-like understanding that homes are personal. Where I part company from traditional positivists is in my belief that such partial, contingent rules rest only on situated experience and not on *a priori* master-rules. Nor do I deny that we can and should try to develop principles that can help us deal more readily with corrective justice and the personal/fungible continuum. Perhaps the difference between my views and those I characterize as belonging to a traditional positivist is one of perspective or of degree. To alleviate the perpetual disarray of the takings issue, as it appears from the traditional point of view, it is important to understand rules or principles as open-ended and inseparable from context.

Those who tend toward traditional positivism may be less able to evade contextuality when the focus is explicitly on politics. There is an affinity between traditional legal positivism and the liberal political theory now known as interest-group pluralism. Interest-group pluralism is a log-rolling or deal-making theory of politics in which interest groups try to maximize their self-interest by bringing about favorable government action, forming strategic coalitions with other groups, and making concessions to competing groups when these are strategically necessary.[43] For someone who accepts a deal-making theory of politics, the takings issue brings contextuality to the fore in a way that cannot easily be evaded. All the typical questions we might ask about a particular transaction—How large is the loss?

How much does this kind of loss interfere with personhood or dignity?—are counterbalanced, in fact engulfed, by questions about the political context. Why? Because in any particular case a claimant's loss can seem a paradigmatic taking of her property and yet be a bargained political quid pro quo.

Suppose local landlords are forced by a new ordinance to dedicate 25 percent of their units to free housing for the homeless, and the landlords claim this is a taking requiring compensation. Before deciding whether to pay them off, we should ask, at least on the deal-making theory of politics, whether the landlords bargained away these units in return for a greater gain elsewhere, for example a giant tax break. If the landlords bargained for their loss in expectation of greater gain, then no compensation should be due them.

The general point is that any loss on a particular transaction may turn out to be the price paid for gains extracted elsewhere.[44] If so, then to pay compensation is to compensate twice. Although in this political theory, at least, the self-interested claimant should be expected to try this gambit, the gambit must be defeated or politics will come to a halt. Logrolling will be foiled by a logjam.

The general point must be understood to have a temporal dimension as well. The landlords who acquiesce in the ordinance giving over some of their units to the homeless may be buying political benefits for the future rather than paying for government favors already granted. It would still be double compensation for the government both to make good on the deal and to pay them off when they scream "taking."

The deal-making theory of politics places every takings case in a virtually unbounded dynamic context. The context is dynamic because deals, according to this theory, are always part of an ongoing process; they get unmade and remade as political give-and-take goes on. The context is unbounded because deals can be made at all levels of government. They can be made for the benefit of other groups sympathetic with one's own, or linked to one's own by a merely passing coalition. You scratch my back, I'll scratch yours. They can be made for past and future payoffs over an indefinite period. The payoffs can occur anywhere in the system and need not be observably connected with claimants' property. What if the landlords cared more for restricting abortion than for maintaining high profits in the rental business? Rent-seeking and restricting abortion make strange bedfellows. The deals can be made even when the expected payoff is uncertain, or even risky, if the interest group finds the risk to be worthwhile.

The deal-making theory of politics does not tell us how to find out what deals have actually been made. It does not tell us how to draw the boundaries of context, nor when to stop the clock and freeze the action. It commits itself, probably in spite of itself, to contextualized pragmatic decisions. Each case requires a look at the political universe.

Suppose, though, that we reject the liberal theory of interest-group pluralism. One prevalent alternative is a version of civic republicanism.[45] Under the tenets of civil republicanism, as reinterpreted by left-liberal thinkers, a political contextuality concern still poses a deep problem for taking decisions.[46] Republicanism rests on a commitment to the flourishing of citizens in a community by means of their self-government. Most modern republicans understand that some groups have more power than others to define and constitute the political community. In keeping with this understanding, taking decisions should be viewed through a lens of political empowerment. Groups that have power to control the legislature, or other government action, and hence actually participate, even if informally, in the lawmaking that affects their holdings, should, when they experience losses in their holdings, be more readily understood as sacrificing some of their private interests for the public interest than should less powerful groups that are largely excluded from actual participation in lawmaking. If landlords have a dominant voice on the city council, whether formally or informally, then we may judge giving over some of their units to the use of the homeless as an appropriate contribution to their community's political well-being. On the other hand, we might, as republicans, properly be more skeptical about the appropriateness of the sacrifice if low-income tenants were being asked to relinquish their units, or any important entitlements associated with tenancy.[47] This concern means that the contextual circumstances of political power, of inclusion and exclusion from the

actual governing of the community, become relevant in cases
where a taking is claimed.

II. THE RULE OF LAW AND CONTESTED CONCEPTS: TWO
PROBLEMS FOR LIBERAL PROPERTY THEORY AND PRACTICE

Perhaps no one would seek an *a priori* general rule-like solution
to the takings issue if it were not for the ideal of the Rule of
Law. Perhaps no one would be dismayed that all the courts are
able to do is muddle through.[48] But the liberal ideal of the Rule
of Law, in its traditional form, requires that people be governed
by general rules that predate the action to be judged by them,
and that these rules be understandable by, known to, and capable of being met by, those to whom they are addressed.[49] Mud-
dling through does not seem to meet these criteria.

The most prevalent rationale for the requirements of the
Rule of Law is that liberty depends upon them, and hence the
very justifiability of government in the liberal scheme depends
upon them.[50] The liberal commitment to equality—like cases
must be treated alike—also seems to require a regime of general rules. The takings issue, like the death penalty, poses a
crisis for the ideal of the Rule of Law, because no one has been
able to bring the issue satisfactorily under a general rule or a
regime of general rules.[51] If private property, a cornerstone of
the complex of liberal commitments, cannot be protected in a
way that lives up to the requirements of the Rule of Law, then
how can governmental action affecting holdings ever be justified?[52]

I shall not attempt here to prove a negative, to demonstrate
irrefutably that it is impossible to solve the takings issue with
formal rules.[53] It should be clear, at least, that each of the
concerns I have delineated is at best extremely resistant to reduction to rules in the traditional sense. In that sense of rules,
their preexisting meaning is supposed to dictate results of its
own force. In a more modern understanding of rules, the ap-
prehension of an action as rule-governed depends upon social
consensus after the fact and not upon some *a priori* formal
logical force. While I have not denied that partial rules, in the
modern sense, are possible, the traditional sense of rules is the

sense embedded in the ideal of the Rule of Law.[54] The need for shifting situational judgment in dealing with baseline problems, person/fungible distinctions, and political contextuality highlights the inutility of the traditional conception of rules and of the traditional ideal of the Rule of Law.

One basic difficulty with the takings issue, then, is that the inherited ideal of the Rule of Law impels us to seek preexisting formal solutions where only practice-based contextual solutions are to be had. Another basic difficulty, implicitly apparent, I am sure, in the very controversiality of much of what I have said so far, is our deep pluralism regarding the values that drive these practice-based partial and temporary solutions. Property is a perennially contested concept, as are the concepts of liberty, personhood, and polity on which it is supposed to rest. We do not have consensus on the requirements of corrective justice, on the significance, if any, of the personal/fungible continuum, or on the appropriate way to theorize about politics and to construe our political practice. This pluralism does not mean that there cannot be better and worse answers, solutions, or principles associated with the takings issue. It means only that the better—the right—answers will not have the open-and-shut quality that we expect from rules and that drives the old ideal of the Rule of Law.

In my view these two intertwined difficulties, the problem of trying to achieve formal rules in the face of the stubborn relevance of circumstances, and the problem of pluralism in basic liberal values, together account for much of the disarray in takings jurisprudence. They render the takings issue resistant to general solutions. The resistance stems in part from recalcitrant theory: the continuing contestedness of moral and political theory relating to property and our need to make decisions with broad philosophical ramifications while the philosophers are still arguing, as they always will be. The resistance arises also from recalcitrant practice: the stubborn situatedness of people and their property, and the endless variations in property relations. This protean aspect of property is part of the reason why property, like liberty, is a central value in liberal schemes, but ironically, it is also the reason why property problems resist the liberal commitment to rules.

All of this is not intended to say that we cannot make takings jurisprudence better by seeking to include principles of corrective justice, personal/fungible distinctions, and dynamic contextuality in our thinking about it. We can and should seek principles and wrestle with their conjoined application. If the tacit concerns come to light and we talk about them directly, and if the traditional rhetoric of rules is relinquished, at least in its single-mindedness, then thought and decision making about taking must benefit. Once we do this, though, we must recognize that we cannot meet the requirement of the traditional Rule of Law that government act by self-evident application of preexisting general rules.

III. The Taking Issue and the Tension Between Ideal and Nonideal Thinking About It

As a first cut at the problem, it seems that three pervasive and intractable problems interact to make a general solution to the takings issue elude us. It also seems that their intractability is due largely to their connection with contested concepts crucial to liberal property theory and their lack of amenability to solutions in the form of rules in the traditional sense. Now we can look at the problem another way: to understand that the takings issue presents both intractable ideal issues and intractable nonideal issues, and to examine their interaction as a problem of transition.

By ideal issues I mean issues about how we should decide the takings problem in a frictionless world of perfect good faith and perfect knowledge, including knowledge of justified theories of property and politics. In the ideal world of theory, those charged with carrying out law unfailingly do it correctly. By nonideal issues I mean issues concerning how we should decide the taking problem in our world of ignorance, including theoretical disagreement and uncertainty, mistakes, and bad faith. The problem of transition concerns how much deviance from our ideals we should mandate in practice in our present nonideal world to make the best progress toward our ideal world of theory. If our ideal, for example, is more caring interaction between landlords and tenants, should we try to implement that ideal now, in the midst of a market-oriented world, by greatly increasing landlords' duties of habitability and curtailing their profits? Or will this backfire and make the gulf between landlords and tenants even worse? Or should we stick with a largely free-market regime, hoping for happy, generous landlords and a trickle-down effect? Or will this further entrench the nonideal market order and push our ideal farther away?

The problem of transition to a better world, to the world of our theories of justice, is the problem of politics. The transition never ends; we are always *in medias res*. In making our decisions in practice we must recognize that those decisions not only move either toward or away from our ideals, they also continually help us to reshape those ideals, for better or for worse.

The intractability of the takings issue arises not just from the multiplicity of issues, and not just from the difficulties with contestedness and the Rule of Law, but also from our inability to specify in any general way when we should be governed by the ideal and when we should pay attention instead primarily to the nonideal. Always in the midst of the transition, we are always unsure when we should lean toward theory and our hopes for progress and when toward practical politics and our realistic appraisal of the world as it is.

The overriding ideal concern that makes the takings issue intractable is that a general solution demands a fully worked-out theory of justified property holding, which depends upon a theory of politics and the person. The contestedness of moral and political theory relating to property renders our ideals uncertain and conflicting. Perhaps we should consider its very contestedness to be nonideal. At any rate, this central ideal problem with our world of theory shades over into the nonideal, into corrective justice, our deep commitment that wrongs about property must be righted.

The need for corrective justice reflects our nonideal circumstances: wrongs happen. Corrective justice nevertheless has an aspect that relies on ideal theory. Commitment to a theory of justified property holding is necessary to identify cases of wrongful holding in which corrective justice is called for. Corrective justice also has a more immediate nonideal aspect. Corrective justice fades out in favor of the status quo. It fades out for the primary nonideal reason that otherwise the continuance of the institution of property would be under threat. When and how corrective justice should be allowed to fade will always be a serious problem of transition, a matter of controversy and pain.

Does the contestedness of ideal theory translate into ineradicable difficulties on the level of individual decisions? It seems that if theories of property are contested, because theories of politics and the person are contested, then the takings issue must remain contested. Interest-group pluralism and civic republicanism yield different patterns of justified holdings and different levels of tolerance for rearrangements. Neo-Lockeans find entrenchment where other kinds of liberals find none, and counsel corrective justice where others find no need for it. The relevance of the personal/fungible continuum remains contested, as do recognizable stopping places upon it.

To this one might try to respond that at least some paradigm cases must count as a taking under any plausible theory we can hope to devise.[55] If this response succeeds it is still only a partial solution. But I think this response must likely fail, given the range of competing political theories currently on the scene, and particularly because of the force of the deal-making theory, interest-group pluralism. Suppose we say a paradigm case might be one in which government takes over all ownership indicia except the nominal title. In other words, say that a paradigm case looks just like an undeclared case of eminent domain. It seems that this kind of paradigm is too narrow to help much with the array of takings problems that arise. But worse, as we have seen, even what looks like a paradigm case can flip-flop, either because it runs into the nonideal problem of corrective justice, or because it runs into the nonideal problem of political context. As we have seen, the problem of political context is especially acute for the political theory of interest-group pluralism.

The Rule of Law is another ideal problem confronting us in takings, as everywhere in a liberal regime of legality. In a sense the Rule of Law ideal is rooted in the nonideal from its source. It asks us to recognize that a regime of general rules is necessary to implement the political ideal of negative liberty, in light of the tendency of government to overreach, and in light of the shortcomings of judges and administrators.[56] The irony about the Rule of Law is that it requires general, well-understood, and self-evidently applicable rules about property, but if we were able to develop such well-behaved rules we would be more confident of decision makers' ability to make correct decisions and therefore less in need of the constraints of the Rule of Law.

Part of the complex of nonideal issues surrounding the Rule of Law is an old debate about institutional priorities. Given our theoretical uncertainties and the various possibilities of error and bad faith, should legislatures almost always have their way? Or should courts be active in attempting to correct them? The Rule of Law is often understood to include legislative deference: judges are to "apply" not "make" the law.[57] Constitutional protection of property against taking, however, is countermajoritarian. Its function is to disallow some legislative actions. Judges who are too deferential, however much deference is "too" much, will fail to "apply" the constitution and thereby violate the Rule of Law, no less than they will violate the Rule of Law if they are not deferential enough, however much deference is "enough."

In practice it seems that those who are sure of their ideal theory, their general theory of justified property holding, especially if that theory gives little or no weight to community participation in arriving at what constitutes a system of justified holding, are likely to plump for activist judging.[58] Those who are less sure of their ideal theory, or who hold an ideal theory more dependent upon community, are more likely to favor deference to legislatures, especially at the local level.[59] Just as there are no readily apparent uncontroversial rules for justified property holding, all things considered, so there are no readily apparent uncontroversial rules for institutional priorities in deciding when a claimant has been unjustifiably deprived of property.

CONCLUSION

The lesson of my investigations is modest. We should not seek what we cannot find: decisions that uncontestedly follow from a coherent system of rules. Some of the apparent disarray in the takings doctrine, as applied in practice, disappears if we see the courts as engaged in the pragmatic practice of situated judgment in light of both partial principles and the unique particularities of each case.[60] More still might be further eased if courts became more comfortable with their practice and less oriented toward searching for rules capable of mechanical application.

Just because the takings issue resists rationalization by a coherent master-rule does not mean we should fail to seek principles that can help organize our thinking about it. Nor does the lack of a master-rule mean that there are not better and worse valences for taking jurisprudence. In fact, I hope that taking jurisprudence can be the better for explicit cognizance of the problems I have raised in this chapter. In my investigations I have not sought to say anything novel or surprising, but only to help us see what we already know. Rather than seeking complete theories and a system of rules, we should work more consciously within the framework of the dilemmas of transition, in the tension between ideal and nonideal worlds. We should continue to work on the general principles suggested by the takings issue, but we should accept both that they always "run out" in practice and that practice always changes them. In other words, here as elsewhere in the law, we should recognize the inescapably pragmatic nature of the enterprise.[61]

NOTES

1. Ludwig Wittgenstein, *Philosophical Investigations* (New York: Macmillan, 1958), section 255.

2. The "takings" clause of the Fifth Amendment reads "Nor shall private property be taken for public use, without just compensation." Application of the "takings" clause often coalesces in important respects with the Fifth Amendment's due process clause, which provides that "[No person shall be] deprived of life, liberty, or property, without due process of law." The jurisprudence of these clauses restraining the federal government is applicable to state governments as well through the due process clause of the Fourteenth Amendment. State constitutions have their own "takings" clauses, as well.

3. See, for example, Frank Michelman, "Property, Utility, and Fairness: Comments on the Ethical Foundations of Just Compensation

Law," *Harvard Law Review* 80 (1967); 1165; John Costonis, "Presumptive and Per se Takings: A Decisional Model for the Taking Issue," *New York University Law Review* 58 (1983): 465; and Leslie Bender, "The Takings Clause: Principles or Politics," *Buffalo Law Review* 34 (1985): 735.

4. In *Pennsylvania Coal Co. v. Mahon,* the Court stated that "while property may be regulated to a certain extent, if the regulation goes too far it will be recognized as a taking . . ." 260 U.S. 393, 415 (1922).

5. See, for example, Michelman, "Property, Utility, and Fairness"; Richard Epstein, *Takings: Private Property and the Power of Eminent Domain* (Cambridge: Harvard University Press, 1985); and Bruce Ackerman, *Private Property and the Constitution* (New Haven: Yale University Press, 1977).

6. See, for example, Cass R. Sunstein, "Lochner's Legacy," *Columbia Law Review* 87 (1987): 873.

7. We also need to know how long Susan has been there, and whether the circumstances are such that we ought to treat Susan's claim as paramount to John's in view of the length of time she has been trespassing. If she has been trespassing long enough to have gained title by adverse possession, then she can be treated as the rightful owner. In cases that deviate from this kind of simple paradigm, however, it is much more difficult to say how we should weigh the length of time the wrongful claim has been exercised, as against its wrongfulness at its inception. I will have more to say about this problem in section A.3 below.

8. The problem is further complicated by the fact that it may matter whether the value is lowered only in the current holder's perception, or whether indeed the market value is lowered (that is, the value is lowered in the perception of what we would consider an "average" holder). It also may matter whether the injury appears normatively to be merely a lowering of monetary value, or whether the personhood of the holder appears to be infringed upon. (See section I.B below.) These concerns may pull in opposite directions, further complicating the issue. That is, we may intuitively feel that "mere" lowering of value in one's own perception is not entitled to as much weight as lowering of market value, yet we may feel that injury to personhood is entitled to more weight than "mere" lowering of market value.

9. See *Restatement (Second) of Torts,* American Law Institute, (1979), Sec. 882. (For nontrespassory invasion to be the source of liability it must be (i) intentional and unreasonable (ii) unintentional and otherwise actionable under the rules controlling liability for negligent or reckless conduct, or for abnormally dangerous conditions or activities.)

10. The avenues of appropriateness explored in the rather extensive literature on nuisance are both utilitarian (focusing on economic efficiency) and nonutilitarian (focusing either on rights or on custom). See, for example, Robert G. Bone, "Normative Theory and Legal Doctrine in American Nuisance Law: 1850–1920," *Southern California Law Review* 59 (1986): 1101.

11. See Michelman, "Property, Utility, and Fairness."

12. 276 U.S. 272 (1928).

13. 239 U.S. 394 (1915).

14. 56 Wis. 2d 7 (1972).

15. See Margaret Jane Radin, "Market-Inalienability," *Harvard Law Review* 100 (1987): 1849, 1915–17.

16. See, for example, Margaret Jane Radin, "Residential Rent Control," *Philosophy & Public Affairs* 15 (1986): 350.

17. See Louis Kaplow, "An Economic Analysis of Legal Transitions," *Harvard Law Review* 99 (1986): 511.

18. The problem is further complicated by the question of the extent to which we might be morally inclined to honor holdings we come to recognize as wrongful, simply because of their entrenchment (this is the problem of "settled expectations" or "vested rights"). Even if we are not positivists, and admit that property rights are not properly accepted to be exactly what the government or society in general proclaims or allows, we still might think that (some of the time? always?) we should honor wrongfully granted or wrongfully condoned property claims. This could be either because we think repose is necessary (analogous to one strand of the rationale for adverse possession), or because we think there is affirmative moral force to settled expectations that at some point can outweigh the wrong in holding (analogous to another strand in the rationale for adverse possession). This difficulty will be discussed in section A.3 below.

19. There is intuitive appeal in Austin's and Bentham's critique of the notion that a bad law is not a law. See H. L. A. Hart, "Positivism and the Separation of Law and Morals," *Harvard Law Review* 71 (1958): 593. We should face the fact that we do have some bad laws, and deal with it. Yet there is also intuitive appeal in the notion that people can have rights even if the government fails to recognize them, which means that property rights cannot be entirely positivist creatures.

20. See J. S. Mill, *Principles of Political Economy* (Harmondsworth, Middlesex; Penguin, 1970), bk. II, chap. II, § 2, p. 370. For other strands of rationale about adverse possession, see Margaret Jane Radin, "Time, Possession, and Alienation," *Washington University Law Quarterly* 64 (1986): 739.

21. See, for example, *Hadacheck v. Sebastian,* 239 U.S. 394 (1915); *Pendoley v. Ferreira,* 345 Mass. 309 (1963).

22. Congress passed a special statute of limitations so that the Sioux Indians could sue today for the loss of the Black Hills in the time of Custer. We might want to say that even without the intervention of Congress we should not consider their claim to have lapsed. See *United States v. Sioux Nation of Indians,* 448 U.S. 371 (1980).

23. See *Mugler v. Kansas,* 123 U.S. 623 (1887) (upholding enforcement of a state prohibition on the sale of alcohol that destroyed plaintiff's brewery business).

24. G. W. F. Hegel, *Philosophy of Right,* trans. T. M. Knox (1942) as *Hegel's Philosophy of Right,* section 41 (New York: Oxford University Press, 1967). Cf. section 39 ("personality is that which struggles . . . to give itself reality, or in other words to claim that external world as its own [jenes Dasein als das ihrige zu setzen]"); and Margaret Jane Radin, "Property and Personhood," *Stanford Law Review* 34 (1982): 957.

25. Charles Reich, "The New Property," *Yale Law Journal* 73 (1964): 733, 774; and Robert Nozick, *Anarchy, State and Utopia* (New York: Basic Books, 1974).

26. Karl Marx and Friedrich Engels, *The Communist Manifesto,* in *The Marx–Engels Reader,* 2d ed., ed. R. Tucker (New York: Norton, 1978), 484–85.

27. See Radin, "Property and Personhood"; see also idem, "Market-Inalienability," 1907; and idem, "Residential Rent Control," 362.

28. For example, judicial decisions that enhance a tenant's entitlements and diminish the landlord's often find it significant that the tenant is a person with a home and the landlord is, or is assumed to be, a commercial business entity. See, for example, *Javins v. First National Realty Corp.,* 428 F.2d 1071 (D.C. Circ.), *cert. denied,* 400 U.S. 925 (1970). Landlords' claims that such diminutions of their entitlements vis-à-vis tenants are "takings" regularly fail. See also, for example, *PruneYard Shopping Center v. Robins,* 447 U.S. 74 (1980) (it is not a taking for California law to prevent commercial shopping centers from excluding people engaging in peaceful political speech).

29. A 75 percent diminution in market value was found not to be a taking in the classic case of *Euclid v. Ambler Realty Co.,* 272 U.S. 365 (1926), which validated land use regulation by zoning. Those theorists, often economists, who favor utilitarian or market-oriented tests for taking often find it absurd that the courts tolerate so high a percentage loss (often dismissing it as "mere diminution of market value"). I believe that one reason for this high threshold, which must be incompre-

hensible to those who conceive of all property as fungible, is that legal
practice tacitly gives greater weight to personal interests.

30. Nor is justifiable personal connection expressed through a monetary estimation of consumer surplus. Where consumer surplus is traditionally conceived as a dollar amount over market value that an
individual would demand to relinquish an object or a right justifiable
personal connection is associated with and identified by the personal
pain or anguish that occasions the loss of an object or right.

31. This would be analogous to the common law recognition of
ameliorative waste, giving the right to future interest holders to receive
the property in the same condition, even if the interim holder's changes
increase its market value. The inquiry focuses on a substantial change
in the character of property without reference to the resulting increase
or dimininution of market value.

32. In this the legal system seems committed to an ethic of fungibil-
ity (commodification and exchange value), but the jurisprudence of
taking, with its apparent understanding of the personal/fungible continuum, paradoxically cuts against it. See Margaret Jane Radin, "The
Liberal Conception of Property: Cross currents in the Jurisprudence
of Takings," *Columbia Law Review* 88 (1988): 1667, 1685–86.

33. See ibid., n. 103.

34. See ibid. Modern taking decisions have consistently found the
right to exclude trumped by other rights. See *PruneYard Shopping Center v. Robins*, 447 U.S. 74 1980 (political speech); *State v. Shack*, 58 N.J.
297 (1971) (access to counseling about federal rights).

35. 458 U.S. 419 (1982).

36. See Radin, "The Liberal Conception of Property," 1686.

37. Kathleen M. Sullivan, "Unconstitutional Conditions," *Harvard
Law Review* 102 (1989): 1413. Though not a core liberal ideological
concern in the same way as personhood, we can see an analogy here in
the connection between land holding and group religious or cultural
identity. The Sioux Indians won only an ironic victory when, after one
hundred years of effort, they persuaded the Supreme Court that the
U.S. government had "taken" the Black Hills from them such that
monetary compensation was due, for, as the Court itself recognized,
they had been deprived of their chosen way of life. *United States v. Sioux
Nation of Indians*, 448 U.S. 371, 423 (1980).

38. There is a difficult problem lying in wait here for those who
argue that body parts are alienable property. See, for example, Lori
Andrews, "My Body, My Property," *Hastings Center Report* 16 (Oct.
1986): 28, 36 (arguing thoughtfully for a "quasi-property" approach in
which "human beings have the right to treat certain physical parts

of their bodies as objects for possession, gifts, and trade"); Comment, "Retailing Human Organs under the Uniform Commercial Code," *John Marshall Law Review* 16 (1983): 393, 405 (arguing that "society should not view the sale of human organs any differently than the sale of other necessary commodities such as food, shelter, and medication").

39. See *PruneYard Shopping Center v. Robins;* note the tortured distinction of *PruneYard* in *Nollan v. California Coastal Commission,* 107 S.Ct. 3141, 3145 n.l. (1987).

40. In a case analytically similar to *PruneYard Shopping Center,* in that it involved state law diminishing a landowner's exclusion rights, the New Jersey Supreme Court declared, on normative grounds, that an agricultural landowner's property rights simply did not include the right to exclude Office of Economic Opportunity (OEO) workers who wished to counsel farmworkers about their federal rights. Hence the landowner could not claim trespass, or a deprivation of his supposed right to exclude others, when the federal workers entered his land without permission. *State v. Shack,* 58 N.J. 297 (1971).

41. In an article similar in spirit to this chapter, Carol Rose locates here (in the tension between liberal and republican theories of politics and property) the reason why the taking issue is still a "muddle." Carol Rose, "Mahon Reconstructed: Why the Takings Issue Is Still a Muddle." *Southern California Law Review* 57 (1984): 561.

42. See part II below on the Rule of Law.

43. The affinity between positivism and the interest-group theory of politics may simply lie in the compatibility of both with Hobbesian assumptions. See, for example, Frank Easterbrook, "Foreword: The Court and the Economic System," *Harvard Law Review* 98 (1984); 4.

44. Cf. Michelman, "Property, Utility, and Fairness," 1238 (sweepstakes discussion); *Penn Central Transportation Co. v. New York City,* 438 U.S. 104, 137 (1978) (Court's discussion of valuable rights afforded Penn Central through the City's transferable development rights program).

45. See, for example, "Symposium: The Republican Civic Tradition," *Yale Law Journal* 97 (1988): 1493.

46. See Frank Michelman, "Takings, 1987," *Columbia Law Review* 88 (1988): 1600.

47. See Radin, "The Liberal Conception of Property," 1693.

48. On occasion the courts are quite clear that that is how they understand their task. See *Penn Central Transportation Co. v. New York City,* 438 U.S. 104, 124 (1978) (taking decisions are "essentially ad hoc").

49. See Margaret Jane Radin, "Reconsidering the Rule of Law," *Boston University Law Review* 69 (1988): 781.

50. See John Rawls, *A Theory of Justice* (Cambridge: Harvard University Press, 1971), sec. 38, 235–43.

51. Mention of two ways of failing to render taking jurisprudence rule-like may be instructive. One way corresponds roughly to the liberal entitlement theory of property and one corresponds roughly to the liberal utilitarian view. Richard Epstein asserts that there is one canonical concept of property and any diminution of its scope is a taking. Epstein, *Takings,* 85; Richard Epstein, "An Outline of *Takings,*" *University of Miami Law Review* 41 (1986): 1 (synopsis of *Takings*). This definitional coup might satisfy lay libertarians, but fails to convince any who understand property to be both a contested concept and one that evolves historically. See Thomas Grey, "The Malthusian Constitution," *University of Miami Law Review* 41 (1986): 21. It also fails to convince any who think the personal/fungible continuum both normatively significant and observable in our practice of property. See Margaret Jane Radin, "The Consequences of Conceptualism," *University of Miami Law Review* 41 (1986): 239. Epstein undermines his own attempt to make takings rule-like by admitting the issues of corrective justice (especially the nuisance aspect and the reliance aspect) and political reciprocity, for his attempts to render these issues rule-like in turn fail to convince.

Frank Michelman, in an early but still important article, found that a utilitarian solution to the taking problem would have a "quasi-mathematical structure." Michelman, "Property, Utility, and Fairness," 1214. But the algorithmic structure was achieved by excepting the class of cases in which corrective justice is relevant, without trying to demonstrate that the exception could be algorithmically delineated, and by ignoring (largely, though not completely) the problem of political contextuality, that is, the dynamic nature of the problem.

For reflections on the jurisprudential problems posed by the death penalty, see Margaret Jane Radin, "Risk-of-Error Rules and Non-Ideal Justification," *NOMOS XXVIII; Justification* (New York: New York University Press, 1985); idem, "Cruel Punishment and Respect for Persons: Super Due Process for Death," *Southern California Law Review* 53 (1980): 1143.

52. For reflections on justifying takings decisions when they do not look very rule-like, see Michelman, "Takings, 1987," 1614; Radin, "Property and Personhood," 1002.

53. Nor am I addressing here the question whether it is possible to solve anything with rules. My own view is that a pragmatic reinterpretation of rules does indeed speak well to many legal situations; Radin,

"Reconsidering the Rule of Law." See also Frederick Schauer, *Playing by the Rules: A Philosophical Examination of Rule-Based Decisionmaking in Law and Life* (unpublished manuscript, 1989, forthcoming Oxford University Press, Clarendon Series).

54. See Radin, "Reconsidering the Rule of Law."

55. In other words, perhaps we possess an "overlapping consensus" about property. See John Rawls, "The Idea of an Overlapping Consensus," *Oxford Journal of Legal Studies* 7 (1987): 1.

56. Radin, "Reconsidering the Rule of Law."

57. See, for example, Rolf Sartorius, *Individual Conduct and Social Norms* (Encino: Dickenson 1975).

58. See, for example, Richard Epstein, "Needed: Activist Judges for Economic Rights," *Wall Street Journal*, Nov. 14, 1985, p. 32, col. 4; Robert Ellickson, "Suburban Growth Control," *Yale Law Journal* 86 (1977): 385.

59. See Frank Michelman, "Tutelary Jurisprudence and Constitutional Property," in Howard Dickman and Ellen Paul, eds., *Liberty, Property, and the Future of Constitutional Development* (Albany: SUNY Press, 1990).

60. Compare Susan Rose-Ackerman, "Against Ad-Hocery: A Comment on Michelman," *Columbia Law Review* 88 (1988): 1697, with Michelman, "Takings, 1987." Compare *Penn Central Transportation Co. v. New York City*, 438 U.S. 104, 124 (1978), (taking decisions are "essentially ad hoc") with *Loretto v. Teleprompter Manhattan CATV Corp.*, 458 U.S. 419 (1982) and *Nollan v. California Coastal Commission*, 107 S.Ct. 3141 (1987) (seeking *a priori* rules).

61. Stephen Munzer, in chapter 8 of this volume, writes in what I take to be a pragmatic spirit when he advocates a pluralistic intuitionist approach that denies the possibility of a "formula or calculus" and seems to accept that appropriate principles may be conflicting and undecidable except for situated judgment. His treatment does not highlight, however, what I take to be important points: the scope of the political contextuality problem, and the close connection between a theory of justified property holding and a theory of justified government (that is, of politics and the person).

Munzer deviates from the pragmatic spirit, perhaps, when he implies that there is a clear line between a tax and some other kind of regulation that might count as a taking, and when in his penultimate paragraph he suggests both that we might "elaborate subordinate rules" to be applied more readily than the general complex of principles, and hints that the takings problem might be helped by "an account of institutional competence." These suggestions seem to imply, contrary to the pragmatic approach, that there may after all be some *a priori* across-the-board method that can order the taking problem in advance of the practice of deciding cases. Both nonpragmatists and pragmatists alike will be troubled by Munzer's failure to confront the problem presented for the Rule of Law by his multiprincipled intuitionist approach. Nonpragmatists will find it invites arbitrary judicial ad hoc decisions, and pragmatists will find that in omitting the Rule of Law (except for this final hint), Munzer's theory omits a central and pervasive feature of our practice.

PART V

LEGAL CULTURES

11

THE LIMITS OF COMPENSATORY JUSTICE

CASS R. SUNSTEIN

The model of compensatory justice is the staple of Anglo-American legal systems.* One person harms another; the purpose of the lawsuit is to ensure that the victim is compensated by the aggressor. Drawing from this basic understanding, the model of compensatory justice is organized around five basic principles.

1. The event that produced the injury is both discrete and unitary.
2. The injury is sharply defined in time and in space.
3. The defendant's conduct has clearly caused the harm suffered by the plaintiff. The harm must be attributable to the defendant, and not to some third party or to "society."
4. Both plaintiff and defendant are identifiable and a bilateral relation exists between them.

*I am extremely grateful to participants in the annual meeting of the American Society for Political and Legal Philosophy, the Yale University seminar on American Political and Institutional Development, and the University of Chicago Law School workshop for valuable comments. Bruce Ackerman, Jon Elster, Larry Kramer, Peter Schuck, David Strauss, and Robin West also offered helpful suggestions.

5. Apart from the goal of compensation, narrowly defined, existing entitlements are held constant. The purpose of the remedy, and of the legal system, is to restore the plaintiff to the position that he would have occupied if the unlawful conduct had not occurred. It is not to engage in any kind of social reordering or social management except insofar as those functions are logically entailed by the principle of compensation. Noncompensatory disruption of the existing distribution of wealth and entitlements, and particularly injuries to innocent parties, are barred.

Principles of compensatory justice are the defining feature of the common law of tort, contract, and property. In all of these areas, those principles are usually thought to perform reasonably well, in the sense that they capture intuitions that underlie diverse conceptions of the role of the legal system in settling disputes and in remedying illegality. In particular, compensatory principles can be associated with approaches to law that draw on utilitarian and deontological conceptions deriving from such otherwise diverse thinkers as Locke, Bentham, and Kant.[1] These principles might serve to protect a realm of private autonomy, reflecting principles of both entitlement and desert, and at the same time to promote optimal deterrence of socially undesirable activity.

In numerous areas of public and private law, however, traditional principles of compensatory justice are unattractive, or at least serve to rule out quite plausible alternatives. The basic problem is that in ways large or small, those principles are ill-matched to the best theories that underlie the plaintiff's claim. In these contexts, the relevant harm is not sharply defined, and it cannot be connected to a discrete event; the problem involves a collective risk rather than an individual right; the defendant is not easily identifiable, or has a highly ambiguous relation to the harm; causation itself is doubtful; the injured party cannot be specified in advance; the notion of restoration to a status quo ante seems logically incoherent, unworkable, or based on fictions; and/or the status quo should itself be questioned, or taken as endogenous to the legal rule or the decision at issue. In cases of this sort, the harms in question may be described as *regulatory*. When a regulatory harm is at stake, principles of compensatory justice may generate a regime of legal rules that is perverse.

Here I make two basic claims. The first is explanatory. A number of areas of doctrinal disarray in both private and public law, I argue, are produced by the importation of principles of compensatory justice into a context in which those principles are highly contested. The source of the difficulty is the controversial character of applying compensatory principles in those settings.

Indeed, the rise of administrative agencies and the dramatic displacement of the common law courts in the twentieth century are partly attributable to dissatisfaction with the compensatory model. Both the New Deal period and the "rights revolution" of the 1960s and 1970s saw self-conscious responses to the inadequacy of compensatory principles. The rise of institutions foreign to the original system of tripartite government reflects models of the role of the legal system that depart from compensatory ideas. An extraordinary anomaly of the American system of public law is the continued use of the compensatory model in defining the content and reach of the very initiatives that were created to displace it.

My second claim is normative. Legislatures and administrative agencies, I suggest, should sometimes abandon compensatory principles, and courts should be receptive to such efforts at abandonment. To say this is emphatically not to say that courts should frequently venture in that direction without legislative or administrative authorization. But in many contexts, the engrafting of compensatory principles onto programs built on quite different premises has produced results that are incorrect, even nonsensical. In such contexts, compensatory ideas ought to be rejected in favor of alternative conceptions of the function of legal controls. In particular, two conceptions seem to provide superior accounts of a large area of the disputed territory.

The first substitutes for notions of compensatory justice a principle of *risk management*. Many modern legal standards are designed to diminish and manage risks, not to vindicate individual rights or furnish compensation to injured parties. Under risk management, social ordering is indeed the goal of legal rules, in the form of systematic, ex ante restructing of the incentives faced by private actors.

The second conception, departing from compensatory justice in distinct ways, introduces a principle of *nonsubordination*. This principle is not simple to define, and I will have to be somewhat imprecise and tentative about it. In discrimination law, the instinct underlying the plaintiffs' claim is poorly captured when put in terms of compensatory principles. At least some of the time, blacks, women, the disabled, and others bringing discrimination suits do not claim that they have been injured by a discrete actor at a specific time. Nor are their claims connected in any simple way with past discrimination, and certainly not with acts of discrimination that can be tightly connected with their particular complaint. Nor are they seeking to hold existing entitlements constant; on the contrary, existing entitlements are the precise object of attack. Their argument is that a difference irrelevant from the moral point of view has been turned, without sufficient reason, into a social disadvantage in important spheres of life.

In these cases, a tort-like conception of discrimination produces strange results. Above all, the problem is that it holds too much constant. A compensatory model of discrimination misconceives the basis of the relevant action. It follows, perhaps jarringly, that in these cases past discrimination is largely immaterial. Principles of nonsubordination provide the basis for statutory and on occasion judicial initiatives in the area of race and sex discrimination and, perhaps most strikingly, disability. Compensatory principles present a sharp contrast, although they have frequently been invoked to define the content of discrimination law.

Principles of risk management and nonsubordination, I contend, better capture the dynamics of a number of disputes currently conceived in terms of compensatory justice. Indeed, a large part of the shift from private to public law consists of the progressive abandonment of traditional principles of compensatory justice. This shift is one of both substantive principle and institutional design. The dramatic movement from adjudication to administration; the New Deal reformation of the 1930s and the rights revolution of the 1960s and 1970s; the design of programs, especially in the environmental area, to redress individually small but collectively large injuries; occasionally dramatic softening of traditional requirements of causation; recognition of "rights" against risks, especially in the law of the environment, the workplace, and consumer products; substitution of public for private initiative and enforcement; deterrence of injuries that are probabilistic and systemic in character—all these are part of the basic movement I wish to describe.

At the same time, and this is my central complaint, compensatory principles exert a tenacious hold on the legal mind, and are often applied in adjudicative contexts in which they are anachronistic or have little or no place. Whether because of the lawyer's acculturation, judges' emphasis on their own institutional limits, or (most probably) substantive disagreements about the appropriate and actual role of law in society, there are continuing tensions between an adjudicative culture operating under a compensatory model and a legal system based on quite different ideas. These tensions account for many of the most important dilemmas in modern public law and public policy as well.

I. Compensatory Principles in Surprising Places

My goal in this section is to outline a series of controversies in which principles of compensatory justice are used in areas in which they are highly contested and quite plausibly do not belong. The contested character of compensatory principles accounts for contemporary doctrinal disputes.

In these areas, a legal system founded on compensatory principles often confronts a set of statutory initiatives built on different foundations. In the nineteenth century, from which many of the current debates arise, compensatory principles were especially dominant in both private and public law. On this view regulatory legislation—minimum wage or maximum hour laws, for example—was often unconstitutional because it represented an impermissible "taking" from one group for the benefit of another.[2] "Redistribution" was constitutionally out of bounds. With only a few exceptions, the legal system could take wealth

or property from one person only in the service of compensatory goals. Existing distributions of wealth and entitlements were
off-limits to law. Unless changes were in the interest of compensatory justice, narrowly defined, they were barred.

This framework came under attack with a recognition that
the existing distributions were themselves a product of law rather
than an aspect of "the state of nature." This understanding was
accompanied by the view that regulatory legislation superim-
posed one set of legal controls on another; it did not displace,
with law, spontaneous or prepolitical interactions. This set of
ideas can be found in both academic and political debate. Thus
Franklin Roosevelt argued for social security by pointing to
harms that could not be wholly avoided in this "man-made
world" of ours, and urged, "We must lay hold of the fact that
the laws of economics are not made by nature. They are made
by human beings."[3] Ideas of this sort were part of a process of
denaturalizing existing distributions of property and wealth, by
showing that they are a product of social custom and indeed of
law itself.

These ideas helped fuel the rise of the regulatory state, which
frequently redistributes property among social groups and no
longer treats existing distributions as sacrosanct. They were
accompanied by a recognition, especially in the 1960s and 1970s,
of the collective action and coordination problems that often
make reliance on private markets inadequate. This is so especially in the area of environmental controls, where the compensatory capacities of the common law are outstripped by virtue
of the enormous difficulties in aggregating individually small
injuries through adjudicative processes. Regulatory programs,
interfering with freedom of contract, find multiple justifications. Occasionally they respond to market failure; sometimes
they attempt to redistribute resources; sometimes they reflect
collective aspirations or considered judgments, departing from
private consumption choices; sometimes they respond to the
perception that private choices are based on an absence of information, on limited opportunities, or on unjust background institutions, all to be counteracted through law.[4]

In their entirety, the resulting shifts, of substantive principle
and institutional design, make compensatory principles a quite

partial and often anachronistic feature of the legal system, both inside and outside of the courts. But a legal system reared on these principles has an exceedingly difficult time in adapting itself.

A. The Small Claim Class Action

Since the Federal Rules of Civil Procedure were amended in the late 1960s, there has been an enormous growth in the use of the class action device, which allows many people to join together in a lawsuit. One of the purposes of the class action device is to ensure vindication, through the courts, of legal claims that are not viable on their own. The major problem here is that small injuries must be aggregated to be litigable; if they must be redressed separately, they will not be redressed at all. Assume, for example, that a defendant engages in fraudulent advertising, causing fifty dollars in damages to each of several thousand purchasers. For each claimant, the expense of bringing suit dwarfs the damages. No person who is alert to costs and benefits will initiate litigation. Since harms of this sort will have to be amalgamated in a class suit to be remedied at all, the class action guarantees that the relevant wrongs will be punished and deterred.

In a number of ways, the small claim class action, collecting individually small but collectively large injuries, strains compensatory principles.

(a) Notice. It is not unusual for small claim class actions to carry costs of notice that are so high as to exceed the potential recovery for one or even many class members. Rule 23 says that in class actions, courts should give "the best notice practicable, including individual notice to all class members who can be identified through reasonable effort."[5] Does this provision require the class representative to provide individual notice to all class members in the small claim class action?

In *Eisen v. Carlisle & Jacquelin*,[6] the Supreme Court concluded that it does. The Court's holding is a straightforward adaptation of compensatory justice ideas drawn from private law. On this view, any person whose legal rights are at stake has a right to be notified before the case is adjudicated. But in the small claim class action, claims are not viable individually. The case will go forward as a class action or not at all. Moreover, the expense of giving notice to a huge group of members will be so high as to prevent the action from proceeding. In these circumstances, a requirement of individual notice seems perverse.

The point may be put in a slightly different way. The purpose of notice is to protect those whose legal interests will be affected by adjudication; if one's interests are at stake, and will be foreclosed by the ruling, one has a right at least to know about it. But if the consequence of notice is to prevent rights from being vindicated at all, it is quite odd to say that notice must be given in the interest of protecting the rights of those affected. In the small claim class action, the use of principles of notice reflexively drawn from compensatory models is irrational and serves no purpose.

(b) Distribution of Damages. How should damages be distributed in small claim class actions? Suppose, for example, that the defendant has engaged in securities fraud against millions of purchasers, that the average purchaser was defrauded of between fifty and one hundred dollars, and that the total damages amount to nearly a billion dollars. Suppose also that the court has made efforts to permit purchasers to recover their damages, by providing notice in the newspapers and elsewhere; but that after these efforts, several million dollars remain in the fund produced by the extraction from the defendant of his ill-gotten gains.

The problems here are similar to those that arise in the context of notice. If the court is required to ensure that the funds are actually distributed to class members, the fund will be depleted. The costs of identification of and distribution to those defrauded will take a huge chunk out of the total. Indeed, those costs may exceed the damages for individual plaintiffs. The problem is a product of the fact that it is exceptionally expensive to identify all class members in the small claim class action. Even exhaustive efforts may fail.

In these circumstances, there are several possibilities for the distribution of damages. First, the damages might revert to the defendant on the ground that compensatory goals cannot be satisfied by any sensible system of distribution. If the injured parties cannot be identified, it might be thought best to allow the defendant to keep the money, a conclusion that seems to follow naturally from compensatory principles. Second, the court might allow for "fluid class recovery." Under this approach, the defendant's illegal profits might be applied to reduce the prices charged by the defendant in future transactions, so that people who are securities purchasers, even if not necessarily injured parties, might benefit. Under another approach, the damages might go to various good works, including, for example, an institute for the study of the securities market. In yet another perspective, the damages might go to the government.

In general, the federal courts are hostile to the fluid class recovery and to noncompensatory remedies, suggesting that the damages should remain with the defendant if they cannot be used for the benefit of injured parties. But attitudes of this sort seem to misconceive the aim of the small claim class action. Here the goal is not to compensate the plaintiffs, but instead to deter and punish the risk-creating behavior. Nothing is gained by allowing the defendant to keep funds that have been unlawfully obtained. Despite its lack of fit with the traditional model, non-compensatory remedies have much to be said in their favor.

B. Probabilistic Torts

Often regulatory schemes and sometimes modern litigation are designed to respond to risks of injury that cannot be tightly connected with any specific harm to any individual. Prominent recent illustrations are lawsuits over the harms caused by substances such as Agent Orange. The problem here is that any particular harm, or incidence of cancer, may or may not be attributable to exposure. It is possible that some carcinogen was responsible for the death of someone who died of cancer after exposure, or for her infertility. But it is possible as well that the person would have had the same problems in any event. The problem is complicated by the fact that a plaintiff might be unable to attribute her injury to an identifiable seller of the risk-creating substance.

In these circumstances, judicial treatment of the problem is murky. Standards have yet to be developed.[7] One possibility, rooted in traditional compensatory principles, is to deny recovery altogether unless and until the injury has occurred. But if that route is followed, it is unclear that the plaintiff would recover at all. The difficulties in establishing causation may prove insuperable; there are extraordinary evidentiary problems here. Another possibility would be to allow people to be compensated, either before or after the harm, in dollar equivalents for increased risks of disease. But there are severe problems here as well. The legal system does not ordinarily compensate people for increased risks as opposed to "actual harms"—a legacy of traditional and probably anachronistic understandings. Moreover, when the harm has occurred, compensation for the risk alone might seem, to many observers, to be far too low. Whether or not the harm has occurred, the problem of valuation remains, and this problem is especially troublesome where assessment of probabilities is so difficult. Importation of principles of compensatory justice has made it extremely difficult to develop sensible solutions to the problem of probabilistic torts.

C. Regulatory Harms

In recent years, courts have frequently been confronted with social and economic regulation that is designed to prevent harms that are probable, systemic, or regulatory in nature. These harms consist of risks rather than concrete injuries. The magnitude of these risks is typically highly disputed; no clear relation can be established between an injured party and a harm-causing actor. The goal of the program is to manage social risks rather than to vindicate individual rights. In numerous respects, the decision to create a system redressing regulatory harms represents a rejection of traditional compensatory principles.

Consider, for example, the decisions of the National Traffic Safety Administration to require passive restraints in automobiles, of the Occupational Safety and Health Administration to reduce levels of benzene from 10 to 1 part per million, and of the Environmental Protection Agency to impose fuel efficiency requirements on new automobiles. Many courts show antagonism to measures of this sort, requiring agencies to demonstrate that discrete harms to identifiable actors have occurred or will occur. For this reason they have invalidated agency rule making in such contexts on the ground that the relevant harms are too speculative.[8] When the government is unable to show a tight causal connection between the requirements it imposes and discrete injuries, or when the injuries would occur in the future and are speculative in character, the judiciary tends to be skeptical. The problem here is that a governmental actor is seeking to "reorder society" by demanding measures from someone who has not been shown to have been a tortfeasor, and whose behavior may not in fact produce future injury.

By contrast, courts are hospitable to administrative proceedings that fit the compensatory model more neatly. Backward-looking, remedial measures are treated with far less suspicion. In the context of automobile regulation, the basic paradigm is the recall proceeding, in which automobiles sold to identifiable persons and actually shown to be defective are taken off the market. In the area of automobile regulation, the result of the courts' simultaneous hostility to prospective rule making and endorsement of recalls is to press national policy into a system of safety regulation almost entirely through recalls—in all likelihood, an irrational way to reduce automobile accidents and injuries.[9] The continuing strength of compensatory justice ideas is the principal motivating force here. In a variety of areas of contemporary law, courts require administrators to satisfy the requirements of the traditional compensatory model, despite the fact that the model is awkwardly adapted to systemic or regulatory harms.

D. Standing: Access to Judicial Review

Who is entitled to seek review of the action, or inaction, of a regulatory agency? The problem arises when the beneficiaries of government programs—victims of pollution, discrimination, securities fraud, toxic substances in the workplace—attempt to bring suit against regulatory inaction, or action on their behalf that they think inadequate.

In recent years, the Supreme Court has held that plaintiffs

challenging administrative decisions must show (1) that their injury is a result of the conduct complained of and (2) that their injury is likely to be redressed by a judicial decree in their favor. These requirements are described as involving "redressibility" or "causation"; they are clear holdovers from compensatory principles.

Notions of this sort are used to support a variety of judicial conclusions: that parents of children attending schools undergoing desegregation may not challenge the grant of tax deductions to segregated private schools;[10] that poor people may not challenge the change of tax regulations so as to reduce hospitals' incentives to provide medical services to the indigent;[11] that prospective purchasers of fuel-efficient cars may not challenge the EPA's decision to give retroactive benefits to automobile manufacturers.[12]

In all of these cases, denial of standing is based squarely on principles of compensatory justice. If a plaintiff cannot show that a discrete harm to him is a result of the government's action, judicial redress should be unavailable. The basic model for the lawsuit consists of discrete injury and discrete remedy. If the suit does not fit that format, no legally cognizable harm exists at all.

The problem with these ideas is that in the cases at issue, the plaintiffs' injury is regulatory or systemic in character. Plaintiffs contend that the harm they suffer takes the form of an increased risk, not of a discrete injury. If their injury is recharacterized to involve an increased risk, or a systemic harm, there is no doubt that an injury has been suffered. For example, plaintiffs might urge that their injury consists in an impairment of the opportunity to obtain medical services under a regime undistorted by unlawful tax incentives; that they have been deprived of the opportunity to undergo desegregation in school systems unaffected by unlawful tax deductions; that their opportunity to purchase fuel-efficient cars has been constrained. The question for the courts is whether increased risks are a legitimate basis for judicial intervention.

When the administration of governmental programs becomes an issue in court, it is frequently because of harms that are regulatory rather than tightly connected to a discrete plaintiff and a discrete defendant. The programs exist precisely because the compensatory capacities of the courts are outstipped in these settings. The problem raised by the standing cases is whether the courts ought to see, as judicially cognizable, actions that attempt to prevent harms that statutes were written to redress, but that do not fall within compensatory principles. This is the question that has produced doctrinal disarray.

E. Racial Discrimination

In its most important recent decisions on racial discrimination, the Supreme Court has concluded that plaintiffs alleging a violation of the equal protection clause must plead and prove "discriminatory purpose" on the part of the governmental actor.[13] A showing of discriminatory effects is insufficient. These decisions have had enormous consequences, immunizing from attack a wide range of practices that have disproportionate discriminatory effects on blacks, women, and others. Discriminatory purpose is extremely difficult to prove.

The requirement of discriminatory purpose is a clear outgrowth of compensatory principles. Indeed, it defines the constitutional concept of equal protection by reference to traditional tort principles; in this respect, it attests to the tenacity of those principles in the legal culture. The basic notion is that the government violates the equality principle when it acts like a private law tortfeasor, intentionally harming someone. But when there is no identifiable act by an identifiable actor who intends to cause harm, legal redress is not forthcoming. Equality, on this view, is itself rooted in traditional compensatory ideas. To be treated unequally is to be treated "differently" by a particular actor at a particular time. The equality norm is understood in terms of discrete rights and responsibilities, owed by identifiable perpetrators to identifiable victims.

A possible response here would be to suggest that if traditional private law principles were taken seriously, discriminatory purpose would not be required. Reasonably foreseeable harm-producing effects are usually sufficient in private law. It is surely foreseeable that verbal tests and the like will have racially discriminatory effects. On one version of the compensatory model, then, discriminatory effects would indeed be questioned.

Ironically, however, the Court has rejected the reasonably foreseeable effects test for reasons that are ultimately traceable to the compensatory model. If such effects were sufficient to draw government action into doubt, the compensatory model would itself be thrown into question insofar as it attempts to promote its own central goals: holding existing entitlements constant, avoiding social reordering or redistribution, and preventing injuries to innocent parties. In most societies, including our own, disproportionate effects along lines of race and sex are almost always foreseeable. To say that such effects raise constitutional issues would be to call for wholesale reallocation of social benefits and burdens as between blacks and whites and men and women. The costs of such a reallocation would have to be borne by people who played little or no role in "causing" the current inequalities of blacks and women. It is here that the deeply substantive foundations of the compensatory model fit well with a requirement of discriminatory purpose.

But the Court's approach to the problem is highly controversial.[14] The current distribution of benefits and burdens as between blacks and whites and women and men is not part of the state of nature but a consequence of past and present social practices. This idea is itself congenial to the New Deal attack on the compensatory model; recognition of the role of law in allocating wealth and entitlements is central to both the rise of regulation and to the attack on the discriminatory purpose requirement. The status quo, reflective as it is of both law and injustice, presents a questionable baseline from which to distinguish between partisanship and neutrality, or action and inaction. In these circumstances, nothing is neutral in the use of criteria that, while not discriminatorily motivated, entrench those practices or ensure that they will have important current consequences. Indeed, critics of the intent requirement argue that the use of compensatory principles misconceives the nature of the equality claim by ensuring that nothing, or close to nothing, will be done about existing inequality. The inability to make a tight causal connection between the current pattern of distribution along racial and gender lines and identifiable past acts by identifiable actors ought not, in this view, to be taken as an obstacle to legal objections to practices that perpetuate the social subordination of various groups. The problem of inequality is not at all understandable in traditional compensatory terms.

Similar issues arise in the context of sex discrimination. Consider, for example, *Personnel Administrator v. Feeney,*[15] in which the Supreme Court was asked to decide whether a veterans' preference program, relegating to clerical positions most women in the Massachusetts civil service, violated the equal protection clause. The Court held that there was no violation because the plaintiff was unable to show discriminatory intent. In the Court's view, the plaintiff must show that a particular measure was enacted "because of rather than in spite of" its effect on a disadvantaged group. But perhaps an intent requirement, properly understood even under compensatory principles, would have required the Court to ask: Would the Massachusetts legislature have enacted the veterans' preference law if men, rather than women, had been hurt by it? That question is probably impossible to answer. An effort to ascertain what the treatment of veterans' preference laws would have been in a world unaffected by sexism leads to insoluble logical conundrums.[16] In any case, both the use of and the controversy over the discriminatory intent requirement are products of the awkwardness of using traditional compensatory principles in this setting.

F. School Desegregation

Suppose that a school district engaged in de jure segregation until 1954, and that in 1958, 1968, or 1978 a judge issues a finding to the effect. The example is far from hypothetical. What remedy ought to be imposed? The Supreme Court's cases are exceptionally complex on the point.[17] The Court's basic approach to the problem seems to involve an attempt to restore the status quo ante. Hence the desegregation cases ask whether the remedy proposed will restore the system to what it would have been if not for past acts of segregation. Under this rationale, the Court has invalidated "freedom of choice" desegregation plans, emphasizing that they will bring about less desegregation than would have occurred if there had been no segregation in the first instance.[18]

Principles of compensatory justice play a prominent, indeed central role here. They define the very nature of the inquiry. Some justices, for example, emphasize the difficulty of finding a good causal connection between post-1970 practices and pre-1954 discrimination.[19] For them, the weak causal connection with past illegality means that the law should not make people restructure present practices. By contrast, other justices emphasize the legacy of past discrimination and what they see as its undeniable connection with present injustice.

Both sides appear, however, to downplay the fact that issues of causation, and the compensatory principles that underlie them, appear to have little coherence in this context. An inquiry into the amount of racial integration that would have occurred in a world unaffected by racial segregation is likely to be empirically unanchored, indeed chimerical. Social scientists, let alone judges, are simply unequipped to answer that question—and not because of the lack of the appropriate tools, but because the question itself is of uncertain epistemological status. To try to resolve issues bearing on desegregation remedies in terms of compensatory principles is a recipe for confusion.

G. Affirmative Action

In cases involving affirmative action, the Supreme Court has frequently indicated that race-conscious measures are permissible only as a "remedy" for identifiable acts of purposeful discrimination undertaken by the institution engaging in affirmative action.[20] Affirmative action grounded in an effort to overcome "societal discrimination" is generally impermissible. In so holding, the Court has emphasized that the victims of affirmative action are either employers or, much more frequently, white people or men who never engaged in discriminatory conduct. The problem of innocent victims appears to be a principal impetus behind the requirement of a showing of past discrimination. Under current law, affirmative action can be defended most easily in tort-like terms, as an effort to restore a status quo ante that has been unsettled by identifiable acts producing identifiable harms to identifiable actors.

All of these ideas are an outgrowth of the use of principles of compensatory justice in the affirmative action setting. One could, however, imagine a different model, one having roots in the New Deal attack on compensatory principles. For example, forward-looking justifications might be brought into play: justifications that point not to discrimination by the affirmative actor in the past, but to the need for race-conscious measures to eliminate workplace caste, to promote diversity in the educational process, to ensure a balanced police force in the interest of community service, or to accomplish a range of other goals.[21] Concepts of compensatory justice seem to miss, indeed to distort, some of the principles that underlie affirmative action programs.

More generally, affirmative action might be understood not as a remedy for discrete acts by discrete actors, or as a response to identifiable breaches of past and present duty, but as an effort to overcome the social subordination of the relevant groups. On this view, whose details remain to be worked out, the problem of racial discrimination is systemic rather than episodic in character. It is not controlling and perhaps not even relevant that the harms that affirmative action attempts to redress cannot be understood in the usual compensatory terms. The purpose of the "remedy" is, to be sure, to respond to injustice. But the nature of the problem guarantees that the legal response cannot take the form of discrete remedies for discrete harms.

H. Disability

For the most part, the disabled have nothing to gain from the equal protection clause.[22] If the deaf and blind bring suit to challenge their exclusion from public jobs designed by and for people who hear and see, or if people using wheelchairs attack a transportation system to which they are denied access, the answer is identical: they have been treated "the same" as the able-bodied, and the equal protection clause imposes no "affirmative" obligation on government to restructure its business.[23]

The reason for these perhaps jarring results is the use of

compensatory principles to give content to constitutional equality principles. In the ordinary course of affairs, no distinct, tort-like wrong has been committed against the disabled. The use of stairs, or inaccessible buildings, or practices and norms established for the able-bodied, does not easily fall into a compensatory model.

Advocates of legal rights for the handicapped are operating pursuant to a different conception of legal injury. Their complaint, pointing to a systemic harm, is that practices designed by and for the able-bodied predictably create a range of obstacles to the disabled. Largely those practices, and not disability "itself," a highly ambiguous concept, are responsible for the daily handicaps faced by the disabled. The objection from the standpoint of equality is that such systems turn a difference into a systemic disadvantage and must accordingly be justified or changed. Complaints of this sort have had some impact on Congress.

I. Summary

We have seen a number of different areas in which compensatory principles raise serious questions; it is now time to sort out those questions. In the small claim class action, the problem simply involves the costs of notice and of distributing damages. The departure from the compensatory model is the relatively trivial one of transactions costs in bringing about compensation. In the case of regulatory harms, the compensatory model is tested more severely; here the requirements of identifiable plaintiffs and defendants and of clear causation are drawn into doubt. Causation is speculative, and one knows neither plaintiffs nor defendants ex ante. In the area of discrimination, the challenge to the compensatory model is most fundamental. The plaintiffs are seeking significant social reordering; they do not want to hold existing entitlements constant; they question the status quo.

There are of course similarities as well as differences. Above all, the courts' skepticism about ex ante rule making, about discriminatory effects tests, and about probabilistic injuries has a similar foundation, namely, in the perception that the existing distribution of wealth and entitlements forms the neutral baseline against which to assess the propriety of legal intervention, and the associated belief that social reordering, through law, ought not to be permitted except in the service of compensation to identifiable plaintiffs injured by identifiable defendants at discrete times. This approach appears to be undergirded by an understanding that existing distributions are not themselves unjust, are not the product of law, or at least are not to be challenged in the context of the issue at hand.

It is here that the compensatory model, despite its apparently formal character, is rooted in a deeply substantive, and controversial, conception about the appropriate role of law. Here the relevant disputes embody a disagreement about first principles. Those disputes, revisiting arguments during the New Deal, involve the actual and appropriate place of law in the social structure. Is redistribution off-limits? Are existing distributions unjust or already a product of law? Can the legal system impose costs on people who have not produced traditional injuries? Questions of this sort underlie many of the relevant debates.

II. Substitutes for Compensatory Justice

The analysis so far should be sufficient to reveal that principles of compensatory justice have played an important role in a number of areas. The legal culture is permeated by them, from the first year in law school to the very structuring of adjudication. In part for this reason, compensatory principles have given content and shape to programs built on quite different foundations. But there are alternative ways of understanding the role of the legal system in these settings. Compensatory principles are a controversial choice among competing possibilities.

In this section, I explain how the persistence of principles of compensatory justice has had an important distorting effect in many areas of current law. More concretely, I suggest that legal issues have been approached through compensatory principles when those issues might better be understood in terms of principles of *risk management* or *nonsubordination*. These principles, I suggest, are best adopted by legislatures and administrators rather than by courts; but when the former institutions have

acted, courts ought not to define the reach of the relevant
programs by reference to compensatory notions.

It is notable that such principles do not entirely reject compensatory ideas. Even in cases falling within their domain, they
require a showing of both injury and a kind of causation. Without some version of these notions, regulatory harms and even
racial discrimination would be far less intelligible. But the risk
management and nonsubordination principles do not require a
clear causal connection between an identifiable actor and an
identifiable victim. They call for the redress of injuries that are
systemic rather than sharply defined. And they are intended to
bring about a kind of social reordering rather than a restoration
to some status quo ante. It is important as well that risk management and nonsubordination principles are different from each
other, and depart from the compensatory outlook in distinctive
ways.

The development of risk management and nonsubordination
principles has been tentative; it can be found mostly in the work
of Congress and administrative agencies. A large task for the
next generation is to elaborate them in some detail, and to
encourage the legal culture to shift in their direction. I venture
a preliminary treatment.

A. Risk Management

Many regulatory programs are designed not to prevent an ascertainable harm to an ascertainable actor, but instead to manage and diminish risks that affect large classes of people. Here
a close connection exists between development of principles of
risk management and the understandings that underlay the
New Deal and the rights revolution, especially insofar as the
latter involved environmental degradation. Systemic restructuring rather than compensation of injured parties is the overriding task. The aim is optimal deterrence of harmful conduct.

This aim is to be achieved in the presence of several problems: (1) difficult issues of causation; (2) victims and aggressors
who are not readily identifiable; (3) complex technical issues
and scientific uncertainty; and (4) severe collective action and
coordination problems making it difficult to rely, as the tort

system does, on private initiative. Statutes protecting the environment, consumers, and occupational safety and health are conspicuous examples. In these cases, the goal of public law cannot realistically be understood in compensatory terms. No concrete event produced an identifiable harm stemming from an identifiable defendant to an identifiable plaintiff. The purpose of the regulatory system is not to restore a status quo ante.

These points have implications for a variety of contested issues. Consider, for example, the question of standing. In recent cases, some courts have suggested that to have access to judicial review, a plaintiff must show that he would suffer an identifiable harm as a result of the defendant's action. A "speculative" injury is not enough. But whether the harm is speculative depends on how it is defined. In the celebrated *Bakke*[24] case the plaintiff challenging an affirmative action scheme was said to have standing because his injury consisted of deprivation of an "opportunity to compete." By characterizing his harm as an "opportunity"-type injury, the Court was able to avoid the difficulties that would have been produced in terms of causation if the injury had been described as, for example, a failure to be admitted to medical school.

The device of recharacterizing the injury as implicating an "opportunity" is relatively rare in the cases. But as we have seen, modern regulatory schemes are typically designed to redress probabilistic or systemic harms. In these circumstances, the consequences for any person are inevitably "speculative." The plaintiff attempts to redress an increased risk, not a discrete injury. In these cases, the question is whether a regulatory harm should be a sufficient basis for standing. And in light of the purposes of the relevant regulatory scheme, there is no reason that it should not be. Regulatory harms should quite generally be a sufficient basis for judicial review.

Principles of risk management would call for reformation of many of the doctrines described above. If regulatory programs were understood in these terms, and traditional compensatory principles were abandoned, one would expect a number of novel developments. I outline some possible directions.

1. Reviewing courts should be far more hospitable to agencies trying to counteract regulatory or systemic harms. Use of com-

pensatory principles has distorted several regulatory programs, especially automobile regulation. The judicially mandated shift from rule making to recalls, founded in compensatory notions, has led to far less rational regulation. It would have been better for courts to permit regulatory controls to redress harms that could not be confidently described ex ante. This is so particularly in the environmental area, but it applies to all programs attempting to manage and reduce risks.

2. The legal system should abandon compensatory principles in dealing with the small claim class action. The *Eisen* case, mandating notice in such cases, should be overruled by statute or rule. Moreover, courts should not, in the setting of the small claim class action, insist that the damages be transferred to the injured parties. The purpose of these actions is not compensation at all. Courts should be permitted to experiment with remedial strategies that include fluid class recovery.

3. Devices should be developed to allow for damages or punishment in cases of probabilistic harms, as in the context of exposure to toxic substances. Exposure to risk should itself be a liability-creating event. The development of some sort of mixed public and private enforcement mechanism, supplementing the tort system, would be a natural development.[25]

4. A major task for modern public law is to develop strategies of risk management that attempt to control the most serious risks most cheaply. As first steps, it will be necessary to permit many risks, especially those that are *de minimis* in character. A system that bars trivial risks will create serious distortions in the allocation of enforcement and compliance resources. It will also be necessary to develop a system of priorities putting limited funds for enforcement where they will do the most good. A major advance here would be to impose, in all regulatory programs, a proportionality principle calling for attention to the costs and benefits of regulatory action.

Risk management principles will also call for coordination of regulatory systems now diffused over many statutes and agencies, and for recognition of the high potential costs of both action and inaction in the face of inadequate information. The general task of developing risk management strategies is made far more difficult by the persistence of compensatory principles.

Many of those principles must ultimately be abandoned or at least significantly altered.

B. Nonsubordination

We have seen that courts often approach questions of equality by way of traditional principles of compensatory justice. The courts' approach here has been based on a narrow conception of compensation, but a broader conception, with some roots in the cases, would draw on the same model in favor of far more victories for blacks and women. It is doubtful, however, that such an approach would make much sense. The search for a status quo ante is likely to be chimerical. What would the world look like if it had been unaffected by past discrimination on the basis of race and sex? As in the case of school desegregation, the question is unanswerable, not because of the absence of good social science, but because of the obscure epistemological status of the question itself. Moreover, it is unclear what the relevance of past discrimination is to the present status of blacks and women. Whether such discrimination is a necessary or sufficient condition for "remedial" efforts is by no means self-evident.

In these cases, the plaintiffs' claim, best understood, is not for compensation in the traditional sense, but instead for an end to, or a reduction of, a form of social subordination. The concept of subordination is by no means self-defining, and I will have to be tentative and somewhat vague about it. A concept of this kind will certainly point in the direction of an alternative understanding of the nature of equality and inequality, one that has little to do with discrete harms to discrete persons as a result of identifiable conduct by discrete actors.

The motivating idea behind a nonsubordination principle, Rawlsian in character, is that differences that are irrelevant from the moral point of view ought not without good reason to be turned, by social and legal structures, into disadvantages. They certainly should not be permitted to do so if the disadvantage is systemic, in the sense that it operates in multiple spheres of life, or if it applies in realms that determine basic participation as a citizen in a democracy.[26] In the areas of race and sex discrimination, and of disability as well, the problem is precisely this sort of systemic disadvantage. A social or biological difference has the effect of systematically subordinating the relevant group, and of doing so in multiple spheres and along multiple indices of social welfare: poverty, education, political power, employment, susceptibility to violence and crime, and so forth. That is the subordination to which the legal system is attempting to respond.[27]

Differences are usually invoked as the justification for disadvantage. The question is not, however, whether there is a difference, but whether the legal and social treatment of that difference can be adequately justified. Difference need not imply inequality; and only some differences have that implication. For these purposes it is not decisive whether a present disadvantage can be tightly connected to an intentionally discriminatory act by a public "tortfeasor," even if it is relevant that the subordination is in some sense a consequence of past and present public action. This intuition, I suggest, provides the principal impetus behind antidiscrimination efforts. That impetus is but the most recent version of the same intuition that originally produced a rejection of compensatory principles.

A few disclaimers are necessary. The nonsubordination principle, if taken seriously, would call for significant restructuring of social practices. The principle is better set out and implemented by legislative and administrative bodies, with their superior democratic pedigree and fact-finding capacities, than by constitutional courts. Moreover, it is important to acknowledge that for good Rawlsian reasons a wide range of differences are morally arbitrary, and in a market economy those differences are quite frequently translated into social disadvantages. Consider educational background, intelligence, strength, existing supply and demand curves for various products and services, even willingness to work hard.

A nonsubordination principle that would attempt, through law, to counteract all of these factors would be difficult indeed to sustain. In general, the recognition of such factors is inseparable from the operation of a market economy, which is an important source of freedom, prosperity, and respect for different conceptions of the good. The use of such factors is at least sometimes in the interest of the least well-off, and when this is so a nonsubordination principle that would bar them seems perverse. Moreover, a nonsubordination principle that would override all morally irrelevant factors would impose extraordinary costs on society, both in its implementation and administrative expense and in its infliction of losses on a wide range of people; and those costs are high enough to make such a global principle immensely unappealing. The nonsubordination principle therefore has greatest weight in discrete contexts, most notably including race, sex, and disability, in which gains from current practice to the least well-off are hard to imagine; in which there will be no global threat to a market economy; and in which the costs of implementation are not terribly high. The most general question is whether members of the disadvantaged group, or people who might find themselves in that category, could be persuaded that there are good reasons for the practice under attack. Here the answer will frequently be negative.

Although nonsubordination principles have a degree of overlap with those that underlie the risk management formula, they depart from compensatory principles in different ways. Risk management has clear connections to long-standing compensatory goals and is rooted in broadly analogous notions of entitlement, desert, and deterrence. Above all, risk management is supported by a belief that compensatory principles are inadequate in light of difficulties in establishing causation, in identifying perpetrators and victims, and in overcoming the collective action problems inherent in individually small but collectively large harms. Paretian criteria might well lead to exactly this shift from compensation to risk management, particularly in the environmental setting.[28] People who start from the compensatory tradition, broadly conceived, can often be led, without serious reluctance, to endorse risk management.

The nonsubordination model is not so readily defensible on Paretian grounds. Because it represents a conspicuous rejection, as unjust, of the status quo ante, those who accept the model are not bothered if some are made worse off by the results for which it calls. For example, affirmative action does not appear an impermissible "taking" of an antecedent entitlement. Because the existing distribution of benefits and burdens between blacks and whites and men and women is not natural and sacrosanct, and because it is in part a product of current laws and practices having discriminatory effects, it is not decisive if some whites and men are disadvantaged as a result. This idea is a direct application of the New Deal attack on compensation.

Moreover, nonsubordination offers a different and perhaps competing conception of entitlement. The idea that differences are systematically, and illegitimately, turned into disadvantages is foreign to the compensatory scheme. And while nonsubordination does have a compensatory feature—past and present discrimination, controversially defined, is at least an ingredient here—its normative foundations will seem foreign or objectionable to many who are schooled in the compensatory tradition as it is generally understood.

The nonsubordination conception of equality suggests a norm that cannot be captured by standard ideas about compensation. If accepted, this model would also have a series of consequences for present law.

1. At the very least, public and private actors ought generally be permitted to engage in voluntary race-conscious efforts even when the requirements of compensatory justice cannot be satisfied, that is, no identifiable defendant has "caused" the plaintiff's injury. Societal discrimination is a sufficient predicate for remedial action. Measures that are designed to overcome the effects of discrimination, by advantaging members of minority groups, cannot be assimilated to ordinary discrimination. Above all, race-conscious measures designed to reduce social subordination are supported by purposes and effects clearly opposite to those designed to bring it about.[29]

2. Forward-looking reasons for race-conscious measures[30] provide a legally sufficient justification for them, quite apart from the backward-looking reasons that the Supreme Court has generally required. Race-conscious efforts to get diversity in education, or otherwise to improve the performance of public institutions, ought generally to be permitted.

3. A showing of discriminatory effects should be sufficient to trigger a requirement that government justify its behavior in persuasive terms. If a law has a disproportionate impact on members of minority groups, or on women, the state should

demonstrate that the law is well supported by nondiscriminatory considerations. A test that excludes more blacks than whites, or a veterans' preference law having the effect of excluding women from high-level civil service jobs, would on this view be invalidated unless shown to be substantially related to an important state interest. Probably a test of this sort should be set out by legislatures rather than courts, because of the superior democratic pedigree and fact-finding competence of the former; judicial creation of an effects test would raise serious questions of democratic legitimacy. Many civil rights laws straightforwardly reject compensatory criteria in favor of standards that point to discriminatory effects.

4. Disabled people should have a prima facie claim of inequality in the use of standards and practices that have the effect of excluding them from important areas of public and private life. Inequality is produced when people who need wheelchairs cannot enter buildings; blind people are not given the means to read materials that the sighted take for granted; deaf people cannot hear fire alarms or act on equal terms in the courtroom. The usual response is to suggest that problems of this sort raise no equal protection issue because the handicapped are "different" and therefore not discriminated against. But this way of understanding discrimination is seriously mistaken. A system that turns differences into social disadvantages should be taken as a form of discrimination.

This is not to suggest that a world designed for the able-bodied must be redesigned to generate substantive equality for the handicapped. The meaning of a norm of substantive equality is ambiguous in this context. The costs of social change are relevant, and would be very high. In any event, it is hard to see how such a norm might be administered by the judiciary. The principal remedies must come from legislative and bureaucratic bodies. But a large category of cases raises issues of discrimination that call for some justification by the state. To point to the fact that handicapped people are different is insufficient. The legal and social consequences of the differences are the questions at issue. Any such differences are made relevant largely by human decisions.

III. Conclusion

Anglo-American legal systems are comfortable with principles of compensatory justice. Those principles provide the foundation for the common law of property, tort, and contract. They are emphasized throughout law school, particularly in the influential first year. And even in a heavily industrialized nation, with a large administrative apparatus, they must continue to play an important role. In many areas of modern law, however, doctrinal disarray is a predictable consequence of the importation of compensatory thinking.

But the problem goes deeper than disarray. Substance and not mere form is at the heart of the compensatory model. That model holds existing entitlements constant, and it sees revision of the status quo, or the infliction of costs on third parties, as impermissible partisanship or "redistribution" unless in the service of compensation, narrowly defined. The result is administrative, legislative, and judge-made doctrine that misconceives the most persuasive basis for the plaintiff's claim, producing decisions that are, on occasion, positively perverse, and that shut off exploration of alternatives. The rise of regulatory programs has frequently been responsive to alternatives that depart dramatically from the compensatory paradigm. While compensatory principles have had significant advantages, they have introduced serious pathologies as well.

The shift from private to public law, partly a recognition of this problem, remains tentative and halting. Courts continue to invoke compensation to define the nature and reach of programs developed in self-conscious repudiation of that imperative. And while courts generally ought not to undertake significant social restructuring on their own, no such barriers apply to legislative and administrative officials; when those officials have acted, courts should treat their efforts hospitably, and not cabin them by reference to compensatory ideas. Alternative conceptions, drawn from emergent principles of risk management and nonsubordination, reveal the limitations of compensatory justice as an understanding of the role of the legal system in the alleviation of public and private harm.

NOTES

1. See, for example, Richard A. Epstein, "A Theory of Strict Liability," *Journal of Legal Studies* 2 (1973): 151–204; Ernest J. Weinrib, "Causation and Wrongdoing," *Chicago-Kent Law Review* 63 (1987): 407–50; Richard A. Posner, *Economic Analysis of Law,* 3d ed. (Boston: Little, Brown, 1986).

2. See *Lochner v. New York,* 198 U.S. 45 (1905); *Adkins v. Childrens Hospital,* 261 U.S. 525 (1923).

3. F. D. Roosevelt, Speech Accepting the Nomination for the Presidency (July 2, 1932), in *The Public Papers and Addresses of Franklin D. Roosevelt,* 1938, vol. 1, *The Genesis of the New Deal,* 657; and F. D. Roosevelt, Annual Message to Congress (Jan. 3, 1936), in *The Public Papers and Addresses of Franklin D. Roosevelt,* vol. 5 *The People Approve,* 13.

4. For a catalogue, see Cass Sunstein, *After the Rights Revolution: Reconceiving the Regulatory State,* chapters 1 and 2 (Cambridge: Harvard University Press, 1990).

5. Fed. Rules of Civ. Proc. 23(d).

6. 417 U.S. 156 (1974).

7. See generally David Rosenberg, "The Causal Connection in Mass Exposure Cases: A 'Public Law' Vision of the Tort System," *Harvard Law Review* 97 (1984): 849–929.

8. See *Industrial Union v. American Petroleum,* 448 U.S. 607 (1980); and Jerry L. Mashaw and David L. Harfst, "Regulation and Legal Culture: The Case of Motor Vehicle Safety," *Yale Journal of Regulation,* 4 (1987): 257–302.

9. See Mashaw and Harfst, "Regulation and Legal Culture."

10. *Allen v. Wright,* 468 U.S. 737 (1984).

11. *Simon v. Eastern Kentucky Welfare Rights Org.,* 426 U.S. 26 (1976).

12. *Center for Auto Safety v. Thomas,* 847 F.2d 843 (D.C. Cir. 1988) (en banc). In this case, the court divided 5-5, and thus reinstated a previous decision granting standing.

13. *Washington v. Davis,* 426 U.S. 229 (1976); and *Personnel Administrator of Massachusetts v. Feeney,* 442 U.S. 256 (1979).

14. See Owen M. Fiss, "Groups and the Equal Protection Clause," *Philosophy & Public Affairs* 5 (1976): 107–77; Catharine A. MacKinnon, *Feminism Unmodified* (Cambridge: Harvard University Press, 1987); and David A. Strauss, "Discriminatory Intent and the Taming of *Brown,*" *University of Chicago Law Review* 56 (1989): 935–1015.

15. 442 U.S. 256 (1979).

16. See Strauss, "Discriminatory Intent."

17. See Geoffrey Stone, L. Michael Seidman, Cass Sunstein, and Mark Tushnet, *Constitutional Law* (Boston: Little, Brown, 1986).

18. See *Green v. County School Bd.*, 391 U.S. 430 (1968).

19. The various positions can be found in *Dayton Bd. of Educ. v. Brinkman*, 443 U.S. 526 (1979); *Columbus Bd. of Educ. v. Penick*, 443 U.S. 449 (1979).

20. See *City of Richmond v. Croson*, 109 S. Ct. 706 (1989).

21. See Kathleen M. Sullivan, "Sins of Discrimination: Last Term's Affirmative Action Cases," 100 *Harvard Law Review* (1986): 78–98.

22. The exception is that the Court applies "rationality review" to measures disadvantaging the disabled. See, for example, *Cleburne v. Cleburne Living Center*, 473 U.S. 432 (1985). Rationality review is, however, highly deferential, and almost always results in validation.

23. *Greater Los Angeles Council on Deafness v. Community Television of So. Calif.*, 719 F.2d 1017 (9th Cir. 1983) (rejecting suit by hearing impaired persons claiming that television must be made accessible to them); *Gallagher v. Pontiac School Dist.*, 807 F.2d 75 (6th Cir. 1986) (rejecting a claim from a deaf and mentally handicapped student for educational services on the ground that the "essence of his claim does not constitute a valid equal protection challenge. When a handicapped child does not allege that he has been singled out or treated differently from the nonhandicapped child, but rather needs additional special services, the fourteenth amendment is rarely implicated."); *Pinkerton v. Moye*, 509 F.2d 107 (W.D. Va. 1981) (same). See also *Ferris v. Univ. of Texas at Austin*, 558 F. Supp. 536 (W.D. Tex. 1983); and *Dopico v. Goldschmidt*, 518 F. Supp. 1161 (S.D.N.Y. 1981), aff'd in part, rev'd in part, 687 F.2d 644 (2d Cir. 1982).

24. *Regents of the University of California v. Bakke*, 438 U.S. 265 (1978).

25. See Rosenberg, "The Causal Connection."

26. See John Rawls, *A Theory of Justice* (Cambridge: Harvard University Press, 1971), 102; and MacKinnon, *Feminism Unmodified*.

27. Cf. Strauss, "Discriminatory Intent"; and David A. Strauss, "The Myth of Colorblindness," *1986 Supreme Court Review*, 99–134.

28. See Richard A. Epstein, "Nuisance Law: Corrective Justice and Its Utilitarian Constraints," *Journal of Legal Studies* 8 (1979): 49, 77–98.

29. Cf. Strauss, "Discriminatory Intent"; Richard Lempert, "The Force of Irony: Steelworkers v. Weber," *Ethics* 95 (1984): 86–93; and Cass R. Sunstein, "Lochner's Legacy," *Columbia Law Review* 87 (1987): 873–919.

30. See Sullivan, "Sins of Discrimination."

12

COMPENSATION AND RIGHTS IN
THE LIBERAL CONCEPTION
OF JUSTICE

RANDY E. BARNETT

In the previous chapter on "The Limits of Compensatory Justice," Cass Sunstein offers two distinct theses. First, he defines a conception of compensatory justice that he claims lies at the root of Anglo-American legal systems. Second, he contends that in a number of doctrinal areas this model of compensatory justice is incompatible with the best theories that underlie the claims being made by plaintiffs. I will call the first of these arguments the "compensatory justice thesis" and the second the "incompatibility thesis."

In part I of my commentary, I question the accuracy of the compensatory justice thesis and suggest that Sunstein's account neglects a crucial characteristic of the liberal conception of justice that underlies Anglo-American legal systems: the dimension of entitlement. Even so, rejection of the compensatory justice thesis does not entail rejection of the incompatibility thesis. For, when properly understood, the underlying entitlements component of the liberal conception of justice may be nearly as incompatible with some of the legal theories favored by Sun-

311

stein and others. These theories also run afoul of the liberal conception of the rule of law. In part II, I explain how, by acknowledging this basic incompatibility, Sunstein has made an unintended but significant concession to the liberal conception of justice and the rule of law.

Finally, any analysis of limits, whether of compensatory justice or anything else, must be comparative. As Sunstein implicitly acknowledges in his presentation of substitutes for compensatory justice, the limits of a theory support its abandonment only when the superiority of an alternative is established. In part III, I suggest that, for his argument to succeed, Sunstein must come to grips with the limits of legal competence created by the pervasive problems of knowledge, interest, and power. I conclude by briefly summarizing the liberal conception of justice and the rule of law and how they address these problems.

I. The Compensatory Justice Thesis

Let me begin by restating Sunstein's five basic principles of compensatory justice. First, the event that produced the injury is both discrete and unitary. Second, the injury is sharply defined. Third, a clear causal connection exists between the defendant's conduct and the plaintiff's injury. Fourth, a bilateral relation obtains between an identifiable plaintiff and an identifiable defendant. Fifth, the purpose of the remedy and of the legal system is to restore the plaintiff to the position that he would have occupied if the unlawful conduct had not occurred. Presumably, the fifth of these principles gives this model the name of compensatory justice.

If we accept this as a working definition of compensatory justice, it presents at best only a partial view of the conception of justice that informs Anglo-American legal systems. Of course, the fifth principle describing the goal of compensation captures what for a long time has been the presumptive remedy at common law for breaches of certain obligations. But other types of remedies, such as specific performance in contract law and injunctions in tort, were traditionally available at equity and even at common law. These other remedies, although sometimes seen as compensatory, are more accurately viewed as vindicating the *rights* of the aggrieved party. What is missing from Sunstein's account is the rights-based nature of the common law of tort, contract, and property.

The conception of justice that informs the Anglo-American legal system is liberal. Compensation for objective wrongs rather than for subjective "injuries" is fundamental to the liberal conception of justice. The concept of injury is simply too undiscriminating to provide the kind of social-ordering principle that a liberal society requires. Subjective injury is in the eye of the beholder. Any act can subjectively injure another provided only that the performance of the act is bothersome or offensive. For example, the fact that one watches certain movies or listens to certain music may be genuinely offensive to others; consequently knowledge that such conduct is occurring may inflict a real though psychological injury. Therefore, if subjective injury is the criterion for legal relief, any act may potentially be the subject of a legal sanction and there is little way of knowing before one acts whether one is acting in a purely noninjurious way.

Although the existence of a subjective injury may be a necessary condition of prohibiting an action, it cannot be sufficient. Because we all must engage in a variety of acts any of which could inflict a subjective injury upon another, we need some more objective criterion to distinguish permissible from impermissible action, compensable from uncompensable injuries. That the injury sustained by the plaintiff is "discrete and unitary" or "clearly defined" is not enough. More than a "clear causal connection" between the defendant's conduct and the harm to the plaintiff is needed to obtain legal relief. All of these characteristics are usually present with subjective injuries caused by offensive conduct.

In a liberal conception of justice, rights are the concept by which the wrongful nature of an action is identified. That the defendant caused injury *by committing a wrongful act* is what justifies the imposition of legal force to obtain a remedy, and the nature of the plaintiff's rights define the wrong. Without identifying the rights of the parties, one cannot distinguish a legally cognizable harm from the many genuine subjective harms for which no legal remedy is available. Consider a woman charged with shooting a man. Only a proper understanding of her rights permits us to distinguish a noncompensable injury inflicted by the woman in self-defense during the course of his attempt to rape her from a compensable battery that she inflicted wrongfully upon him. Regardless of which description of rights is the more accurate, the injury to the man is quite the same.

In sum, the liberal conception of justice underlying the Anglo-American common law is rights-based not injury-based and Sunstein's definition of compensatory justice misses this crucial entitlements dimension. There are, however, two distinct ways of viewing the rights or entitlements that galvanize the common law. One could adhere to the view of Oliver Wendell Holmes and say that rights of persons are nothing more than the legal remedies they can receive in court. According to the Holmesian conception of rights, the availability of a legal remedy entirely and precisely defines the rights of the parties; the concept of right or entitlement adds nothing to the analysis. The Holmesian identification of rights with remedies is sometimes referred to as the "bad man" theory of law since it views law from the perspective of the person who cares nothing for the law and is influenced only by the prospective legal sanction:

> If you want to know the law and nothing else, you must look at it as a bad man, who cares only for the material consequences which such knowledge enables him to predict, not as a good one, who finds his reasons for conduct whether inside the law or outside it, in the vaguer sanctions of conscience.[1]

In contrast with the Holmesian conception of rights as defined by the availability of legal relief, one can view rights as *justifying* the availability of legal relief. According to the liberal conception of rights, a legal remedy is not identical to the right that justifies its imposition. Rather, a legal remedy vindicates an antecedent right of the plaintiff that was violated by the defendant. In this way, the "legal right" or remedy available in a court is distinguished from the underlying or "background right" that morally justifies the court's imposition of legal force on a defendant.[2] Although this distinction between legal and background rights is correctly associated with natural rights thinking, the term *natural rights* evokes a controversy concerning the origin or source of background rights that is not germane here. For present purposes we need only note that, in contrast with the Holmesian conception of rights, the liberal conception acknowledges background rights, however grounded, that are antecedent to legal rights. In the liberal conception of justice, violating these background rights is unjust and justifies rectification.

Despite their substantial differences, both of these conceptions of rights undercut Sunstein's thesis that the principles of justice informing Anglo-American legal systems are exclusively compensatory. Given the Holmesian view that recognizes only legal rights and equates these rights with available remedies, because other types of remedies besides compensation were always and are still regularly awarded, rights are not exclusively compensatory. And viewed from a liberal perspective that acknowledges both background and legal rights, the common law is not strictly compensatory, since remedies other than compensation may sometimes appropriately vindicate a right.[3] Regardless of which view of rights one adopts, then, it is inaccurate to describe the conception of justice underlying the Anglo-American common law as exclusively compensatory.

Moreover, if the conception of justice that informs Anglo-American legal systems is liberal, then Sunstein's omission of the dimension of entitlement is misleading. It inaccurately suggests that any injury satisfying the first four principles he lists is sufficient to justify legal relief, whether compensatory or injunctive. In fact, the liberal conception of justice also requires that a right be violated before the legal system may justly rectify even a sharply defined injury produced by a discrete and unitary event clearly caused by a defendant's conduct.

By severing the goal of rectifying injuries from the conceptual framework that distinguishes compensable from uncompensable injuries, Anglo-American legal systems may be made to appear unjust by their own standards for failing to rectify many genuine injuries that cannot plausibly be cast in terms of entitlements. Yet the entitlements dimension of the liberal conception of justice functions precisely to limit legal relief to certain injuries and not others. In part III, I shall say something about why this distinction among kinds of injurious action is necessary.

II. The Incompatibility Thesis

If the compensatory justice thesis is mistaken, or at least mis-leadingly incomplete without the dimension of entitlement, does this undermine the incompatibility thesis? I think the answer is both yes and no. On the one hand, viewing Anglo-American legal systems as vindicating entitlements rather than simply as compensating injuries may eliminate some examples of incom-patibility. For example, certain impositions of risk are thought by some rights theorists to be wrongful and potentially tortious in a rights-based conception of justice. Even Robert Nozick's theory of libertarianism accepts the justice of prohibiting some activity that creates a serious risk of a rights violation.[4] The obvious and the traditional Anglo-American remedy for a con-tinuing wrongful imposition of a risk of rights violations is an injunction, not compensation.

Although the treatment of imposed risk is controversial among rights theorists, no one denies that self-defense may rightfully be employed when a person is confronted with a credible threat of a rights violation. The liberal conception of justice does not require that one suffer a battery and then collect compensation afterwards; one can also defend oneself, by force if necessary, when confronted with the imminent prospect or risk of a bat-tery. The imminent threat of receiving a battery is itself defined as a rights violation and is called an "assault."

On the other hand, although the entitlements dimension of justice may deprive the incompatibility thesis of some examples, enough examples of incompatibility remain to give it consider-able descriptive merit. Sunstein's argument is that, in some im-portant cases, compensatory justice simply misses the basic point of the plaintiff's claim and leads to a regime of legal rules that is "positively perverse" from the perspective of the plaintiff's theory of relief. His incompatibility thesis could easily be recast to say that, in many of the same cases, the rhetoric of vindicating individual background rights also misses the basic point of the plaintiff's claim.

For example, consider the case of a plaintiff who has not been discriminated against by a particular employer, but who is a member of a group that has suffered in the past from pervasive discrimination. Suppose this plaintiff sues a particular employer alleging that, because of the long history of discrimination, the group of which she is a member is represented in certain occupations at a substantially lower rate than other groups that had not been similarly subordinated. Sunstein would correctly argue that to characterize this claim as alleging that the conduct of this particular defendant violated the individual background rights of this particular plaintiff would surely be to distort the plaintiff's theory.

Moreover, recasting such claims in terms of a "right to be free from wrongful discrimination on the basis of race or gender" paves the way for the type of reverse discrimination claims that Sunstein and others lament. This sort of rights analysis is simply too "color-blind" to address effectively the injury suffered by members of subordinated groups. Affirmative action plans that use racial quotas to end group subordination may unavoidably entail that some white males are intentionally discriminated against on the basis of their race and gender. To protect these white males from wrongful discrimination would surely be incompatible with the nonsubordination theory underlying the original complaint.

My purpose is not to express an opinion on the merits of these controversial issues, any more than it was Sunstein's purpose to do so. Rather, this is his example of a claim that is incompatible with principles of compensatory justice. My purpose is only to note a similar incompatibility between this claim and entitlements, provided that Anglo-American legal systems implicitly accept the liberal, rather than a Holmesian, conception of justice.

Holmesian legal rights are defined entirely in terms of remedies. If a "nonsubordination" legal remedy is deemed to be available, then this is the plaintiff's right. Therefore, no incompatibility arises between Holmesian legal rights and any judicially enforceable remedy favored by Sunstein. Nor does incompatibility with a Holmesian conception of rights arise when persons are denied judicial review of the "risk management" schemes of administrative agencies. If no remedy is deemed to be available, under the Holmesian conception, there is simply no right to such judicial relief. In this sense, Sunstein's theories are entirely compatible with a Holmesian conception of rights because the Holmesian conception is empty.

To sustain the incompatibility thesis, we must therefore assume that Anglo-American legal systems adopt a liberal conception of justice that assesses legal rights against a normative framework of individual background rights. Only if justice requires the protection of background rights that are antecedent to legislative or judicial action can there be a serious problem of incompatibility. The liberal conception of justice requires that the use of legal force against a defendant be justifiable on the grounds that the defendant has violated a particular background right of the plaintiff's. A claim by a plaintiff seeking an end to the subordination of a particular group, irrespective of whether the defendant has acted wrongfully, cannot be translated into this sort of rights claim without losing something in the translation. In this sense, these two types of claims are genuinely incompatible.

If anything, Sunstein has understated the incompatibility of his legal theories with fundamental notions underlying Anglo-American legal systems. These theories are not only incompatible with a substantive view of justice based on background rights, they are also incompatible with the procedural protections associated with the liberal conception of the rule of law.[5] For example, the rule of law requires that persons be able to know, in advance of acting, whether a particular act is wrongful. This is accomplished by promulgating rules and principles of general application. Yet the sorts of theories advocated by Sunstein would make this difficult, if not impossible, because legal relief is not made to depend on the wrongful nature of the defendant's conduct. The kinds of injuries they redress cannot easily be cast in sufficiently general terms.

In addition, because coercively imposed remedies create serious risks of enforcement error and enforcement abuse, the liberal conception of the rule of law also requires that sufficient evidence of liability must exist and be presented in a neutral forum before a remedy may be imposed. Civil defendants must be proved liable beyond a preponderance of the evidence; criminal defendants must be proved guilty beyond a reasonable doubt. In this way, both the rate of enforcement errors and the potential for enforcement abuse will be reduced.

This requirement of proof will seriously inhibit the feasibility of risk management strategies. Requiring that sufficient evidence of risk imposition be presented in a neutral forum before a legal remedy is imposed means that hunches or guesses or speculation that a defendant's activities may someday, in some way, cause harm to a plaintiff are insufficient to justify a finding that the defendant's conduct is actually risky and subject to coercive regulation. Presumably, even a regulatory regime of risk management would refrain from banning conduct that cannot be shown to create a risk of harm—provided, of course, that this sort of a regime respected a liberal conception of the rule of law.

The background rights of the parties that define the liberal conception of justice, coupled with procedural protections associated with the rule of law, give rise to a heavy presumption in favor of liberty. Even when conduct is shown to create a serious risk of a rights violation, we require those who advocate restricting such conduct to prove that such a restriction is really necessary. The importance of a presumption of liberty is well-accepted when other kinds of genuinely risky conduct not discussed by Sunstein are considered.

For example, even when speech creates a risk of serious emotional and even physical injury to others, a heavy burden falls on those advocating prior restraint to show that this sort of remedy is really warranted. And, despite the demonstrable risks that many accused criminals pose to others, we require a high standard of proof be met before imposing punishment. Proposing "risk management" strategies to handle these kinds of risks of injury has a decidedly different ring from the sorts of risks Sunstein proposes to manage, but no difference in principle exists between them. The very same dangers of managing risk so familiar to us in the areas of speech and crimes exist to an even greater degree with the other more amorphous and speculative kinds of risks he wants to address.

We may summarize the analysis to this point as follows: The compensatory justice thesis misses the dimension of entitlement

that is a crucial part of the conception of justice accepted by the
Anglo-American systems of justice. To sustain the incompatibility thesis requires that this dimension of entitlement be liberal,
rather than Holmesian. For, while a Holmesian conception of
rights is perfectly consistent with any of the theories discussed
by Sunstein, a liberal conception of justice based on individual
background rights is incompatible with at least some of these
theories. Moreover, these theories are also incompatible with
important aspects of the liberal conception of the rule of law.
Consequently, if Sunstein is correct to claim that the fundamental principles of Anglo-American legal systems are incompatible with the theories he describes, then he must concede that
Anglo-American legal systems implicitly accept a liberal conception of justice, a liberal conception of the rule of law, or both.

Of course, given that the reason for formulating the incompatibility thesis was to highlight the normative shortcomings of
Anglo-American legal systems, this may seem more like an in-
dictment of the liberal conception of justice than a "concession."
Yet a concession it surely is. For decades we have been told by
those who accept a Holmesian view of rights that because any
claim can be cast in terms of a legal right, the concept of rights
in no way assists in deciding among conflicting claims. The
incompatibility thesis undermines this argument. It concedes
that, given the individual background rights that inform the
liberal conception of justice, at least *some* claims simply cannot
be couched in terms of a rights violation without either absurd
or even perverse doctrinal results. To implement legal theories
such as risk management and nonsubordination means abandoning important aspects of the liberal conception of justice
and the rule of law.

The concession implicit in the incompatibility thesis is important in at least two respects. First, the thesis concedes that these
legal theories are indeed iconoclastic, insofar as they cannot
comfortably be fit within long-standing conceptions of corrective justice and long-accepted precepts of the rule of law that
inform Anglo-American legal systems. Of course, to call a legal
theory iconoclastic is in no way to refute it; nothing is intrinsi-
cally wrong with being an iconoclast. Still, candor has its rhetor-
ical price. Genuinely iconoclastic proposals cannot be defended,

as proponents of these theories are wont to do, as mere modest and inevitable extensions of already accepted principles.

Second, and more significantly, legal theories that are candidly incompatible with an entitlements approach are vulnerable to a potent line of criticism: that the "limits" of the liberal conception of justice and the rule of law, not coincidentally, correspond to the limits of legal competence.

III. THE LIMITS OF LEGAL COMPETENCE

Fully to explain the limits of legal competence requires a lengthy analysis of the liberal conception of justice and the rule of law and their relation to the pervasive social problems of knowledge, interest, and power. For obvious reasons, I cannot present a comprehensive analysis here.[6] Instead, to give some flavor of why legal competence is limited, I briefly summarize just a few of the many aspects of the social problems that the liberal conception of justice and the rule of law address. Although I shall not repeat this caveat, it is, in effect, for the balance of this commentary.

Some legal philosophers have argued that institutional features of the judicial system make it an appropriate place to adjudicate claims of right and generally an inappropriate place to settle polycentric disputes that do not involve rights violations.[7] Courts are only competent to decide issues about which they can gain enough facts from the parties to make a knowledgeable decision. While the resolution of any dispute is likely to have unforeseen effects, the sorts of disputes that are amenable to adjudication involve more local and discernible effects than do others. The background rights specified by a liberal conception of justice serve to identify the kinds of disputes that are discrete enough to be adjudicated.

Nonsubordination and risk management theories involve controversies that cannot be couched in terms of liberal rights, in part, because the problems they address involve complex interactions among and wide-ranging effects upon countless people. Likewise, the unforeseen consequences of any judicial decision in applying such a theory to an actual controversy will swamp the immediately perceivable benefits to be gained by this decision. That the outcome of any adjudication of such controversies will be for the better is pure chance.

Moreover, forcing parties to couch their legal claims as claims of right provides a conceptual connection between the legal rights recognized and enforced by a legal system and the background rights specified by the liberal conception of justice. This connection increases the correspondence between the outcomes reached by a legal system and the background rights that define the liberal conception of justice, making for a more just legal system. It also enables the adjudication of legal rights claims constructively to contribute to the evolving understanding of background rights.

If judicial competence is truly limited in this way, to concede that a particular legal theory cannot be couched in terms of a claim of right is to concede that such a claim does not belong in a court of law. To the extent that the incompatibility thesis is correct, then, the goals of nonsubordination or risk management may be inappropriate judicial concerns. In sum, the "limits of compensatory justice" that Sunstein stresses may simply reflect the limits of judicial competence. The mere fact that the liberal conception of justice and the rule of law is limited in this way does not, therefore, support his conclusion that it is normatively objectionable.

But doesn't this limit of judicial competence bolster Sunstein's claim that courts should not interfere when regulatory agencies such as the Environmental Protection Agency or the Occupational Safety and Health Administration adopt risk management policies or when school boards adopt plans to end the subordination of certain groups? In some cases, the limits of judicial competence may indeed justify judicial deference to other institutions. Still, adoption of risk management or nonsubordination strategies by government agencies does not cause the background rights of citizens to evaporate, any more than the adoption of censorship strategies to minimize the harmful risks of speech causes the First Amendment rights of citizens to evaporate.

When the First Amendment is implicated, courts scrutinize legislation or regulations to ensure that the risks alleged by the regulators to be posed by the activity sought to be restricted are serious enough to warrant legal restraint. The courts are not only the best places to adjudicate claims of right, they are virtually the only place where these claims may be vindicated. The liberal conception of justice and the rule of law create a presumption of liberty that places the burden on regulatory agencies of all varieties to justify in a neutral forum any restrictions they may seek to impose on the otherwise rightful actions of citizens. Courts are that neutral forum.

To pursue the goals of risk management and nonsubordination without judicial oversight requires that such efforts be confined to nongovernmental institutions which are not subject to the same degree of scrutiny as government agencies. Of course, the more that government becomes intertwined with other institutions the more difficult it is to permit these institutions to pursue important social goals without judicial review of their actions. This argues for less rather than more legislative activism in these areas, permitting other powerful social institutions to carry the ball.

Incompetence to deal with the polycentric issues raised by Sunstein's theories is not limited to courts. Legislatures and administrative agencies may be incompetent as well. The limits of their competence stem from the pervasive problems of knowledge, interest, and power.

Every society faces a pervasive problem of knowledge that has two dimensions. On the one hand, we must somehow let persons make use of the knowledge that they possess; on the other hand, persons who act on their own knowledge must somehow take into account the knowledge of others of which they are and must be profoundly ignorant. The knowledge problem, then, involves both the radical dispersion of knowledge and the pervasiveness of ignorance. The problem of knowledge may be analogized to a "knowledge glass" that is only partially full. Persons must be able to make use of the part that is full, while somehow taking into account the part that is empty.

We solve the knowledge problem in practice by respecting the particular background rights specified by the liberal conception of justice. The principle of *several property* solves the first dimension of the knowledge problem by allocating jurisdiction over physical resources to the individuals and associations most likely to have access to the dispersed personal and local knowledge of how such resources may best be used. Similarly, the principle of freedom *to* contract enables transfers of these property rights to reflect the personal and local knowledge of current right holders.

The principle of freedom *from* contract addresses the second dimension of the knowledge problem by preventing transfers of property rights without the consent of the right holder. In this way, anyone seeking to displace a current right holder must offer a benefit sufficient to induce a transfer. This forces one who seeks to obtain a given right to take into account the current right holder's knowledge of how this jurisdiction may best be exercised. In the aggregate, consensual transfers of property rights give rise to an irreplaceable set of market prices for physical resources that consolidate in a usable form dispersed worldwide personal and local knowledge of how these resources may be used. Requiring people to respect these market prices forces them to take into account indirectly the knowledge of others to which they could never have direct access.

Theories of risk management and nonsubordination that operate independent of these entitlements face an insuperable problem of knowledge. They require a knowledge of past, present, and future circumstances that may simply be unavailable to any person or group, including legislatures and administrative agencies. Both of these approaches require that we know more about past events and causes, more about everyone's present knowledge and preferences, and more about the future consequences of actions—including the consequences of any lawsuit—than we can possibly know.

Of equal importance, behavior that risks harm may also yield considerable benefits. Indeed, the potential for gain motivates almost all risky action. Few of the benefits we currently enjoy and take for granted came without considerable risks. Moreover, an unappreciated benefit of engaging in risky activity is discovering which courses of actions are beneficial and which are mistaken. Often, until risky conduct is undertaken we cannot know whether it is a mistake or not; only after an action is performed will its mistaken character be discovered. Experiencing mistakes is crucial to the evolution of knowledge of which actions to take and which to avoid. The very idea of risk management underestimates the value of mistakes in the discovery of knowledge. If central planners responsible for risk management could know in advance what they would need to know to balance the cost of these mistakes against the benefits yielded by discovery, there would be nothing to discover.

In a utopia of perfect information where all of this knowledge is freely available, we probably would be wise to reconsider our traditional insistence on rectifying only proven rights violations. In our world, however, empowering anyone—whether judges, legislators, or regulators—to use force to rectify conditions about which we are largely or wholly ignorant virtually ensures the violation of background rights that are needed to solve the pervasive problem of knowledge. With this in mind, Sunstein's call "to develop a careful system of priorities; to coordinate regulatory systems now diffused over many statutes and agencies; and to recognize the high potential costs of both action and inaction in the face of inadequate information,"[8] simply assumes what must be proved: that systemic solutions to these and other serious problems of knowledge can be devised that outperform adherence to the liberal conception of justice and the rule of law. F. A. Hayek refers to this assumption as "the fatal conceit."[9]

Moreover, both risk management and nonsubordination policies create grave and possibly insurmountable problems of power. Using force to achieve compliance with justice raises the severity of erroneous judgments, giving rise to a serious problem of *enforcement error*. The background rights of the liberal conception of justice limits the *severity* of these errors by limiting the scope of enforcement. By extending the use of legal coercion beyond the protection of individual background rights, however, theories such as Sunstein's would expand the severity of enforcement error. The liberal conception of the rule of law reduces the *rate* of enforcement error by allocating burdens of proof and by varying the degree of proof needed to satisfy these burdens. By reversing the burden of proof and by reducing the degree of proof required, these theories risk a serious increase in the rate of enforcement errors.

The problem of enforcement error applies to enforcement decisions made in good faith. The problem of *enforcement abuse*, in contrast, arises when the power to regulate the actions of others by force is used, not to pursue justice, but to serve the interest of the enforcers or others. James Madison called this "the problem of faction":

> By a faction I understand a number of citizens, whether amounting to a majority or minority of the whole, who are united and actuated by some common impulse of passion, or of interest, adverse to the rights of other citizens, or to the permanent and aggregate interests of the community.[10]

This problem is most likely to arise when some persons and groups are given power in the absence of clear standards by which abuses of power may be detected. The liberal conception of justice and the rule of law serve to identify abuses of power when they occur. Identifying abuses is a prerequisite to constraining them.

That the pursuit of certain worthwhile ends, such as the goals of risk management and nonsubordination, requires that precepts of justice and the rule of law be set aside creates enormous opportunities for enforcement abuse. We are all too familiar with regimes of "public interest" being used as a veneer for oppression and injustice. The conceptual and institutional structure that has evolved to cope with both the problems of enforcement error and abuse are the very conceptions of justice and the rule of law that are incompatible with the legal theories Sunstein favors. We abandon them at our peril.

IV. Conclusion: Compensation and Rights

Notice that the liberal conception of justice addresses the problem of knowledge, not with the principle of compensation, but with the concepts of several property rights and freedom of contract. Well-defined rights of several property and freedom of contract are sufficient to solve the knowledge problem without any need for compensation. A principle of compensatory justice is needed only to address two serious problems of interest: the incentive problem and the compliance problem.

Generally, the "problem of interest" refers to a gap that can arise between the requirements of justice and the rule of law and people's perception of their interests. Without a right to compensation for forced transfers of property, persons may lack sufficient incentive to use the liberty that the liberal conception of justice makes possible. Without this incentive the resulting gap between rights and interest will undermine the ability of the strategy of decentralized jurisdiction to address the knowledge problem. And the compliance problem is the need to close the gap between the rights that define the requirements of justice and the interest of persons who would violate these rights. Compensation that deprives rights violators of the gains derived from their wrongful conduct provides an incentive to comply with the requirements of justice.

By addressing these pervasive problems of interest, a right to compensation for injustice is an important aspect of the liberal conception of justice, but the injustice that is to be rectified is defined by the rights of several property and freedom of contract that are needed to address the knowledge problem. Seeing how these other background rights perform a function distinct from that performed by the right to compensation makes it easier to appreciate why rights precede and justify remedies in the liberal conception of justice. Each of these rights reflects different dimensions of justice addressing different social problems.

Proponents of legal theories that are incompatible with the liberal conception of justice and the rule of law cannot rest content with observing the limitations of compensatory justice or of the entire liberal conception of justice and the rule of law. They must confront seriously the pervasive problems of knowledge, interest, and power that impose real limits on legal competence and that require for their solution the very conception of justice that conflicts with these legal theories. Before we may safely jettison the liberal conception of justice and the rule of law that addresses these problems, we must be shown persuasively that alternative conceptual and institutional arrangements are available that can transcend these limits.

Yet Sunstein is remarkably casual about urging the abandonment or modification of these principles because they stand in the way of these legal theories while leaving the "large task" of elaborating principles of risk management and nonsubordination to the next generation. But surely this expression of preference is premature, if not supremely risky. Risk management in the realm of political and legal theory requires that one first establishes the ability of a legal system enforcing these as yet unelaborated principles of risk management and nonsubordination to deal with the pervasive social problems that are currently being addressed by the conception of justice and the rule of law it would supplant. Only then would the observation that the conception of justice underlying Anglo-American legal systems is limited be of normative significance. Wishing does not make it so.

NOTES

1. Oliver W. Holmes, Jr., "The Path of the Law," *Harvard Law Review* 10 (1897): 459.

2. An important caveat: Although the Holmesian view is to equate legal rights with remedies, to be distinguishable from the term *background right* the term *legal right* need not be synonymous with *legal remedy*. Legal right could refer as well to the legal rules and principles used by a legal system to reach the conclusion that a remedy is justified. These concrete rules and principles need not, and typically will not, be the same as the abstract concepts defining the background rights of the parties. I am adopting the Holmesian usage of *legal right* in the text strictly for the purpose of criticizing it.

3. See, for example, Randy E. Barnett, "Contract Remedies and Inalienable Rights," *Social Philosophy and Policy* 4 (Autumn 1986): 179–203 (discussing the appropriateness of the remedy of specific performance for breach of contract).

4. See Robert Nozick, *Anarchy, State, and Utopia* (New York: Basic Books, 1974), 73–84.

5. For a discussion of this distinction, see Randy E. Barnett, "Foreword: Can Justice and the Rule of Law Be Reconciled?" *Harvard Journal of Law and Public Policy* 11 (1988): 597–624.

6. The analysis presented in this part draws upon a lengthy work in progress. For a brief and early summary of this approach, see ibid., 588–622.

7. See, for example, Lon L. Fuller, "The Forms and Limits of Adjudication," *Harvard Law Review* 92 (1978): 353–409.

8. Chapter 11 of this volume, p. 302.

9. See F. A. Hayek, *The Fatal Conceit* (Chicago: University of Chicago Press, 1989).

10. *The Federalist* No. 10 (James Madison) (New York: Modern Library, 1937), 54.

13

BEYOND COMPENSATORY JUSTICE?

DAVID JOHNSTON

According to Cass Sunstein, principles of compensatory justice are misplaced in numerous areas of public and private law. Attempts to apply these principles to cases involving claims of probabilistic or systemic harm, or racial or gender discrimination have led to numerous and needless legal disputes and confusions as well as to incorrect, nonsensical, or irrational results. In these areas of law, compensatory notions ought to be abandoned in favor of alternative conceptions of the function of legal controls. Sunstein proposes that some of these cases can best be understood by reference to principles of risk management, while others should be adjudicated in accordance with a principle of nonsubordination.

I am sympathetic toward the normative objectives that underpin Sunstein's claims.[1] But the arguments he makes to advance these objectives are defective because he conflates questions about models of adjudication with questions about the purposes of legal regulations. Although these two kinds of questions are related to one another, they are not identical. To see the difference, think of legal regulations as primary rules, in H. L. A. Hart's sense, that require human beings to act in certain ways and to abstain from acting in others.[2] These primary rules may serve various purposes. They may be intended like some traffic regulations merely to help coordinate human actions. Or they may be designed to advance other substantive objectives of an economic, political, or social nature. Adjudication is a procedure that helps enforce primary rules. The rules that govern adjudication are parasitic upon or secondary to the primary rules of a legal system. These secondary rules may embody the substantive values a legal system is designed to advance, but the basic relation between procedures of adjudication and primary legal regulations is that of a means to an end. Questions about the purposes of legal regulations are political questions. To answer these questions we must ask ourselves about the substantive values we wish to see the legal system promote. Questions about models of adjudication are quasi-technical in nature, since the principal purpose of adjudication is to help enforce the primary rules of a legal system.

Sunstein's conflation of questions about models of adjudication with questions about the purposes of legal regulations weakens his argument in two ways. First, it vitiates his explanatory claims. Sunstein explains the fact that doctrinal disarray prevails in some areas of law as a consequence of the misapplication of compensatory principles in inappropriate contexts, due in part to their tenacious and unwarranted hold on the legal mind. Yet he offers his readers no reason to believe that this disarray would diminish if his alternative principles were adopted. The principal source of the disarray to which Sunstein alludes is disagreement about the purposes the legal system ought to serve. Sunstein is aware that disagreement about these substantive purposes exists, but his argument proceeds misleadingly as if this disagreement could be resolved by the quasi-technical means of adopting alternatives to the prevailing compensatory model of adjudication.

Sunstein's conflation of these two kinds of questions also weakens his normative claims. By focusing on the effects of legal education and legal culture he creates the impression that the substantive values behind his proposals are less problematical than they really are. This strategy of argument conceals a host of difficulties. Sunstein has little to offer by way of defense or even explanation of the values that are supposed to support his proposals and has even less to say about the values embodied in compensatory principles. He is particularly vague about the conception of equality that would support his nonsubordination principle. Moreover, he does not even attempt to formulate an alternative to the compensatory model of adjudication, apparently because he regards his proposals about the objectives the legal system ought to serve as a substitute for that model. Sunstein exhorts us to go beyond the limits of compensatory justice in the areas of legal regulation with which he is concerned. But he tells us very little about what we should expect to find when we venture into that territory.

In this chapter I discuss some of the issues that would have to be confronted in any serious effort to map this territory. My principal concern is with whether and in what ways compensatory principles ought to be revised to promote substantive values they may be thought to impede. I also describe an approach to defining equality that I hope may be of some use in discussions of this topic. To put the issues into perspective and to begin laying the groundwork for my treatment of the norm of equality, I begin by sketching two visions of state and society that capture some rudimentary assumptions underlying public discussion of these matters.

I. Two Visions of State and Society

Much of the legal reasoning employed in cases involving claims of probabilistic or systemic harms, racial or gender discrimination, and the like is rooted in one or the other of two conceptions of state and society, which I shall call the classical liberal and managerial views. These two views are not the only ones that might be relevant to legal reasoning in general, but in recent years they have been the most prominent in the areas of legal regulation with which I am concerned. In this section I describe the main features of these two views and discuss the relation between them and principles of compensatory justice. The main point of this analysis is to suggest that the two conceptions capture contrasting, but equally essential, normative and empirical features of modern societies. They are like two views of a cathedral,[3] both of which would have to be taken into account by any satisfactory effort to address the problems raised by probabilistic and systemic harms.

A. The Classical Liberal Conception

The classical liberal conception of state and society is defined by two major features.

Individualism. First, individuals are assumed to be the only significant actors in society. Legal "persons," including partnerships and limited liability corporations, eventually were recognized as actors by some of the theorists who formulated this liberal view in the eighteenth and nineteenth centuries, but neither informal groups nor the more clearly defined status rankings of the ancien régime were believed to deserve legal recognition. One implication of this assumption is that it is nonsensical to treat groups either as agents or as objects of action except in a metaphorical sense. John Stuart Mill expressed this view when he insisted that voluntary actions should be prohibited only when they impose "perceptible hurt" upon some "assignable individual" other than the actor or violate some "specific duty" to the public.[4]

Voluntary Transactions. Second, voluntary actions and transactions among individuals enjoy a special status in this conception. State intervention to restrict voluntary actions and transactions is viewed as an evil, though in some circumstances a necessary one. In general the purpose of intervention should be only to enforce voluntary transactions by ensuring that the parties involved keep their promises and to prevent involuntary harms. John Locke appears to have had something like this conception of social order in mind when he argued that *"the end of Law is not to abolish or restrain, but to preserve and enlarge Freedom"* conceived as *"a Liberty* to dispose, and order, as he lists, his Person, Actions, Possessions, and his whole Property, within the Allowance of those Laws under which he is."[5]

Proponents of the classical liberal view generally believe that society is fundamental and primary while legal and political structures are superstructural and secondary. For most purposes society is considered self-sufficient. The legitimate internal functions of the state are limited to enforcement of agreements, prevention of harm, and adjudication of disputes. Often liberals depict the state as a kind of umpire supervising the activities of players in a game rather than a player in its own right.

The theoretical foundation of the classical liberal view is the idea of a person as an agent of choice who is responsible for his or her own voluntary actions and their effects, but not for effects or events over which he or she has no control. This idea of the person has a long history in Western thought, going back at least to St. Augustine and represented more recently by diverse influential writers, including John Locke, Immanuel Kant, and John Stuart Mill. It is embedded in the institutions and practices of modern constitutional democracies in innumerable places, including, but by no means limited to, their legal systems. The most persuasive justifications of many of these institutions and practices are constructed upon the ethical premise that this idea of the person provides.

Although the classical liberal conception has had powerful detractors since the early stages of its formulation, variations on this view have been defended vigorously and shrewdly throughout the twentieth century.[6] To its early proponents this conception of state and society represented a liberating vision of the future. All citizens were to have equal legal standing based upon recognition of their personhood rather than deference to status. This liberal principle, which has been symbolized for the past two centuries by the French Revolution, justified a wide-ranging program of legal reforms, including abolition of aristocratic privileges, termination of the widely abused institution of benefit of clergy, and abrogation of deeply resented sumptuary laws regulating dress, among other measures. Of course, as early critics pointed out, denial of legal recognition to ascribed differences did not ensure abolition of their social importance. By circumscribing the legitimate role of the state, classical liberalism gave relatively free rein to prejudicial social activities and to the amassing of "private" economic power. This consequence of the liberal program assumed increased importance in the twentieth century, when many, though not all, of the program's formal goals were achieved. Nevertheless, even some of its harshest critics admitted that the program of reform legitimated by the classical liberal view constituted a progressive move away from the evils of the ancien régime.[7]

B. The Managerial Conception

During the first half of the twentieth century classical liberalism came under seige. The instabilities of the period suggested that a regime based principally upon voluntary transactions with a minimum of state control will not produce a stable order.[8] Moreover, economists and social theorists increasingly became aware that voluntary transactions often do not produce beneficial results, most importantly because they frequently have effects upon persons who were not parties to the agreement ("externalities"). These observations helped stimulate the formulation of an alternative conception of state and society based upon claims antithetical to the liberal assumptions sketched above.

Groups. The first component of the managerial view of state and society is the idea that in some instances informal groups should be granted administrative and legal recognition as actors in society with identities of their own. The practical requirements of administration in an industrial society make the task of identifying and recognizing informal groups inescapable. Legal systems that strive to avoid granting recognition to such groups often end up doing so anyway, even if the fact of recognition is disguised by mystifying legal theories.[9] To be sure, the practice of recognizing groups raises difficult problems of identification and definition, since it is often hard to discover reliable criteria for distinguishing the groups intended as objects of administrative or judicial action. In many cases, however, such actions would become impossible, rather than merely difficult, if we were to insist that legal reasoning should take account only of individuals.

Social Management. The rise of modern regulation, which has occurred in the United States mainly since the New Deal, was justified by the argument that in many areas a stable and beneficent social order can be achieved only through deliberate planning and social management.[10] The exemplary instrument of social management is the administrative agency, which is responsible for providing desired results that the market may be unable to deliver. Advocates of this view argue that state intervention in society should be a regular feature of life in a modern industrial society. Intervention is appropriate to prevent harms to persons affected by, but not included as, parties to private agreements and to prevent voluntary transactions on a variety of other grounds.[11] On this view the state appears as a manager and active participant in the game rather than as a mere umpire.

The idea underlying the managerial conception of state and society is that the legal system establishes social order. Legal systems help create the norms that govern social interactions in subtle and unobtrusive ways as well as through overt enforcement. In view of this constitutive relation between law and society, no simple principle can be invoked to draw clear limits to state intervention.

Many of those who contributed to its formulation regarded the managerial approach to state and society as an effort to complete some of the social projects initiated by classical liberals. This understanding is especially persuasive in the area of economic and welfare rights. The general argument is that the formal right to equal legal standing based upon personhood is chimerical unless the possessors of that right are also guaranteed a standard of well-being sufficient to enable them to act as full participants in the society. On the basis of this argument the modern regulatory state is sometimes justified as a necessary extension of the legal reforms initiated at the time of the French Revolution.[12] Nevertheless, adoption of this approach in modern administrative and legal practices historically has gone hand in hand with abandonment or attenuation of some of the central postulates of earlier liberals. Liberals who embraced the managerial conception discarded their predecessors' distrust of state power with the argument that the key substantive goals guiding the liberal tradition could be achieved only through the actions of state administrative and regulatory agencies.[13] Similarly, the early liberals' insistence that society should be viewed as consist-

ing only of individuals and not of groups was dismissed in favor
of more collectivist conceptions. The idea of individual responsibility, though not abandoned, declined in importance for those
who endorsed the managerial view. The "system" came to be
treated as an agent in its own right, both for the purpose of
social explanation and for that of ascribing responsibility.[14]

C. The Principles of Adjudication

The model of compensatory justice that prevails in the Anglo-
American common law of tort, contract, and property is defined
by three features. First, the model assumes an individualistic
conception of party structure. The parties involved in a lawsuit
are assumed to be individuals or are thought of as if they were
individuals. Second, it assumes a transactional understanding of
causation. The focus is upon discrete or discontinuous historical
events. Third, the model is restorative in its approach to remedies. The purpose of adjudication as defined by the compensatory model is to restore the plaintiff to the position he or she
would have occupied if the injurious event had not occurred.[15]

These features render the compensatory model of adjudication highly consonant with the assumptions of classical liberalism. The individualistic conception of party structure characteristic of this model echoes the individualism of the classical liberal
view in an obvious way. The transactional understanding of
causation reinforces this individualism. From the present perspective the point of this understanding is to ensure that those
and only those persons who have inflicted a harm by virtue of
their voluntary actions will be held responsible for that harm
and to guarantee that the beneficiaries of a legal judgment
deserve their benefits. The restorative approach to remedies is
likewise consistent with classical liberal views. The assumption
behind this approach is that the status quo ante is a normatively
valid point of reference for the purpose of determining a settlement because it can be assumed that that state was the product
of a series of voluntary transactions that was interrupted by the
injurious event under adjudication.

Compensatory adjudication is inherently conservative. The
restorative approach to remedies limits adjudication to the func-

tion of reproducing social reality in its received form. Moreover, the effectiveness of compensatory adjudication as a means of accomplishing even this limited purpose is impaired by its assumptions about party structure and causation. Its individualistic conception of party structure complicates and in many cases prevents the rectification of harms in circumstances where either plaintiffs or defendants are not easily identifiable. The transactional understanding of causation may block the correction of harms that result from continuous and diffuse processes. In short, compensatory adjudication is both useless as a means of transforming social reality and ineffective even as a means of helping maintain social reality in its received form when harms occur in ways that deviate from the standard assumptions of the model.

These limitations suggest that it would be desirable to construct an alternative to the standard compensatory model, either to enable adjudication to be more useful as a tool for transforming social reality or to render it more effective as a means of correcting harms that deviate in form from the standard assumptions, or both. The question is: What form should this alternative take? One possibility might be to devise a structural model of adjudication to accord closely with the managerial conception of state and society.[16] For example, the assumptions about party structure might be revised to accommodate classes or other informal groups. Representatives might be recognized legally as spokespersons for the group as a whole. The well-being of the group could be defined as an object of legal concern distinct from the well-being of its individual members. Similarly, principles could be defined to take account of harms caused by continuous and diffuse processes rather than by discrete historical events. Transactional causation need not be assumed. Finally, alternatives to the restorative approach to remedies could be designed. Adjudication might be regarded as a means to equalize the conditions of the parties involved or to bring social reality into conformity with some other social ideal, without regard for the positions the parties would have occupied if the event precipitating the lawsuit had not occurred.

A structural model of adjudication in the form just described would certainly transcend some of the limitations of the compensatory model. But it is not obvious that such a structural model would achieve superior results overall. One reason is that the model as described defines the well-being of groups as an object of legal concern. It is unclear what justification could be offered for this definition. Groups do not act, think, or experience sensations; their individual members do.[17] Adjudication conducted in accordance with the structural model as described would almost certainly result in the perpetration of injustices toward individuals. Another difficulty with the structural model, at least in the form described, is that it fails to offer a satisfactory account of the procedures through which the public values and social ideals guiding adjudication should be defined. While it would be possible on the one hand for adjudicatory procedures themselves to play this role, there are good reasons for objecting to the use of adjudication for this purpose. Procedures of adjudication are fundamentally undemocratic. Access to these procedures is highly restricted. The outcomes of adjudicatory procedures are determined by the arguments and thinking of the members of a tiny elite group of legal professionals. It seems undesirable to allow public values and social ideals to be determined by such relatively closed procedures. On the other hand, this difficulty cannot be resolved simply by suggesting that the courts should follow wherever legislatures and administrators have taken the initiative in formulating alternatives to compensatory principles. Within the American constitutional structure, it is appropriate for the judiciary to apply independent standards to the actions of legislatures and administrators. These standards should not be invulnerable to criticism and reform, but they also should not be abandoned altogether.

I do not offer these observations to suggest that the compensatory model of adjudication is satisfactory after all, or even to arouse the thought that the compensatory model may be preferable on balance to all possible alternatives. The standard compensatory model could be revised to mitigate its limitations; the structural model as described above could be modified and supplemented to meet objections. Adjudication might take any one, or more than one, of many possible forms. My point is that to devise the most satisfactory feasible form of adjudication we must think carefully about the purposes we would like adjudication to serve and the likely consequences of adopting one model of adjudication rather than another. It is not difficult to identify the limitations of the compensatory model. But it is not useful to do so, either, unless one is prepared to offer a feasible alternative, or at least make some constructive suggestions about the considerations that ought to be taken into account in designing an alternative.

Sunstein offers no alternative to the compensatory model, and while his proposals identify purposes he believes the legal system ought to serve, the reasoning behind these proposals is so underdeveloped that they are of little use in helping us think about how to go about constructing one. In the second half of the present chapter I develop some reasoning relevant to the design of principles of adjudication that might be applied in areas of legal regulation in which standard compensatory principles seem problematical. I make no attempt to design an alternative to the compensatory model, but I do try to suggest how the putatively desirable legal objectives identified by Sunstein's proposals might be pursued without excessive cost to other values.

II. Assessing the Proposals

The normative objectives of Sunstein's proposed risk management and nonsubordination principles appear quite different from one another. More importantly for present purposes, his proposals challenge compensatory principles of adjudication in diverse ways. The proposed risk management principle would discard the individualistic conception of party structure and the transactional view of causation associated with the standard compensatory model. The nonsubordination principle would cast away the traditional restorative approach to remedies as well. Because they raise substantially different issues, I shall discuss his two proposals separately. Throughout my analysis I assume that the means for pursuing the objectives stipulated by his proposals should, as far as is feasible, be consistent with the idea of a person as a responsible agent. I shall not attempt a defense or further explication of this idea of a person except to observe that it describes a substantive value that seems to me central to the public culture of representative democracy in the United States and elsewhere.

A. *Risk Management*

The problem Sunstein seeks to correct by means of his proposed risk management principle is that certain kinds of harms are difficult or impossible to prevent or redress by means of the traditional lawsuit. These harms include those which involve hidden or uncertain effects (for example, flaws in automobile design or construction), externalities (acid rain), or both (toxic substances). Sunstein argues that these problems should be addressed by the formulation of an alternative to the compensatory account of the function of legal controls.

Legal means may be used to manage risks in either of two different ways. One is to control the activities that give rise to the risks by means of ex ante regulation. Most traffic regulations are designed to manage risks in this manner. By laying down rules that regulate speed, direction, and other variables involved in driving an automobile, we seek to reduce the risks entailed in this activity. The other way of using legal means to manage risks is to provide for ex post compensation to persons who have already been harmed or placed at risk of harm.

No good reason exists why ex ante regulations designed to manage risks should not be adopted and enforced, regardless of the nature of the risks in question. Certainly compensatory principles should not be regarded as an obstacle to efforts of this kind. Compensatory principles are designed to facilitate the correction of harms. Ex ante regulations of the kinds with which we are concerned here are designed to facilitate the prevention of harms. Sunstein's argument is misleading insofar as it suggests that effective ex ante regulation designed to manage risks requires the construction of an alternative to the compensatory account of the function of legal controls. All that is needed is a clear understanding of the traditional purpose of compensatory principles, which is to describe a model of adjudication that can be used to enforce primary rules and to secure compensation for injuries suffered, not to offer a comprehensive account of the functions of legal controls.[18]

Ex post compensation for harms involving hidden or uncertain effects raises more difficult issues. A legal system designed to correct ex post for probabilistic harms or for harms in which either perpetrators or victims, or both, are difficult to identify would depart significantly from traditional compensatory principles. The reason is that these harms either cannot be redressed at all or can be redressed only with great difficulty and, in some cases, at very high cost through procedures of adjudication based upon an individualistic conception of party structure and a transactional view of causation. Notice that the problem does not stem from the restorative approach to remedies characteristic of the compensatory model of adjudication. On the contrary, the aim of adjudication designed to correct for these harms would be the same as that of traditional compensatory adjudication, namely to restore the plaintiffs to the positions they would have occupied if the harmful events had not occurred. The difficulty arises because of the assumptions about party structure and causation associated with traditional compensatory principles.

If these assumptions were simply discarded, the cost to values other than the management of risks would be high. These traditional compensatory principles are designed to allocate responsibility for harms to persons who have caused harm by their voluntary actions and to allocate benefits to persons who have actually been injured. They are founded theoretically upon the idea of a person as an agent of choice who is responsible for the effects of his or her voluntary actions (and in some cases inactions), but not for other effects. In abandoning these principles we would be forsaking that idea of a person. On the other hand, in light of contemporary knowledge about the etiology of harms, the cost of rigorous adherence to these principles would also be high. In many instances we can be reasonably certain that harms have occurred even if we cannot explain those harms by reference to transactional causation or achieve certain identification of all the parties involved. In these instances rigorous adherence to traditional legal conceptions of party structure and causation would lead to injustice by preventing us from rectifying genuine harms inflicted by some human beings upon others.

The best solution to the problems posed by the existence of probabilistic and systemic harms would be one designed to compensate victims fully for harms suffered by them *and* to distribute the burdens of compensation as nearly as possible in accordance with the norm that actors should be held responsible for their voluntary actions and not for the actions of others or for effects over which they had no control. This norm would be respected if the basic rules for assessing costs were constructed with regard for the voluntary actions of perpetrators of harms, regardless of whether transactional causation can be demonstrated in a particular case. For example, the individual manufacturers of a substance known to be toxic could each reasonably be held responsible for a portion of the damages resulting from a mishap involving that substance in a case where the actual manufacturer cannot be identified. The amount of any assessment would depend upon a determination of the degree of responsibility borne by each party, but the inability of a plaintiff to demonstrate transactional causation should not be sufficient reason for dismissal of his or her claims if the risks associated with the substance in question are such that some accidents or misuse are foreseeable consequences of its manufacture.[19]

My main conclusion is that traditional principles of compensatory adjudication should be modified to facilitate the correction of harms that cannot easily be rectified when customary assumptions about party structure and causation are applied rigorously. Modifications should not disregard the important concerns behind those assumptions; they should take very seriously the norm that actors should be held responsible only for their voluntary actions. But they should also take seriously the need for a means by which victims can secure compensation for injuries even under circumstances to which traditional assumptions about party structure and causation cannot easily be applied. In this area of legal regulation, the point is not to go beyond compensatory justice, but to modify it.

B. Nonsubordination

The intent of Sunstein's nonsubordination principle is to provide a means to improve the circumstances of groups that suffer from disadvantages caused or abetted by social arrangements. Membership in certain groups defined by race, sex, or other characteristics, including handicaps of various sorts, often imposes disadvantages that cannot be accounted for by legally prohibited acts of discrimination. Sunstein argues that these disadvantages ought to be subjected to amelioration through a reinterpretation of the idea of discrimination, which he believes is too closely wedded to the compensatory justice tradition.

For the past several decades the idea of discrimination has been interpreted in American law through a body of legal doctrine known as the antidiscrimination principle. The legal reasoning behind the antidiscrimination principle is similar to that incorporated in compensatory adjudication. Compensatory adjudication is individualistic because of its conception of party structure; the antidiscrimination principle is individualistic because it casts doubt, through the doctrine of "suspect classification," upon the practice of classification as such.[20] Compensatory adjudication adopts a transactional understanding of causation; the objective of the antidiscrimination principle is to prevent particular acts of discrimination against individuals that cannot be justified by reference to a legitimate purpose. Because of these similarities compensatory adjudication is well suited for the purpose of enforcing the antidiscrimination principle. By the same token, the compensatory model of adjudication might turn out to be a poor means of enforcing an alternative to the antidiscrimination principle. Although Sunstein does not identify the target of his proposal clearly, his point seems to be both that the legal objectives defined by the antidiscrimination principle are too restricted and that the compensatory model of adjudication is ill-designed to advance more appropriate objectives.

Sunstein is right to point out that the legal means provided by the antidiscrimination principle and by the compensatory model of adjudication are woefully inadequate for the purpose of ameliorating the circumstances of groups that suffer from disadvantages that are at least in part the products of existing social arrangements. In this respect the American legal system as presently constituted fails to do justice, and it is a signal virtue of Sunstein's chapter that it calls attention to this fact. But

Sunstein himself fails to describe the norm of equality that informs his critique sufficiently to contribute to the construction of a feasible alternative to existing arrangements. The problem is not that he fails to provide a fully worked-out alternative to either the antidiscrimination principle or the compensatory model of adjudication. To expect this much of his chapter would be unreasonable. The real difficulty is that he tells us so little about the norm of equality upon which his argument supposedly rests that it is impossible to interpret his proposal.

Clearly Sunstein intends the nonsubordination principle to describe a more egalitarian objective for legal regulations than that advanced by the antidiscrimination principle. But equality may be conceived in any one of many different ways. It is impossible to reason constructively about the legal means that might be appropriate for achieving equality in the absence of a clearly formulated conception of that goal. Is equality enhanced or diminished by affirmative action programs that include schemes of preferential treatment in decisions about employment for adult members of disadvantaged groups? The only intelligent way to address this and other related practical questions is to define a conception of equality to serve as a yardstick for future discussion. To propose a legal principle ostensibly designed to guide thinking about the purposes of legal regulations without defining the content of that principle in a more substantive way than Sunstein does is to add nothing to the current rather muddled state of public debate about the idea of equality.

In the remainder of this chapter I describe an approach to equality that seems promising for addressing the practical issues associated with this ideal. The purpose of my analysis is to define the values at stake in a sufficiently precise way to guide deliberation about the construction of an alternative to the antidiscrimination principle and to the compensatory model of adjudication through which that principle has been enforced. I assume that my approach to equality will be controversial. Any attempt to specify substantive values intended to shape legal regulations is likely to evoke disagreement and should do so. The purposes of legal regulations should be determined through political deliberation. We should not expect political deliberation to be a highly consensual process, and we should not pretend that basic differences about ends can be reduced to less fundamental differences about means that are amenable to resolution by technical means.

III. DEFINING EQUALITY

In section I of this chapter I presented the classical liberal and managerial visions as contrasting perspectives on state and society. I also suggested that both perspectives would have to be taken into account by any satisfactory effort to address the problems with which both Sunstein and I are concerned. Now I am in a position to specify more fully the way in which both perspectives should be taken into account. These two visions of state and society are better seen as relevant in different ways to the problem of interpreting and applying the norm of equality than as alternatives to one another.

The managerial view of state and society is best regarded as a primarily descriptive heuristic. It portrays the organization of state and society in the United States, especially since the New Deal, more accurately than the liberal vision. Moreover, the managerial view directs our attention to the fact that the social world is an artifact subject, at least to some degree, to reformation through various means, including legal regulation. This insight is not contingent upon any particular organization of state and society. It applies to America in the eighteenth century as well as to the United States since the New Deal, and it has been grasped by political philosophers at least since 1651, when Thomas Hobbes argued that "by Art is created that great LEVIATHAN called a COMMON-WEALTH, or STATE, (in latine CIVITAS) which is but an Artificiall Man."[21] Despite the antiquity of this insight, some participants in recent political debates about the norm of equality have failed to understand it. The managerial view of state and society, regarded as a descriptive heuristic, usefully calls attention to the artificiality of the social world.

On the other hand, the managerial view is prescriptively empty. In the conversations about equality to which I have alluded in this chapter, the assumptions of the managerial view have been used most prominently by advocates of greater equality among groups. But this notion of equality is extrinsic rather than intrinsic to the managerial perspective. The main features of that perspective, including the emphasis upon the need for deliberate social management and the claim that informal groups should be administratively and legally cognizable, would be as congenial to the proponent of a caste society as they seem to be to the advocates of equality.

By contrast with the managerial view, the liberal vision of state and society is a relatively poor foundation for descriptive or explanatory social theory. Although many enthusiasts have argued that a stable and beneficent social order can be achieved through voluntary transactions among private individuals with a minimum of state control, the empirical relation between the stipulated conditions, especially minimal state control, and results, namely a beneficent social order, is far weaker than the defenders of this thesis sometimes suppose. John Locke, who is widely regarded as the founder of modern liberalism, argued that a system of exchange based upon voluntary transactions without provisions limiting the accumulation of goods would result in great inequality, including "disproportionate and unequal Possession of the Earth";[22] and although he went on to argue that this inequality is justified, he did not claim that it is beneficial, and at times seems to imply that it sometimes is not.[23] In this respect Locke seems to have been less deluded about the advantages of liberal approaches to the organization of state and society than some of his successors in the liberal tradition.[24]

While the liberal vision of state and society is a poor foundation for sociological theory, the idea of a society organized by means of voluntary transactions among individuals is a useful device for specifying norms. When the liberal vision is regarded as a form of sociological theory, this idea is treated as a presupposition or stipulation. In its general form, the argument is that *if* transactions among individuals were voluntary, then certain consequences would follow. Regarded as a normative device, however, the idea of a society organized by means of voluntary transactions becomes a goal. The argument then is that transactions among individuals *should* be voluntary to the fullest extent possible within limitations imposed by considerations of feasibility and by other desirable values. Often liberals have linked these two arguments into a longer chain by arguing that transactions among individuals should be voluntary insofar as possible, in part because of the salutary consequences that would follow if they were. This linkage is unnecessary, and the shortcomings of liberalism as a sociological theory render it undesirable. Voluntariness in transactions among individuals is a worthy goal, independently of assertions about the consequences to which it might lead.

The implication of the liberal vision regarded as a normative device is that individuals should enter into transactions with one another on a voluntary basis rather than under duress. This objective can be grasped most clearly once it is disentangled from the remnants of liberal sociological theory. It entails no assumptions about the means by which the voluntary nature of transactions can be assured. In particular, we have no reason to assume that the voluntariness of transactions is always enhanced by the minimization of regulation. Transactions would be voluntary if those who enter into them were genuinely free to refuse to do so. This freedom to refuse can be enhanced by regulation under some circumstances and harmed under others. In general, persons can enjoy this kind of freedom only if they possess adequate resources to make refusal a feasible alternative.

This line of reasoning can be developed into an interpretation of the norm of equality that can be applied to the problems to which this chapter is addressed. I suggest that the general norm relevant to these problems is that individuals should possess adequate resources to enable them to participate in transactions with others on a voluntary, and to that extent equal, basis. Refusal should be a feasible alternative. The members of a society in which all parties to all transactions enjoyed this freedom to refuse would be one another's equals in the most practical sense.

The most important resources relevant to the norm of equality I have described are skills. Skills are overwhelmingly the most significant resource that can be employed in the pursuit of welfare goals. They are also crucial for participation in political decisions, including decisions about common institutions and about policy matters in general. Lack of the relevant skills places some at a disadvantage in comparison with others, both in deliberations about political matters and in competition in the marketplace for employment and other goods. Although for many purposes skills must be combined with other goods, including financial means or other resources external to the person, an approach to equality that takes into account only external resources cannot be used to give a reliable indication of a person's freedom to refuse to undertake an action or to enter into a transaction.[25]

The norm of equality supported by this line of reasoning differs both from the notion of equality of treatment and from the idea of equality of result. The predominant notion representing the idea of equality in recent political and legal argument has been equality of treatment. The basic idea is that individuals should be treated equally except when they possess different characteristics that are relevant to legitimate public or private purposes. The genesis of these differences is not a relevant consideration when this notion of equality is applied. Background conditions, the factors that give rise to advantages and disadvantages, are ignored. The idea of equal treatment underpins the antidiscrimination principle. The principal alternative contender to represent the idea of equality in recent arguments has been equality of result. The idea behind this interpretation of equality is that in general advantages and disadvantages are unjustified, especially when these differences result from social arrangements that are subject to change. Something like this idea of equality appears to lie behind Sunstein's proposed nonsubordination principle. In contrast to both these notions, the interpretation sketched here focuses upon the possession of resources considered as a means necessary for participation in society, and especially for engaging in transactions on a voluntary basis, rather than as an end in itself. The criterion of adequacy of resources is an outcome of this approach.

This interpretation of the idea of equality is liberal in spirit. Its justificatory focus is upon the freedom of persons to engage in or to refrain from transactions.[26] This focus is founded upon the idea of a person as a responsible agent of choice. Unlike some liberal conceptions, however, the approach to equality I have outlined here does not suppose that persons come into the world as fully formed agents of choice, like Hobbes's famous mushrooms.[27] It assumes on the contrary that persons need resources, internal as well as external, in order to be the agents described by this idea of a person. The most general prescription that can be derived from this conception of equality is that persons should be endowed with adequate resources, both internal and external, to participate fully and voluntarily in a full range of activities, including the making of political decisions, competition in the marketplace, and the various facets of private life, including family membership.[28]

The single most significant step that could be taken today toward applying this conception of equality would be to provide the younger members of society with educational opportunities and resources of a much higher standard than many now receive, together with the provisions for health care, child care, and other forms of support necessary to make use of these resources. The focus of efforts to promote equality should be upon preventing the reproduction of disadvantages by addressing the background conditions that bear the bulk of responsibility for generating those disadvantages. The objective of these efforts should be to cultivate the capabilities that enable individuals to become responsible agents of choice.

Attempts to prevent the reproduction of disadvantages by addressing background conditions should be designed with due regard for other values. Respect for other values may limit the efficacy of attempts to equalize resources beyond some as yet unknown point. In the United States today, however, we are so far from approaching that point that discussions of the limits of egalitarian efforts seem to be of little immediate practical importance.[29]

The idea of equality as adequacy of internal and external resources describes a desirable objective of legal regulations that differs from the objectives of antidiscrimination law, but in an additive rather than contradictory manner. True, this idea of equality mandates inequalities of treatment for persons whose characteristics or circumstances differ from those of others in ways affecting their abilities to acquire or maintain adequate internal or external resources. Special needs due to handicaps, responsibilities for young children or aged adults, or other causes would be recognized as grounds for receiving unequal treatment. But these differences of treatment would be justified by reference to a legitimate public purpose, namely preventing the reproduction of disadvantages. Advancement of this objective should be recognized as one of the central purposes of legal regulation.

NOTES

1. I wish to thank Bruce Ackerman, Owen M. Fiss, Ian Shapiro, Rogers M. Smith, and Dennis F. Thompson for reading a draft of this chapter and providing many helpful comments and suggestions for improvement.

2. For his discussion of legal systems as unions of primary and secondary rules, see H. L. A. Hart, *The Concept of Law* (Oxford: Oxford University Press, 1961), chap. 5, esp. pp. 78–79.

3. The allusion is to G. Calabresi and A. D. Melamed, "Property Rules, Liability Rules and Inalienability: One View of the Cathedral," *Harvard Law Review* 85 (1972): 1089.

4. John Stuart Mill, *On Liberty* (New York: Norton, 1975 [1859]), 76 and chap. 4 generally.

5. John Locke, *An Essay Concerning the True Original, Extent, and End of Civil Government*, para. 57, in *Two Treatises of Government*, revised ed., ed. Peter Laslett (Cambridge: Cambridge University Press, 1963 [1690]); emphasis in the original. Mill's harm principle is rooted in a similar high regard for voluntary actions and transactions.

6. For examples, see Friedrich A. Hayek, *The Constitution of Liberty* (Chicago: University of Chicago Press, 1960); and Ralf Dahrendorf, *Life Chances* (Chicago: University of Chicago Press, 1979).

7. See, for example, Karl Marx, "On the Jewish Question" (1843), in *The Marx-Engels Reader*, 2d ed., ed. Robert C. Tucker (New York: Norton, 1978), 26–52, for both criticism of and grudging admiration for the accomplishments of the liberal program.

8. The most influential formulation of this viewpoint in the English-speaking world was John Maynard Keynes's *General Theory of Employment, Interest, and Money* (New York: Harcourt, Brace & World, 1964 [1936]). See also Karl Polanyi, *The Great Transformation* (Boston: Beacon, 1957 [1944]).

9. For a recent argument to this effect, see Owen M. Fiss, "Groups

and the Equal Protection Clause," *Philosophy & Public Affairs* 5 (1976):107–77 at pp. 123ff.

10. For a classic statement on this point in the field of public administration, see Luther Gulick and L. Urwick, *Papers in the Science of Public Administration* (New York: Institute of Public Administration, 1937). Frank Goodnow and Ernst Freund attempted to apply similar arguments to the teaching and practice of law between the 1890s and the early 1930s, but their early efforts were generally unsuccessful. For an interesting account, especially of Freund's efforts, see William C. Chase, *The American Law School and the Rise of Administrative Government* (Madison: University of Wisconsin Press, 1982).

11. For a recent statement of this view, see Cass R. Sunstein, "Disrupting Voluntary Transactions," in John W. Chapman and J. Roland Pennock, eds., *Markets and Justice: Nomos XXXI* (New York: New York University Press, 1989), 279–302.

12. For an early statement of this argument, see Leonard T. Hobhouse, *Liberalism* (London: Williams and Norgate, 1911).

13. As Bruce Ackerman has pointed out in *Reconstructing American Law* (Cambridge: Harvard University Press, 1984), the legal activism implied by adoption of the managerial view "is entirely consistent with a strong commitment to limited government" (p. 32). For liberals of the managerial persuasion, however, limitations upon the scope of governmental action are determined by weighing the advantages and disadvantages of government intervention in each potential area of intervention, as Sunstein suggests we should do in "Disrupting Voluntary Transactions." This approach to the problem of the limitations of state action reflects little of the distrust of power characteristic of early liberals.

14. See, for example, Steven Lukes, *Power: A Radical View* (London: Macmillan, 1974).

15. For an interesting recent debate about the compensatory model of adjudication, see Owen M. Fiss, "Coda," *University of Toronto Law Journal* 38 (1988):229–44; and Ernest J. Weinrib, "Adjudication and Public Values: Fiss's Critique of Corrective Justice," *University of Toronto Law Journal* 39 (1989):1–18. I have described the model of compensatory justice in terms borrowed from this debate.

16. The structural model as described in this paragraph is borrowed from Fiss's proposal in "Coda."

17. For a more extended discussion, see George Sher, "Preferential Hiring," in Tom Regan, ed., *Just Business* (New York: Random House, 1984), 32–59 at pp. 36–38.

18. Of course, compensatory principles are sometimes applied in

inappropriate ways. For an example, see Jerry L. Mashaw and David L. Harfst, "Regulation and Legal Culture: The Case of Motor Vehicle Safety," *Yale Journal on Regulation* 4 (1987):257–316. In instances of the kind described by Mashaw and Harfst, Sunstein is probably right to suggest that the culprit is a legal culture excessively devoted to tort-like conceptions.

19. The U.S. Supreme Court allowed this approach in a recent product liability case, *Rexal v. Tigue*, 110 S. Ct. (1989). In this case several pharmaceutical companies had appealed a ruling by the New York Court of Appeals that made all manufacturers of a drug linked to serious medical problems potentially liable for damages in proportion to the share they had of the national market for the drug. In a judgment issued in October 1989, the Supreme Court allowed the ruling to stand.

20. For discussion, see Fiss, "Groups," 123–29.

21. Thomas Hobbes, *Leviathan*, ed. C. B. Macpherson (Harmondsworth, Middlesex: Penguin, 1968 [1651]), Introduction, 81.

22. John Locke, *Second Treatise*, in *Two Treatises of Government*, para. 50 (p. 344).

23. Locke argues that

> in the beginning, before the desire of having more than Men needed, had altered the intrinsick value of things, which depends only on their usefulness to the Life of Man; or had *agreed, that a little piece of yellow Metal*, which would keep without wasting or decay, should be worth a great piece of Flesh, or a whole heap of Corn; though Men had a Right to appropriate, by their Labour, each one to himself, as much of the things of Nature, as he could use: Yet this could not be much, nor to the Prejudice of others, where the same plenty was still left, to those who would use the same Industry.

(*Second Treatise*, para. 37) Locke does not say here that under the greatly altered conditions of expanded desires, unlimited accumulation, and scarcity, appropriation of goods by some is prejudicial to others, but he may have believed it. Locke also points out that "in Governments the Laws regulate the right of property, and the possession of land is determined by positive constitutions" (*Second Treatise*, para. 50). This observation seems to suggest a greater sympathy for the managerial perspective on state and society than some of Locke's interpreters have credited him with.

24. Adam Smith was also aware of the limitations of systems of exchange based upon voluntary transactions, though it would be impossible to discover this fact from reading the accounts offered by some of his recent enthusiastic disciples. See his *Inquiry into the Nature*

and Causes of the Wealth of Nations, ed. Edwin Cannan (New York: Random House, 1937 [1776]), bk. I, chap. 10, inter alia.

25. Although the view I describe here focuses upon equality of resources, it differs from Dworkin's view in that it treats both internal and external resources, and not merely the latter, as objects of egalitarian concern. For his contrasting view, see Ronald Dworkin, "What Is Equality? Part I: Equality of Welfare" and "What Is Equality? Part II: Equality of Resources," *Philosophy and Public Affairs* 10 (1981):185–246 and 283–345.

26. This idea of equality is similar to the one Amartya Sen has developed in a series of articles over the past several years. See his "Well-Being, Agency and Freedom," *Journal of Philosophy* 82 (1985):169–221, and for a very broad recent statement see his Agnelli Prize address, "Individual Freedom as a Social Commitment," *New York Review of Books,* June 14, 1990, 49–54.

27. Thomas Hobbes, *De Cive: The English Version,* ed Howard Warrender (Oxford: Oxford University Press, 1983 [1642]), chap. VIII, sec. I.

28. Susan Moller Okin has applied a similar conception of equality to the area of relations within the family in a very useful way in her *Justice, Gender, and the Family* (New York: Basic Books, 1989).

29. Bernard Williams expresses concern about the potential for conflict between the objective of equality of opportunity and other values in "The Idea of Equality," in his *Problems of the Self* (Cambridge: Cambridge University Press, 1973), 230–49. This concern is at the center of James Fishkin's argument in *Justice, Equal Opportunity, and the Family* (New Haven: Yale University Press, 1983). But Fishkin acknowledges that social arrangements in the United States today are so inegalitarian that a great deal could be done to advance equality without threatening the other values he discusses.

INDEX